INCOME TRANSFER ANALYSIS

INCOME TRANSFER ANALYSIS

GORDON H. LEWIS

Carnegie-Mellon University

RICHARD J. MORRISON

Health and Welfare, Canada

THE URBAN INSTITUTE PRESS

Washington, D.C. 1989

THE URBAN INSTITUTE PRESS
2100 M Street, N.W.
Washington, D.C. 20037

Library of Congress Cataloging in Publication Data

Lewis, Gordon H.
Income Transfer Analysis

Includes bibliographical references.

1. Income maintenance programs--United States--Data processing.
2. MAPSIT (Computer program) I. Morrison, Richard J. II. Title.

HC110.I5L469 1989 362.5'82 89-22507

ISBN 0-87766-430-7 (casebound)

Printed in the United States of America.

9 8 7 6 5 4 3 2 1

Distributed by:
University Press of America
4720 Boston Way
Lanham, MD 20706
3 Henrietta Street
London WC2E 8LU ENGLAND

To our parents:

Leslie and Ruth

Bill and Arlene

TABLE OF CONTENTS

LIST OF TABLES

LIST OF FIGURES

PREFACE

Rapid change and increased complexity in governmental programs for income security and taxation make it imperative that policy actors find ways to analyze the interactions that occur among these programs. It is not uncommon that the very legislators who propose and enact changes in income security programs or changes in the tax laws do not, and cannot, anticipate the manifold ramifications of those changes, both behavioral and programmatic. Our principal purpose in writing this book is to present a conceptual framework for understanding why analysis is complicated in this area and to point the direction in which we believe software development should proceed. We do not believe that there is only one way in which to proceed analytically, but we do believe that customary approaches have been inadequate in several respects and are in need of supplementation.

While one of the goals of the book is to identify criteria for effective analysis, the book is not just a normative statement of analytic desiderata. In addition to offering our thoughts on what the elements of an appropriate software system should be, we describe a specific software system, MAPSIT, that has been developed, tested, revised, and retested. It works and has been in daily use, in present or prior versions, since 1976. Although it has been described briefly elsewhere (Lewis and Morrison, 1983), we think that those of you who learn about that modeling package here for the first time will find its capabilities remarkable.

The present work began in Canada when the Department of National Health and Welfare authorized Rick Morrison, a graduate of Carnegie-Mellon University, to investigate the potential for building software that would allow analysts efficiently and effectively to ascertain the impacts of complex systems of tax and benefit programs. The software that is described here as an example of the kind of approach needed for this area is actually the second major pass at constructing appropriate software. Both the first generation (NSTACK) and the second generation have gone through several revisions.

The philosophy of attack we propose follows three guiding principles. First, write software in such a way that it is seldom or never necessary for the analyst to interact with programmers. That is, the programmer should develop software to assist the analyst to model systems of tax and transfer programs, but the analyst should then be able to build models without further input from the programmer. The model-building software should be sufficently comprehensive, robust, error-free, and easy to use that seeking help from programmers will be unnecessary. If the analyst finds it necessary to seek out programming specialists to alter the model-building program so that particular models can be constructed, then the software wasn't properly designed. Second, design the software so that when analysts build models the modelling package will do as much of the drudgery as possible. Third, strive for generality. Employ a minimum of built-in assumptions; let the analyst control the assumptions and the amount of detail desired.

The Department of National Health and Welfare, Canada, and the School of Urban and Public Affairs at Carnegie-Mellon University have both played important roles in the production of this book. In the case of Carnegie-Mellon University, general research support from the School of Urban and Public Affairs made it possible for Gordon Lewis to devote part of his time to work on this book. The authors want to thank Brian J. L. Berry, Dean of the School of Urban and Public Affairs, and Otto A. Davis, former Dean. In the case of the Department of National Health and Welfare, the support for this project came in two ways. First, the Department supported the development of NSTACK and MAPSIT, and without those packages this book would have been mere suggestions about the directions in which such modeling should proceed. Within the Department of National Health and Welfare, Greg Traversy (currently with the Department of Finance) and Dave Beavis provided active support in the development and use of that software. They also specifically granted permission for Rick Morrison to undertake work on this book and the related VolksMap software in a private capacity, a permission which was necessitated by Rick Morrison's position as Chief, Tax/Transfer Simulation Analysis within the Department of National Health and Welfare. We appreciate the several contributions of both Greg Traversy and Dave Beavis.

Others to whom we owe a debt of gratitude include Marvin Avery and William J. Bradley (Analytical Services, National Health and Welfare), Fred Gage (University of Pittsburgh), Bruce Limber (Computer Data Systems, Inc.), John Mercer (AT&T), Greg O'Beirne

(Sperry Corporation), and Rob Williams (Congressional Budget Office).

In addition to these people there is also a large number of Canadian analysts and Carnegie-Mellon University graduate students who have used MAPSIT and thereby contributed to our experience about what works and what doesn't work in an analytical, policy environment and in a university research setting.

To Pamela Lewis and Sue Morrison go our thanks for their forebearance in what has at times seemed like an interminable task. We also want to acknowledge with great appreciation the assistance of Carole McCoy and Judy Lando, who did much of the work involved in word processing, and Laura Peirce, who made many useful suggestions.

During the course of writing this book the division of labor has shifted in one direction and then another. As a result it would be impossible for us to identify either one of us as senior author. We have, therefore, adopted the time-honored procedure of listing our names alphabetically on the title page.

The substance of this book reflects the opinions of the authors. It should not be construed as reflecting positions either of the School of Urban and Public Affairs at Carnegie-Mellon University or of the Government of Canada or the Department of National Health and Welfare.

FOREWORD

Economic analysis, at least of the sort that finds its way into newspaper headlines and opinion columns these days, focuses almost exclusively on the broad aggregates of economic activity--the GNP, the money supply, the unemployment rate, the budget and trade deficits, and so on. Partly that's because large-scale measures are much easier to incorporate into the computerized models that are the stock-in-trade of modern economics. Politicians, however, still feel more comfortable dealing at the level where policies and programs affect the everyday activities of firms and people. It's an understandable--and not always unwise--preference.

Unfortunately for both the analysts and the politicians, it's much harder to develop rigorous descriptions of these "micro" happenings. But, as the authors of this volume observe in their introductory chapter, failure to do so can spell doom for a major policy initiative, no matter how elegant its theoretical underpinnings or how compelling its moral justification. When the Nixon Administration--still glowing from its earlier success in selling the Family Assistance Plan to the House of Representatives--took its case for welfare reform to the Senate Finance Committee, its planned presentation was completely disrupted by the sharp inquiries of Senator John J. Williams of Delaware. Senator Williams, no friend of welfare reform, had hit upon the realization that the various kinds of aid to and taxes on the poor--welfare, food stamps, housing aid, medical benefits together with payroll and income taxes--could, at least for lucky families in generous localities, give rise to a situation in which members of that family gained little if anything from increased work effort.

The Family Assistance Plan, FAP, would not have created, or even noticeably worsened that situation. But the fact that the Department of Health, Education and Welfare was not ready with the required analyses made it much easier for the Senator to put the Administration on the defensive. And that loss of momentum, as Senator Daniel P. Moynihan so vividly describes in his *Politics of a Guaranteed Income*, ultimately led to FAP's demise. HEW would not, of course, have been found unprepared if it had had the advantage of access to the MAPSIT model and the accompanying analysis described in this volume. In fact, the origins of the MAPSIT software system can be traced directly to the FAP incident. I was at the time employed in the Office of the Secretary, HEW and, as one of the few analysts then working on FAP, I helped Alair Townsend prepare some of the tables requested by Sen. Williams and, subsequently, by others. It was mind-destroying work, and all of us made numerous mistakes. The more tables we made, the more variations the policymakers wanted.

A few years later, when I left HEW to join the Urban Institute, Larry Orr, then an economist at the Office of Economic Opportunity, asked me if I could spend a month or so computerizing the process so that none of us would have to suffer through that sort of table-making again. The result was the "Cumulative Tax Rate Model" that Gordon Lewis and Richard Morrison kindly recognize as a precursor of the far more elegant invention, MAPSIT.

The uses of MAPSIT are obvious to those who have tried to construct or redesign any part of an income transfer system while giving any thought to the interactions of that part with other taxes and transfers. This is true not only in the United States, with its hodge-podge of cash and in-kind programs, but also, as Chapter 11 of this book amply illustrates, in other countries such as Canada whose "welfare states" are, in many respects, more advanced than ours. But MAPSIT is equally of interest to anyone who wants simply to understand how tax and transfer programs really work.

It is true of both tax and transfer programs that their effectiveness, efficiency and fairness cannot be judged solely from their formal structures or overall price tags. To measure those qualities you have to see how a tax or transfer, in combination with all the other taxes and benefits, affects families and individuals in different circumstances. From comparisons of this sort, inferences can be drawn about the incentives the programs provide for changes in work effort, saving, spending, family formation or dissolution, residence, child-bearing and so on. From there you can estimate in turn how those responses may impinge upon a program's actual, as compared to theoretical, impacts.

The interactions among programs can, either by design or inadvertence, be very complicated. Chapter 5 gives an example of a policymaker considering whether to take childcare into account in determining food benefits for a family also receiving welfare. That is no abstract possibility. For better or worse, complications of this sort are embedded in all our social programs and, in our federal system, the rules tend to vary from locality to locality. Working through the construction of a MAPSIT model and analyzing its output is certainly one of the best ways to understand the implications of this complexity both for the people affected by it and for the policymaker who may wish to alter it. Having ready access to the capability that MAPSIT provides to assess interactions rapidly and conveniently as alternatives are considered is essential to any participant in the policy process who wants to suggest changes in social programs. That is true whether the ultimate objective is, as was true a decade ago, to improve their adequacy or, as in the current situation, to reduce their costs.

Jodie T. Allen
Editorial Staff
The Washington Post
November 30, 1985

PART I

PROBLEMS AND APPROACH

CHAPTER 1.
INTRODUCTION

Income transfers play an important role in modern society. They make it possible for single parents to work by furnishing day care; they provide support for the unemployed; they supply income for the retired; and they aid the poor through grants for housing and energy. Some of these benefits are cash, some are benefits in-kind, but all of them help to determine the effective income of the recipients. Other programs also have an impact on families' effective incomes by reducing the amount that the individuals or families have to spend. Federal and state income taxes and mandatory contributions for social security are examples.

These programs are important in the lives of millions of families, and the combined effects of these programs are of fundamental concern to the federal and state governments. Nevertheless, many of the problems in analyzing the effects of combinations of income transfer programs have not been adequately addressed in past analytic and methodological efforts. In this book we present a methodology that allows one to analyze systems of income transfer programs. The approach we take is oriented to the recipient unit (family or individual) and is thus a "micro-oriented" analysis. Since major software systems exist that are generally called "microsimulation" we shall return to the characteristics that differentiate that work from ours.

Measures of the impact of income transfers on modern society are to be found in the number of programs, the number of people, and the number of dollars involved. In terms of programs, Lawrence and Leeds (1978) catalogued over 180 federal programs that provide benefits to individuals or families, and they also catalogued a large number of state sponsored programs (Lawrence and Leeds, 1980). In terms of people, estimates from the Office of Management and Budget (1985) indicated that in 1985 approximately thirty-eight million people would receive Social Security; twenty-one million would receive food stamps; twenty-three million would receive Medicaid; and eleven million would receive Aid to Families with Dependent

Children.[1] Finally, in terms of dollars, five of the largest benefit programs (Social Security, food and nutrition, housing, Medicaid, and Medicare) had outlays of $321 billion in 1985 (Office of Management and Budget, 1986). On the tax side the sums are equally impressive. Federal personal income tax amounted to $335 billion in 1985, and over $170 billion was contributed to Social Security through mandatory FICA payments (Office of Management and Budget, 1986).

The magnitude of income transfers is a sufficient cause for interest and analysis, but there are other aspects of income transfer programs that generate interest and concern as well. While on one level these programs involve simple transfers of money or in-kind benefits, on another level they involve important incentives: incentives to work, to move, to marry or divorce, and to have children. Obviously when programs that have an impact on incentives such as these are designed or changed, it is important that one understands the consequences. Unfortunately, assessing such consequences is a difficult problem, in part because the programs are individually complicated and in part because their complexity is greatly magnified when multiple programs interact.

During the past twenty years considerable effort has focused on the development of increasingly sophisticated methods for analyzing income transfers (Pechman, 1965; Brazer, 1968; Wilensky, 1970; McClung, 1970; Beebout and Sulvetta, 1974; Golladay and Haveman, 1976; Orcutt et al., 1976; and Sadowsky, 1977).[2] Based on microsimulation, the major thrust of most of this work has been the estimation of costs and numbers of recipients that would result from changes to specific transfer programs. Until recently there has not been a corresponding focus on the impact of tax and transfer systems on individual families or the sensitivity of those impacts to specific parameters of the system.[3] This book describes a software package, MAPSIT (Modular Analysis Package for Systems of Income Transfers), that permits effective, fast, low-cost analysis of such sys-

---

[1] These are not independent counts since recipients of one program are often recipients of other programs.

[2] For a review of this work see Harris (1978).

[3] There are, of course, exceptions; see, for example, Federal Council on the Aging (1975).

tems. MAPSIT makes it possible for analysts to investigate the nature of program effects and interactions and to perform sensitivity analyses that previously would have been too difficult, too lengthy, or too costly to do.

Part I of this book focuses on the nature of income transfer programs, the analytical concerns that have historically arisen, and the basic features that one would want an analytic technology to possess in order to address those concerns. In Part II MAPSIT itself is introduced, and two chapters provide examples of MAPSIT's application in realistic analyses. The final two chapters in that section demonstrate the types of secondary analyses that can be done with MAPSIT as well as describing other special capabilities. Part III of the book analyzes the art of modeling and illustrates both the applications and problems that arise in practice. The chapters in Part III describe several of the policy issues to which MAPSIT has been applied and how MAPSIT is used within an active policy environment. The final section presents concluding remarks and an assessment of strengths and weaknesses of this technology.

The three major sections of the book complement each other by showing first how MAPSIT enables one to model complex systems of taxes and benefits quickly, rigorously, and economically, and second how this meets the demands imposed by policymakers addressing actual transfer policy issues. Indeed, this latter point is made primarily through description of MAPSIT's extensive use by the federal government in Canada, where MAPSIT was developed, and by the Congressional Budget Office, the House Ways and Means Committee, and the Department of Agriculture in the United States.

The purpose of the remaining portion of this first chapter is to indicate areas in which analysis is needed and sketch roughly the dimensions and problems of such analysis.

HISTORICAL STATUS OF INCOME TRANSFER ANALYSIS

Because welfare reform is prominent economically, politically, and morally, it has generated a fair amount of analysis. Historically, much of this analysis has been focused on macro-level issues, although the analytic tools employed sometimes involve microsimulation or micro-accounting (Harris, 1978; Anderson, 1980; Employee Benefit Research Institute, 1981). For example, analyses often involve computations of the dollars spent on various programs (Hoagland, 1984), projections of the dollar figures for future years (Congressional

Budget Office, 1982), or estimations of the number of dollars that would be required by various proposed programs (Mills and Palmer, 1983). Analysts have also computed the percent of population lifted from poverty by a particular program or set of programs (Congressional Budget Office, 1977; Danziger and Plotnick, 1982). Or again, the analysis may focus on the number of households or individuals participating in or eligible for a given program (Boland, 1973; Danziger and Plotnick, 1981). In Canada much of this analysis has been done using estimation technologies such as BENTAX and SIMTAB (Morrison, 1984). In the United States several programs have been developed to produce estimates of the effects of welfare programs. Three of these models, TRIM (Beebout and Sulvetta, 1974; Sulvetta, 1976), MATH (Sadowsky, 1977) and DYNASIM (Orcutt et al., 1976), are based on "microsimulation;" they utilize a "sample" population and calculate the benefits received and the costs of the welfare programs as they would be received by the families of this hypothetical population, appropriately weighted. While these software packages allow one to view both aggregated and disaggregated costs and benefits, they are not especially amenable to allowing the analyst a detailed look at program interactions.

Governments are fairly proficient at macro-oriented analyses, even though there are perennial problems of appropriate data, data confidentiality, questions about the weighting of sample data to produce national or state figures, and about appropriate demographic and financial growth rates. Governments are proficient at these analyses because they have to be; these issues arise naturally in the course of legislative debate on new programs, in the review of existing programs, and in budget construction.

But despite the analysis, and despite the attempts to reform welfare by each new administration, there has developed a virtual litany of the complaints against the welfare system:[4]

1. *"The system is inequitable."* People with similar needs often receive very different benefits, and people who are manifestly better off often receive more benefits than people who are worse off (Bennett, 1979).

[4] This list contains elements found in many sources: Marmor (1971:86–90), Storey (1972:8–22), Jencks (1974:60–68), Lurie (1974:4–14), Aaron (1980:52–57), and Danziger and Plotnick (1981:134–136).

2. *"There is often a lack of meaningful work incentives."* Economic outcomes for additional work effort may be directly in opposition to social pressures to increase work effort. Aaron (1973:31-46) produces some compelling analyses showing how programs can interact to produce high or confiscatory effective tax rates. The disincentives for work occur both because effective tax rates are very high (in many cases over 80 percent) and because of "notches," points at which, if the person earns only slightly more income, he or she may be much worse off financially. Similar problems are noted by Appel (1972), Feldstein (1973, 1975), Smith (1974), Viscusi and Zeckhauser (1977), Anderson (1978), and Joe (1982).[5]

3. *"There are inappropriate regional disparities."* Many regional differences in benefits exist that are larger than any difference in cost of living between the regions. In 1985, Aid to Families with Dependent Children (AFDC) benefit levels for a family of three were $96 per month in Mississippi and $555 per month in California (Office of Family Assistance, 1985).

4. *"The present system is inefficient."* Many families receiving benefits are not "poor," at least in terms of some official poverty line, and many of the families receiving benefits are not entitled to them under present regulations (Anderson, 1978:35).

5. *"The present system is ineffective."* The transfers that the present system provides do not eliminate poverty. Again, the estimates differ, but many analysts agree that a minimum of 11 to 12 percent of the U.S. population still falls below the officially defined poverty level, even after transfers (Lynn, 1977:90; National Advisory Council on Economic Opportunity, 1980:704).

---

[5] Blinder and Rosen (1985) argue that while notches create serious work disincentives for persons with low earnings potential, the existence of notches in certain programs is sometimes desirable.

6. *"There are too many programs."* The number of programs varies according to "how one counts," but most sources agree that the large number of programs leads to confusion, inequities, and administrative inefficiencies (Aaron, 1980:55).

7. *"Programs in the present system are ill coordinated."* Differing levels of government, differing goals for differing transfer programs, multiple semi-autonomous agencies, differing types of benefits, differing definitions of income, differing definitions of families, differing definitions of need, and separated physical locations of offices combine to compound paper work. These factors virtually guarantee that programs in the system will be working at cross purposes (Aaron, 1973).

8. *"The present system interferes with family structure decisions."* Especially controversial instances include potential incentives for families to have additional children, and incentives for fathers to desert their families in order to make them better off financially and incentives for the elderly to divorce or not marry. Family structure issues are raised by Green (1966), Cutright and Scanzoni (1973), Honig (1974), Ross and Sawhill (1975), Hannon et al. (1977), MacDonald and Sawhill (1978), Moles (1979), Angel and Tienda (1982), Goodwin (1983), Usher and Griffith (1983), Murray (1984), and McLanahan (1985).

Most of these problems are not addressed via macro-oriented analysis because they are not simply cost and clientele problems. Before analyzing some of the aspects of these problems and what they do imply about the type of analysis needed, some other observations should be made.

In 1973 Moynihan ascribed the death of the Family Assistance Plan in the Senate Finance Committee to the fact that Senator John J. Williams demanded to see the combined effects of a set of income transfer and benefit programs on specific types of families. Senator Williams wanted to see the combined effects for a four-person, female-headed family in each of several states. According to Moynihan, it was these examples of the effects on individual families that killed the bill (cf. Moynihan, 1973:474-483).

In 1976 in Canada the Department of National Health and Welfare completed a three-year Social Security Review. In initiating that review, Marc Lalonde, then Minister of Health and Welfare, summarized objections to the system as follows:

> The deficiencies in (Canada's) social security system become apparent, really, when one looks at how it affects individual Canadians. This is perhaps where the experts and indeed governments have gone wrong: they have tended to concern themselves rather more with the general programmes needed to help particular groups of people, and rather less with the way in which these programmes affect the individuals they are designed to help -- or indeed the way they affect other people (Lalonde, 1973:9; emphasis in original).

Thus, Lalonde charged that the failure to use microanalyses has resulted in programs going off in wrong directions, and Moynihan observed that microanalyses can be a powerful tool precisely because they focus attention on the effects of programs and program systems on people.[6]

Two other comments are also worth considering. In his earlier book on welfare, Aaron concluded that:

> The welfare system is a hodgepodge of uncoordinated but interacting programs, enacted for diverse motives, each written without regard for most of the others. From the standpoint of the recipients, at least, these programs form a system -- a very complex and often arbitrary system. A major step forward in thinking about welfare reform would be widespread recognition of this fact (1973:70).

---

[6] Some argue that focusing on the effects on people is natural since people are the intended beneficiaries of the programs. Others argue that the individuals are irrelevant to the government's policies which have more to do with items such as the total amount of money in circulation. It is not necessary to resolve that debate, however, if one assumes that even if the latter position is correct (1) Congress and the public at large are not indifferent to the effects of social experimentation or (2) the income redistribution effects are at least of some concern.

Shortly thereafter, in one of the papers in the Studies in Public Welfare series produced for the Joint Economic Committee, Mirer (1974) suggested that:

> The whole set of welfare or transfer programs might be thought of as a system. It is properties of the system as a whole--its equity, and its work incentive features--rather than those of individual programs which are most important. The design of links between various programs must be aimed at the goals of the system rather than those of its individual elements (1974).

These four observations have in common the assertion that policy analysts and decision makers have failed to carry out the necessary microanalyses that describe the effects of systems of programs on individuals or families. They also share the belief that micro-level analyses are a necessary precursor to intelligent welfare reform.[7]

IMPLICATIONS

The previous list of typical objections against the welfare system reinforces this concern for a system-oriented microanalysis of income transfer programs. Most of the objections contain at least one component that can be addressed only through micro-level or systems-level analysis:

Equity. The assertion that persons with similar needs are receiving very different benefits is not particularly meaningful unless one is talking about the net benefits from an entire set of programs. This requires that one can assess and compare the net effects for each of the parties. Another common meaning of equity is that for two similar parties eligible for a given program, the party with a higher income should not receive more benefits than the party with the lower income. This requires that one be able to assess for these two income levels, or preferably for all income levels, the level of the benefits received. While inequities do occur, they usually occur not

---

[7] While these observations have all focused on the income transfer systems in the United States and Canada, the need to analyze systems of programs has also been recognized as a general problem by the Organisation for Economic Co-operation and Development (1978).

within a program but in the interaction of multiple programs. This requires, therefore, that one be able to do analyses not only across possible incomes but also across sets of programs.

Work incentives. In discussing welfare issues, the term work incentives typically takes on one of two meanings. In the first, receipt of benefits may be conditioned on the recipient's working at a job, or at least actively searching for a job. In the second definition, a work incentive is said to exist if disposable income rises with increases in work effort (longer hours worked at the same wage rate or the same hours worked at a higher wage rate, and therefore presumably at a more demanding job). The faster disposable income rises for a unit increase in earnings, the greater the work incentive. Since disposable income depends on the net effect of all the programs with which the family interacts, overall work incentives cannot meaningfully be discussed in the context of a single program. Rather, one must examine the total impact for the entire system of relevant programs. Since program benefits or taxes for many programs depend on family size, it is also clear that one must carry out the calculation of this second form of work incentive for multiple family sizes at multiple levels of earned income. It is not sufficient simply to examine a two-parent, two-child family at some median income level. One must also measure work incentives in terms of some economically relevant income definition (earned income is often used) rather than some arbitrary program definition of income.

Regional disparities. To analyze the real extent of regional disparities, and more generally of horizontal equity effects, one must be able to model an identical family and its treatment by the relevant transfer programs in different jurisdictions. It is inappropriate simply to compare the guarantee levels of single programs in different locales, because other programs in the relevant systems may reinforce or attenuate the differences in any one program, and because not all families receive the full amount of program guarantees. Furthermore, for a meaningful comparison, the analyst must take local living costs and wage rates into account.

Inefficiency. When the definition of inefficiency is expressed in terms of families above a poverty line receiving benefits, it is important that the analyst be able to determine program breakevens for individual programs (expressed in terms of any relevant income definition) and the levels of income at which any family surpasses the poverty line. Clearly these determinations will depend on the characteristics of the families under examination, the particular system of programs under examination, and the particular definition of income being used.

Ineffectiveness. Once again, the analyst is dealing with a micro phenomenon. To determine effectiveness for a given family, the analyst must take into account the particular programs that have an impact on that family and be able to compare the net effect of that impact against some poverty line. As before, the characteristics of the family may make a difference. A given combination of programs may be effective in reducing poverty for one class of families but ineffective for another. It is important to recognize that the analyst can seldom simply add up program guarantees to determine system effectiveness.

Too many programs. Some analysts have suggested that all program combinations be analyzed, but that suggestion is hardly attractive. With several hundred programs, the number of possible combinations is vast.[8] This presents a serious obstacle to any attempt at a definitive analysis of "the system." Yet a microanalysis of particular program combinations is extremely important. It is not grand program averages that affect individual families; it is specific sets of program regulations.

Coordination. There is a general consensus that the present system is not well coordinated. However, aside from the institution of a single new program, there is little indication of what a coordinated system would look like. Presumably a minimum criterion for coordination would require that changes in the parameters of any one program, adopted in pursuit of that program's legitimate goals, would not be appreciably undone by the reactions of other programs in the system. Measurement of this form of coordination thus requires the ability to model arbitrary systems of transfer programs as they affect arbitrary families, with the added complication that the modeling must be able to incorporate changes in existing programs. In more technical terms, measures of program coordination would involve the comparison of relevant total and partial derivatives with respect to any parameter in any of the programs in the system and with respect to variables relevant for the target families.

Family structure. To ascertain the extent to which family structure concerns may be valid, an investigator must be able to com-

---

[8] For n independent programs, the number of combinations is 2^n. As few as twenty-eight independent programs would produce more combinations than there are people in the United States.

pare the financial implications of alternate family structures. For arbitrary combinations of programs and for families with arbitrary characteristics, the analyst must be able to determine the consequences for a family of assuming different nominal or real configurations, like family splitting, desertion by the head, choosing to bear or adopt an additional child or to expel an older child from the family. This is not to say that nonfinancial considerations are irrelevant. However, the financial incentives that combinations of transfer programs induce with respect to family structure should not be accidental or capricious.

In sum, micro-level, system-oriented analyses are crucial if one is to address many of the objections often raised against the present system of income transfer programs. We are not suggesting that macro-level considerations are irrelevant. Quite the contrary, questions such as "How much would it cost to change program regulations in this way?" or "How many people would be affected if a particular eligibility condition were changed?" are vitally important. But the balance of analytic resources expended on micro versus macro approaches must also be considered. We believe that analytic difficulties have often resulted in too few, and too limited, microanalyses.

The next chapter explores why microanalyses have been so difficult and illustrates the kind of calculation that has historically been necessary to obtain even limited results on a micro basis. The second part of Chapter 2 addresses some early attempts to build a methodology appropriate to the need for micro-level systems analysis.

CHAPTER 2.
CONCEPTS AND COMPLEXITY

In Chapter 1 we discussed some of the reasons why the present set of benefit and tax programs is considered by laymen, program analysts, and policymakers alike to be difficult to understand. The arguments introduced there indicated a need for more micro-level, systems-oriented analyses. This chapter examines some of the difficulties that arise when one attempts to analyze sets of income transfer programs. In the course of doing this, we consider the complexity of individual programs, the difficulties created by interactions among programs and the basic responses to these problems. The chapter begins with a discussion and delineation of some of the concepts that will be used. Readers who have dealt with income transfer programs may wish to omit this first section and proceed to the example in the second section of this chapter.

CONCEPTS

Transfers. The basic notion of a transfer is obvious and needs no definition. The distinction between a "positive" and a "negative" transfer, however, is arbitrary and requires that we clarify the manner in which we plan to use these terms.

In this book we will focus primarily on individuals and families who are recipients of transfers. Hence, transfers that place money (or its equivalent) in the hands of individuals or households will be called "positive" transfers. Transfers that take money (or its equivalent) away from individuals or households will be called "negative" transfers. Obviously, what is a positive transfer from the standpoint of the individual is in general a negative transfer from the standpoint of the government, and vice versa. As we shall show, the methods subsequently described handle both types of transfers with equal facility.

Typically a positive transfer program specifies some payment (in cash or kind) to an individual (or other unit) as a function of some definition of income of the unit.[9] One characteristic of most positive transfer programs is that they are monotonic nonincreasing, which means that the benefit to a unit with a higher income is less than, or equal to, the benefit to a unit with a lower income. An example of a very simple transfer function is shown in Figure 2.1.

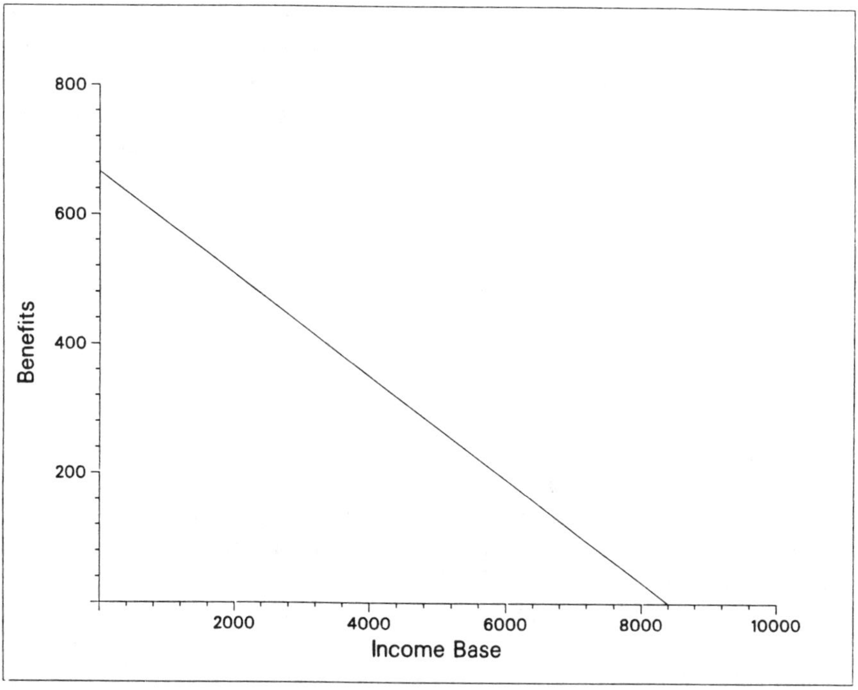

Figure 2.1: Benefits as a Function of the Income Base

This particular form can also be described mathematically, within the relevant domain, as a linear equation:

$$T = G - t\,Y, \qquad \text{for } 0 \leq Y \leq Y*$$

where T is the transfer (or benefit to be paid), G is the guarantee (or zero-income benefit), Y is the value of the income base on

---

[9] Demogrants, benefits which do not change with any change in income, are merely a special case in which the function is a constant.

which the benefit is calculated, t is the tax-back rate (or benefit reduction rate), and Y* is the income base value at which the benefit first reduces to zero. Several of these concepts warrant further comment.

Income base. The income base consists of the various sources of income from which the amount of the transfer is calculated. It may include only earned income. It may include earned income plus benefits from other specified programs, as in the case of the Food Stamp program where the income base includes not only earnings but benefits received from AFDC. It may include earned income less deductions, such as work-related expenses or taxes. In general, the income base may be any combination of these alternatives; that is, the income base might be the sum of earned (and other) income, plus benefits from specified programs, minus allowable deductions.[10] Typically, the value of the income base increases with earned income and benefits from other programs, and may decrease with negative transfers and work expenses.

In many cases "floors" and "exemptions"are also specified. Floors are typically used to keep the value of the income base from being negative, which could happen, for example, if taxes and allowable deductions exceeded earned income. More generally, floors and ceilings are used in the case of specific transfer programs to keep the value of the transfer or some deduction from being below or above some fixed value. Exemptions are used so that a fixed portion of the income or benefits being received is not taxed back. A well known example in the United States is the "30 and 1/3" rule for AFDC. Under prescribed conditions, the first $30 of income, and 1/3 of the rest of the earned income for the month, is not counted in establishing the income base for the person for that month.

Tax-back rate. Both "tax-back rate" and "benefit reduction rate" are used in the literature on income maintenance. We shall adopt the former since it calls attention to an important characteristic of this rate: namely, a benefit reduction has the same effect as a tax. For each additional dollar in its income base, the unit gives up

---

[10] Just as the set of elements contained in the income base of a specific transfer program varies across programs, so too the set of elements contained in the definition of income varies across analyses. The paper by Danziger and Plotnick (1982) illustrates several definitions of income often found in the literature.

("pays back") a portion of the benefit that it otherwise would have received. Thus the reduction affects work incentives just as if a corresponding amount had been taken from the unit by the tax system.

The tax-back rate is a critical factor in income transfers since each of several programs that provide positive transfers may use the same income component (earned income, for example) as part of the base on which the transfers are defined. Thus, increases in that component may cause not just one but several simultaneous reductions. The total effect of such a set of programs may be a higher effective tax on additional income than may have been intended by any of the programs individually, and indeed in some cases the net result may be a reduction in benefits greater than the increase in income. We shall return later to some examples of this type.

Breakeven point. The breakeven point for a positive transfer program is the point at which the benefits cease. In Figure 2.1, Y* is the breakeven for the hypothetical program because at that point benefits first equal zero.

In the special example of Figure 2.1 it is also clear that G, t, and the breakeven point, Y* are interdependent; any two determine the third since $Y* = G/t$. That this algebraic relationship should simplify understanding of the constraints for an income transfer function of this type seems obvious, yet Hausman (1975) found it necessary to emphasize this point. Many legislators, he noted, want to make the guarantee, G , as high as possible to encourage adequacy of benefits, to make t as low as possible to encourage work, and to make Y* as low as possible to minimize the total costs of the program by terminating benefits to people with incomes beyond a certain level. As he also pointed out, these three goals are in conflict. One cannot simultaneously approach all three.[11]

Multiple tax-back rates. Figure 2.1 was a special case in which the transfer function can be expressed as a single linear equation. Figure 2.2, on the other hand, shows another common transfer function. It is piecewise linear; it has a constant tax rate over each segment (Y_{i-1}, Y_i), but the rates for different segments of the income base may vary. Thus, although the transfer function is not linear in Y over its whole domain, the domain can be broken into segments

[11] Even more recently Gueron and Nathan report that the empirical results from "the negative income tax experiments highlighted the difficulty of simultaneously meeting the objectives of adequacy, work incentives, and minimal cost" (1984:5).

such that, within each segment, the function is linear in Y. Points Y_0, Y_1, Y_2, Y_3, Y_4, and Y* serve as the endpoints for these segments in Figure 2.2. For an income base value Y falling within segment i, the level of the benefit can be written as the linear function:

$$T = G - \Sigma_{j=1}^{i-1} t_j(Y_j - Y_{j-1}) - t_i(Y - Y_{i-1})$$

or

$$T = K - t_i Y, \text{ where } K = G - \Sigma_{j=1}^{i-1} t_j(Y_j - Y_{j-1}) + t_i(Y_{i-1})$$

Coefficient t_j is the tax-back rate of the j-th segment of the function, and Y is the value of the income base, such that Y occurs at an end point or within a single line segment (Y_i, Y_{i-1}). Thus,

$$T = G - t_1(Y - Y_0) \qquad \text{for } Y_0 \le Y \le Y_1$$

$$= G - t_1(Y_1 - Y_0) - t_2(Y - Y_1) \qquad \text{for } Y_1 \le Y \le Y_2$$

and

$$T = G - t_1(Y_1 - Y_0) - t_2(Y_2 - Y_1) \ldots$$

$$\ldots t_{i-1}(Y_{i-1} - Y_{i-2}) - t_i(Y - Y_{i-1}) \qquad \text{for } Y_{i-1} < Y \le Y_i$$

Other tax rate concepts. The literature on income transfers also contains reference to at least three somewhat different types of tax rates: average, marginal, and cumulative-marginal. The average tax rate is computed over a given range, usually from zero to a specified upper limit of income.[12] In Figure 2.2, for example, the average tax at Y_3 is equal to the reduction in benefits divided by the change in income, $(G-T_2)/(Y_3-Y_0)$; at Y_4 the average tax rate is $(G-T_1)/(Y_4-Y_0)$. If transfer functions are continuous and piecewise linear, then the

---

[12] Occasionally one finds in the literature average tax rates which are taken on a domain not including Y_0.

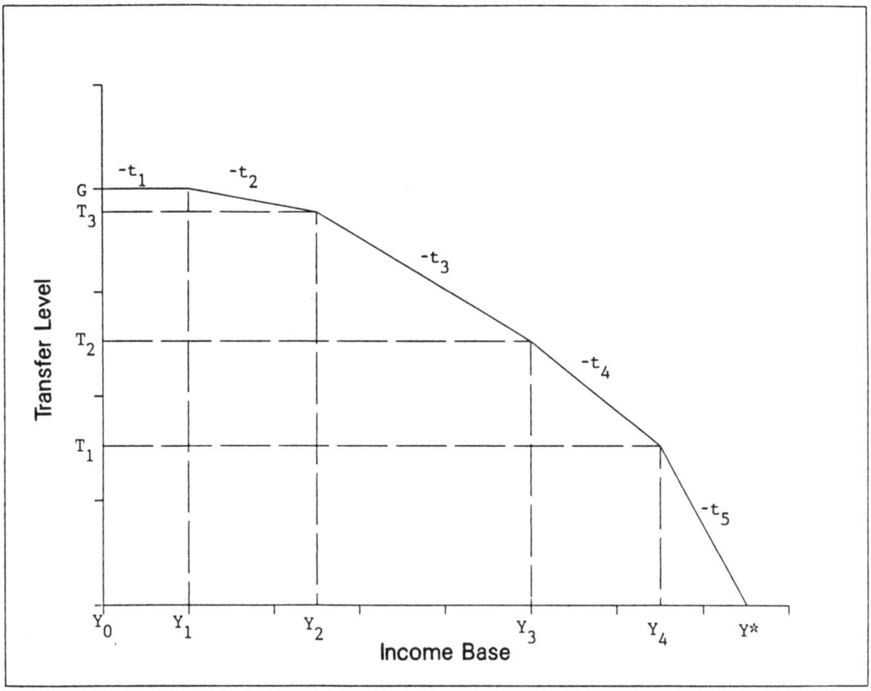

Figure 2.2: A Piecewise Linear Transfer Function

average tax rate will be a weighted average of the individual reduction rates, with the weights proportional to the domains over which the individual rates apply.

The marginal tax rate, which occurs more frequently in the literature, is effectively the amount of the benefit reduction per dollar increase in the income base and is closely related to the derivative of the transfer function at a given point. Marginal tax rates are especially important since they are the effective tax rates actually faced by individuals or families as they alter amounts of work effort. That is, marginal tax rates can be used to measure work incentives. For a given value of the income base there is a specific marginal tax rate, although the marginal tax rate may change as the value of the income base increases or decreases from that point. Only by chance does a family find itself paying the average tax rate. Marginal tax rates, therefore, are of intrinsic interest when one wants to know the incentives that exist for a family to increase or decrease work effort.

The tax-back rates, t, to which we have previously referred might be called the "true marginal tax rates," to distinguish them from the "cumulative-marginal tax rates." Because the analyst usually does not know and cannot compute the endpoints of the piecewise linear transfer function, cumulative-marginal tax rates are usually calculated by dividing the domain of the transfer function into arbitrary segments, and the tax rate for each segment is then found. Obviously, the smaller the segments, the more closely one can approximate the true marginal tax rates.

Offsets. The last of the concepts to be introduced in this section is the offset. Offsets occur when the benefit from the transfer program under consideration is reduced by some fraction of the amount to be paid from one or more other transfer programs. Algebraically, offsets can be represented as a simple reduction of the transfer:

$$T = \begin{cases} G - t(Y_B) - F & \text{if } G - t(Y_B) > F \\ 0 & \text{if } G - t(Y_B) \leq F \end{cases}$$

where F is the offset. Offsets are often used where benefits from different programs are direct substitutes for one another. In so doing, one avoids duplication of benefits and unreasonably high benefits to families getting transfers from several programs.

Thus, the presence of multiple benefits can be handled in two ways. First, income from other programs can be included in the income base, causing the benefit to be reduced by the prevailing tax-back rate, or second, income from other programs can be treated as an offset and fully (or partially) deducted from the benefit that would otherwise be paid.

Having specified our use of these terms, we shall now turn to an example that illustrates some of the complexity in the ways in which transfer programs can be interrelated and some of the difficulties that are encountered in the analysis of actual systems of programs.

CHARACTERIZING THE PROBLEM

Since almost all transfer programs can be represented as linear functions or piecewise linear functions of income, it might be imagined that transfer analysis would be a simple matter, and in some few cases it is. If one has a set of programs in which the benefits from one program are not affected by the benefits from any other program, if the definitions of the income bases are identical and the definitions of the recipient[13] are identical, and if the programs are reasonably uncomplicated, calculating the net transfer is not always a difficult matter. But life is seldom this simple. Typically the analyses one wants to do involve programs that interact, either because the benefits or taxes for one of the programs enter into the definition of the income base for another program, because some of the benefits from part of the programs are treated as offsets by other programs, or because the definition of parts of the system (such as recipient) differs by program. The following example illustrates some of these problems.

An Example

Let us assume that an analyst wanted to, or was directed to, examine the consequences of a set of welfare and taxation programs in existence at a specific point in time. (This is essentially the type of analysis that Senator Williams demanded from HEW and that, according to Moynihan, signaled the death of the Family Assistance Plan.) The analyst chooses earned income as the independent variable for the analysis and net (disposable) income for the family as the major dependent variable. In the United States the major factors that affect net income for lower income families include AFDC, Food Stamps, Medicaid, employment expenses, FICA contributions, federal and state income taxes, the earned-income tax credit, and of course, the unit's own earnings.

Although MAPSIT allows one to analyze sets of transfer programs across the entire domain of the independent variable, our present purpose is merely to illustrate the ways in which transfer programs interact. Consequently, for this illustration we shall not deal with the entire earned income domain but rather shall choose a specific value for earned income and illustrate the steps necessary to calculate the net income for a specific (albeit hypothetical) family. In particular we shall assume for our illustration that the family contains a single earner who receives $6700 per year from wages (working full time at the minimum wage, $3.35 per hour) and that the person has no other source of income except for the transfers from the programs listed above.

---

[13] We shall use "recipient" generically. In various programs recipients are known by various names, such as "assistance unit," "filing unit," "household," or "adult unit."

Transfers to and from a family often depend on the characteristics of the family. For example, transfers from a welfare program may depend on the number of adults in the family, the number of children, their ages, and the state and even city of residence. In our example we shall assume the family consists of a single parent less than sixty years old and three children, all less than eighteen years old, that none of the family members is disabled, and that the family resides in Pennsylvania, a state that computes state income taxes as a simple proportion of taxable income. Finally, we shall adopt 1984 as the year of analysis.

Having defined the family unit, its location, and the time period for the analysis, the second step in our illustration is the description of each of the programs.

State Income Tax. This is quite simple since the tax rate in Pennsylvania in 1984 was a constant proportion (.0245) of state taxable income, and state taxable income in Pennsylvania essentially included all income, with virtually no exclusions or deductions. Figure 2.3 represents this slightly simplified form of the state income tax. (In that figure the abscissa and the ordinate are drawn on different scales for greater clarity.)

Federal Income Taxes. Since we have assumed that, aside from transfers, the family has no sources of income (dividends, interest, rent, royalties, and so forth) other than earnings, earned income is the sole component of "taxable income," the income base for federal taxes. At the same time, however, the income exclusion of $1000 per person, or $4000 for the present family, and the dependent care tax credit for child care expenses are relevant for the present analysis.

To calculate income taxes, the tax schedule for single person head of household, Schedule Z, is used.[14] The schedule of taxes payable as a function of taxable income is shown in Table 2.1.

It is important to remember that the independent variable in Table 2.1 is taxable income, total income less exemptions, and not simply total income. Second, it is important to note that even in terms of

---

[14] For the family we are examining, federal tax law allows Schedule Z to be used only if the parent provides at least 50 percent of the cost of maintaining the home. If not, Schedule X for single persons must be used. In the present case the point at which the parent has to begin paying federal tax is beyond the point where the home maintenance rule is satisfied, so we have simplified the example by excluding Schedule X.

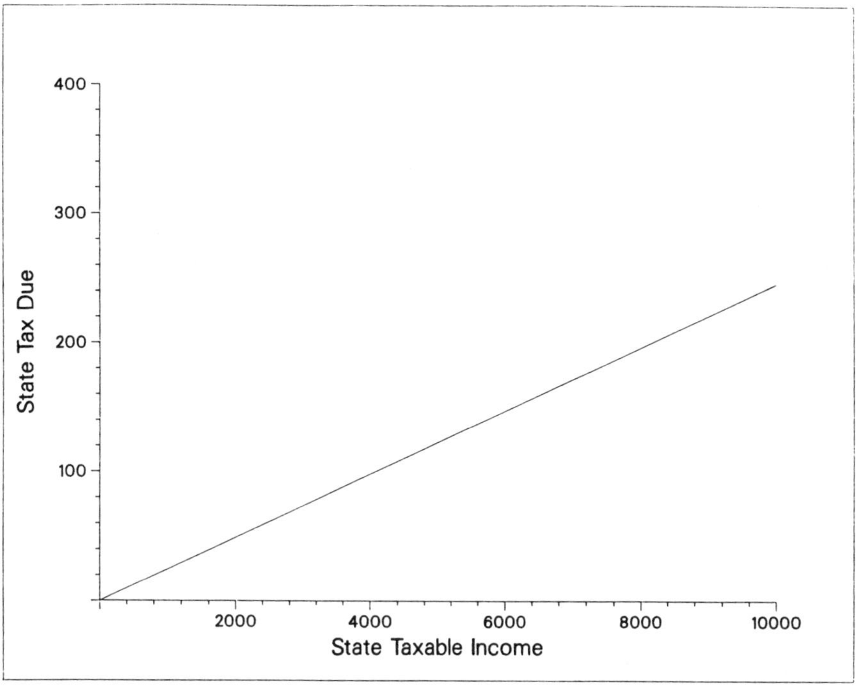

Figure 2.3: State Tax as a Function of Taxable Income, Pennsylvania

Table 2.1: Federal Taxes as a Function of Taxable Income, Schedule Z, 1984

Taxable Income	Tax Payable	Taxable Income	Tax Payable
2300	0	23500	3806
4400	231	28800	5290
6500	483	34100	6986
8700	791	44700	10696
11800	1318	60600	17374
15000	1894	81800	26914
18200	2534	108300	39634

taxable income there is no tax due until one has more than $2300 of taxable income. Finally, the arrangement of Table 2.1 is such that between any two values of taxable income one can find the amount of tax due by linear interpolation. This reflects the fact that the basic tax table contains fourteen separate tax rates, or equivalently, the transfer function consists of a piecewise linear function with fourteen line segments.

FICA. In 1984 the Social Security (FICA) tax was 6.70 percent of earnings up to the maximum contribution of $2532.60, which was reached at earnings of $37,800. This is shown in Figure 2.4. Note that for earnings above the maximum contributory amount, the FICA contribution remains constant.

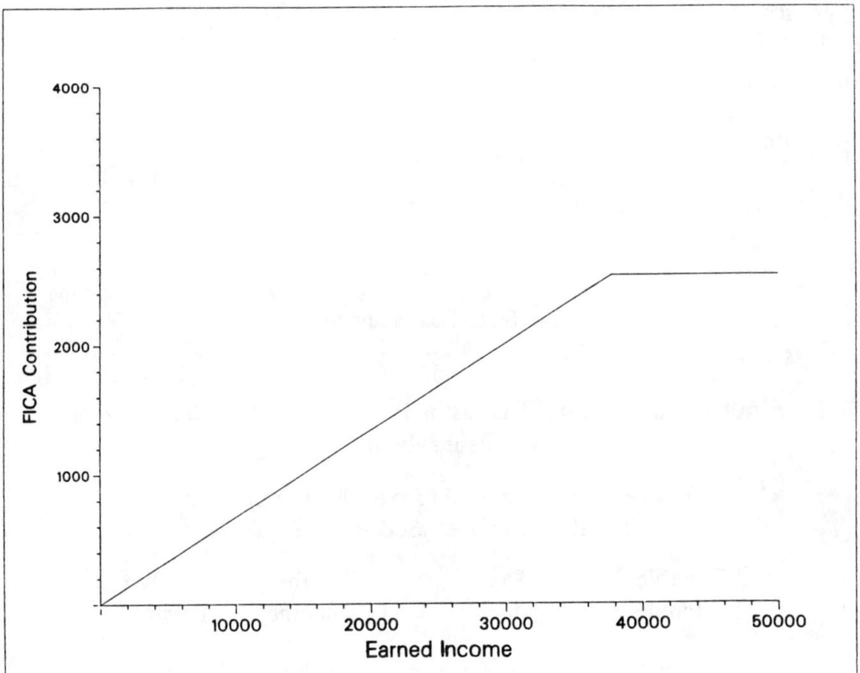

Figure 2.4: FICA Contribution as a Function of Earned Income, 1984

Earned-Income Tax Credit (EITC). The Federal government provides an earned-income tax credit for families with children. For families with income only from earnings, in 1984 the credit was a piecewise linear function with the following limits: if the earned income was between $0 and $5000 the credit was 10 percent of earnings. From $5000 to $6000 it was $500, and from $6000 to $10,000 it decreased by 12.5 percent of the amount by which earnings exceeded $6000. This can be written algebraically:

$$\text{EITC} = \begin{cases} .1Y & \text{if } 0 \le Y < 5000 \\ 500 & \text{if } 5000 \le Y < 6000 \\ 1250 - .125Y & \text{if } 6000 \le Y < 10,000 \\ 0 & \text{if } Y \ge 10,000 \end{cases}$$

and depicted graphically as in Figure 2.5.

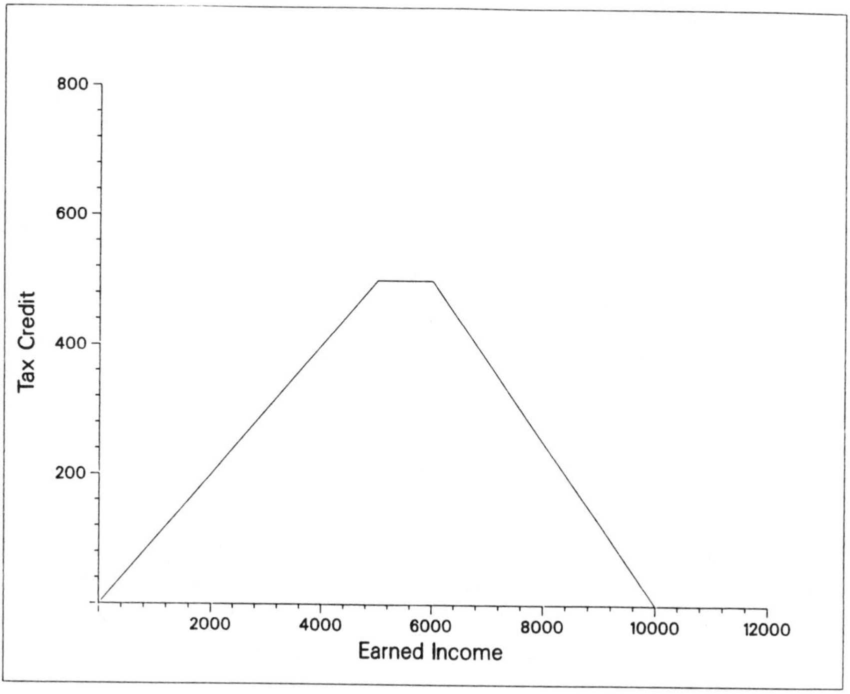

Figure 2.5: Earned Income Tax Credit as a Function of Earned Income

The Dependent Care Tax Credit. The tax credit for dependent care expenses can be used to help offset the cost of day care. We shall assume in the present case that one of the children is of pre-school age and needs day care and that the other two require no day care. For the child in the day care center we shall allow only those day care expenses incurred during the hours that the parent is working, and even these expenses are allowable only if the parent is supplying more than 50 percent of the cost of running the household. The credit is 20 percent of the actual expenses, but the credit cannot exceed the amount of the tax due or the maximum of $400 for one child ($800 for two or more.) Finally, unlike the earned income credit, this credit can be used only to reduce the federal tax payable, and cannot be taken as a refund.

AFDC. The income base for Aid to Families with Dependent Children includes both earnings and the Earned-Income Tax Credit (EITC), as well as other (unearned) income. When the parent is working, deductions are allowed for work-related expenses and for child care expenses. The work expense deduction is $75 per month, prorated for less than full-time work; the child care expense deduction is limited to the actual costs of child care necessary for employment, up to a maximum of $160 per child per month. In addition, there is an earned income exemption if the parent has been employed for less than four months while on AFDC. The earned income exemption is $30 per month plus one-third of the net earned income, where net earned income is earned income plus the earned income tax credit minus the deductions for work expenses, child care expenses, and the first $30 per month.

In general, the benefit is a result of subtracting available income (the income base) from the state specific payment standard. However, if the family's gross income (earned and unearned income plus the earned income tax credit) is greater than 1.5 times the payment standard, the family is ruled ineligible for any benefit.

The amount of the payment standard is determined by the state. In most states there is a single payment standard for a given size family, but in some states payment standards vary by region or other specification.[15] Figure 2.6 illustrates the relation between the benefit level and the AFDC income base for our four-person family in the specified areas of Pennsylvania in 1984.[16] The slope of -1 reflects the fact that every dollar increase in the income base results in the loss of one dollar in AFDC benefits.

---

[15] Pennsylvania is divided into four sets of counties based on the cost of living, and each of the four sets has its own benefit schedule. For the present discussion we shall adopt the benefit schedule for the set that includes Philadelphia and Pittsburgh.

[16] In this example we shall adopt an annual accounting period. Thus, although AFDC and food stamps are both calculated on a monthly basis, we shall treat these and other programs as if they were calculated on an annual basis. This procedure is adopted to simplify the problems raised by the fact that various programs have different accounting periods. It is possible to demonstrate that simple conversion from monthly to annual basis, or vice versa, is not always appropriate.

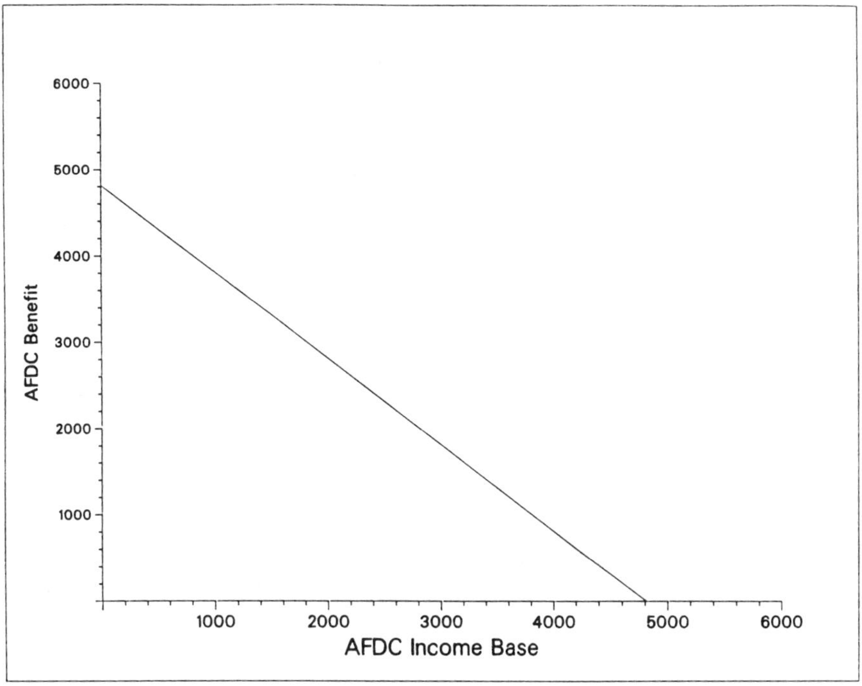

Figure 2.6: AFDC Benefits as a Function of AFDC Income Base

It is important to remember that the abscissa is the "income base" and not simple earned income or even gross earned income (earned income plus EITC). If we graphed the relation between earned income and benefits, we would also have to specify whether the family was eligible for the earned income deduction, how much was being paid for necessary child care, and the effect of the maximum gross income eligibility condition. If the abscissa were earned income and if (1) the family were eligible for the earned income deduction or (2) the family had sufficiently large child care costs, there would be a segment of the benefit function with a vertical slope where the benefits were terminated because gross earned income exceeded the maximum gross earned income limitation. As we shall later see, graphing relations like these is simple when one is using MAPSIT.

Food Stamps. The income base for food stamps in 1984 includes earned income, unearned income, and transfers such as AFDC and SSI. From this sum one subtracts 18 percent of earned income, a standard deduction of $1020 per year ($85 per month), and child care costs up to a maximum of $1380 per year ($115 per month).

There is also a shelter cost deduction. Monthly shelter costs in excess of 50 percent of the household's net monthly income (income less the earned income deductions, the standard deduction, and the child care deduction) may be deducted from net monthly income.[17] The size of the shelter cost deduction plus the child care, however, cannot exceed the annual equivalent of $1380 ($115 per month). Finally, for households containing persons age sixty or over, there is a medical expense deduction, but in the present example we have assumed that the parent is under age sixty.

Given the calculation of available income for food stamp purposes one obtains the monthly food stamp allotment by subtracting 30 percent of the household's net monthly income from the maximum monthly benefit for that household size. The relation between the income base and the food stamp allotment is shown in Figure 2.7, in annual terms, for a four-person household in 1984. The abscissa indicates the value of the income base (total income less deductions) and the ordinate indicates the food stamp allotment. The horizontal portion of this transfer function arises from the further stipulation that as long as the household's net available income is less than the maximum, the family receives a food stamp allotment of $10 per month. In 1984 the maximum net available income was $1,073 per month ($12,876 per year) for a four-person household.

Medicaid. Medicaid is available to people under several conditions. Of particular relevance to this analysis, it is categorically available to anyone who is receiving AFDC. In the present example we shall assume that the value of the medical expenses reimbursed by Medicaid can be treated as a cash benefit.[18]

Since the form of the transfer function for Medicaid is different

---

[17] For food stamp purposes, shelter costs include rent or mortgage, property taxes and insurance on structure, cost of heating and cooking fuel, electricity, water, garbage disposal, and a basic allowance for telephone service.

[18] We recognize the controversy concerning the treatment of in-kind benefits as if they were cash payments. The argument is especially relevant for medical expenses when they are paid not to the family but to the vendor. We have included their value to the family as the average cost reimbursed per person in AFDC on the (admittedly tenuous) assumption that medical consumption would remain the same and that the payments would have to be financed some way in the absence of Medicaid, either through out-of-pocket payments or through the purchase of medical insurance that would presumably cost as much as the average cost of services consumed. For an analysis of in-kind benefits, cf. Schmundt et al. (1975).

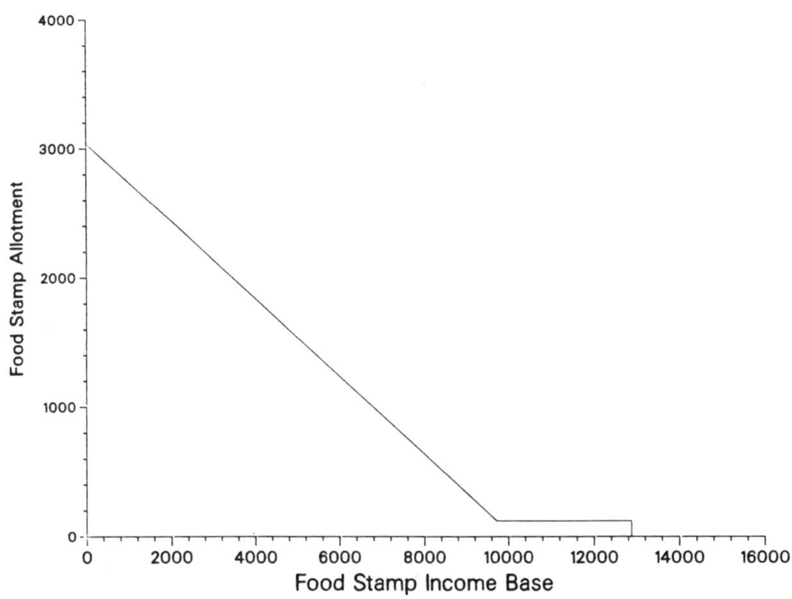

Figure 2.7: Food Stamps as a Function of Food Stamp Income Base

from any of the others, it is shown in Figure 2.8. The breakeven point for the Medicaid program is at point X on the abscissa, where X is the point at which the AFDC benefits cease to exist.[19]

This completes the list of programs and assumptions about their operation. The next step is to compute the net benefit for our hypothetical family. The various benefits and deductions are recorded in Table 2.2.

The first item in Table 2.2 is earned income, which we have as-

---

[19] Technically it is possible for a family to be eligible for Medicaid by virtue of their AFDC status even though they receive no AFDC payment. In particular, if the calculated AFDC benefit is greater than $0 and less than $10, the family is considered ineligible for AFDC but eligible for Medicaid. We have included this provision in the model to be presented in Chapter 5. It is also possible in some states to qualify for Medicaid if one is "medically needy," but we have ignored that computation since it depends entirely on the specific medical expenses incurred by the family.

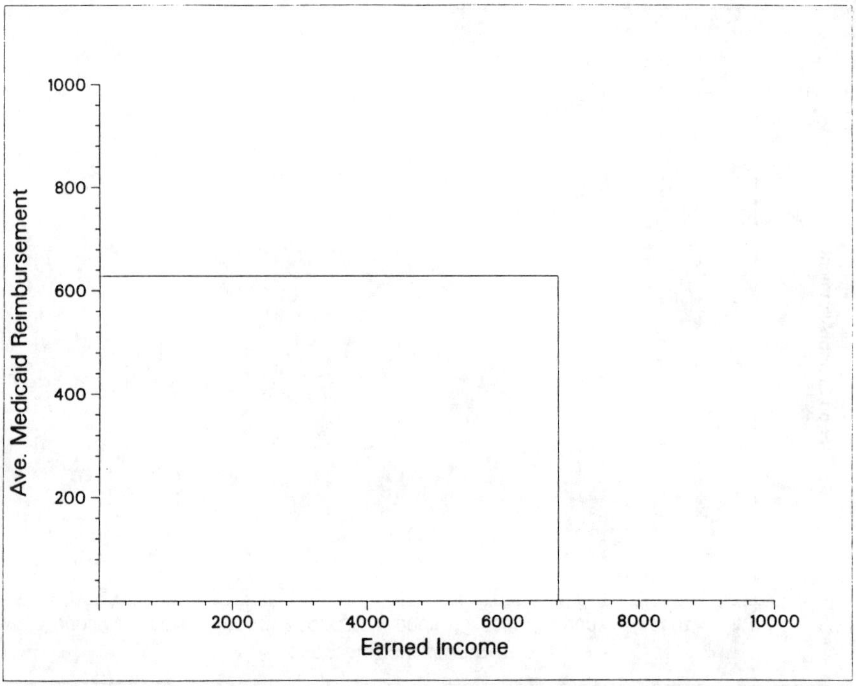

Figure 2.8: Average Medicaid Reimbursement by Earned Income

sumed is $6700 for this family. The next items are the state income tax of 2.45%, or $164.15, and FICA, calculated at 6.70% of earned income, or $448.90. Federal income tax is calculated by first deducting the $1000 exemption per person, reducing the taxable income to $2700. Interpolation from Table 2.1 shows a tax payable of $44.

Before calculating the AFDC benefit we need to calculate day care expenses. In the present example we assume that the parent is working full-time and that one of the three children is receiving full-time day care. Based on a sample of day care centers in Pittsburgh in May 1980, the average cost of full-time day care was $35 per child per week, or $1750 for fifty weeks. Updating this by an average of 5 percent per year for assumed increases in day care costs from 1980 to 1984, we obtain the estimated cost for full-time day care in a private day care center of $2735 per child per year.

The first of the positive transfers is AFDC. For AFDC purposes, the available income is the sum of earnings ($6700) and the earned income tax credit [$500 - .125(6700-6000)], minus the full work

Table 2.2: Calculation of Net Income for Example 1

Program	Transfer Positive	Negative
Earnings	6,700.00	
Taxes		
State Income		164.15
FICA		448.90
Federal Income		44.00
AFDC	519.50	
Food Stamps	1,951.95	
Medicaid	2,512.00	
EITC	412.50	
Depend. Care Credit	44.00	
	12,139.95	657.05

Total = $12,139.95 - $657.05 = $11,482.90

expense deduction ($900; $75 per month) and the maximum day care allowance ($1920; $160 per month.) Available income for this family is thus $7112.50 - $2820 or $4292.50, which is subtracted from the maximum benefit, $4812 for a family of four living in Philadelphia or Pittsburgh in 1984. The difference, $519.50, has been entered in Table 2.2.

To find the food stamp benefits, one begins with earned income ($6700) and subtracts the 18 percent earned income deduction leaving an adjusted earned income of $5494. One adds to this the AFDC benefits, and subtracts the standard deduction ($1020 per year), the maximum child care expenses of $1380 ($115 per month), and excess shelter costs. For the present illustration we shall assume that the shelter costs are $3600 per year, which is more than one-half of the adjusted net income, but since the child care deduction has already reached $1380 there is no further allowable deduction for excess shelter costs. Thus the available income for food stamp purposes is $3613.50, which on a monthly basis ($301.13) is less than the maximum net monthly income ($1073.00), so the family qualifies for a food stamp benefit. For a family of four, the benefit would be

$1951.95 for the year.[20]

The third benefit in Table 2.2 is Medicaid. We have included the value of the medical expenses reimbursed by Medicaid as a cash value, ignoring the fact that the value to the family may be less than the total amount of reimbursements. To estimate the amount of the medical reimbursement we have started from the data cited by Hausman (1975, p.45), that average expenditures for AFDC recipients in Illinois in 1971 were $222 per person. Between 1971 and 1980 the consumer price index for medical care increased from 128 to 263, a compound rate of 8.33% per year. Extrapolated to 1984 the average expenditures per person would be $628 per year, or $2512 for the family.

Finally there are two tax credits. Since we have assumed no unearned taxable income, the earned income tax credit is a simple calculation: $500 - .125(6700 - 6000), or $412.50. The dependent care tax credit, however, requires more work.

We have already stated our assumptions about the costs of day care. Here it is necessary to compare the expenditures to the maximally allowed expenses and verify that the appropriate limits are imposed: the costs of child care cannot exceed the earnings of the parent, and the parent must provide (not including benefits from AFDC) more than 50 percent of the costs of maintaining the home. In the present case the earnings are greater than the cost of day care, and the parent is clearly providing more than 50 percent of the costs of maintaining the home since earnings are $6700 and AFDC provides only $519 for the year. Nevertheless, the full $2735 of expenses is not allowable, since it exceeds the maximum amount for one child, $2000. Nominally the child care credit would be $400 since it is 20 percent of the allowable expenses, but it is also constrained to be no more than the actual taxes due, in this case $44. That amount is then entered in Table 2.2.

The net effect of all these programs is also shown in Table 2.2. Our hypothetical family with earnings of $6700 received a total of $5439.95 in benefits and paid $657.05 in taxes and mandatory FICA contributions. As a result of all these transfers their effective net income was $11,482.90, although from this they must pay $2735 in child care expenses, and we recall that the Medicaid benefit is a reimbursement and not paid directly to the family.

---

[20] We have chosen to ignore the fact that food stamp program rounds all calculations to the closest dollar and uses a step function with three dollar increments of available income.

Comment

We chose this example to illustrate some of the characteristics of transfer programs and the ways in which they can interact. The full complexity of even this problem is not portrayed in our example since we made a considerable number of simplifying assumptions to keep the complexity of the problem within reasonable exposition. (1) We simplified the income base for AFDC and food stamps by assuming away a number of potential sources of income, such as interest, rents, self-employment income, and pension income. (2) We simplified the tax system by ignoring a variety of possible income sources and by ignoring a variety of deductions and credits that might be relevant for many families, such as moving expenses, excess medical expenses, charitable donations, political contributions, and interest expenses. (3) We omitted a number of programs or pseudo-programs that a family would take into account when making decisions: mandatory company deductions for life and disability insurance, school lunch programs (and their effect on the food stamp program), state tax reductions based on earned income credits, and other non-monetary benefits, like free company health programs. (4) In modeling AFDC and the food stamp program we ignored complications such as eligibility tests, asset tests, and the possible existence of special needs for medical reasons. (5) We have converted all of the programs to an annual accounting period, eliminating in one fell swoop all of the difficulties associated with reconciliations due to income fluctuations and overpayments or underpayments. Nevertheless, we think that the analysis still preserves enough of the complexity to serve as an adequate illustration of both the ways in which programs are and can be linked and some of the problems that arise even in a straightforward analysis.

We also simplified the example in another important way. We calculated the effect of this set of programs for a single filing unit with a specific earnings level. While there is value in such a calculation, what the analyst usually wants to know is how programs interact across the entire range of the independent variable, in this case earned income. Even treating earned income as a discrete variable, there is a very large number of calculations that one might have to do to obtain a complete picture of the program interactions.

Although the example just presented was simplified in these respects, it still demonstrates a number of characteristics frequently found in actual analyses: (1) when one is interested in the entire domain of the independent variable, there may be more relevant programs than can easily be analyzed by hand, usually too many for any given analysis to be comprehensive and certainly too many for completeness. (2) The regulations that govern any given program may be complex, a fact easily verified by looking even at summaries of program regulations. (3) Different programs in a given system often employ different definitions of income, in part because the enabling legislation defines the appropriate treatment of transfers from other programs in the system. (4) Programs may employ different conditions for eligibility, either directly in terms of family characteristics, or indirectly in terms of eligibility for, or participation in, other programs. (5) Programs differ greatly in the extent to which, and the manner in which, they are linked: one may be part of the income base of another (as AFDC was for food stamps), or it may even be used to help define the eligibility for another (as AFDC did for Medicaid). (6) Often programs must be considered in sequential fashion; the complexity of the system is increased by the fact that the relationships among programs can be indirect as well as direct. Program A may affect program K because A affects the income base of B, which is an offset for program C, which . . . is an offset or part of the income base or an eligibility condition for K.[21]

A simplified representation of the relationships among programs used in our example is depicted in Figure 2.9. As shown there, child care expenses have a direct effect on food stamps (as well as on federal taxes and AFDC), but they also have an indirect effect on food stamps through their effect on AFDC. The net result of these (and the other) simultaneous relationships is not superficially apparent.

Our experience in using MAPSIT leads us to the conclusion that "judgment" and "intuition" are not always sufficient for understanding systems of income transfers. There are often surprises when systems are modeled; new things become "obvious" (Lewis, 1983).

EFFECTS ON ANALYSIS

To perform a competent microanalysis, the analyst must determine the relevant logic governing each of the programs and consistently resolve program differences regarding definitions of family, income,

---

[21] One of the requirements for the modeling package to be described is that one know the "chains of relationship," although one only has to know the "one step" relationships. Working backward, if M is affected by L and L is affected by K, and so forth, a sufficient picture of the network can be established for the algorithm in the modeling package to work.

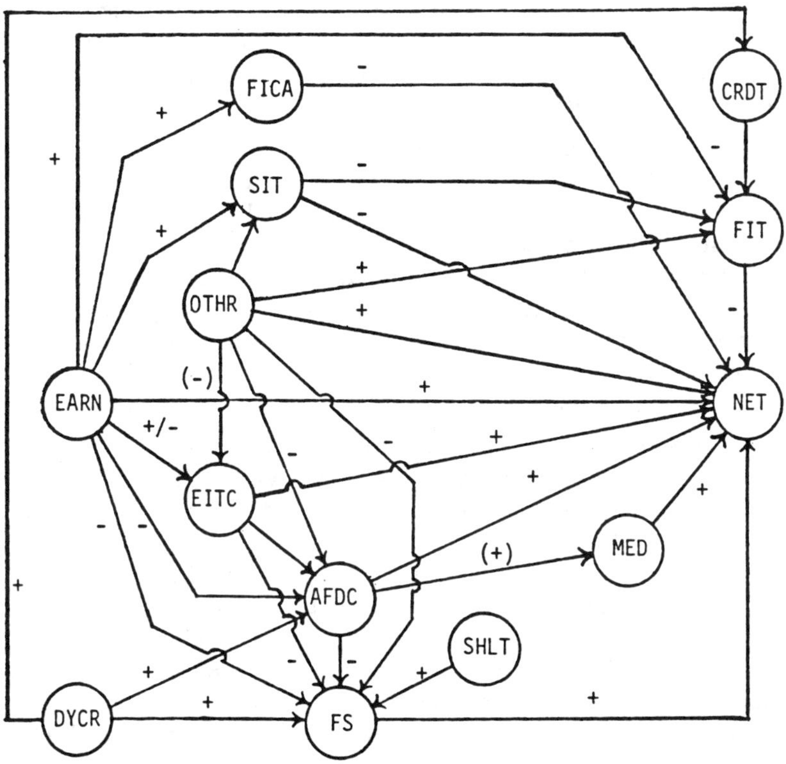

AFDC	Aid to Families with Dependent Children	FS	Food Stamps
CRDT	Dependent Care Tax Credit	MED	Medicaid
DYCR	Day Care Expenses	NET	Net Income
EARN	Earned Income	OTHR	Other Income
EITC	Earned Income Tax Credit	SHLT	Excess Shelter Costs
FICA	Social Security Contribution	SIT	State Income Tax
FIT	Federal Income Tax		

Figure 2.9: Relationships among Programs and Factors Affecting Net Income for a Low Income Family with Children

eligibility, accounting periods, and so forth. These demands frequently combine to ensure that microanalysis is rather expensive and that results actually achieved are unlikely to generalize.

Additional implications of such difficulties for microanalysis are also clear. Many important analyses will never be undertaken because committing resources to a project that is likely to be expensive, and whose results are likely to be rather limited, will often be considered inappropriate. For analyses that are done, their character will reflect the difficulties encountered:

1. When the analyst is operating under significant time and resource constraints there will be a tendency to build verbal models (cf. Lampman, 1971). This may be a rational approach, but unfortunately this approach often limits the analyst to rather a general level of recommendations, such as "limit the number of programs in which a family may participate in order to limit the possibilities for inappropriate program interactions." Such a position may or may not be appropriate in the end, but it tells the policymaker little about how current programs could be altered to improve system impacts.

2. There will be a tendency to produce analyses that include only a few hand-calculated examples from which the reader is implicitly or explicitly expected to generalize (cf., Appel, 1972; Sanger, 1982). Often, for clarity of presentation, details that may be relevant for actual families are omitted. For example, an analyst may choose to ignore certain mandatory deductions from gross pay, such as company pension contributions, life insurance, health insurance, and local wage and school taxes. In other cases even major programs, such as state and federal personal income taxes, are omitted (cf., Bergmann et al., 1980; Danziger, 1980; and Burkhauser and Quinn, 1981).

3. Stemming from pressure for generality there will be a tendency to produce analyses that concentrate on the most common cases (cf., Haveman et al., 1973; Plotnick, 1977). Analyses will deal primarily with "typical" families--the two-parent, two-child family is legendary--and only with major programs, despite the fact that participation in one or two of the less common programs can substantially alter the character of the system's impact on a family.

4. When analyses do involve computer models, the analyst will tend to program one subroutine for each program to be modeled. An executive program will then call the relevant program subroutines and coordinate the inputs and outputs for the subroutines. Modeling additional transfer programs or changing parameters in existing transfer programs often involves writing or rewriting the source code for the subroutines. Modeling more complex changes, especially those that change the order in which transfers must be calculated, typically involves rewriting both the executive program and the subroutines. This common limitation is particularly important when one recognizes that

programming and debugging are time-consuming and expensive tasks, and that analysts are not always competent programmers.

5. When computer models are built, they frequently do not generalize easily to alternative independent variables. Most computer models for microanalysis focus, either implicitly or explicitly, on earned income as the independent variable for the analysis. However, other variables, such as the proportion of earnings earned by the secondary earner, tax-back rates for a given program, number of weeks worked, or hourly wage rates, may often be appropriate for an analysis. Models keyed to earned income, because it is the most common independent variable, often cannot cope with the change to a different independent variable.

6. In addition, in many computer analyses the major portion of the labor investment goes into the development of the necessary logic, with insufficient attention to documentation and output. The lack of good documentation means that the system will be hard to maintain, it will be "people dependent," and more likely than not the built-in and hidden assumptions will become lost. Over time even the output may become difficult or impossible to decipher.

7. Without going into detail here, many analyses also display important shortcomings when measured against the criteria that are set forth in Chapter 3.

SOME PRIOR WORK

There is one very important exception to the generalizations just presented. It is the "Cumulative Tax Rate Model" by Allen (1972), a computer tool to help analysts overcome several of the difficulties just described. It is not a model per se, but rather a model building package--a piece of software that greatly simplifies the analyst's job of modeling whatever system of transfer programs and whatever particular type of family is of interest.

The model identifies several common types of programs and also embodies a more general type that subsumes the others as special cases. Specific transfer programs are thus modeled by substituting specific parameter values for the symbolic arguments of the various program types, and the analyst can build a model by constructing a data set that provides the particular parameters and also specifies the order in which the transfers from the system programs are to be computed. Constructing a new model then requires the construction of a new data set rather than the writing of new source code or assembler level code. Even though the data set construction bears some similarity to ordinary programming, this approach constituted a major advance over previous models.

In a paper presented in 1983, Watson et al. appear to have independently discovered both the importance of turning points for the analysis of systems of piecewise-linear programs and the sequential nature of the necessary calculations. Although their analysis includes more programs than are usually found in hand calculated analyses, the analysis also reflects many of the limitations of a non-computerized methodology.

Finally, there have also been a couple of attempts to understand the nature of possible program interactions by examining the ways in which pairs of programs can interact. Apparently independently, Dickinson and MacDonald (1974), in Canada, and Mirer (1975), in the United States, approached the problem of understanding program interactions through examination of the possible relations that could occur as a function of properties of transfer functions. While we shall not attempt to recount their analyses here, it is fair to say that in their attempts to understand the system they found it necessary to consider only highly simplified situations, using, for example, only two transfer functions, both of which are single, linear equations. Even then the results showed a high degree of complexity. Although some useful information has come from these analyses, it is quite clear that given the complexity of transfer programs and the differing sets of programs that enter into a given analysis, the effort to find a taxonomy of transfer interrelations in large systems is not going to be fruitful.

The limitations of the previous analyses are not the result of any unprofessionalism or shortsightedness on the part of the analysts or those responsible either for identifying issues to be addressed or for allocating the various resources to be used in performing the analyses. The kinds of shortcomings discussed are understandable as rational responses to the complexities and difficulties described. Traditional models of individual and organizational decision making would lead one to predict the general responses that have been observed.

Looked at in one way, the particular shortcomings mentioned above, and the example of Allen's Cumulative Tax Rate Model, indicate the broad manner in which the various problems can be eliminated, or at least alleviated. The "solution" to the difficulties does not lie in the construction of better models of specific substantive situations, but rather in the development of more sophisticated model building approaches, approaches specifically intended to address and reduce the major difficulties in building good micro-system models of transfer programs. The features that one would want in such a methodology are the subject of Chapter 3.

CHAPTER 3.
BASIC APPROACH AND DESIGN CRITERIA

In the preceding chapter we argue that analysts require a better technology for executing income transfer analyses and that the Allen Cumulative Tax Rate Model illustrates a useful approach. In principle, a modeling package of this sort can be very attractive. After one has paid the costs of developing the package itself, one can create a wide variety of specific models quickly and inexpensively. These benefits, however, are attainable only with a package designed and implemented to standards that are appropriate for the analyses to be conducted and for the policy environment in which the analysis will take place. Thus, even if one grants the assertion that a package can be useful, two very pragmatic questions remain.

1. What analytic difficulties will the package reduce and how will it effect these reductions?

2. If the Allen model only illustrates the approach, what specifically is being proposed?

This chapter takes up the first of the questions, with the answer to the second forming the central theme of Part II of this book. Thus, here we set out specific criteria that we believe are relevant and crucial for conducting analyses of tax/transfer systems as they affect individuals and families. Two characteristics of the discussion reflect our concern for practicality. First, for each criterion we describe the analytic consequences that ensue if the criterion is not met. Second, we indicate how MAPSIT attempts to satisfy the criterion. We recognize that the latter discussion must remain at a fairly general level since we have not yet provided a detailed description of MAPSIT. However, the discussion may be viewed in one sense as a problem-centered first pass at a description of MAPSIT. From this perspective, Part II of the book then provides a more structured, concrete description, and Part III merges the problem-centered and MAPSIT-centered descriptions by focusing on the role that the MAPSIT technology plays within an active policy environment.

For presentational purposes we group the criteria into three categories: generality, convenience, and cost. Generality includes those aspects of the package pertaining to the range of models one can build with the package, the degree of detail required or permitted, and the choice and character of the models' independent and dependent variables. Convenience includes the package's ability to render the construction and solution of models natural and error free, to provide or encourage the documentation of models and analytic results, and to generate results quickly. Costs includes those features that permit results that are undemanding of scarce resources such as analysts' time, computer time, and dollars, and secretarial and programming services. Clearly, economies in these areas are also relevant for obtaining results quickly.

GENERALITY

If a model-building package is to have an appreciable impact on the way in which income transfer analyses are executed, it must be general and flexible with respect to the models that one can build using it. If a model-building package cannot be used for a fairly broad range of problems, then the costs of learning to use the package are spread over fewer analyses, and thus the package is less likely to be used. Fewer uses and more widely spaced uses also mean, given learning and retention curves, that skill levels will tend to be lower and analyses less economical or less satisfactory. Limited applicability means that fewer analysts will learn or use the package, there will be less sharing of expertise, less standardization and improvement of conventions and terminology, and greater problems with personnel turnover. Fewer or inferior analyses mean that fewer policymakers will hear of or use the package. Thus, there will be less opportunity for the package to be applied, even to those areas in which it is appropriate. All of these difficulties can be linked loosely to a sort of "critical mass effect." The more general and flexible the package, the more likely potential users are to hear of it, to recognize its applicability to their problems, and to be able to use it successfully. As this discussion suggests, the broad topic of generality includes several criteria that are rather more specific.

Theoretical Foundations

The theoretical foundations on which a modeling package rests should be solid. The basic concepts should be well-defined, easy to understand, and consistent with standard modeling practices. The package's algorithms should be well-specified and should either handle all reasonable inputs or at least fail gracefully with an explicit warning to the user. Where the characteristics of the algorithms are not readily apparent, mathematical proofs are appropriate.

Should a package lack solid foundations or algorithms, then it is only a matter of time until anomalous results emerge from the package and are correctly identified as stemming from defects in the package rather than from models built using the package. Encounters with such results then breed suspicion of the entire technology and of its results, even though some of the results may be shown to be independent of the shaky portions of the package. Beyond actual errors in the foundations, appearances themselves are important. If the foundations do not look solid, potential users will hesitate to use the package or its results even though the foundations may in fact be solid. For sound, ethical policy analyses and recommendations, any suspicions, qualms, and uncertainty are anathema.

A substantial amount of material has been written to explain how MAPSIT works and what it allows users to do. Materials include pocket cards, reference manuals, mini-manuals, in-line comments in the source code, technical documentation, background papers, theorems, and algorithm descriptions. Communication of the foundations is quite tractable in the sense that the mathematics of piecewise linear functions is rather simple. We have included some of the more important concepts and results in Appendix A.

During the development of MAPSIT considerable attention was given to the appearance that the package presents, with the recognition that the naturalness and "surface validity" of the package would have a major impact on user confidence. Modeling operations were drawn primarily from the spectrum of computations appearing on the types of forms used in the administration of transfer programs, such as the IRS Form 1040. The reporting module of the package was designed to produce as outputs all of the tabular and graphic formats that analysts regularly use in their examinations of income transfer systems and their effects. Aggressive error checking in the package reinforces users in their attempts to generate accurate, meaningful results. The design philosophy calls for the user to be able to ascertain how the automatically generated results are produced, as evidenced, for example, by the inclusion in the package of one module devoted entirely to debugging and validating models built using the package.

Scope

To be really useful, a package must be able to build models that address a wide variety of substantive issues relevant to income transfer analyses. For example, one should be able to conduct analyses reflecting most or all of the categories that Storey (1972) identifies:

1. **Adequacy** - Given a definition of income adequacy, one should be able to build models for arbitrary family types that ascertain the degree of adequacy provided by arbitrary combinations of existing and proposed programs.

2. **Incentives** - One should be able to build models that produce meaningful measures of work incentives or other incentives over variables of interest to the analyst, including both earnings levels and policy parameters. The measures might include average, marginal, or cumulative marginal tax rates, slopes and derivatives, and transfer system reactions to decisions under family control.

3. **Equity** - One should be able to build models that address vertical and horizontal equity issues. One should be able to compare, directly within a given model or across different models, transfer system impacts on identical families interacting with different systems or different families interacting with a common transfer system.

4. **Family Structure** - One should be able to build models that identify the incentives that transfer systems provide for families to alter or misrepresent family size or structure. Relevant issues falling under this category include family splitting, adoption, marriages of convenience, common law living, young unmarried mothers keeping their children, and bearing additional children.

5. **Consequences of Administrative Error** - One should be able to build models that identify clearly the financial impacts of administrative errors in determining program eligibility or benefit levels. The identification should include the total impact of the errors, including the reactions of other programs in the system as they alleviate or aggravate the error, rather than purely first round effects.

6. **Administrative Complexity** - One should be able to use the package to investigate the administrative complexity in transfer systems, primarily in ascertaining what parts of the systems interact and the forms of those interactions.

7. **Program Inefficiencies** - One should be able to build models that ascertain the extent to which the various programs in a transfer system may be working at cross purposes, with respect to either adequacy or incentives. For example, one should be able to build a model to ascertain the extent to which increases in the benefit from one program go to benefit the family or to increase revenues or decrease costs for other programs in the system.

To the extent that a modeling package does not permit the construction of models that address all of these issues, users will be forced to rely on a variety of approaches in conducting analyses, and it will be more difficult to produce unified, internally consistent analyses and presentations. In our extensive Canadian and U.S. applications of MAPSIT we have built models and conducted analyses incorporating all of the issues just described, plus others, including analyses of the potential for system or program abuse. Chapter 10 contains descriptions for several of these analyses and issues.

Flexibility

The modeling package should allow an analyst complete flexibility in the choice of the transfer programs that will make up the transfer systems being modeled. The analyst should be able to model any transfer program, past, present, or hypothetical, and should be able to include in the systems any and all required linkages between pairs of transfer programs. Furthermore, the package should permit the analyst to model programs and systems as they apply to any relevant family type, size, and structure. The package should not impose assumptions on the substance of the models thus constructed; rather, the analyst should have total control over the assumptions in the models.

In the absence of these characteristics, the analyst will be constrained by the types of families, programs, and systems that can be modeled, and considerable effort will be diverted into trying to "outsmart" the package -- to get it to answer questions beyond the constraints. The resulting approximations and circumventions will erode the quality of the results. Furthermore, as the analyst is forced to devote more attention to the means of producing the results rather than the substance of the results, the quality of the results will further decline, and responsiveness will decrease. MAPSIT provides the required flexibility by giving the analyst a modeling language that contains no built-in assumptions about programs (other than piecewise linearity), and that has thus far allowed us to model income transfer programs or systems to any desired degree of accuracy.

Levels of Analytic Detail

The package should permit an analyst to build and solve models across the entire spectrum of levels of detail. Consider these two extreme cases. If the analyst wishes to specify directly a relationship between a model's independent variable and federal income taxes payable, the package should permit this. If, however, the analyst finds it necessary or appropriate to model the calculation of income taxes in all its detail, with a variable or relationship for every line in the tax forms and supplementary schedules, then the package should also permit this. Obviously, the package should also permit intermediate levels of detail.

If the modeling package constrains the analyst in the choice of levels of detail, then the analyst either will waste resources in trying to model more subtle considerations than the package permits, or will be forced to provide unreasonably large numbers of inputs and face higher computer charges than the analyses warrant. MAPSIT addresses the issue of levels of detail by providing the analyst with a universe of instructions that the analyst can combine at will into a model of any desired level of detail.

Independent Variable

The package should give the analyst the freedom to choose the independent variable for an analysis. Our experience has shown that for most income transfer analyses, the analyst wishes to ascertain the values of key dependent variables, usually program transfers or disposable income, along the entire domain of a single independent variable (annual earnings, wage rate, or guarantee level for example), while holding constant a configuration of other parameters (such as family size and structure, place of residence, and various policy parameters). Two aspects of the independent variable are particularly important: the choice of an independent variable for an analysis and the treatment of that variable as a continuum.

Taking the choice aspect first, we believe an analyst ought to be able to treat any reasonable variable in a system as the independent variable for an analysis, and indeed, ought not have to know or choose that variable when modeling the system of interest. In the absence of such freedom, an analyst will not be able to gauge the response of a system to changes in its variables, even when willing to "freeze" the values of all the other variables and parameters that are inputs to the model. Such a restriction would be an immense handicap to meaningful sensitivity analyses, for the analyst would, at best, be forced to edit or rebuild models to conduct such analyses, and at worst, be unable to ascertain the system sensitivity to changes in its inputs.

Turning to the second aspect, the use of a continuous independent variable, we believe that most of the variables an analyst might wish to use as independent variables are inherently continuous; our previous examples of earnings, wage rate, guarantee level, or a policy parameter such as an amount of exempted income are, for practical purposes, continuous variables. For other potential independent variables, such as the number of children in a family, even though the variables are only meaningful for a subset of points on the continuum, there is no harm done in treating the variables as continuous in one's models, while looking at results only for integer values of the variables. What is particularly important is that the analyst not be forced to specify beforehand explicit values of the independent variable that will be of concern. The package, rather than the user, should bear the burden of ascertaining precisely where on the continuum taxes cut in, benefits break even, or tax brackets change, or across what income domains a specified set of programs is taxing back additional earnings. Such knowledge is crucial to an appreciation of what is happening in a transfer system and should automatically evolve from analyses, with little or no effort on the part of the analyst. If the analyst must actively search out or derive this information rather than receive it automatically, time demands will ensure that the seeking remains undone and both the what and how of the system operation remain unclear.

In MAPSIT, fundamental design criteria include both the freedom of choice for independent variables and the continuity of independent variables, in association with the automatic derivation of all the independent variable values at which "things happen." The analyst builds models virtually without regard for the specific variable to be later used as the independent variable for an analysis. Subsequently, when an analysis is desired, the analyst chooses the specific variable that is to serve as the independent variable. Thus, the analyst models a given system only once, even though several different variables in that system may eventually be used as the independent variable for analyses. MAPSIT then treats an indicated variable as a continuum, deriving the dependent variables as functions of it, complete with the automatic derivation of all cut-ins, breakevens, tax bracket changes, and so forth. The analyst is free, of course, to have the dependent variables displayed either at specifically chosen values of the independent variable, like round numbered thousands of dollars, or at those values where "something happens" as derived automatically by the package. Moreover, MAPSIT can further indicate why each of these latter values shows up in a solution of the transfer system.

Parameter Configurations

The package should provide the analyst with the capacity to specify conveniently alternate parameter configurations for variables not used as independent variables. If analysts cannot conveniently ascertain the implications of different values for different solutions of a model, then the quality of sensitivity analyses will suffer, and analysts will be unable to explore effectively the workings of transfer systems. At the same time, analysts should not continually have to respecify those parts of the transfer system that remain fixed across analyses. MAPSIT responds to this set of needs by permitting analysts to "hardwire" parameter values into models, to read them from disk files, or to supply them individually in response to user-specified prompts when a model is solved.

Dependent Variables

The package should provide the analyst with substantial flexibility regarding the dependent variables that models generate. Although an analyst will most often be concerned with the transfers to and from the various income transfer programs as the dependent variables in analyses, many other dependent variables may be relevant for particular analyses. Examples include measures of net or disposable income, ratios of transfers, implicit marginal or average tax rates, tax cut-ins and benefit breakevens, the size of penalties for nonoptimal decisions, or difference comparisons across systems. If an analyst is unable to generate the desired dependent variables or must put up with crude proxies for them, then the analysis itself may remain undone.

The design of MAPSIT addresses this issue by providing a language that permits the analyst to employ any dependent variable that can be created by some sequence of instructions in the language. Chapters 5 and 6 illustrate many such variables, but the possibilities are constrained primarily by the analyst's imagination.

CONVENIENCE

If a model-building package is to have an appreciable impact on the execution of income transfer analyses, it must be convenient to use. To serve as an effective decision support system or policy tool, the package must address the various analytic tasks by means that simultaneously maintain rigor and provide the analyst with a natural framework of concepts and procedures relevant for income transfer analyses. The greater the convenience of the package, the greater the fraction of time that the analyst can devote to issues of substance rather than to the mechanics of the analysis. Furthermore, to the extent that the available tools are natural rather than contrived, the analyst is less likely to make errors. As with generality, the broad classification of convenience has several subcategories.

Language

The package should provide a natural "language" for modeling programs, program components, and program interrelationships. The language should provide statements or instructions corresponding to all of the calculations used in ascertaining program eligibility or computing taxes or program benefits. In addition, it should provide additional statements for calculations of a more analytic nature, it should enable the analyst to shift freely among income definitions, and it should permit comparisons across programs and systems of programs. The language should be rigorous and precise as well as understandable to the several groups that may use it -- analysts, clerks, programmers, policymakers, and administrators.

If the modeling language does not reflect the calculations used to administer transfer programs, then analysts will be unable to build models that parallel those forms. The models consequently will be more difficult to build, harder to understand (especially for those not technically skilled), and more likely to contain errors. If the modeling language does not provide for analytic needs in modeling, then analysts will be forced to abandon certain approaches or to make do with approaches that only hint at what is really wanted.

The building block instructions for MAPSIT were chosen as a union of the calculations appearing on forms used to administer tax and benefit programs. Others were chosen because of their suitability for the kinds of analytic tasks regularly undertaken. In both cases the phrasing of the instructions was carefully chosen, user tested, and adapted for consistency across instructions and in response to user comments. The resulting language is so natural that it can be read by persons who are not familiar with MAPSIT, and so natural that the MAPSIT models of programs are sometimes used to introduce staff to the logic of transfer programs.

Diagnostics

The package should provide meaningful diagnostic messages for the things that can go wrong during the creation of models, their solution, and the presentation of results. These messages should incorporate, when feasible, the analyst's variable names and the relevant operation numbers from the models involved. Without such references, the analyst may be unclear about the exact location or nature of the error. The package should be "smart enough" to generate diagnostic messages for at least some substantive errors, as well as purely mechanical ones. For example, the package should be able to warn the analyst if the model attempts to add two relations that are not functions of the same independent variable, and should be capable of detecting instructions with missing arguments. In the absence of this capability, the user may accidentally, through carelessness or typographical errors, enter models incorrectly and not discover the errors until it is too late and results have already been generated and distributed. MAPSIT contains extensive diagnostic capabilities for model entry and consistency checking as well as for printing analytic results. In addition, the wording of the diagnostics makes extensive use of the analysts' names and the models' operation numbers so that the messages, which are for the most part in sentence form, can be readily understood. Furthermore, the diagnostics, as well as the dialogue for interacting with the package, are available in multiple levels of detail, allowing the analyst to choose the desired level.

Package Documentation

The package should include extensive, accurate documentation materials and should be self-documenting as well. In the absence of sound documentation, analysts will have a difficult time learning to use the package and will be especially reluctant to try new or complicated analyses. MAPSIT possesses an extensive users' manual, plus additional material including a mini-manual, a reference card, and assorted background papers. All of these are written for both didactic and reference use.

The package should be self-documenting where feasible. In the absence of this feature, analysts will be forced to carry the documentation to the terminal or to guess when in doubt. MAPSIT provides self-documentation in three important respects, documentation that can be accessed interactively in the middle of whatever task the analyst is pursuing. First, whenever the analyst must choose from a fixed menu of keywords or a menu of analyst-provided variable names, MAPSIT can display, on request, the complete menu. Second, when the analyst is unsure of the meaning of a prompt, and is not already operating at the most detailed dialogue level, the next more detailed version of the prompt can be displayed by entering a question mark response to indicate uncertainty. Third, the analyst can request, by means of the HELP command, a textual description of any of the MAPSIT keywords in any of the modules and their subsystems.

Analytic Documentation

The package should facilitate the documentation of models and analytic results. Models are algorithms that inevitably include whole collections of assumptions and relationships; at times the reasoning behind these assumptions is as important as the specific assumptions actually made. If a package does not actively support the inclusion of good documentation within a model, or does not provide for convenient updating of that internal documentation, then it is only a matter of time until whatever documentation exists becomes outdated or even harmful to an understanding of what is happening in the model. Given the time pressures under which many analyses are conducted, it is vital that the package document models automatically wherever possible.

MAPSIT supports both user documentation and automatic documentation. The user can enter comments, section headings, and descriptions of variables and transfer programs as a formal part of a model. MAPSIT then carries these items through successive versions of the model unless the analyst alters them, and in this latter case, maintains the altered versions of the documentation items. Furthermore, much of the documentation is carried through the solution of the model and is made available as legends, descriptions, or parameter configurations to the module that reports on analytic results.

The documentation of analytic results has another dimension as well. The analyst has a right to expect well-formatted, unambiguous presentations of analytic results, whether in tabular or graphic form, without having to pay the price of specifying those formats explicitly. At the same time, the analyst should be able to override the default formats for customized presentations. Insofar as possible, the outputs should be in final form or "camera ready." A shortcoming on either of these counts is serious. If results appear in ambiguous formats, then they are subject to misinterpretation and are possibly inferior to having no results at all. If results appear in other than final form, then their eventual use is subject to both unwanted time delays and the possibility of transcription error during conversion to the desired final form. MAPSIT's design pays special concern to all of these issues. The report generation module provides a variety of formats for the most commonly used forms of presenting results, from tables of breakevens and the documentation of the parameter configurations used in analyses, through summary tables of transfers and incomes across a domain of the independent variable, to specialized presentations for marginal and average tax rates and for determining isoquants. The default formats have been revised as a result of extensive usage so that they are easy to understand and especially resistant to misinterpretation, but MAPSIT still allows the analyst to override those defaults for special audiences. These efforts have been successful enough for photocopies of MAPSIT output to appear regularly in the reporting of analytic results.

Responsiveness

One of the most important characteristics a package should have is responsiveness. That is, an analyst must be able to use the package to get results quickly. The nature of an active policy environment serves to ensure that results are always needed yesterday; if results cannot be obtained quickly, they are frequently irrelevant to the discussions at hand. Even when comfortable lead times are available, there will always be last minute changes in parameter configurations, decisions to include additional detail in some corner of the model, or a newer interpretation about how some transfer program actually works. Policymakers need to know, in a matter of minutes or hours, the implications of these changes, so that the automated derivation and presentation of results is mandatory.

A second aspect of analytic speed is also relevant. Part of an analyst's stock in trade is the ability to interact creatively with models, to dig back into them to discover the causes of unexpected findings. Any significant lag between the time the analyst initiates an analysis and the time that the results are available severely inhibits this interaction. MAPSIT's interactive nature and the automated calculations for solving models and presenting results make it extremely responsive. Most models can be constructed in a few hours. Solutions and presentation of results requires only minutes. Solving an existing model under an alternative parameter configuration, printing the implications of that configuration, and displaying the differences between the implications of a base configuration and those of the new configuration may take as little as five minutes.

COSTS

If a modeling package is to have an appreciable impact on the way in which income transfer analyses are executed, it must be economical to use. In describing economy we shall employ a fairly broad notion of costs, including personnel costs and time costs as well as the more traditional direct computer costs. Any failure of a package to be economical on these counts imposes severe limitations on the policy impact that the package can have. First, if an analysis is expected to be expensive, it may not be authorized for execution. Clearly, an analysis that is not performed can have no direct impact on policy. Indirectly, of course, the failure to execute an analysis can have substantial impact if an inferior decision results. Second, if an analyst is using an expensive package as opposed to an economical one, a greater proportion of the effort will focus on cost reduction devices and a lesser proportion on the problem substance. Possibly this shift of effort will lead to greater attention paid to what is really wanted, but any such gain is likely to be small relative to a tendency to perform cheaper "make-do" analyses rather than to generate what is actually wanted. Third, when analysis is expensive, analysts will feel obliged to attempt generalizations on the basis of a relatively small number of cases. Our analyses using MAPSIT have shown that the impacts of systems of income transfer programs may be sensitive to several of the system parameters and that what are reasonable impacts for one family structure and income level may turn out to be utterly perverse for another structure and income level.

Economy of a modeling package is, of course, relative. One measure of economy is a comparison to the cost of doing the same analysis using another technology. We estimate that, on this measure, MAPSIT analyses average about one-tenth the cost, on both computer dollars and staff days, with the cost measured in terms of what else could be done with those resources. The computer dollar figures are given for interactive use at prime-time commercial rates. We break them down in terms of the three main stages of analysis: modeling and model entry, model validation and solution, and presentation of results.

Modeling and Model Entry

In this stage the analyst fleshes out the problem and models the relevant transfer system in terms of sequences of MAPSIT operations, probably drawing heavily on the MAPSIT library of transfer programs already modeled. The stage also includes the entry of these instructions, via the MAPSIT editor, into a specially formatted disk file. Because of MAPSIT's completeness and consistency checking, this stage is usually the most expensive of the three. A typical analysis may require something less than one staff day and less than $200 of direct computer costs. A relatively large model may require five staff days and $1000 of computer costs. The preceding estimates are for models that an analyst constructs from scratch. Most of the analyses that use MAPSIT are at least grossly similar to analyses that have been done previously, and so the earlier models can be edited, or at least used as "templates" to further reduce modeling costs.

Model Validation and Solution

In this stage the analyst validates the model, by checking to ensure that the calculations performed when MAPSIT derives a model's implications are the ones actually desired, and then requests solutions of the model for the relevant parameter configurations. Because the MAPSIT editor checks the model for logical completeness and many forms of internal consistency, the validation in this stage can ignore these mechanical details and concentrate on the substance of the problem. Typically an analyst validates a model by requesting one or two solutions of the model for specific parameter configurations and then requests detailed printouts of intermediate and final results. The actual validation consists of reproducing a subset of these results by hand, with the checked values chosen for their centrality to the desired results. An hour or two of hand calculation is usually sufficient. The computer dollar cost of solving a model is typically about five dollars, with a large model costing perhaps twenty dollars. Because the solution process is automated, the staff cost of such solution is literally a matter of minutes and is primarily a function of the number of parameters whose values are asked for at solution time rather than being "hardwired" into the model.

Presentation of Results

In this stage the analyst generates the specific presentations of results. The substance of these results may be as simple as tabulations of amounts of transfers at different levels of income, or may be more esoteric, involving marginal tax rates, the derivation of isoquants, or the relative contributions of relevant transfers to a family's disposable income. The costs associated with such presentations, although higher than those for solving models, are quite reasonable. A typical session focused on presenting results takes less than half an hour and generates perhaps twenty dollars in computer charges. For a large session involving many tables and the concatenation of results from several solutions, the session might take an hour and a half and cost $100. The design of MAPSIT's report generation capabilities has two major cost reduction thrusts. First, the variety of available output forms means that the analyst usually can get exactly what is wanted, and thus there is no need to compile partial results into a format suitable for final processing. Savings in both the analyst's time and computer resources result. Second, the high quality of the output formats, combined with the ability to get what is wanted and the ability to customize the formats further when desired, means that the results are usually in final copy form. This capability eliminates the need for secretarial resources that would otherwise be required for retyping or redrawing the output, and also reduces the potential for transcription error. Some indication of the quality of results may be gleaned from the fact that direct photocopies of MAPSIT output have been sent to the Canadian Cabinet for use in Cabinet discussions, while in other cases of MAPSIT analyses used by Cabinet, the formats have been retained, but results were retyped to provide a different type face -- more a comment on the available printer than on MAPSIT formatting. In the United States, plots generated directly from MAPSIT tables were used by the staff of the House Ways and Means Committee as background material on the programs of the Committee (Committee on Ways and Means, 1982).

CONCLUDING REMARKS

This chapter has outlined the characteristics that an income transfer analysis package should have if it is to make a meaningful impact on the way one analyzes income transfer problems. Our main concern has been to identify desirable characteristics, to indicate the nature of the penalties paid if a package does not possess those characteristics, and to describe, usually in rather general terms, MAPSIT's performance on the characteristics. Although our choice and emphasis on characteristics is inevitably colored by our experience with MAPSIT, we believe that they represent a fair cross section of the requirements for an effective policy package for income transfer analyses.

With respect to generality we conclude that MAPSIT is applicable to a wide range of problem areas. It enables analysts to build models in multiple levels of detail, and it imposes no hidden assumptions on analyses. Furthermore, it provides considerable flexibility in the choice of independent and dependent variables, of sensitivity analyses, and of alternate parameter configurations. MAPSIT is also convenient. It provides a modeling language that is simultaneously natural, powerful, and rigorous; it provides extensive diagnostic facilities for modeling and for the automated solution of models; and it provides results responsively, with extensive facilities for including both automatic and user-supplied documentation along with analytic results proper. In the area of costs, we believe that the coordinated package approach yields high quality results, often at a mere fraction of the corresponding costs of other technologies whether measured in computer dollar costs or staff days. Our experience in conducting or observing MAPSIT applications in a variety of policy environments, from departments of the Canadian federal government, through provincial governments across Canada, to departments of the U.S. government, convinces us that MAPSIT meets the demands of income transfer analysis as it is presently practiced and as analysts and policymakers would like to see it practiced.

The perspective we have taken in this chapter has been that of an observer looking at the general topic of income transfer analyses and considering the nature of a technology that would allow analysts to address the many substantive issues in a manner that is simultaneously effective, rigorous, and practical at the same time that it is responsive and economical. Although this perspective allows us to conclude that a modeling package is a virtual necessity as a decision support system for these issues, and further allows us to ascertain the major characteristics of such a package, it does not provide a useful way of describing coherently a specific modeling package such as MAPSIT. Thus, in Part II, we switch our perspective from the general level of income transfer analyses, to a narrower focus on MAPSIT itself. Subsequently, in Part III, we illustrate the application of the specific package MAPSIT to the general problems we have been describing here.

PART II

THE MAPSIT PACKAGE

CHAPTER 4.
MAPSIT

On the basis of the criteria established in Chapter 3, an acceptable technology for income transfer analyses will need to be computerized. Computer assistance is necessary both to achieve the degree of accuracy desired over the extensive calculations required for a typical analysis and to minimize transcription errors in the presentation of results. In addition, computer assistance is necessary to produce analyses quickly, including the time it takes to validate a model, to derive results under alternative parameter configurations, and to do the detailed calculations required for the presentation of results.

Where Part I addressed general issues and a basic approach for income transfer analyses, Part II takes up MAPSIT as a specific implementation of that approach, that is, describes MAPSIT as a software package built to supply a coherent technology for performing income transfer analyses. In this first chapter of Part II, the focus rests on the software per se as seen from two distinct perspectives: (1) the modules that make up the package and the tasks they perform, and (2) the flow of control among and within the modules during analyses. Later in Part II, Chapters 5 and 6 develop two detailed examples to illustrate how an analyst can use MAPSIT to model income transfer systems, Chapter 7 illustrates the broad range of report generation facilities available, and Chapter 8 completes the description of MAPSIT with a catalog of other major features.

STRUCTURE OF THE MAPSIT PACKAGE

One way of depicting MAPSIT is through a structural overview diagram such as Figure 4.1.[22] In the center column of the diagram the small boxes with solid perimeters represent the several modules of

---

[22] Figure 4.1 is reproduced from MAPSIT (Modular Analysis Package for Systems of Income Transfer, Version 5), courtesy of the Department of National Health and Welfare, Ottawa, Canada.

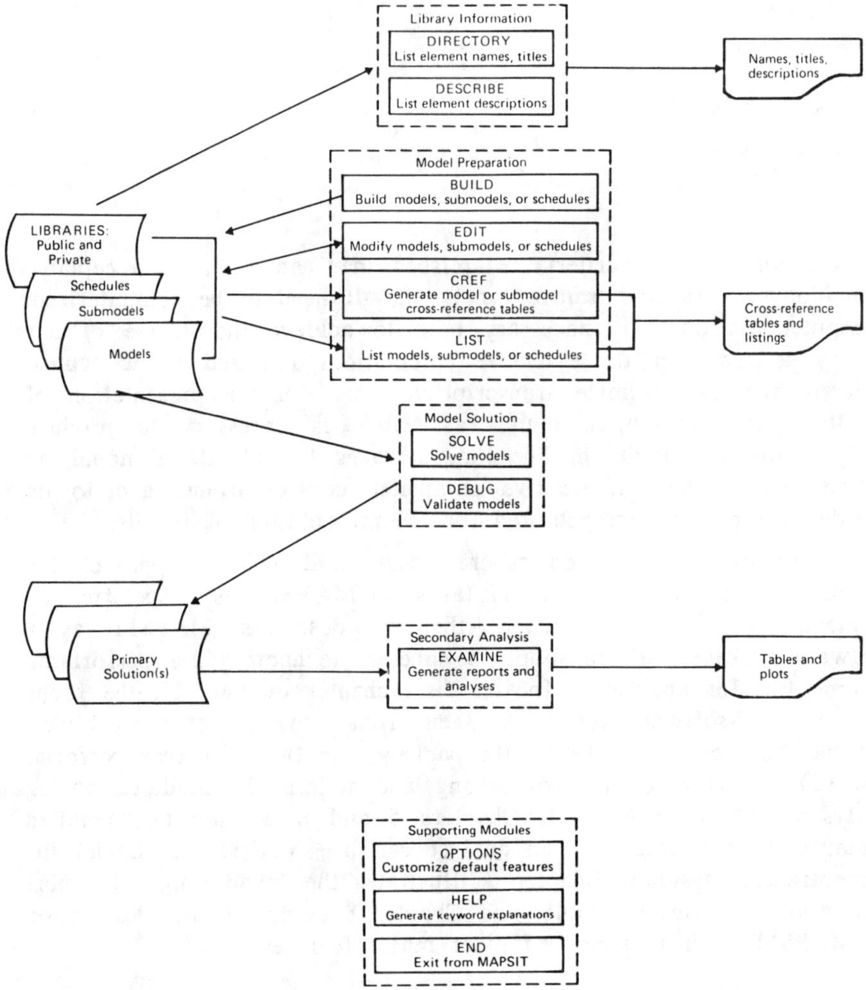

Figure 4.1: Structure of MAPSIT

MAPSIT. The dashed boxes surrounding groups of them divide the modules into related functional areas; for example, both the DIRECTORY and DESCRIBE modules enable the analyst to retrieve information about the elements of the Library.[23] Appearing in the

---

[23] Throughout the book we use the convention adopted in MAPSIT of capitalizing the names of the modules (DIRECTORY, DESCRIBE, BUILD, and so forth) as well as the acronym MAPSIT, Modular Analysis Package for Systems of Income Transfers.

right-hand column are the major "hard copy" outputs available from MAPSIT, although, technically speaking, many of these may also appear in disk files or on a video display terminal. Arrows pointing to these outputs identify the modules that produce them. The left-hand column of the diagram indicates the major disk files relevant, from the analyst's viewpoint, to the operation of MAPSIT. However, MAPSIT also employs several other files, such as files containing dialogue and error messages, with which the analyst does not interact directly.

The diagram has been constructed so that the general analytic flow, for typical analyses, runs from the top of the diagram to the bottom. Illustratively, an analyst begins an analysis by querying the Library, via the Library Information Retrieval modules, to ascertain what existing material can be reused. Next, the analyst employs the Model Preparation modules to build or edit a model appropriate to the problem at hand. The Model Solution modules then assist in the validation of the model and the derivation of its numerical implications. Finally, the Secondary Analysis module, EXAMINE, permits the analyst to obtain specific desired results in the form of tables, plots, or documentation. The diagram also includes, at the bottom, other "Supporting" modules that the analyst may access from time to time as needed.

In the present section we shall take up the constituents of the diagram one by one. We shall describe each item and indicate the part that it plays in the overall operation of MAPSIT. Our discussion, given its purpose here as an overview, is at a general level. Readers wishing more technical detail should consult the MAPSIT Reference Manual (Morrison, Bradley, et al., 1985).

The MAPSIT Libraries

One of the most prominent features of the diagram is the central position of the MAPSIT Libraries which provide inputs to all of the functional areas except secondary analysis and the supporting modules. The underlying logic is that it is typically much easier to attack a modeling problem by modifying something similar that already exists than to build something new from scratch, and that if one does have to do original modeling, it is easier to assemble prefabricated pieces of models than to simulate the logic in full. By these means, MAPSIT analysts are immediately able to draw on any relevant modeling that has already been done. In turn, models or pieces of models that are created by the analyst automatically become part of the Library, with no "librarianship" required on the part of the analyst.

Three separate libraries are relevant. First, there is a library of models that pertain to whole systems of transfer programs. Second, there is a library of submodels, which are pieces of models, each of which typically corresponds to the logic of a specific transfer program. These submodels are effectively subroutines that the analyst can link to a model by using a single MAPSIT command. Third, there is a library of schedules, which are relationships such as those that describe taxes as a function of taxable income. The analyst can call a schedule into a model or submodel with a single instruction, thereby eliminating the possibility of transcription error that would arise if each schedule had to be entered by hand. Taken together, the libraries provide the analyst with a valuable, low-overhead stockpile that allows economies of scale and permits more responsive analyses.

Library Information Retrieval

If an analyst is to use models or pieces of models as inputs to an analysis, information about those items must be available. The DIRECTORY and DESCRIBE modules provide the means for retrieving this type of information. In essence, these two modules act as automatic librarians, giving analysts information about the names and contents of the items in the library.

The DIRECTORY module enables the analyst to ascertain names of the library elements. Recall that when a model, submodel, or schedule is created, it automatically becomes part of the MAPSIT library. The DIRECTORY "recognizes" such elements via the distinctive extensions that are part of their file names (for example, files with the extension "MOD" are MAPSIT models). To minimize the staff overhead associated with MAPSIT, the Canadian government has dispensed with issuing periodic indices of the library's contents. Instead, a user can get an up-to-the-second index by requesting one from the DIRECTORY module. The result is a listing of all of the relevant files, complete with one line titles, with the user able to control the type of element indexed (model, submodel, or schedule) and, security provisions permitting, the "public" library disk area or the private disk areas associated with individual MAPSIT accounts.

The DESCRIBE module permits an analyst to obtain information about library elements at a more detailed level than is possible in the one line titles available through the DIRECTORY module. Each model or submodel contains a block of text, typically about two-thirds of a page in length, describing the purpose of the element, its major assumptions and its references. The analyst retrieves this information by submitting the file name for an element as a command to the DESCRIBE module. Still more detailed information, in the form of a complete listing of the file's instructions, or its logic, is available through the LIST module described in the next section.

Model Preparation

Models are the starting points for MAPSIT analyses. A model is a set of instructions describing the derivation of desired relationships. Thus the model preparation modules, modules that enable an analyst to build, edit, list, or analyze models, play a central role in MAPSIT. It is these modules that enable an analyst to access elements from the library and to create new elements for the library.

The BUILD module enables the analyst to construct models, submodels, and schedules from scratch. It prompts the analyst in an orderly and consistent manner for all of the instructions, linkages to other library elements, and documentation that make up the elements. During this process the analyst benefits from a variety of defaults, error recovery procedures, and consistency checks that facilitate the construction of elements.

The EDIT module, more commonly used than BUILD, enables the analyst to use an existing element as a starting point, delete portions that are incorrect or simply not wanted, and to insert any relevant new material. It includes all of the defaults, error recovery, and consistency checking of the BUILD module. It also provides features usually associated with editors, such as backup files and renaming, the ability to list all or part of what is being edited, and renumbering.

The LIST and CREF modules, though they do not create or alter models, supply valuable support functions. The models, submodels, and schedules constructed by BUILD or EDIT are formatted for computer efficiency and are not particularly easy for analysts to read. Consequently, the LIST module translates these elements into versions that analysts can easily understand and use. Chapter 6 and Appendix B illustrate output from LIST. The CREF module is a bit more technically oriented. Taking a model or submodel as input, it produces cross reference output showing, for each mapping in an element, information including where the mapping is created, where it is used, and how it is used. The module also displays the locations of all linkages to submodels and identifies the specific submodels used. In addition, the CREF module identifies missing or extraneous material that usually indicates inefficiency or errors in logic.

Solution of Models and Primary Solutions

Because a MAPSIT model, as constructed by the BUILD or EDIT modules, consists of an algorithm or set of instructions that indicates how the desired relationships are to be derived, it remains to carry out these derivations and to solve the model. MAPSIT provides two modules to execute this task, the DEBUG and SOLVE modules. Each of them takes as input a model, including any linkages to relevant submodels, and produces as output a solution that consists of the derived relationships accompanied by appropriate documentation.

The DEBUG module, as its name indicates, serves primarily to validate models. With it the analyst initiates the automated derivation process, but in such a manner that the solution can be suspended at any point in the model and partial results can be examined for correctness or possible errors in the model. The capacity to investigate intermediate results without having to alter the model itself is a major aid in producing error-free models.

The SOLVE module is used to generate results more quickly and with minimal analyst participation when one already has a model that is believed to be correct. Typically, the only analyst involvement is answering the prompts built into the model itself. File extensions on the solution files produced allow the analyst to distinguish among multiple solutions of the same model under different parameter configurations.

The solution files produced by the SOLVE and DEBUG modules are termed "primary" solutions. They contain the relationships derived during the solution of the model and documentary information. The latter includes the name, title, and description of the model, the date and time of the solution, and the parameter configuration used in the solution (characterized as the model's prompts and the analyst's responses to them). The solution is called "primary" because, although it does not directly contain all of the tabular and graphic results an analyst will wish to see, it does contain all of the information required for their derivation. The derivation itself is left for the EXAMINE module.

Secondary Analysis

The EXAMINE module assists the analyst in conducting secondary analyses, conversions of the information contained in primary solutions to the specific tabular and graphic outputs that the analyst desires. In essence, EXAMINE is a report generator that is both powerful and easy to use. The analyst uses it to obtain results quickly and accurately in formats that are pleasing to the eye and resistant to misinterpretation.

Chapter 7 and parts of Chapter 8 provide considerable detail on both the kinds of results one can obtain using the EXAMINE module and the variety of support features built into that module. Here we indicate only a sparse sampling of its capabilities.

- The analyst can choose among tables of mappings, implicit marginal or average tax rates, breakevens, ratios, and isoquants.

- The analyst can make presentations of results in terms of prespecified values of the independent variable, natural system inflection points, or can present results in terms of alternative income definitions.

- The analyst can choose from a variety of documentation facilities including model descriptions, mapping descriptions, titles, legends, specialized labeling, parameter configurations, and warning messages.

- The analyst can conveniently override module defaults for a variety of appearance-oriented features such as field width, numbers of decimal places, labeling, line types and colors, and legend locations.

- The analyst can employ a number of timesaving convenience features ranging from controllable defaults to the ability to define, name, store, and access repeatedly-used constructs within and across sessions with the EXAMINE module.

- The analyst can record sessions with the EXAMINE module, and then execute them using other solutions to generate, very rapidly, equivalent secondary analyses for alternative parameter configurations and to generate sensitivity analyses.

Supporting Modules

Although the sets of modules previously described (Library Information Retrieval, Model Preparation, Model Solution, and Secondary Analysis) form the core of MAPSIT, other modules provide useful support for analysts. Apart from the END command that allows the analyst to leave MAPSIT, these supporting modules include HELP and OPTIONS. The HELP module allows the analyst to request documentation on line during a session with MAPSIT. By entering the HELP module and supplying the name of a MAPSIT module, the analyst can receive a description of the module and its purpose. Within a module, HELP provides definitions of any of the module's keywords.

In the OPTIONS module the user can ascertain or alter the status of several options within MAPSIT. Options subject to user control include dialogue level for prompts and listings, the desired degree of automatic error checking performed by the BUILD and EDIT modules, the ability to overwrite existing files without notifying the analyst, and a number of parameters and features relevant to the EXAMINE module (for example, number of decimal places to be used in printing abscissa values in tables, the degree of identification for the independent variables in tables, and the field width for columns in tables).

Taken together, the various components of MAPSIT supply an effective modeling environment or decision support system for the analyst. The library maximizes the utility of previous modeling efforts. The BUILD and EDIT modules ensure that the analyst enters the logic of a transfer system precisely, in response to understandable prompts. The use of a model as a constructively oriented, algorithmic statement of system logic permits solution of the same system, repeatedly and automatically, under alternative parameter configurations without any need to reenter the logic. The LIST and CREF modules enable the analyst to obtain accurate, up-to-date, readable versions of models, in varying levels of detail, with negligible effort. The SOLVE and DEBUG modules assist in the validation of models and make the quick derivation of the models' implications trivial in terms of the analyst's effort and low-cost in terms of computer resources. In turn, the EXAMINE module converts the implications automatically into the desired formats, and because EXAMINE uses the "primary solution" files as input, a model need not be re-solved each time new presentations are desired. In sum, the several modules of MAPSIT automate tasks inherent in modeling income transfers systems within a logical and natural framework, permitting the analyst to concentrate on the substance of problems rather than the machinery for solving them.

MAPSIT AND THE MODELING PROCESS

The discussion to this point has been somewhat one-sided. It has identified the major components of MAPSIT and their purposes, but has not shown how those pieces fit together into a unified whole; it has addressed the question "What?" without giving much attention to the questions "How?" or "Why?". In the remainder of this chapter we begin to illustrate the process of using MAPSIT to conduct income transfer analyses, thereby introducing a theme developed more fully in the remainder of Part II and in Part III. In particular, we initiate a process-oriented view of MAPSIT and income transfer analyses by focusing on the flow of control among the several modules and on the basic usage patterns within the modules. Our primary device for this exposition are Figures 4.2A and 4.2B.[24]

The pentagonal box at the top center in each of these diagrams represents the MAPSIT Executive. From the Executive level the analyst can access any of the modules in the package. The modules themselves appear in the diagram as pentagons beneath the Executive level. Because of the number of different modules, the diagram is shown in two parts, but it is only one system, consisting of the following modules: BUILD, EDIT, CREF, OPTIONS, LIST, DIRECTORY, SOLVE, DEBUG, EXAMINE, DESCRIBE, HELP, ?, and END.

Effectively, the Executive asks the analyst for the name of the desired module. The analyst responds by typing the relevant keyword, such as EDIT, or an abbreviated form sufficient to distinguish the desired module from the other modules, ("ED" for "EDIT" as opposed to "EX" for "EXAMINE"). Suppose that the analyst chooses the BUILD module in order to construct a new model or submodel. BUILD first prompts for some documentary material, a one line title

---

[24] Figures 4.2A and 4.2B are adapted from MAPSIT (Modular Analysis Package for Systems of Income Transfer, Version 5), courtesy of the Department of National Health and Welfare, Ottawa.

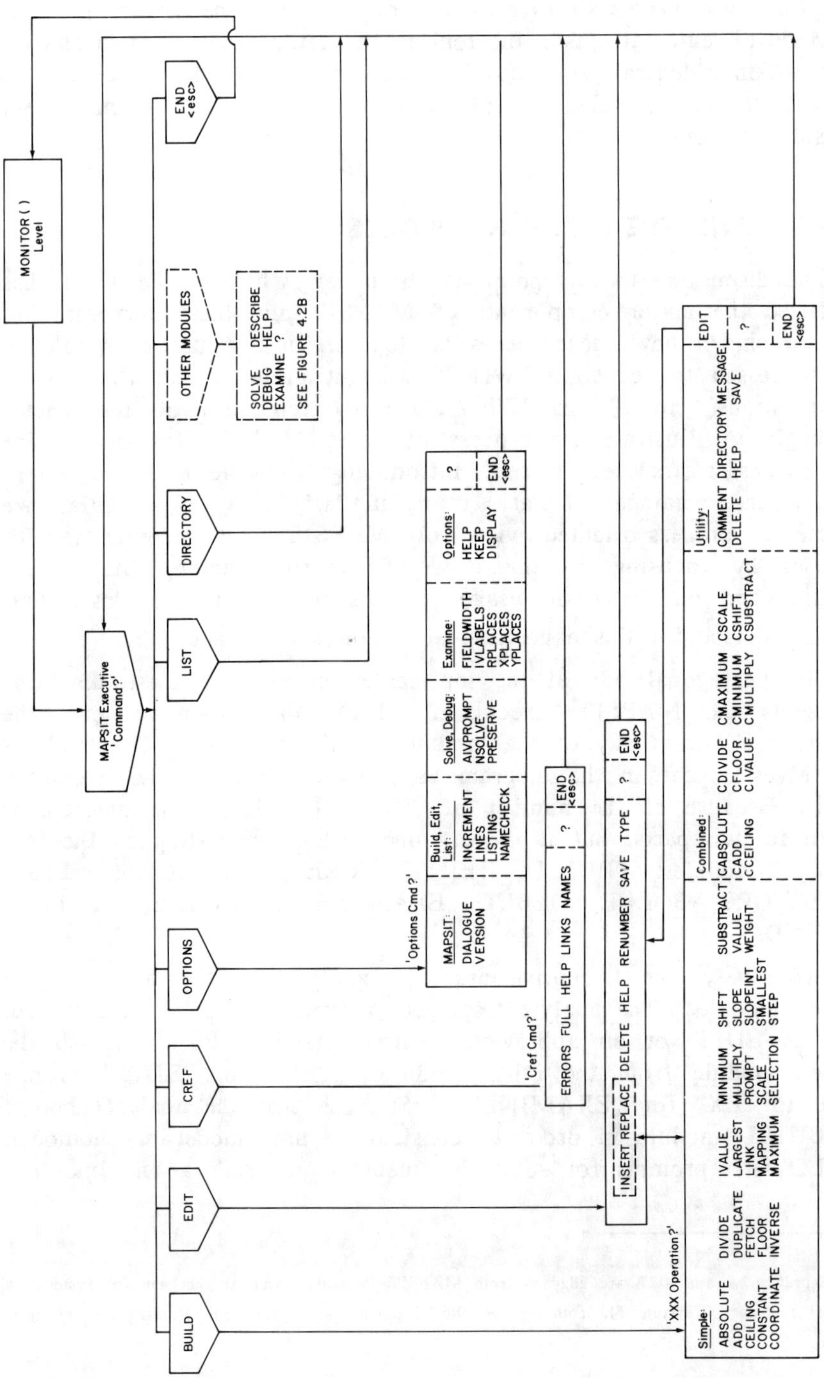

Figure 4.2A: MAPSIT Flow of Control

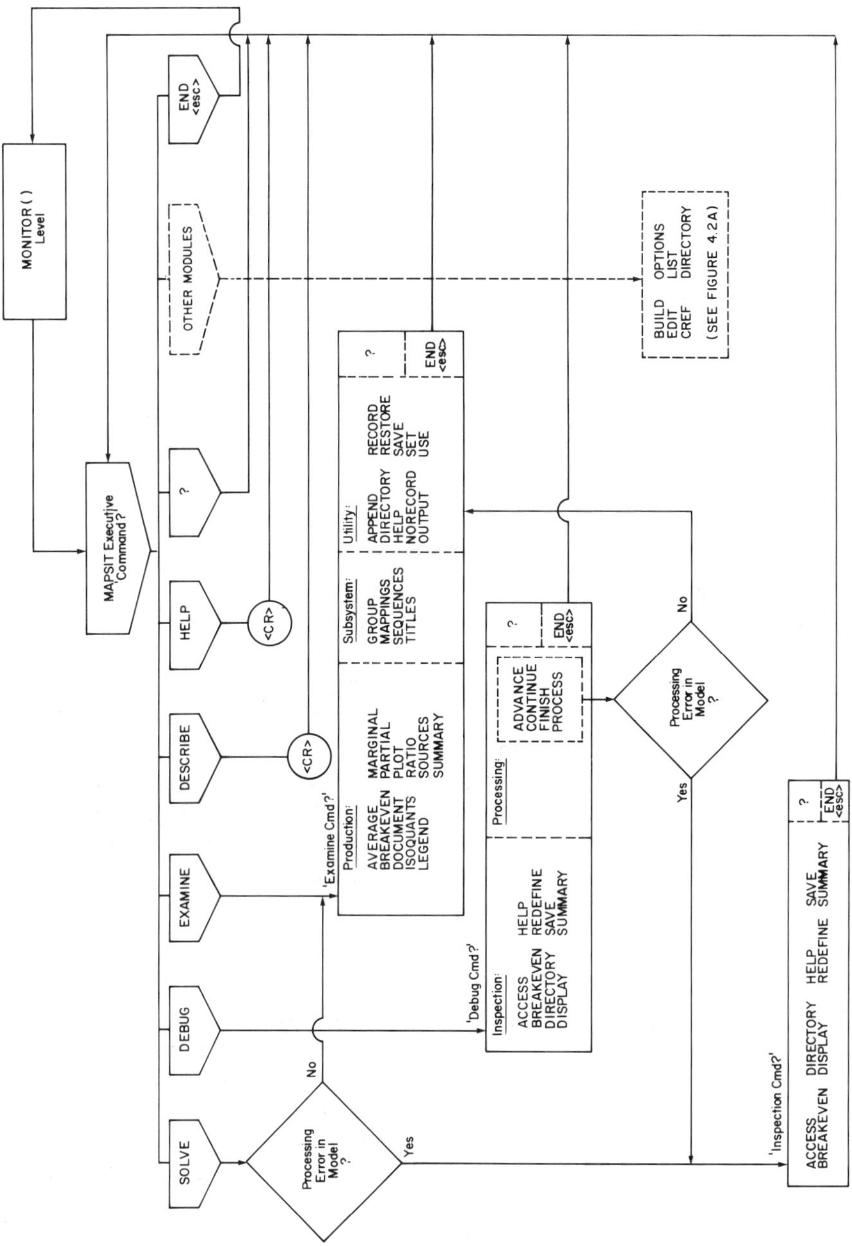

Figure 4.2B: MAPSIT Flow of Control, continued

and a multiple line description, that becomes part of the model and that can be accessed via the DIRECTORY and DESCRIBE modules, shown in Figures 4.2A and 4.2B, respectively. This material also remains part of the model and is copied into any solutions of the model to serve as documentation of the results. Typically, the title and description contain information about the purpose and major assumptions for the model.

Next, BUILD ascertains from the analyst the sequence of operations that, when executed, derive the desired relationships. The analyst enters a loop, each cycle of which specifies the identity of the next desired operation and then the arguments for the operation. The analyst chooses the operation from a fixed menu shown in the bottom left-hand corner of Figure 4.2A by entering an appropriate keyword, such as ABSOLUTE or ADD, or an acceptable abbreviation. When the identity of the operation is clear, BUILD prompts the analyst for all of the arguments necessary for the subsequent execution of the operation.

Most of these arguments are mappings, that is, named, piecewise-linear relationships between pairs of variables. Most operations serve to create mappings, such as taxable income as a function of gross earnings, or annual disposable income as a function of weeks worked at a given wage. The relationships are characterized by the coordinates of the end points of the linear segments, with MAPSIT taking care of all of the computational details. Typically, the analyst will supply the name of a mapping to be derived in the operation, a textual description for the mapping, the names of any mappings used as arguments for the operation, and any required numerical constants. When BUILD completes the acceptance of the arguments, it cycles back to prompt the analyst for a new keyword to identify the next operation to be inserted.

Throughout the cycle, BUILD carries out error checks that catch many entry errors at the point where they are made and give the analyst the opportunity to correct them immediately. It checks to ensure that names and text strings are not too long and do not contain prohibited characters that would prevent subsequent solution of the model. It checks to ensure that mappings specified as arguments (precedents or inputs) to operations exist at the point in the model where they are used. Most importantly, it employs a prompt oriented approach to ensure that the analyst does not accidentally omit any of the arguments that the operations require.

The analyst, having entered all desired operations, exits from

BUILD by responding with END or EDIT to the prompt for the next operation keyword. When END is used, control returns to the MAPSIT Executive. When EDIT is used, control transfers directly to the EDIT module so that the analyst can begin to edit the material just entered. Since BUILD does not allow the analyst to alter operations once they have been completely entered and the cycling has gone on to a new operation, and since entry sessions are unlikely to be completely error free, this "short circuit" of the Executive is quite convenient.

The EDIT module contains the standard features that have come to be associated with many editors. The analyst can rename the input file, delete existing material no longer wanted, insert new material, display or replace existing material, renumber the operations, save the current version onto a disk file, and leave the editor. The analyst chooses the desired action by entering the appropriate command keyword or an acceptable abbreviation; in Figure 4.2A these commands appear in the rectangle suspended from the EDIT pentagon. Two of the commands, INSERT and REPLACE, naturally require the analyst to supply new operations, keywords, and arguments, while both of these commands allow the analyst to cycle through sequences of operations in the model, and to abandon the cycling at any desired point. Both of them provide the same error checks as in BUILD. When EDIT completes a cycle, or any of the other commands, it returns control to the "EDIT Cmd?" prompt, permitting the analyst to choose the next desired command. When the editing is complete, the analyst responds to this prompt with the command END, causing EDIT to write a copy of the edited model to disk and to return control to the MAPSIT Executive.

When the entry of a model or submodel is complete, the analyst will typically wish to inspect or validate it prior to any attempted solution. Two modules, CREF and LIST are valuable for this purpose. CREF provides the analyst with a cross reference version of a model or submodel, with the analyst choosing one of three different formats. First, a full cross reference indicates the operation number at which each mapping is defined, and the operation numbers for all instances in which the mapping appears as an argument, plus additional information on the form of the usage. Second, the analyst can get this same information for specific mappings or sets of mappings, a useful feature if the analyst intends to change a mapping name and wants to effect the change everywhere the mapping is used. Third, the analyst can request that CREF identify instances where mappings are used questionably (as a precedent without being defined, or defined but never used). In effect, CREF supplies the analyst with a snapshot of a model from the perspective of the mappings, indicating where they are created, plus where and how they are used.

The LIST module offers a different perspective on a model, one that focuses on the operations that constitute the logic of the model. Because a model is a disk file that is more suited to the computer's needs than to the analyst's, LIST provides the analyst with a "human readable" version. LIST generates, for the model's operations taken in sequence, an annotated listing of the model and its logic. The annotation consists of MAPSIT-generated text that turns each of the operations into a declarative statement documenting the effect of the operation's logic. The resulting text, identical to that appearing when the operations are typed in the EDIT module, can often be read even by persons unfamiliar with MAPSIT. When LIST has finished listing a model or submodel, it returns control to the MAPSIT Executive level.

The flow of control for the SOLVE module (Figure 4.2B) is conditional on the solvability of the argument model. In the usual case, when the analyst is solving a model all of whose operations can meaningfully be executed, the flow is rather simple; SOLVE executes each of the operations in sequence. On completing the solution, SOLVE writes out the primary solution to a disk file and then transfers control to the EXAMINE module, which in turn reads in the solution and prompts the analyst for secondary analysis commands. This flow automatically provides the routing for the most common case -- the analyst has solved a model and now wishes to present its results. MAPSIT also provides a capability, not shown in the diagram, for the analyst to generate multiple solutions of a model, typically to reflect multiple parameter configurations of interest, before control transfers to the EXAMINE module.

If, during the course of solving a model, SOLVE encounters an operation that it cannot execute, for example if a nonexistent mapping is given as an argument to the operation, a different control flow obtains. Within SOLVE, the analyst is placed in a command loop that permits inspection of the partial solution to that point. For example, the analyst can generate summary tables that include mappings available at that point, ascertain breakevens and departures, and retrace the calling sequence back to the main program should the error occur inside a submodel. The array of possibilities is suggested by the box headed "Inspection Cmd?" in the lower left corner of Figure 4.2B. When the analyst has inspected the partial solution to the extent desired, entry of the END command transfers control back to the MAPSIT Executive level. Note that in this context, any error is fatal, because normal processing of the model cannot resume, and control cannot proceed directly to the EXAMINE module.

The flow for the DEBUG module is similar to that for the SOLVE module, but allows the analyst greater control over the solution of models. SOLVE sees its primary application in the solution of models that are believed free from errors; DEBUG sees its primary usage in the validation of models.

The added capabilities in DEBUG permit the analyst to control the solution so that it can be suspended at any point, and the partial solution inspected to ascertain whether the intended results are being derived. As shown in Figure 4.2B, this capability is provided by the analyst supplying one or more of the commands shown in the dashed box with the set of DEBUG commands. Taken together with the Inspection commands, these commands enable the analyst to initiate suspension at specified locations in a model or one of its subsidiary submodels, or to execute a specified number of operations before suspending the solution for inspection. The Inspection commands play the same role they play in the SOLVE module.

If there are no errors in a model and the analyst continues to ask DEBUG to execute operations, processing eventually reaches the end of the model. At this point, like the SOLVE module case, control transfers automatically to EXAMINE. If an error exists, at the conclusion of any desired inspection, the analyst initiates transfer of control back to the MAPSIT Executive level by means of the END command, since he cannot continue with model execution. Note also that the analyst can transfer directly back to the Executive level at any point in the command loop by using END.

With the possible exception of the EDIT module, the EXAMINE module has the most powerful and involved control flow. As shown just above the center of Figure 4.2B, the analyst may initiate entry to EXAMINE from the MAPSIT Executive level or may be sent there automatically by either the SOLVE or DEBUG modules. Exit from EXAMINE is always to the Executive. However, it is within the module that the flow, reflecting the tasks that analysts wish to perform, involves its greatest flexibility. Three examples, one from each of the three subsets of EXAMINE commands (Subsystem, Production, and Utility) will illustrate this flexibility.

First, EXAMINE is the only MAPSIT module to have subsystems or module commands, each of which initiates a command loop for a new menu. Four subsystems are relevant, one for each of the major constructs serving as arguments to the EXAMINE commands, specifically:

sequences:	ordered sets of scalars, usually serving as row headings in tables,
groups:	sets of mapping names, usually serving as column headings for tables,
titles:	headers for tabular output, and
mappings:	relationships, which can be created in EXAMINE as well as read into EXAMINE from primary solutions.

Each subsystem has an array of commands for defining, displaying, manipulating, and deleting the relevant constructs. For example, the MAPPINGS subsystem allows the analyst to create new mappings as weighted sums of existing mappings, a very useful feature for constructing alternative income definitions or conducting comparative/difference analyses. The analyst enters the relevant subsystems to create arguments that may be used repeatedly, and then transfers back to the "Examine Cmd?" prompt by responding with END to the subsystem's command prompt. The individual commands in the subsystems may themselves involve loops necessary to ascertain open-ended argument lists.

Second, the EXAMINE Production commands, those commands that effect the presentations for the analyst, may involve control flow. Typically, a Production command prompts for the arguments it requires and then prints out the result. However, if an argument corresponds to one of the four construct types, then the analyst need not necessarily supply the name of an existing argument of that type. Instead, EXAMINE permits the analyst to create the argument "on the fly" (equivalent to a short circuit into the DEFINE command of the relevant subsystem) or to formally enter the subsystem to perform whatever commands are appropriate. In this latter case, exit from the subsystem leads not to a return to the "Examine Cmd?" prompt, but to a repeat of the prompt from which the subsystem was entered, permitting the analyst to pick up the provision of arguments to the Production command exactly at the point where it was interrupted.

Third, among the Utility commands in EXAMINE, the USE command permits the analyst to transfer control of the EXAMINE session to a specified file. Instead of taking instructions from the analyst, EXAMINE then looks in the indicated file for the commands and arguments, returning control to the analyst through the "Examine Cmd?" prompt only when the instructions in the file have been exhausted. This control feature, extremely convenient when the same tables are to be generated for multiple parameter configurations, allows the analyst to build and employ a library of standard analyses, possibly delegating secondary analysis to support staff who then require only the sketchiest of knowledge about MAPSIT in general or EXAMINE in particular. Taken together, these three examples illustrate how EXAMINE enables analysts to automate repetitive aspects of secondary analysis and to maintain flexibility within the order of tasks.

In the OPTIONS module, Figure 4.2A, the analyst picks from a fixed menu of options and commands to save or display the options. To change an option, the analyst enters the name of the option in response to the "Options Cmd?" prompt, for example, answering DIALOGUE in order to control the level of detail in the dialogue or prompts that MAPSIT uses to communicate with the analyst. OPTIONS responds by asking for the desired choice, perhaps REGULAR as in our dialogue example. Control then returns to the "Options Cmd?" prompt, until the analyst elects to leave OPTIONS by answering with END, at which point control returns to the MAPSIT Executive.

The control flow for the remaining modules is very simple. The DIRECTORY command automatically returns control to the Executive after it has fulfilled the analyst's request for a directory of library elements. The DESCRIBE and HELP modules both offer the analyst the opportunity to enter open-ended lists of arguments, library elements to be described or module names for which help is desired, respectively. When the analyst has no more arguments to offer, a carriage return response returns control to the Executive level "Command?" prompt. Finally, of course, the END "module" returns control to the monitor level, allowing the analyst to conclude the MAPSIT session.

The flow of control as described here is one of the pillars of the MAPSIT design. The general structure is hierarchical, but where certain "shortcuts" are appropriate, like the BUILD-EDIT and SOLVE-EXAMINE connections, MAPSIT provides for them. Within modules, the command loop flow guarantees the analyst substantial flexibility to perform the tasks in the most natural order. For example, the analyst, while in the EXAMINE module, can jump into one of the subsystems at the point where a construct is needed, rather than being forced to anticipate that need. The flow of control is one element in the overall philosophy that MAPSIT should be a decision support system that assists the analyst to operate naturally, rather than be a Procrustean framework to which the analyst must adapt.

CHAPTER 5.

ANALYZING RELATIONSHIPS IN WELFARE AND TAXATION SYSTEMS, EXAMPLE 1

This chapter illustrates how an analyst can take a problem of interest, develop a model for the problem using MAPSIT, and perform analyses. We focus on a specific problem in this chapter, but we want to stress that this model is only an illustration of the type of modeling that can be done using MAPSIT. Chapter 10 presents a more representative overview of the range of problems that have been analyzed using MAPSIT.

As a first example we shall take the problem presented in Chapter 2, but in this case we shall address the broader question of what the net transfers look like across the entire spectrum of possible earned income, rather than calculating the net transfers only for a particular value of earned income, as we did in Chapter 2.

The first section of this chapter contains a brief restatement of the essential elements of the problem introduced in Chapter 2. The second section shows how one can use MAPSIT to translate this problem into a solvable model, using the various modules and operations which were described in Chapter 4. The third section discusses the analysis of results from the model. It illustrates how the model documents a solution and shows a few of the types of tables available: transfer levels, marginal tax rates, and so forth. The final section discusses the ease with which the model can be changed to extend the range of questions which one might want to examine. Again, we stress that the illustration in this chapter is merely one of hundreds that have been built and that might have been chosen to illustrate the workings of MAPSIT.

Before beginning to develop this first model, we offer two further caveats. First, like all software systems, MAPSIT has undergone a number of changes since it was initially developed. In the discussion to follow, the model is built and solved using MAPSIT Version 3.0. Those using a more current version of MAPSIT may find differences between this description and MAPSIT as they know it. These changes are, however, irrelevant to our example. The purpose of this chapter is simply to illustrate the general manner in which one can use MAPSIT to model a system of interest, not in any sense to document the latest version of the software package.

Second, although this chapter presents a view of how the analyst might use MAPSIT to solve a particular problem, the chapter does not attempt to be a "users' guide." Users' guides or manuals are necessary for any nontrivial software package, but they are usually reference works first and training devices second, if at all. They typically describe the mechanics of using a software package to perform a specific task, but they usually fall short in telling a user how to decide which task to perform. Our purpose in this chapter is to illustrate how one can use MAPSIT to solve a typical problem in the analysis of interrelationships. Persons wanting to see documentation of MAPSIT should read the extensive formal user's manual (Morrison, Bradley, et al., 1985) or the more compact mini-manual (Duguay and Morrison, 1979).

This chapter focuses primarily on the transition from the statement of the problem to the construction of a model that represents the system of interest. We give little emphasis to the analysis of results generated from the model, since that topic is taken up at length in Chapter 7. As is appropriate for an illustrative analysis, our example addresses a particularly common form of stacking analysis, one in which the analyst wishes to model a transfer system and to ascertain the transfers from programs in the system as functions of a family's earnings. The programs in the system have been chosen so that the system is reasonably realistic, but sufficiently straightforward so that the details do not obscure the basic thrust.

STATEMENT OF THE PROBLEM

Before the modeling can begin, the analyst must understand the system to be modeled. The analyst must know both the basic programs and parameters associated with the system and be able to specify at least broadly the results he or she expects to get from the analysis. Fundamentally, the relevant information about the system falls into three main categories: general problem characteristics, family unit characteristics, and transfer program characteristics. This section describes these three categories in turn.

General Problem Characteristics

The general problem characteristics involve items that serve to define the broad scope of the analysis. Questions include: Is the accounting period for the analysis on a weekly, monthly, or annual basis? What particular period is being analyzed (the first week of 1984, January 1984, or the year 1984, for example)? What are the proposed independent variables for the analysis? (MAPSIT permits one continuous variable per solution as an independent variable for the analysis, plus an arbitrary number of other parameters that are fixed as constants in the model.) For what purpose is the analyst building the model? What type of numerical results are expected? What transfer programs make up the system being analyzed?

In the example presented here, we employ an annual accounting period based on the calendar year 1984. Because we wish to examine the work incentives associated with the transfer system, we choose earned income as the only independent variable for the analysis. With respect to numerical results, we wish, in the course of our analysis, to ascertain the relationships between the independent variable and the transfers from each of the programs in the system. We also wish to know the relationship between the independent variable and the disposable income for the family.

Our interests lead us to concentrate on a particular system of transfer programs. The basic variables and transfers are:

- Earned income
- FICA (social security) contributions
- State income tax
- Earned-income tax credit
- Aid to Families with Dependent Children, AFDC
- Food stamps
- Medicaid
- Federal income tax
- Dependent care expense tax credit

- Net federal income taxes

- Disposable income

Here we will need to specify each of these variables as functions of earned income, the independent variable chosen for the analysis, though in principle we could choose to solve the model in terms of some other independent variable.

Family Unit Characteristics

The transfers to and from the family often depend on the characteristics of the family. For example, transfers from a welfare program may depend on the number of adults in the family, the number of children, their ages, and the place of residence. Since we are carrying out our analysis at the microlevel, we must specify the characteristics of the subject unit. Specifically, we must make assumptions about any aspect of the family that affects transfers from any of the programs in the system.

Because of the way in which several of the programs in the system are structured and because we want to use this model primarily for illustrative purposes, we have restricted this analysis to a family with the following characteristics:

- there is a single parent less than sixty years old and not disabled,

- there is at least one child in the family, and all children are less than eighteen years old,

- other than income from transfer programs, all family income consists of wages and salaries earned by the parent,

- the family resides in a state that uses a proportional income tax and has no applicable tax credit or tax reduction regulations.

We wish to make as few assumptions as possible about the characteristics of the family because we do not want to restrict unnecessarily the generality of the results. Here, the assumptions about family structure and residence are necessary for the tax and social assistance program calculations. Additionally, the calculation of income taxes requires assumptions about the sources of income and about relevant state tax regulations.

Transfer Program Characteristics

Clearly, the analyst must also make assumptions about the programs included in the transfer system. This subsection highlights the basic assumptions pertaining to the eight major programs as they existed in 1984.[25] The assumptions appear in a fairly general form, with specific numerical values left, for the most part, until the model generation section of this chapter.

- **FICA:** The FICA (Federal Insurance Contribution Act -- Social Security) contribution is modeled as a fixed percentage of earnings up to the specified limit.

- **State Income Tax:** In this example we shall assume that state income tax is a simple percentage of gross earnings and other taxable income less any state exemption.

- **Earned Income Credit:** We shall treat the earned income credit as a separate program since the computation is independent of any federal tax paid or due and the value of the credit beyond any tax due is fully refundable to the taxpayer. The actual credit depends on the level of earnings, or for adjusted gross income above $6,000, the level of total income.

- **AFDC:** Aid to Families with Dependent Children provides benefits to single-parent families and to two-parent families under certain conditions. Children must be (i) under age eighteen, or (ii) under age nineteen and a full-time student in secondary school or an equivalent level of a vocational or technical school. The income base for AFDC includes earnings, the earned income tax credit, and other unearned (nontransfer) income, less deductions for work expenses, child care expenses, and the earned income exclusion, if applicable. The work expense deduction is $75 per month, prorated for less

---

[25] We shall refer to the various program regulations in the present tense although in all cases the assumptions made refer to the 1984 regulations.

than full-time work; the child care expense deduction is limited to $160 per child per month and applies only if the child care is necessary for the parent to work. The earned income exemption is available only if the parent has been working for less than four months, but in that case it provides for the deduction of the first $30 of earned income per month and one third of the net earned income (earned income after the first $30 and the deductions for work related expenses and child care expenses have been subtracted). The amount of the benefit is a function of state-specific assistance levels. After available income is established, available income is subtracted from the need standard to arrive at the deficit. The need standard is a function of family size. We shall assume that the state pays the full amount of the deficit and that the state does not impose a maximum payment less than the payment standard.

- **Food Stamps:** The income base for food stamps includes 82 percent of the earned income and all unearned income, including transfers such as AFDC and SSI. From this sum one subtracts a standard deduction of $90 per month, child care expenses up to $115 per month, excess shelter costs which, combined with the previous deduction for child care expenses, cannot exceed $115 per month, and medical expenses for persons over age sixty. The result of these calculations is "available income" for food stamp purposes. The benefit amount of food stamps provided to the household is calculated by subtracting 30 percent of available income from the maximum benefit for that household size. The benefit amount is also constrained so that as long as the household qualifies for any benefit at all, the minimum monthly amount is $10. We shall assume that the nominal value of the food stamp bonus can be treated as a cash benefit of that amount.

- **Medicaid:** Medicaid benefits are categorically available to families receiving AFDC or SSI. For simplicity, we shall assume here that the value of the services paid for or reimbursed by Medicaid can be treated as a cash benefit to the family.

- **Federal Income Tax Withholding:** We shall assume that taxable income, the income base for federal taxes, is equal to earned income and unearned, nontransfer income, less deductions for personal exemptions. The taxes are computed from the appropriate tax schedule, Schedule Z in this case since we are dealing with a single-parent family.

- **Dependent Care Expense Credit:** In the problem at hand, we shall assume that there are no disabled persons in the family and therefore that the only expenses to be considered are those for child care necessary for the parent to work. Since there is only a single parent, conditions relating to two parent families can be ignored. We will not ignore, however, the conditions that require that the parent provide at least 50 percent of the costs of running the home and that child care expenses in excess of earned income are not allowable. Finally, the credit is equal to 20 percent of the allowable expenses up to a maximum credit of $400 for a single child and $800 if there are two or more children. The credit can be used to reduce the federal income tax, but if the credit is greater than the tax due, the excess credit is not refundable.

- **Net Federal Tax:** Since the initial computation of federal income tax did not reflect the credit for dependent care expenses, we need to adjust the federal tax by subtracting the amount of that credit.

- **Disposable Income:** For present purposes we shall define disposable income as earned income, plus benefits from AFDC, food stamps, Medicaid, and the earned income credit, minus FICA, state and federal taxes, after the last item has been corrected for the dependent care expense credit.

ENTERING THE MODEL

There is a natural order to the major portions of a MAPSIT model. The first part usually consists of preliminary documentation of the model, the next introduces those transfer programs that do not depend on other transfer programs, the third develops the more complicated programs, and the final section includes the operations which constitute the "wrap-up" portion of the model. This order is required by MAPSIT, but it is also the order in which hand-calculated analyses would naturally and inevitably be done.

In describing the manner in which the model is entered into MAPSIT, we shall treat the operations in the model individually or in small groups. For each operation a standard format is used. The first item is a line number and a prompt for an operation keyword: "XXX Operation?", where XXX is a number. After the analyst has indicated the desired operation, the system responds with a characterization of that operation and a request for the "Mapping name?", the mapping to be created, the "Mapping description?", and other necessary responses. The characterization of the operation occurs between angle brackets (< >), and is one of the features of MAPSIT that can be controlled by the analyst.[26]

In the illustration to follow we shall show MAPSIT-generated comments by using mixed upper and lower case letters, and we shall show the analyst's responses to the MAPSIT's prompts by using all upper case responses. For the most part the input by the analyst is close to the output version from the listing module. A complete listing of the model is contained in Appendix B, however, and the reader may wish to compare the "LIST" version of the model with the input to the model building module.

Since the function of this chapter is to illustrate how an analyst might build a MAPSIT model to solve a problem such as the one just described, we shall proceed fairly directly with the development of the model, ignoring the steps related to "logging in" and gaining access to the software package. In addition we shall ignore the process of planning a model. We shall assume that the planning process discussed in Chapter 9 is complete and concentrate on model entry. Finally, we assume that the analyst has already entered the MAPSIT command level and specified that he or she wants to use the model building module.

---

[26] While the analyst can specify that these characterizations are not wanted, doing so is not generally a good idea until the analyst has become fairly experienced in using MAPSIT.

Title and Model Description

Since we are already in the model building module the first prompt we receive will be

Title?

MAPSIT allows the analyst to enter an identifying title of up to seventy characters. After we have entered the title, concluding it with a carriage return, MAPSIT again prompts us for documentary material:

Description?
line

This message too is important. Generally, the more complete the response the better, although excessively long descriptions add costs to the editing, solution, and report generation stages of analysis. Some of the elements that are helpful include (1) author, (2) creation or revision date, (3) project under which the modeling was carried out, (4) basic purpose of the model, and (5) major assumptions of the model, plus perhaps a reference to a more complete description of the model, if one exists.

The analyst enters the model description by typing the description as a series of lines, each line up to seventy characters in length. At the end of each line a carriage return is typed and the description is continued on the next line.[27] When the analyst has completed the description, a carriage return is entered as the first item on a new line. The resulting pair of consecutive carriage returns signals MAPSIT that the description is complete.

In this particular session the interaction appears as follows:

---

[27] Throughout the illustration, obvious carriage returns are omitted; nonobvious carriage returns are indicated by "(CR)". Thus it is important that the reader interpret the occurrence of (CR) as a carriage return and not as a string of four particular characters.

```
Title? WELFARE AND TAXES FOR THE SINGLE-PARENT FAMILY

Description?
 line   AUTHORS: GORDON H. LEWIS AND RICHARD J. MORRISON
 line   .
 line   CREATED: JANUARY 1984
 line   .
 line   THE EXAMPLE ILLUSTRATES HOW MAPSIT CAN  MODEL AN  INCOME TRANSFER
 line   SYSTEM AS IT AFFECTS A FAMILY OVER A CONTINUUM OF GROSS EARNINGS.
 line   ALTHOUGH  THE  MODEL IS  REASONABLY  REALISTIC,  ITS  FOCUS  LIES
 line   CONSIDERABLY  MORE  WITH  ILLUSTRATING  THE  "FLAVOR" OF STACKING
 line   ANALYSIS  THAN WITH  THE  CONSTRUCTION  OF  AN ABSOLUTELY PRECISE
 line   DESCRIPTION OF  AN  EXISTING  SYSTEM.   AS A GENERAL PRINCIPLE IN
 line   THIS MODEL, WHERE THE DETAILS  NECESSARY FOR A PRECISE  REPRESEN-
 line   TATION WOULD HAVE  ENCUMBERED THE FLOW OF THE MODEL FOR ILLUSTRA-
 line   TIVE PURPOSES,  WE HAVE  UNHESITATINGLY  EXCISED  THE  DETAIL AND
 line   SUBSTITUTED WHAT WE CONSIDER REASONABLE PROXIES. PARENTHETICALLY,
 line   IN ALL SUCH  SUBSTITUTIONS, MAPSIT IS FULLY  CAPABLE  OF MODELING
 line   THE DETAILED FORM OF THE  RELEVANT TRANSFER PROGRAM OR PROVISION.
 line   .
 line   THE  MODEL  INCLUDES THREE  DIFFERENT  WELFARE/SOCIAL  ASSISTANCE
 line   PROGRAMS (AFDC, FOOD STAMPS, AND  MEDICAID),  THREE  TAXES (FICA,
 line   FEDERAL  INCOME  TAX, AND A  HYPOTHETICAL STATE INCOME TAX),  THE
 line   DEPENDENT CARE TAX CREDIT, AND THE EARNED INCOME  TAX CREDIT.  IN
 line   CALCULATING THESE TRANSFERS THE MODEL ALSO  GENERATES A NUMBER OF
 line   INTERVENING  VARIABLES,  E.G. PRESUMED  CHILD  CARE  EXPENSES AND
 line   SHELTER COSTS.
 line   .
 line   THERE ARE A NUMBER OF SPECIAL ASSUMPTIONS  AND CHARACTERISTICS IN
 line   THE MODEL:
 line      (1) THE CALCULATIONS APPLY TO A SINGLE PARENT FAMILY, BUT
 line          THE MODEL PERMITS THE ANALYST TO SPECIFY ANY NUMBER OF
 line          CHILDREN.
 line      (2) THE SIMULATION EMPLOYS A TIME PERIOD OF ONE YEAR.
 line          PROGRAMS ADMINISTERED ON A SHORTER PERIOD ARE THUS
 line          "SCALED UP" TO ANNUAL EQUIVALENTS.
 line      (3) THE MODEL ASSUMES THAT THE WORKING PARENT RECEIVES WAGE
 line          AND SALARY INCOME AT A CONSTANT RATE THROUGHOUT THE YEAR.
 line      (4) THE ANALYSIS IS LIMITED TO FAMILIES WITH GROSS EARNINGS
 line          (WAGES AND SALARIES) LESS THAN $100,000.
 line      (5) WHEN A SINGLE PARENT IS WORKING, THE FAMILY MAY BE
 line          ELIGIBLE FOR A TAX CREDIT FOR CHILD CARE EXPENSES.
 line          SECTION 9 CONTAINS THE SPECIFIC ASSUMPTIONS ABOUT THAT
 line          CREDIT.
 line      (6) THE MODEL ASKS WHETHER THE PARENT HAS BEEN EMPLOYED
 line          FOR MORE THAN FOUR MONTHS, SINCE THIS AFFECTS
 line          WHETHER THE ASSISTANCE UNIT IS ELIGIBLE FOR THE EARNED
 line          INCOME DEDUCTION IN AFDC.
 line      (7) THE MODEL ASSUMES THAT ALL CHILDREN ARE (A) UNDER AGE
 line          18 OR (B) UNDER AGE 19 AND A FULL TIME STUDENT IN
 line          SECONDARY SCHOOL OR AN EQUIVALENT LEVEL OF A VOCATIONAL
 line          OR TECHNICAL SCHOOL.
 line      (8) THE VALUE OF FOOD STAMPS IS TREATED AS A CASH BENEFIT.
 line      (9) THE VALUE OF THE MEDICAL EXPENSES REIMBURSED BY MEDICAID
 line          IS TREATED AS A CASH BENEFIT.
 line     (10) THE FIXED PARAMETERS IN THE MODEL EMPLOY NUMERICAL VALUES
 line          APPROPRIATE FOR 1984.
 line   (CR)
```

We are now ready to enter the operations that create the mappings needed to model the several programs in this system of transfer programs.

Parameter Entry

As soon as the description is complete, the module responds:

100 Operation ?

indicating that it is ready for the first operation, number 100.[28]

We are ready to begin entering the various programs and mappings that will make it possible to solve the problem described in the previous section. In the present case we begin with a comment and a set of "prompts," instructions to the system to request information about key parameters. These prompts allow the user conveniently to vary, from solution to solution, variables important to the derivation of the transfers. Thus, they make the model more general.

The comment (Operation 100) is self explanatory. Following the comment are two prompts to establish the number of children age five or younger and the number of children age six or older. We divide the age range in this way because later we shall assume that day care is needed only for pre-school aged children (age five and younger.)

```
       100  Operation  ? COMMENT
  < Enter the LINES of the comment, up to 70 characters per line >

  line  SECTION 1:  PROVISION OF VARIABLES THAT MAY CHANGE FROM SOLUTION TO
  line  SOLUTION, AND DEFINITION OF THE MODEL'S INDEPENDENT VARIABLE.
  line  (CR)

       200  Operation  ? PROMPT
  < Define MAPPING NAME as a constant for all values of x, with
    the constant to be entered during the solution stage in response
    to the prompting message, PROMPTING MESSAGE >

 Mname ? CHLDN_LE_5
 Mdesc ? NUMBER OF CHILDREN AGE 5 OR YOUNGER
 Prompt ? HOW MANY CHILDREN ARE THERE AGE 5 OR YOUNGER?

       300  Operation  ? PROMPT
  < Define MAPPING NAME as a constant for all values of x, with
    the constant to be entered during the solution stage in response
    to the prompting message, PROMPTING MESSAGE >

 Mname ? CHLDN_GE_6
 Mdesc ? NUMBER OF CHILDREN AGE 6 OR OLDER
 Prompt ? HOW MANY CHILDREN ARE THERE AGE 6 OR OLDER?
```

Operation 400 then adds together the number of children in each cat-

---

28 Line operation numbers ordinarily occur in increments of 100. This leaves room for subsequent lines to be inserted when one is editing an existing model.

egory, and Operation 500 adds the number of children to the number of parents, which in this case we are assuming is one.

```
       400  Operation   ? ADD
  < Make MAPPING NAME equal to ADDEND MAPPING 1 + ADDEND MAPPING 2 +
    ADDEND MAPPING 3 + ... >

Mname ? N_CHILDREN
Mdesc ? NUMBER OF CHILDREN IN THE FAMILY
Addend 1? CHLDN_LE_5
Addend 2? CHLDN_GE_6
Addend 3?

       500  Operation   ? ADD
  < Make MAPPING NAME equal to ADDEND MAPPING 1 + ADDEND MAPPING 2 +
    ADDEND MAPPING 3 + ... >

Mname ? FAMILYSIZE
Mdesc ? NUMBER OF PERSONS IN THE FAMILY
Addend 1? N_CHILDREN
Addend 2? 1
Addend 3?
```

This completes our information about family structure.

The next set of operations provides information about other variables needed in the model: a prompt to indicate whether the parent is eligible for the earned income exemption in AFDC (Operation 600), a prompt to establish the amount of income other than earned income that the family has (Operation 700), a prompt to set the annual shelter costs (Operation 800), and two prompts (Operations 900 and 1000) to provide information that will be needed to compute the state income tax (the amount of income exempt from the state income tax and the tax rate for the simplified tax program assumed in this model).

```
       600  Operation   ? PROMPT
  < Define MAPPING NAME as a constant for all values of x, with
    the constant to be entered during the solution stage in response
    to the prompting message, PROMPTING MESSAGE >

Mname ? AFDCINCEXM
Mdesc ? AFDC INCOME EXEMPTION (30 AND 1/3)
Prompt ? HAS THE PARENT BEEN EMPLOYED FOR MORE THAN 4 MONTHS? (1=YES;0=NO)

       700  Operation   ? PROMPT
  < Define MAPPING NAME as a constant for all values of x, with
    the constant to be entered during the solution stage in response
    to the prompting message, PROMPTING MESSAGE >

Mname ? YTXBLOTHER
Mdesc ? DOLLAR VALUE OF TAXABLE INCOME (OTHER THAN EARNINGS) FOR THE FAMILY
Prompt ? DOLLAR VALUE OF TAXABLE INCOME (OTHER THAN EARNINGS) FOR THE FAMILY?
```

```
       800  Operation  ? PROMPT
  < Define MAPPING NAME as a constant for all values of x, with
    the constant to be entered during the solution stage in response
    to the prompting message, PROMPTING MESSAGE >

Mname ? SHELTRCOST
Mdesc ? ANNUAL SHELTER COSTS INCLUDING HEAT, ELEC, WATER, & PHONE?
Prompt ? ANNUAL SHELTER COSTS INCLUDING HEAT, ELEC, WATER, & PHONE?

       900  Operation  ? PROMPT
  < Define MAPPING NAME as a constant for all values of x, with
    the constant to be entered during the solution stage in response
    to the prompting message, PROMPTING MESSAGE >

Mname ? STATE_EXEM
Mdesc ? DOLLAR VALUE OF TOTAL INCOME EXEMPT FROM STATE INCOME TAX
Prompt ? DOLLAR VALUE OF TOTAL INCOME EXEMPT FROM STATE INCOME TAX?

       1000  Operation  ? PROMPT
  < Define MAPPING NAME as a constant for all values of x, with
    the constant to be entered during the solution stage in response
    to the prompting message, PROMPTING MESSAGE >

Mname ? STATE_RATE
Mdesc ? STATE INCOME TAX RATE ON TOTAL INCOME LESS EXEMPTION
Prompt ? STATE INCOME TAX RATE ON TOTAL INCOME LESS EXEMPTION?
```

The last operation of this section (Operation 1100) is used to limit the independent variable, earned income, to a maximum of \$100,000. We have imposed this limit for two reasons: first, it is at least ample for the purposes of the model, and second, incomes beyond that upper limit would necessitate different assumptions and modeling concerning the federal income tax system, issues that are irrelevant for our present purposes.

```
       1100  Operation  ? COORDINATE
  < Define MAPPING NAME segment endpoints by typing in X and Y
    coordinate pairs >

Mname ? EARNINGS
Mdesc ? GROSS EARNED INCOME (WAGES AND SALARIES) FOR THE FAMILY'S EARNER
1? 0 0
2? 100000 100000
3?
```

For each of the prompts the resultant mapping is constant valued. Thus, the mapping for shelter costs (SHELTRCOST) has a constant value regardless of the value of the independent variable, earned income. Obviously this is a simplification of reality. We could also build our model by assuming that shelter costs are a monotonic increasing function of income and/or that they are conditional on family size. Our purpose in pointing this out is to stress that it is easy for the reader to find the simplifications that have been made, and as we shall show later on, it is easy to modify a model to alter them as appropriate. It is a fundamental design principle that MAPSIT should be able to implement whatever assumptions the analyst wants, rather than imposing assumptions on the analyst.

The "Simple Programs"

Since we have now made provisions for entering the parameter values that we shall need, we turn to the simple programs, transfers that do not depend on other transfer programs: FICA and the hypothetical state income tax. Again, we begin with a descriptive statement that tells the reader about the logic of the succeeding operations.

```
     1200  Operation  ? COMMENT
< Enter the LINES of the comment, up to 70 characters per line >

line  SECTION 2:  CALCULATION OF TRANSFERS FOR PROGRAMS THAT HAVE NO
line  OTHER PROGRAMS AS INPUTS
line     (1) FICA CONTRIBUTIONS ARE CALCULATED USING 1984
line         PARAMETERS AS 6.7% OF EARNINGS UP TO A MAXIMUM CONTRI-
line         BUTION OF $2532.60 (OCCURRING AT AN EARNINGS LEVEL OF
line         $37,800).
line     (2) STATE INCOME TAXES ARE CALCULATED AS THE GIVEN PROPOR-
line         TION TIMES THE QUANTITY "TOTAL INCOME (EARNINGS PLUS OTHER
line         TAXABLE INCOME) LESS THE GIVEN EXEMPTION."
line  (CR)
```

The actual creation of the FICA mapping is done by a CCEILING operation:[29]

```
      1300  Operation  ? CCEILING
 < Make MAPPING NAME equal to the lesser of [ SOURCE MAPPING weighted
   by WEIGHT FACTOR ] and the ceiling value, CEILING VALUE >

Mname ? FICA
Mdesc ? FICA PREMIUMS PAID BY THE EARNER
Source ? EARNINGS
Weight ? .067
Ceiling ? 2532.60
```

The result of this operation is a mapping, FICA, that is equal to 6.70% of earnings up to a maximum contribution of $2532.60.

The calculation of state income taxes requires three steps: (1) adding together earned income and other taxable income, (2) subtract-

---

[29] The CCEILING operation is a "combined" ceiling operation. A list of operations is contained in Appendix A.

ing the amount of any exempt income, as provided by the response to the prompt in the preceding section, and (3) multiplying the total amount of taxable income by the relevant tax rate. These three steps are carried out in Operations 1400, 1500, and 1600:

```
      1400  Operation  ? ADD
 < Make MAPPING NAME equal to ADDEND MAPPING 1 + ADDEND MAPPING 2 +
   ADDEND MAPPING 3 + ... >

Mname ? TOTAL_INC
Mdesc ? TOTAL_INCOME (GROSS EARNED INCOME PLUS OTHER TAXABLE INCOME)
Addend 1? EARNINGS
Addend 2? YTXBLOTHER
Addend 3?

      1500  Operation  ? CSUBTRACT
 < Make MAPPING NAME equal to [ MINUEND MAPPING * MINUEND WEIGHT
   FACTOR ] minus [ SUBTRAHEND MAPPING 1 * WEIGHT FACTOR 1 ],
   [ SUBTRAHEND MAPPING 2 * WEIGHT FACTOR 2 ], ...   optionally imposing
   a floor of FLOOR VALUE on the results of each subtraction >

Mname ? YTXBLSTATE
Mdesc ? TAXABLE INCOME FOR STATE INCOME TAX CALCULATIONS
Minuend ? TOTAL_INC
Weight 1
Subtrahend 1? STATE_EXEM
Weight 1? 1
Floor 1? 0
Subtrahend 2?

      1600  Operation  ? WEIGHT
 < Make MAPPING NAME equal to SOURCE MAPPING weighted by WEIGHT
   FACTOR >

Mname ? STATEINCTX
Mdesc ? STATE INCOME TAXES PAYABLE BY THE HEAD
Source ? YTXBLSTATE
Weight ? STATE_RATE
```

More Complicated Programs

In this part of the model we move into the operations necessary to set up the more complicated programs and expenses: the earned income tax credit (EITC), day care expenses, AFDC, food stamps, Medicaid, and federal income taxes, including the dependent care expense tax credit. To assist later readers of the model, each of these programs (or quasi-programs) is treated as a separate section within the model and is preceded with a comment. We begin with the earned income tax credit and day care expenses because they are both needed in the computations for AFDC.

Earned Income Tax Credit. The introductory comment for the earned income tax credit explains the basis on which that credit is to be computed.

```
      1700  Operation   ? COMMENT
 < Enter the LINES of the comment, up to 70 characters per line >

 line   SECTION 3:  CALCULATION OF THE EARNED INCOME CREDIT.
 line   .
 line   AFTER DEFINING THE EARNED INCOME CREDIT SCHEDULE, THE MODEL
 line   COMPUTES THE CREDIT ON TWO BASES:
 line      (1) USING EARNINGS AS THE INCOME BASE, AND
 line      (2) USING ADJUSTED GROSS INCOME (TOTAL_INC) AS THE INCOME BASE.
 line   .
 line   IT THEN SELECTS (1) OR (2) RESPECTIVELY AS ADJUSTED GROSS INCOME
 line   IS LESS THAN OR GREATER THAN $6000 (CF. THE EARNED INCOME CREDIT
 line   WORKSHEET IN THE IRS DOCUMENT, "INSTRUCTIONS FOR PREPARING
 line   FORM 1040").
 line   .
 line   THE PRESENT MODEL USES TOTAL_INC AS A SURROGATE FOR ADJUSTED GROSS
 line   INCOME.  (IF THE MODEL WERE TO BE USED FOR MORE THAN ILLUSTRATIVE
 line   PURPOSES ONE MIGHT WANT TO INCLUDE MORE DETAIL IN THE CALCULATION OF
 line   ADJUSTED GROSS INCOME, E.G. INCLUSION OF THE DEDUCTION FOR A MARRIED
 line   COUPLE WHEN BOTH WORK.)   FINALLY, THE CREDIT IS "DISALLOWED", I.E.
 line   SET TO 0, IF THERE ARE NO CHILDREN IN THE FAMILY.
 line
```

The first task is to construct the nominal schedule of EITC as a function of EITC income. This is done through a COORDINATE operation.

```
      1800  Operation   ? COORDINATE
  < Define MAPPING NAME segment endpoints by typing in X and Y
    coordinate pairs >

 Mname ? EICTABLE
 Mdesc ? EARNED INCOME CREDIT TABLE
 1? 0 0
 2? 5000 500
 3? 6000 500
 4? 10000 0
 5?
```

The next task is to construct a mapping for "adjusted gross income," the construct called for in the IRS instructions on computing the earned income tax credit (1983 IRS document "Instructions for Preparing Form 1040"). In the present case this is equivalent to the mapping already constructed for the state income tax, TOTAL_INC. Consequently we shall merely copy it, with a DUPLICATE operation, and use it as ADJGROSS in the computation of EITC.[30]

---

[30] We could simply use TOTAL_INC, but since we may want to use this logic in later models we choose to construct a separate mapping to remind us that the relevant mapping is indeed adjusted gross income, which may under other circumstances differ from our definition of total income.

```
      1900  Operation  ? DUPLICATE
  < Make MAPPING NAME a duplicate of SOURCE MAPPING >

Mname ? ADJGROSS
Mdesc ? ADJUSTED GROSS INCOME
Source ? TOTAL_INC
```

To find the earned income credit as a function of earnings and as a function of total income requires only two simple MAPPING operations:

```
      2000  Operation  ? MAPPING
  < Make MAPPING NAME [Z(X)] by combining Z(Y) MAPPING and Y(X)
    MAPPING >

Mname ? EICEARNNGS
Mdesc ? EARNED INCOME CREDIT USING INCOME BASE OF EARNINGS
Z(Y) ? EICTABLE
Y(X) ? EARNINGS

      2100  Operation  ? MAPPING
  < Make MAPPING NAME [Z(X)] by combining Z(Y) MAPPING and Y(X)
    MAPPING >

Mname ? EICTOTAL
Mdesc ? EARNED INCOME CREDIT USING INCOME BASE OF ADJUSTED GROSS INCOME
Z(Y) ? EICTABLE
Y(X) ? ADJGROSS
```

Since for earned income greater than $6000 one must take the lesser of these two EITC mappings, we use the MINIMUM operation first to find the lesser of the two values and then use the resulting mapping as a switch mapping in a SELECTION at Operation 2300:

```
      2200  Operation  ? MINIMUM
  < Make MAPPING NAME equal to the minimum of ARGUMENT MAPPING 1,
    ARGUMENT MAPPING 2, ARGUMENT MAPPING 3, ... >

Mname ? LESSER
Mdesc ? LESSER OF EICTOTAL AND EICEARNINGS (CF. WORKSHEET 6C)
Argument 1? EICTOTAL
Argument 2? EICEARNNGS
Argument 3?

      2300  Operation  ? SELECTION
  < Make  MAPPING NAME by selecting:
    GE MAPPING where SWITCH MAPPING is at least COMPARISON VALUE, and
    LT MAPPING where SWITCH MAPPING is less than COMPARISON VALUE >

Mname ? EITC
Mdesc EARNED INCOME CREDIT FOR THE FAMILY (BEFORE CONSIDERING CHILDREN)
Switch ? ADJGROSS
Value ? 6000
GE ? LESSER
LT ? EICEARNNGS
```

Finally, the earned income credit for the family is allowable only if there is at least one dependent child living at home. This final test is accomplished through another SELECTION operation:

```
     2400  Operation  ? SELECTION
  < Make  MAPPING NAME by selecting:
    GE MAPPING where SWITCH MAPPING is at least COMPARISON VALUE, and
    LT MAPPING where SWITCH MAPPING is less than COMPARISON VALUE >

Mname ? EITC
Mdesc EARNED INCOME CREDIT FOR THE FAMILY
Switch ? N_CHILDREN
Value ? 1
GE ? EITC
LT ? 0
```

Child Care Expenses. The next three operations establish child care expenses that are needed for AFDC, food stamps, and the dependent care expense tax credit. In all three of these cases, the allowable day care expenses are those incurred when the eligible person was working full-time. While we could build the model so that it prompted us for a specific wage rate and then computed the total annual wages that would be paid for full-time work, we shall make the simplifying assumption that part-time work is at the minimum wage ($3.35 in January, 1984) and that if the earnings were more than $6700 per year the person was employed full time and hence eligible to report full-time day care expenses for preschool children. As in the case of EITC we begin with a comment inserted into the model to inform others (and to remind ourselves) about the nature of the assumptions made in computing child care expenses.

```
     2500  Operation   ? COMMENT
  < Enter the LINES of the comment, up to 70 characters per line >

  line   SECTION 4:  CHILD CARE EXPENSES
  line   SINCE SEVERAL PROGRAMS (AFDC, FOOD STAMPS, AND THE DEPENDENT CARE
  line   TAX CREDIT)  USE  INFORMATION  ABOUT  CHILD  CARE  EXPENSES, THIS
  line   SECTION MAKES THE INITIAL CALCULATIONS.  THE FOLLOWING ASSUMPTIONS
  line   ARE RELEVANT:
  line      (1) DAY CARE USE IS PROPORTIONAL TO WORK EFFORT AND THAT AT
  line          $3.35/HR (MINIMUM WAGE IN JANUARY 1984) EARNINGS OF $6700
  line          CORRESPOND TO FULL TIME EMPLOYMENT.  THUS, EARNINGS OF $1675,
  line          $3350, $5025, AND $6700 IMPLY 25%, 50%, 75%, AND 100% EMPLOY-
  line          MENT, RESPECTIVELY.  INCOME ABOVE $6700 IS ASSUMED TO BE THE
  line          RESULT OF FULL TIME EMPLOYMENT AT A HIGHER WAGE RATE.
  line      (2) FULL TIME DAY CARE EXPENSES ARE ASSUMED TO BE $54.70 PER CHILD
  line          PER WEEK, OR $2735 FOR 50 WEEKS, BASED ON A SURVEY OF DAY CARE
  line          CENTERS IN PITTSBURGH IN MAY 1980 AND UPDATED BY AN AVERAGE OF
  line          5% PER YEAR FOR ASSUMED INCREASES IN DAY CARE COSTS FROM 1980
  line          TO 1984.
  line      (3) THE MODEL ASSUMES THAT DAY CARE IS NEEDED ONLY IF THE CHILD
  line          IS PRE-SCHOOL AGE (FIVE OR YOUNGER).
  line
```

Only three operations are needed to compute the day care expenses: the first (2600) creates the mapping that is a surrogate for the proportion of time that the person was working, the second weights this by the cost of child care, and the third multiplies the costs per child by the number of preschool age children to obtain the total child care expenses.[31]

```
      2600  Operation  ? COORDINATE
  < Define MAPPING NAME segment endpoints by typing in X and Y
    coordinate pairs >

Mname ? PROP_FULL
Mdesc ? PROPORTION OF FULL TIME EMPLOYMENT
1? 0 0
2? 6700 1
3?

      2700  Operation  ? WEIGHT
  < Make MAPPING NAME equal to SOURCE MAPPING weighted by WEIGHT
    FACTOR >

Mname ? COSTPERCHD
Mdesc ? DAY CARE COSTS PER CHILD
Source ? PROP_FULL
Weight ? 2735

      2800  Operation  ? WEIGHT
  < Make MAPPING NAME equal to SOURCE MAPPING weighted by WEIGHT
    FACTOR >

Mname ? CHLDCAREEX
Mdesc ? TOTAL CHILD CARE EXPENSES
Source ? COSTPERCHD
Weight ? CHLDN_LE_5
```

AFDC. Our usual practice is to include an explanatory comment in the model at this point, and indeed in the actual modeling session we have done exactly that (cf. Operation 2900 in the LIST version in Appendix B). Such comments are extremely important because they make MAPSIT models virtually self-explanatory, even to untrained readers. Nevertheless, since we shall be discussing the purpose of the various operations as well as the overall strategy of each section of the model, we have omitted the text of this and subsequent comments so as not to impede the flow of the discussion.

We begin, therefore, directly with the development of the AFDC need standards or monthly guarantees. We use a COORDINATE operation to establish the maximum benefit per month for family sizes one to six, and, by linear interpolation, for families up to size

---

[31] Implicitly we are assuming that people can buy any proportion of full-time care that they want.

twenty.[32]

Next we convert these monthly values to an annual basis and use a VALUE operation to select the appropriate maximum as a function of the family size being analyzed.

```
      3000  Operation   ? COORDINATE
  < Define MAPPING NAME segment endpoints by typing in X and Y
    coordinate pairs >

Mname ? AFDCMOGUAR
Mdesc ? AFDC MONTHLY GUARANTEE AS A FUNCTION OF FAMILY SIZE
1? 1 172
2? 2 262
3? 3 335
4? 4 401
5? 5 460
6? 6 501
7? 20 1313
8?

      3100  Operation   ? WEIGHT
  < Make MAPPING NAME equal to SOURCE MAPPING weighted by WEIGHT
    FACTOR >

Mname ? AFDCYRGUAR
Mdesc ? AFDC ANNUAL GUARANTEE AS A FUNCTION OF FAMILY SIZE
Source ? AFDCMOGUAR
Weight ? 12

      3200  Operation   ? VALUE
  < Make MAPPING NAME equal to the value of SOURCE MAPPING where x
    equals X-VALUE >

Mname ? AFDC_GUAR
Mdesc ? AFDC ANNUAL GUARANTEE FOR THIS FAMILY
Source ? AFDCYRGUAR
X ? FAMILYSIZE
```

We turn next to the calculation of the income base, "AFDC available income."

As explained in the discussion of program characteristics, there are three possible deductions from earned income: the work expense deduction which is $75 per month if the person is working full time and is prorated if the person is working less than full time, the child care deduction which has a maximum of $160 per child per month,

---

32 Since this model is for illustrative purposes we have used a COORDINATE operation rather than a FETCH operation to enter the schedules for AFDC and food stamps. The COORDINATE operation allows the reader to see the values of those schedules without turning back to the LIST version in Appendix B. In standard analysis, however, we would always use the FETCH operation, as we shall for Schedule Z of the federal income tax (Operation 7300), thereby reducing entry costs and the possibility of entry error.

and the earned income exemption if the person has been working for less than four months while receiving AFDC.

The annual work expense mapping is easily created using a WEIGHT operation:

```
     3300  Operation  ? WEIGHT
  < Make MAPPING NAME equal to SOURCE MAPPING weighted by WEIGHT
    FACTOR >

Mname ? WORKEXPDED
Mdesc ? ANNUAL WORK EXPENSE DEDUCTION ($75 PER MONTH)
Source ? PROP_FULL
Weight ? 900
```

The child care expense deduction, on the other hand, requires a series of steps. One WEIGHT operation is used to establish the maximum amount of day care if the parent were working less than full time. Another WEIGHT operation is used to adjust the maximum to reflect the number of children receiving day care. A MINIMUM operation is used to limit day care expenses to the lesser of the maximum allowance and the actual expenses.

```
     3400  Operation  ? WEIGHT
  < Make MAPPING NAME equal to SOURCE MAPPING weighted by WEIGHT
    FACTOR >

Mname ? MAXDCPERC
Mdesc ? MAXIMUM DAY CARE PER CHILD PER YEAR ($160 X 12)
Source ? PROP_FULL
Weight ? 1920

     3500  Operation  ? WEIGHT
  < Make MAPPING NAME equal to SOURCE MAPPING weighted by WEIGHT
    FACTOR >

Mname ? MAXDAYCARE
Mdesc ? MAXIMUM DAY CARE CONSIDERING ALL CHILDREN AGE 5 OR YOUNGER
Source ? MAXDCPERC
Weight ? CHLDN_LE_5

     3600  Operation  ? MINIMUM
  < Make MAPPING NAME equal to the minimum of ARGUMENT MAPPING 1,
    ARGUMENT MAPPING 2, ARGUMENT MAPPING 3, ... >

Mname ? ADCDAYCARE
Mdesc ? DAY CARE EXPENSES ALLOWABLE IN COMPUTING AFDC
Argument 1? CHLDCAREEX
Argument 2? MAXDAYCARE
Argument 3?
```

Before constructing the available income for AFDC purposes, it is necessary to construct two related income measures: gross income as defined by the AFDC program and net income (before the earned income exemption) for the AFDC program. The first of these is a simple ADD operation, combining total income and EITC. The second includes earnings and EITC minus the work expense deduction and the child care expense deduction.

```
      3700  Operation  ? ADD
  < Make MAPPING NAME equal to ADDEND MAPPING 1 + ADDEND MAPPING 2 +
    ADDEND MAPPING 3 + ... >

Mname ? AFGROSSINC
Mdesc ? GROSS INCOME FOR AFDC
Addend 1? TOTAL_INC
Addend 2? EITC
Addend 3?


      3800  Operation  ? CADD
  < Make MAPPING NAME equal to [ ADDEND MAPPING 1 * WEIGHT FACTOR 1 ]
    + [ ADDEND MAPPING 2 * WEIGHT FACTOR 2 ] + [ ADDEND MAPPING 3 *
    WEIGHT FACTOR 3 ] +... , optionally imposing a floor of FLOOR VALUE
    on the result of each addition >

Mname ? AFDCNETINC
Mdesc ? NET INCOME FOR AFDC
Addend 1? EARNINGS
Weight 1? 1
Addend 2? EITC
Weight 2? 1
Floor 2?
Addend 3? WORKEXPDED
Weight 3? -1
Floor 3?
Addend 4? ADCDAYCARE
Weight 4? -1
Floor 4? 0
Addend 5?
```

The next three operations develop the AFDC earned income exclusion. This exclusion, commonly known as "thirty and a third," allows an AFDC unit to exclude $30 per month of earned income and one-third of the remaining earned income (after the work and child care deductions have been subtracted) in calculating available income for AFDC purposes. The first two of the operations reflect the fixed amount ($30 per month) and the proportion (.33) that can be excluded if the parent has not been employed for more than four months since receiving AFDC, though we simplify the presentation by permitting the deduction for the entire year if the prompt indicates eligibility for the deduction. Operation 3900 uses the earned income exemption value (AFDCINCEXM) to establish whether the amount to be deducted is $360 or nothing. Operation 4000 uses AFDCINCEXM to establish whether the proportion to be deducted is one-third or zero. Operation 4100 subtracts the applicable fixed amount from earned income, and Operation 4200 reduces earned income further by applying the applicable proportional reduction. Finally, Operation

4300 adds other taxable (unearned) income to the net earned income less exemptions to obtain the income base for AFDC--available income.

```
      3900  Operation  ? SELECTION
  < Make  MAPPING NAME by selecting:
    GE MAPPING where SWITCH MAPPING is at least COMPARISON VALUE, and
    LT MAPPING where SWITCH MAPPING is less than COMPARISON VALUE >

Mname ? EXEMPT_VAL
Mdesc EARNED INCOME EXEMPTION IF APPLICABLE (30 PER MONTH)
Switch ? AFDCINCEXM
Value ? 1
GE ? 0
LT ? 360

      4000  Operation  ? SELECTION
  < Make  MAPPING NAME by selecting:
    GE MAPPING where SWITCH MAPPING is at least COMPARISON VALUE, and
    LT MAPPING where SWITCH MAPPING is less than COMPARISON VALUE >

Mname ? EXEMPTPROP
Mdesc EARNED INCOME EXEMPTION:  PROPORTION EXCLUDED
Switch ? AFDCINCEXM
Value ? 1
GE ? 0
LT ? .333333333

      4100  Operation  ? CSUBTRACT
  < Make MAPPING NAME equal to [ MINUEND MAPPING * MINUEND WEIGHT
    FACTOR ] minus [ SUBTRAHEND MAPPING 1 * WEIGHT FACTOR 1 ],
    [ SUBTRAHEND MAPPING 2 * WEIGHT FACTOR 2 ], ...   optionally imposing
    a floor of FLOOR VALUE on the results of each subtraction >

Mname ? YELESSEXM1
Mdesc ? AFDC NET INCOME LESS FIXED VALUE EXEMPTED
Minuend ? AFDCNETINC
Weight 1
Subtrahend 1? EXEMPT_VAL
Weight 1? 1
Floor 1? 0
Subtrahend 2?

      4200  Operation  ? CSUBTRACT
  < Make MAPPING NAME equal to [ MINUEND MAPPING * MINUEND WEIGHT
    FACTOR ] minus [ SUBTRAHEND MAPPING 1 * WEIGHT FACTOR 1 ],
    [ SUBTRAHEND MAPPING 2 * WEIGHT FACTOR 2 ], ...   optionally imposing
    a floor of FLOOR VALUE on the results of each subtraction >

Mname ? YELESSEXEM
Mdesc ? EARNINGS LESS APPLICABLE EARNED INCOME EXEMPTION
Minuend ? YELESSEXM1
Weight 1
Subtrahend 1? YELESSEXM1
Weight 1? EXEMPTPROP
Floor 1?
Subtrahend 2?

      4300  Operation  ? ADD
  < Make MAPPING NAME equal to ADDEND MAPPING 1 + ADDEND MAPPING 2 +
    ADDEND MAPPING 3 + ... >

Mname ? YAVAILAFDC
Mdesc ? INCOME DEEMED AVAILABLE BY AFDC
Addend 1? YELESSEXEM
Addend 2? YTXBLOTHER
Addend 3?
```

The only steps remaining in the calculation of the benefit are to subtract the available income from the "guarantee" (Operation 4400), to eliminate any benefits that are less than $10 per month (Operation 4500), to test whether the maximum gross income limit has been exceeded (Operation 4700), and to certify that benefits exist only if there is at least one child in the family (Operation 4800). Before testing whether or not the maximum gross income has been exceeded, it is necessary to construct that value, which is done in Operation 4600.

```
      4400  Operation   ? CSUBTRACT
  < Make MAPPING NAME equal to [ MINUEND MAPPING * MINUEND WEIGHT
    FACTOR ] minus [ SUBTRAHEND MAPPING 1 * WEIGHT FACTOR 1 ],
    [ SUBTRAHEND MAPPING 2 * WEIGHT FACTOR 2 ], ...    optionally imposing
    a floor of FLOOR VALUE on the results of each subtraction >

Mname ? AFDC1
Mdesc ? AFDC BEFORE ELIMINATING BENEFITS UNDER $10
Minuend ? AFDC_GUAR
Weight 1
Subtrahend 1? YAVAILAFDC
Weight 1? 1
Floor 1? 0
Subtrahend 2?

      4500  Operation   ? SELECTION
  < Make  MAPPING NAME by selecting:
    GE MAPPING where SWITCH MAPPING is at least COMPARISON VALUE, and
    LT MAPPING where SWITCH MAPPING is less than COMPARISON VALUE >

Mname ? AFDC2
Mdesc AFDC AFTER ELIMINATING BENEFITS UNDER $10
Switch ? AFDC1
Value ? 10
GE ? AFDC1
LT ? 0

      4600  Operation   ? WEIGHT
  < Make MAPPING NAME equal to SOURCE MAPPING weighted by WEIGHT
    FACTOR >

Mname ? AFDCMAXINC
Mdesc ? MAXIMUM INCOME FOR AFDC ELIGIBILITY
Source ? AFDC_GUAR
Weight ? 1.5

      4700  Operation   ? SELECTION
  < Make  MAPPING NAME by selecting:
    GE MAPPING where SWITCH MAPPING is at least COMPARISON VALUE, and
    LT MAPPING where SWITCH MAPPING is less than COMPARISON VALUE >

Mname ? AFDC3
Mdesc AFDC BENEFIT BEFORE TESTING FOR PRESENCE OF CHILDREN
Switch ? AFGROSSINC
Value ? AFDCMAXINC
GE ? 0
LT ? AFDC2
```

```
      4800  Operation  ? SELECTION
 < Make  MAPPING NAME by selecting:
   GE MAPPING where SWITCH MAPPING is at least COMPARISON VALUE, and
   LT MAPPING where SWITCH MAPPING is less than COMPARISON VALUE >

Mname ? AFDC
Mdesc AFDC BENEFIT
Switch ? N_CHILDREN
Value ? 1
GE ? AFDC3
LT ? 0
```

Food Stamp Benefits. We shall divide the calculation of food stamp benefits into three steps: the first derives the nominal benefit schedule (benefits as a function of the food stamp income base), the second derives the income base as a function of earnings, and the third derives the benefit as a function of earnings.

The first task in establishing the nominal food stamp benefit schedule is to find the appropriate maximum benefit for the size family being simulated. Since we shall undoubtedly want to analyze families of different sizes we begin by including in the model the maximum monthly bonus as a function of family size and then use an operation to pick out the appropriate maximum food stamp bonus for the particular family size. Again, the first of these tasks would ordinarily be done by a FETCH, but to display the actual values we shall use COORDINATE. The second task involves a VALUE operation:

```
      5100  Operation  ? COORDINATE
 < Define MAPPING NAME segment endpoints by typing in X and Y
   coordinate pairs >

Mname ? MAXBONUSCH
Mdesc ? MONTHLY MAXIMUM FOOD STAMP BONUS BY FAMILY SIZE (JAN 1984)
1? 1 75
2? 2 139
3? 3 199
4? 4 253
5? 5 300
6? 6 360
7? 7 398
8? 8 455
9? 9 512
10? 10 569
11? 20 1139
12?

      5200  Operation  ? VALUE
 < Make MAPPING NAME equal to the value of SOURCE MAPPING where x
   equals X-VALUE >

Mname ? MAXBONUSMO
Mdesc ? MONTHLY MAXIMUM FOOD STAMP BONUS FOR THE FAMILY
Source ? MAXBONUSCH
X ? FAMILYSIZE
```

Finally, since the result of Operation 5200 is in monthly terms we need to weight this amount to get the annual equivalent.

```
      5300  Operation  ? WEIGHT
 < Make MAPPING NAME equal to SOURCE MAPPING weighted by WEIGHT
   FACTOR >

Mname ? MAXBONUSYR
Mdesc ? ANNUAL MAXIMUM FOOD STAMP BONUS FOR THE FAMILY
Source ? MAXBONUSMO
Weight ? 12
```

A similar strategy is followed to obtain the monthly maximum allowable income by family size. The schedule of maxima by family size is established, provision is made to select the appropriate value from that schedule, and the result is multiplied by 12 to obtain the annualized value of the maximum.

```
      5400  Operation  ? COORDINATE
 < Define MAPPING NAME segment endpoints by typing in X and Y
   coordinate pairs >

Mname ? MAXINCSCH
Mdesc ? MONTHLY MAXIMUM ALLOWABLE INCOME BY FAMILY SIZE (JAN 1984)
1? 1 527
2? 2 709
3? 3 891
4? 4 1073
5? 5 1255
6? 6 1437
7? 7 1619
8? 8 1801
9? 9 1983
10? 10 2165
11? 20 3985
12?

      5500  Operation  ? VALUE
 < Make MAPPING NAME equal to the value of SOURCE MAPPING where x
   equals X-VALUE >

Mname ? FSMAXINCMO
Mdesc ? FOOD STAMP MAXIMUM ALLOWABLE INCOME FOR THE FAMILY (MONTHLY)
Source ? MAXINCSCH
X ? FAMILYSIZE

      5600  Operation  ? WEIGHT
 < Make MAPPING NAME equal to SOURCE MAPPING weighted by WEIGHT
   FACTOR >

Mname ? FSMAXINCYR
Mdesc ? FOOD STAMP MAXIMUM ALLOWABLE INCOME FOR THE FAMILY (ANNUALLY)
Source ? FSMAXINCMO
Weight ? 12
```

Using the maximum food stamp bonus and the maximum family income, we derive the nominal schedule in two steps. The first step applies a 30 percent reduction rate (with respect to the food stamp income base) on the maximum bonus for the family and imposes a $10 per month ($120 per year) minimum on benefits payable. The second step uses a SELECTION operation to insure that no benefits are payable for incomes exceeding the maximum allowable income.

```
     5700  Operation  ? CSUBTRACT
  < Make MAPPING NAME equal to [ MINUEND MAPPING * MINUEND WEIGHT
    FACTOR ] minus [ SUBTRAHEND MAPPING 1 * WEIGHT FACTOR 1 ],
    [ SUBTRAHEND MAPPING 2 * WEIGHT FACTOR 2 ], ...   optionally imposing
    a floor of FLOOR VALUE on the results of each subtraction >

Mname ? TENTNOMFS
Mdesc ? NOMINAL FOOD STAMP BENEFIT SCHEDULE (BEFORE MAX INC PROVISION)
Minuend ? MAXBONUSYR
Weight 1
Subtrahend 1? INDEP
Weight 1? .30
Floor 1? 120
Subtrahend 2?

     5800  Operation  ? SELECTION
  < Make  MAPPING NAME by selecting:
    GE MAPPING where SWITCH MAPPING is at least COMPARISON VALUE, and
    LT MAPPING where SWITCH MAPPING is less than COMPARISON VALUE >

Mname ? NOMFSSCH
Mdesc NOMINAL FOOD STAMPS BENEFIT SCHEDULE FOR THE FAMILY
Switch ? INDEP
Value ? FSMAXINCYR
GE ? 0
LT ? TENTNOMFS
```

The next step in obtaining food stamp benefits is to calculate the income base for the food stamp program. This is obtained by taking the sum of earned and unearned income, which we have previously computed as TOTAL_INC, adding to this the benefits from federal or federally aided public assistance programs, in this case AFDC, and then subtracting relevant deductions: (1) 18 percent of earned income, (2) a standard deduction of $85 per month ($1020 per year), (3) a dependent care deduction, (4) a deduction for medical costs in excess of $35 per month for persons age sixty and over, and (5) an excess shelter costs deduction. We start by adding together the various streams of income:

```
     6000  Operation  ? ADD
  < Make MAPPING NAME equal to ADDEND MAPPING 1 + ADDEND MAPPING 2 +
    ADDEND MAPPING 3 + ... >
```

```
Mname ? FSTOTALINC
Mdesc ? TOTAL INCOME COUNTED BY FOOD STAMPS
Addend 1? TOTAL_INC
Addend 2? AFDC
Addend 3?
```

Next we need to compute the dependent care expense deduction. We shall assume that the actual expenses are equal to the child care expenses that were previously defined in this model and that there are no other dependent care expenses, but we also need to represent the fact that the deduction is limited to $115 per month ($1380 per year). This is done using a MINIMUM operation in Operation 6100.

```
     6100  Operation   ? MINIMUM
  < Make MAPPING NAME equal to the minimum of ARGUMENT MAPPING 1,
    ARGUMENT MAPPING 2, ARGUMENT MAPPING 3, ... >

Mname ? CHDCAREDED
Mdesc ? FOOD STAMP CHILD CARE DEDUCTION
Argument 1? CHLDCAREEX
Argument 2? 1380
Argument 3?
```

Since we don't plan to use this model to analyze families with members over age sixty, we shall ignore the medical expense deduction. The last deduction to consider, then, is that for excess shelter costs. Excess shelter costs are defined as shelter costs in excess of 50 percent of the net income (income after the earned income deduction, the standard deduction, the medical expense deduction, and the dependent care deduction). These excess expenses are deductible up to a maximum of $115 per month ($1380 per year), but the combined deduction for dependent care expenses and excess shelter costs cannot exceed $115 per month ($1380 per year).

To find excess shelter costs it is necessary first to compute the net food stamp income, income less all of the other deductions. This is done in Operation 6200 in which we start with FSTOTALINC as the minuend and subtract 18 percent of earnings, the standard deduction of $1020 and the food stamp child care deduction.

```
     6200  Operation   ? CSUBTRACT
  < Make MAPPING NAME equal to [ MINUEND MAPPING * MINUEND WEIGHT
    FACTOR ] minus [ SUBTRAHEND MAPPING 1 * WEIGHT FACTOR 1 ],
    [ SUBTRAHEND MAPPING 2 * WEIGHT FACTOR 2 ], ...    optionally imposing
    a floor of FLOOR VALUE on the results of each subtraction >

Mname ? FSNETINC
Mdesc ? NET FOOD STAMP INCOME
Minuend ? FSTOTALINC
Weight 1
Subtrahend 1? EARNINGS
Weight 1? .18
```

```
Floor 1?
Subtrahend 2? 1020
Weight 2? 1
Floor 2?
Subtrahend 3? CHDCAREDED
Weight 3? 1
Floor 3? 0
Subtrahend 4?
```

The next step is to compute the shelter allowance by taking the amount by which shelter costs exceed 50 percent of net food stamp income. This is done in Operation 6300 by subtracting 50 percent of FSNETINC from SHELTRCOST and imposing a floor of 0 (that is, the shelter allowance cannot be negative).

```
    6300  Operation  ? CSUBTRACT
  < Make MAPPING NAME equal to [ MINUEND MAPPING * MINUEND WEIGHT
    FACTOR ] minus [ SUBTRAHEND MAPPING 1 * WEIGHT FACTOR 1 ],
    [ SUBTRAHEND MAPPING 2 * WEIGHT FACTOR 2 ], ...   optionally imposing
    a floor of FLOOR VALUE on the results of each subtraction >

Mname ? TSHELALLW
Mdesc ? TENTATIVE SHELTER ALLOWANCE, BEFORE MAX ALLOWABLE DEDUCTION
Minuend ? SHELTRCOST
Weight 1
Subtrahend 1? FSNETINC
Weight 1? .5
Floor 1? 0
Subtrahend 2?
```

In addition, however, there is the restriction that the excess shelter cost deduction, together with the dependent care expense deduction, cannot exceed $115 per month. We model this in two steps. First, Operation 6400 computes the maximum shelter cost deduction as $1380 per year minus the amount of the dependent care expense deduction, and second, Operation 6500 takes the minimum of the actual excess shelter costs and the maximum allowable shelter deduction.

```
    6400  Operation  ? CSUBTRACT
  < Make MAPPING NAME equal to [ MINUEND MAPPING * MINUEND WEIGHT
    FACTOR ] minus [ SUBTRAHEND MAPPING 1 * WEIGHT FACTOR 1 ],
    [ SUBTRAHEND MAPPING 2 * WEIGHT FACTOR 2 ], ...   optionally imposing
    a floor of FLOOR VALUE on the results of each subtraction >

Mname ? MAXSHLTDED
Mdesc ? FOOD STAMP MAXIMUM SHELTER DEDUCTION
Minuend ? 1380
Weight 1
Subtrahend 1? CHDCAREDED
Weight 1? 1
Floor 1? 0
Subtrahend 2?
```

```
     6500  Operation  ? MINIMUM
 < Make MAPPING NAME equal to the minimum of ARGUMENT MAPPING 1,
   ARGUMENT MAPPING 2, ARGUMENT MAPPING 3, ... >

Mname ? FSSHELALLW
Mdesc ? FOOD STAMP SHELTER ALLOWANCE
Argument 1? TSHELALLW
Argument 2? MAXSHLTDED
Argument 3?
```

Finally, the value of the food stamp income base is obtained by subtracting the last of the deductions, allowable excess shelter costs, from the net food stamp income (Operation 6600) and using this in a "mapping of a mapping" to find the food stamp benefits as a function of earned income (Operation 6700).

```
     6600  Operation  ? CSUBTRACT
 < Make MAPPING NAME equal to [ MINUEND MAPPING * MINUEND WEIGHT
   FACTOR ] minus [ SUBTRAHEND MAPPING 1 * WEIGHT FACTOR 1 ],
   [ SUBTRAHEND MAPPING 2 * WEIGHT FACTOR 2 ], ...   optionally imposing
   a floor of FLOOR VALUE on the results of each subtraction >

Mname ? FSINCBASE
Mdesc ? FOOD STAMPS INCOME BASE FOR THE FAMILY
Minuend ? FSNETINC
Weight 1
Subtrahend 1? FSSHELALLW
Weight 1? 1
Floor 1? 0
Subtrahend 2?

     6700  Operation  ? MAPPING
 < Make MAPPING NAME [Z(X)] by combining Z(Y) MAPPING and Y(X)
   MAPPING >

Mname ? FOODSTAMPS
Mdesc ? FOOD STAMPS BENEFIT PAYABLE TO THE FAMILY
Z(Y) ? NOMFSSCH
Y(X) ? FSINCBASE
```

Medicaid. The next section of the model computes Medicaid benefits. As mentioned earlier, we shall assume that the Medicaid benefits can be treated as if they were cash. Furthermore, for earnings levels at which the family receives a positive benefit from AFDC, Medicaid is assumed to reimburse the family for its medical expenses; otherwise the family is assumed to pay the medical expenses itself. Hausman (1975, p. 45) reported average expenditures for AFDC recipients in Illinois in 1971 as $222 per person per year. Between 1971 and 1980 the consumer price index for medical care increased from 128 to 263, a compound rate of 8.33% per year. Extrapolated to 1984 the average expenditures per person would be $628 per year.

Only three steps are needed to incorporate expected medical benefits into the model: (1) weighting the expected benefits per person by the number of people in the family, (2) testing whether the family is eligible for Medicaid by virtue of AFDC eligibility, regardless of whether or not they receive a check from AFDC, and (3) testing whether the family exceeds the gross income test in AFDC.[33] To exceed the gross income limit would automatically terminate eligibility for AFDC.

```
      6900  Operation  ? WEIGHT
  < Make MAPPING NAME equal to SOURCE MAPPING weighted by WEIGHT
    FACTOR >

Mname ? MEDICALEXP
Mdesc ? MEDICAL EXPENSES INCURRED BY THE FAMILY
Source ? FAMILYSIZE
Weight ? 628

      7000  Operation  ? SELECTION
  < Make  MAPPING NAME by selecting:
    GE MAPPING where SWITCH MAPPING is at least COMPARISON VALUE, and
    LT MAPPING where SWITCH MAPPING is less than COMPARISON VALUE >

Mname ? PMEDICAID
Mdesc PRELIMINARY MEDICAID CALCULATION
Switch ? AFDC1
Value ? 0
GE ? MEDICALEXP
LT ? 0

      7100  Operation  ? SELECTION
  < Make  MAPPING NAME by selecting:
    GE MAPPING where SWITCH MAPPING is at least COMPARISON VALUE, and
    LT MAPPING where SWITCH MAPPING is less than COMPARISON VALUE >

Mname ? MEDICAID
Mdesc MEDICAID BENEFIT
Switch ? AFGROSSINC
Value ? AFDCMAXINC
GE ? 0
LT ? PMEDICAID
```

Federal Taxes. We shall model federal income tax in three steps: obtaining the relation between taxes payable as a function of taxable income, constructing the amount of taxable income as a function of earned income, and finally, computing the taxes payable as a function of earned income. The first task is accomplished by using a FETCH operation to obtain Schedule Z from an on-line library of tax schedules. (The reader will find the values for that schedule printed

---

[33] At present, AFDC benefits less than $10 are "rounded-down" to zero. In these cases the family is classified as "ineligible" for AFDC, but rounding down does not change the family's eligibility for Medicaid.

in the LIST version of the model, Appendix B.) To construct taxable income as a function of earned income, we start with total income and subtract the personal exemption ($1000 per person), imposing a limit so that taxable income cannot be less than zero. Taxable income is then used in a MAPPING operation to obtain federal taxes due as a function of earned income. These three actions are shown in Operations 7300 through 7500:

```
      7300  Operation  ? FETCH
 < Fetch MAPPING NAME from schedule file SCHEDULE FILE NAME >

Mname ? SCHEDULE_Z
File ? USZ84.SCH

      7400  Operation  ? CSUBTRACT
 < Make MAPPING NAME equal to [ MINUEND MAPPING * MINUEND WEIGHT
   FACTOR ] minus [ SUBTRAHEND MAPPING 1 * WEIGHT FACTOR 1 ],
   [ SUBTRAHEND MAPPING 2 * WEIGHT FACTOR 2 ], ...   optionally imposing
   a floor of FLOOR VALUE on the results of each subtraction >

Mname ? TAXABLEINC
Mdesc ? TAXABLE INCOME FOR THE FAMILY
Minuend ? TOTAL_INC
Weight 1
Subtrahend 1? FAMILYSIZE
Weight 1? 1000
Floor 1? 0
Subtrahend 2?

      7500  Operation  ? MAPPING
 < Make MAPPING NAME [Z(X)] by combining Z(Y) MAPPING and Y(X)
   MAPPING >

Mname ? FEDINCTAX
Mdesc ? FEDERAL INCOME TAX
Z(Y) ? SCHEDULE_Z
Y(X) ? TAXABLEINC
```

Dependent Care Expense Credit. Previously we computed the total child care expense (CHLDCAREEX) for this family, using the number of children age five or younger as a surrogate for whether there were children who needed day care at all. In computing the dependent care tax credit we shall make use of CHLDCAREEX, together with the regulations concerning that tax credit. There are three regulations of special interest in the present case: (1) the family is not eligible for any deduction unless the parent is providing at least 50 percent of the costs of maintaining the home, (2) there is a maximum expense that the parent can claim ($2000 if there is only one child, and $4000 if there are two or more children receiving day care), and (3) the credit is limited to 20 percent of the maximum expenses or 20 percent of the actual expenses, whichever is less.

To model the restriction concerning home maintenance, we construct a mapping that is the difference between total income (earned and unearned income plus EITC) and AFDC. That mapping is constructed using a CADD operation:

```
     7700  Operation  ? CADD
  < Make MAPPING NAME equal to [ ADDEND MAPPING 1 * WEIGHT FACTOR 1 ]
    + [ ADDEND MAPPING 2 * WEIGHT FACTOR 2 ] + [ ADDEND MAPPING 3 *
    WEIGHT FACTOR 3 ] +... , optionally imposing a floor of FLOOR VALUE
    on the result of each addition >

Mname ? HOMEMAINT
Mdesc ? PARENTAL CONTRIBUTION TO RUNNING HOME IN EXCESS OF BENEFITS RECEIVED
Addend 1? TOTAL_INC
Weight 1? 1
Addend 2? EITC
Weight 2? 1
Floor 2?
Addend 3? AFDC
Weight 3? -1
Floor 3?
Addend 4?
```

The credit is then computed by selecting the appropriate maximum expense limit (Operation 7800), restricting the maximum allowable child care expense to the lesser of the limit and actual child care expenses, and then multiplying the allowable expenses by .20 (Operation 8000). Finally, we restrict the credit to those situations in which the parent has provided at least 50 percent of the costs of maintaining the home. These actions are shown in operations 7800 through 8100.

```
     7800  Operation  ? SELECTION
  < Make  MAPPING NAME by selecting:
    GE MAPPING where SWITCH MAPPING is at least COMPARISON VALUE, and
    LT MAPPING where SWITCH MAPPING is less than COMPARISON VALUE >

Mname ? LIMIT
Mdesc MAXIMUM ALLOWABLE CHILD CARE EXPENSE (2441, LINE 4)
Switch ? CHLDN_LE_5
Value ? 2
GE ? 4000
LT ? 2000

     7900  Operation  ? MINIMUM
  < Make MAPPING NAME equal to the minimum of ARGUMENT MAPPING 1,
    ARGUMENT MAPPING 2, ARGUMENT MAPPING 3, ... >

Mname ? MAXALLWEXP
Mdesc ? MAXIMUM ALLOWABLE CHILD CARE EXPENSE
Argument 1? LIMIT
Argument 2? CHLDCAREEX
Argument 3? EARNINGS
Argument 4?
```

```
     8000  Operation  ? WEIGHT
 < Make MAPPING NAME equal to SOURCE MAPPING weighted by WEIGHT
   FACTOR >

Mname ? PCREDIT
Mdesc ? PRELIMINARY CHILD CARE CREDIT
Source ? MAXALLWEXP
Weight ? .2

     8100  Operation  ? SELECTION
 < Make  MAPPING NAME by selecting:
   GE MAPPING where SWITCH MAPPING is at least COMPARISON VALUE, and
   LT MAPPING where SWITCH MAPPING is less than COMPARISON VALUE >

Mname ? CHLDCRCRDT
Mdesc CHILD CARE CREDIT
Switch ? HOMEMAINT
Value ? 0
GE ? PCREDIT
LT ? 0
```

Unlike the earned income tax credit which is refundable to the taxpayer, the tax credit for child and dependent care expenses can be used only to reduce the family's tax liability.

Net Federal Taxes. Since the dependent care expense credit is not reimbursed to the taxpayer but can be used only to reduce the taxes payable, the last programmatic step in the model is to perform a reconciliation of taxes: subtracting the tax credit from the federal taxes due (FEDINCTAX), while setting the minimum value to zero.

```
     8300  Operation  ? CSUBTRACT
 < Make MAPPING NAME equal to [ MINUEND MAPPING * MINUEND WEIGHT
   FACTOR ] minus [ SUBTRAHEND MAPPING 1 * WEIGHT FACTOR 1 ],
   [ SUBTRAHEND MAPPING 2 * WEIGHT FACTOR 2 ], ...    optionally imposing
   a floor of FLOOR VALUE on the results of each subtraction >

Mname ? NETFEDTAX
Mdesc ? FEDERAL INCOME TAX AFTER CHILD CARE EXPENSE CREDIT
Minuend ? FEDINCTAX
Weight 1
Subtrahend 1? CHLDCRCRDT
Weight 1? 1
Floor 1? 0
Subtrahend 2?
```

Final Operations. The last mapping that we need to construct is disposable income. In the present case we shall adopt a rather broad definition of disposable income, including all income sources for the family (earnings, other taxable income, and all program benefits) and then deducting involuntary outflows (FICA premiums and federal and state income taxes).

```
     8500  Operation  ? CADD
  < Make MAPPING NAME equal to [ ADDEND MAPPING 1 * WEIGHT FACTOR 1 ]
    + [ ADDEND MAPPING 2 * WEIGHT FACTOR 2 ] + [ ADDEND MAPPING 3 *
    WEIGHT FACTOR 3 ] +... , optionally imposing a floor of FLOOR VALUE
    on the result of each addition >

Mname ? DISPOSABLE
Mdesc ? DISPOSABLE INCOME FOR THE FAMILY
Addend 1? EARNINGS
Weight 1? 1
Addend 2? YTXBLOTHER
Weight 2? 1
Floor 2?
Addend 3? AFDC
Weight 3? 1
Floor 3?
Addend 4? FOODSTAMPS
Weight 4? 1
Floor 4?
Addend 5? MEDICAID
Weight 5? 1
Floor 5?
Addend 6? EITC
Weight 6? 1
Floor 6?
Addend 7? FICA
Weight 7? -1
Floor 7?
Addend 8? STATEINCTX
Weight 8? -1
Floor 8?
Addend 9? NETFEDTAX
Weight 9? -1
Floor 9?
Addend 10?
```

The command to compute the disposable income mapping completes the specification of the numerical computations to be performed by the solution module. However, one last element of the model remains. The analyst must still specify the mappings to be included in the file produced by the solution module. To carry out this final task, the analyst uses the SAVE operation.

Essentially, the SAVE operation collects three pieces of information about every mapping that is to appear in the output from the solution module. The first is the name of the mapping. In our example the analyst wishes to see all mappings that represent transfers to or from the family, provided the mappings are expressed as functions of earned income. These mappings include AFDC, FOODSTAMPS, MEDICAID, EITC, FICA, STATEINCTX, and NETFEDTAX. Obviously, the analyst also wishes to see disposable income. Additionally, we shall include the initial computation of federal income taxes, FEDINCTAX, and the dependent care expense credit in the solution.

The second piece of information is a mapping description. This is really an opportunity to document further the substance of the model in a manner that is carried through to the output from the model. The analyst can make up a new description for the mapping, or default to the one that was used when the mapping was created. The descriptions are transmitted to the output file where they can be accessed by the secondary analysis module and used as legends for the various forms of output.

The third piece of information for each mapping is the tax factor. The tax factor is used to indicate the appropriate formula for computing the tax rate implicit in the mapping. The necessity of such an indicator can be seen in the following examples. If disposable income increases by $50 when earned income rises by $100, the tax rate implicit over the range is 50 percent. If transfers from a given benefit program decrease by $50 over a $100 range of earned income, then the program is said to impose a 50 percent tax rate on earned income in that range. The general rule of thumb is that if the mapping includes the independent variable as part of a sum, for example, if the mapping is an income measure, it receives a tax factor of "true" ("Y"). Otherwise it receives a tax-factor of "false" ("N"), which is also the default value. Here, only DISPOSABLE receives the value "true".

MAPSIT continues to prompt the analyst for additional mappings to be saved until the analyst responds with a carriage return to indicate that the list is complete. Finally, the analyst indicates that the model is finished by responding to the "Operation ?" prompt with the keyword END.

The interaction appears at the terminal as follows:

```
     8700  Operation  ? SAVE
< Save the specified mappings, descriptions, and tax factors:
  SAVE MAPPING 1, DESCRIPTION, TAX FACTOR;  SAVE MAPPING 2, DESCRIPTION,
  TAX FACTOR; ... >
Sname1? AFDC
Sdesc ?
Tax factor ? N
Sname2? FOODSTAMPS
Sdesc ?
Tax factor ? N
Sname3? MEDICAID
Sdesc ?
Tax factor ? N
Sname4? EITC
Sdesc ?
Tax factor ? N
Sname5? FICA
Sdesc ?
Tax factor ? N
Sname6? FEDINCTAX
Sdesc ?
Tax factor ? N
```

```
Sname7? CHLDCRCRDT
Sdesc ?
Tax factor ? N
Sname8? NETFEDTAX
Sdesc ?
Tax factor ? N
Sname9? DISPOSABLE
Sdesc ?
Tax factor ? Y
Sname10?

      8800  Operation  ? END
```

This completes the model, although it is not the only model that we could have built for this particular problem. Typically there are several ways in which a given mapping can be constructed, and in this example we have used only a relatively small number of the total set of operations available in BUILD. Some of the mappings in this section could have been built more efficiently (with a smaller number of operations), but only at the expense to the reader of having to do more work to follow the logic. There is often a trade-off between minimizing the number of operations and making the logic of the final model stand out as clearly as possible. Thus, throughout the example we chose a more explicit formulation where we thought it would make the logic easier to follow. One advantage of MAPSIT is that it has a rich set of operations, allowing the analyst considerable freedom in developing mappings.

In addition to illustrating the ways in which mappings can be constructed we have tried to illustrate several other features of model building that we think are important: use of clear and comprehensive documentation at the beginning of the model, generous use of comments within the model, division of the model into sections, and orderly placement of operations within a section. Some of these characteristics result naturally from the need to consider "first things first," but there is typically a fair amount of freedom left to the analyst, freedom that is best used to develop a logical and orderly model.

Finally, this section has illustrated the assistance that MAPSIT provides to the analyst, especially the reminders at the start of each operation of what is being done and what responses will be required of the analyst, although this feature of MAPSIT can be suppressed when desired.

Now that the model has been built, it remains merely to solve it.

SOLVING THE MODEL

At the command level in MAPSIT the analyst indicates that he or she wants to solve a model, gives the model name, and is then asked for responses to the model's prompts. This process is shown in the following excerpt from a session at a terminal:[34]

```
Command? SOLVE

Model? ILLUS4.MOD

Version? 1

HOW MANY CHILDREN ARE THERE AGE 5 OR YOUNGER?      1
HOW MANY CHILDREN ARE THERE AGE 6 OR OLDER?      2
HAS THE PARENT BEEN EMPLOYED FOR MORE THAN 4 MONTHS? (1=YES,0=NO)      1
DOLLAR VALUE OF TAXABLE INCOME (OTHER THAN EARNINGS) FOR THE FAMILY?  0
ANNUAL SHELTER COSTS INCLUDING HEAT, ELEC, WATER, & PHONE?  3600
DOLLAR VALUE OF TOTAL INCOME EXEMPT FROM STATE INCOME TAX?  0
STATE INCOME TAX RATE ON TOTAL INCOME LESS EXEMPTION?      .0245

Solution completed and stored in file "ILLUS4.1   ".
```

This particular model, ILLUS4, takes only a couple of seconds to solve, and all but the first three instructions were responses to the prompts of the specific model. Additional solutions could be run to look at the results of different numbers of children, differing ages of the children (those needing day care versus those in school while the parent is working), variations in shelter costs, tax rates, and so forth. At the same time it should be recalled that this model is not a totally general model, and was built using parameters and regulations for Pennsylvania in 1984. We could have built a more general model that would have prompted for the characteristics of a particular state or we could have built a still more generalized model that relied on no state in particular (although it would also allow only general types of conclusions that would characterize no state in particular). The point is that once the model is built it can also be modified to allow different kinds of generalization.

As soon as the analyst has solved the model, MAPSIT moves to the EXAMINE module to allow the analyst to perform whatever secondary analyses are desired. Some typical output from ILLUS4 is shown in the next section.

---

[34] The sixth line of this session shows a prompt regarding whether the parent has been employed for more than four months. If the prompt had been answered with "0", indicating eligibility for the earned income deduction, the model's results would be interpreted as the annual rate equivalents for the four months of the deduction.

RESULTS

Since Chapter 7 contains an extensive description of various types of analyses that one can perform, we shall confine the discussion here to three simple tables that the analyst would probably request initially. Each of these tables can be constructed directly from the solution file, ILLUS4.1, based on the results of the responses to the prompts in the preceding section.

The first of these, Table 5.1, shows each of several transfer programs as a function of the independent variable, which in the present model is earned income. The values for the independent variable, labeled "X" in the table, are shown in increments of a thousand dollars from zero to ten thousand, in increments of five-thousands from ten to thirty thousand, and at forty thousand. Finally, the value 6700 is also included.[35]

The entries in Table 5.1 give the values of the various dependent variables which occur at the values of the independent variable indicated in column 1. Thus, at an earned income of $6700 the AFDC benefit is $519.50, the food stamp benefit is $1951.95, and the disposable income for the family is $11,482.90. These are the same values shown in Table 2.2 (Chapter 2), where the values were calculated by hand.

It is interesting to contrast Table 5.1 with Table 5.2, where the values for the independent variable are chosen to be the "turning points" for the various mappings. In Table 5.2 the values of earned income jump from $0 to $5000.00 and include others like $6820.50 and $14,780.49. The strange nature of these values for the independent variable is produced by the fact that these are the points at which at least one of the mappings has a turning point, or change of slope; the second row heading ($5000.00) is the value of earned income at which the earned income tax credit first reaches its maximum. The fourth ($6700) occurs because, by our assumptions about full-time employment at the minimum wage, it is at this point that two of the mappings, child care expenses and work related expenses, used in calculating AFDC benefits change slope.

---

[35] There is no necessity that a table of mappings be printed out in this manner; in fact, the most common form of this table is one that takes as the values for the independent variable the values of the turning points for any of the dependent variables. Such a table is illustrated in Table 5.2 and discussed at some length in Chapter 7.

Table 5.1: Summary of Benefits and Tax Levels at Specified Values of Earned Income

X	AFDC	FOODSTAMPS	MEDICAID	EITC	FICA	STATEINCTX	NETFEDTAX	DISPOSABLE
0.00	4812.00*	2312.40*	2512.00	0.00*	0.00*	0.00*	0.00	9636.40*
1000.00	4132.90	2270.13	2512.00	100.00	67.00	24.50	0.00	9923.53
2000.00	3453.79	2227.86	2512.00	200.00	134.00	49.00	0.00	10210.65
3000.00	2774.69	2185.59	2512.00	300.00	201.00	73.50	0.00	10497.78
4000.00	2095.58	2143.33	2512.00	400.00	268.00	98.00	0.00	10784.90
5000.00	1416.48*	2101.06*	2512.00	500.00*	335.00	122.50	0.00	11072.03*
6000.00	837.37*	2028.79*	2512.00	500.00*	402.00	147.00	0.00	11329.16*
6700.00	519.50*	1951.95*	2512.00	412.50	448.90	164.15	0.00	11482.90*
7000.00	0.00	2034.00	0.00	375.00	469.00	171.50	0.00	8768.50
8000.00	0.00	1788.00	0.00	250.00	536.00	196.00	0.00	9306.00
9000.00	0.00	1542.00	0.00	125.00	603.00	220.50	0.00	9843.50
10000.00	0.00	1296.00	0.00	0.00*	670.00	245.00	23.00	10358.00*
15000.00	0.00	120.00	0.00	0.00	1005.00	367.50	782.00	12965.50
20000.00	0.00	0.00	0.00	0.00	1340.00	490.00	1694.00	16476.00
25000.00	0.00	0.00	0.00	0.00	1675.00	612.50	2806.00	19906.50
30000.00	0.00	0.00	0.00	0.00	2010.00	735.00	4106.00	23149.00
40000.00	0.00	0.00	0.00	0.00	2532.60	980.00	7251.00	29236.40

Table 5.2: Summary of Benefits and Tax Levels at Values of Earned Income Corresponding to Turning Points for the Mappings

X	AFDC	FOODSTAMPS	MEDICAID	EITC	FICA	STATEINCTX	NETFEDTAX	DISPOSABLE
0.00	4812.00*	2312.40*	2512.00	0.00*	0.00*	0.00*	0.00	9636.40*
5000.00	1416.48*	2101.06*	2512.00	500.00*	335.00	122.50	0.00	11072.03*
6000.00	837.37*	2028.79*	2512.00	500.00*	402.00	147.00	0.00	11329.16*
6700.00	519.50*	1951.95*	2512.00	412.50	448.90	164.15	0.00	11482.90*
6820.50	414.06*	1953.94*	2512.00*	397.44	456.97	167.10	0.00	11473.86*
6820.57	0.00*	2078.14*	0.00*	397.43	456.98	167.10	0.00	8672.06*
9808.33	0.00	1343.15	0.00	23.96	657.16	240.30	0.00*	10277.98*
10000.00	0.00	1296.00	0.00	0.00*	670.00	245.00	23.00	10358.00*
10500.00	0.00	1173.00	0.00	0.00	703.50	257.25	83.00*	10629.25*
12700.00	0.00	631.80	0.00	0.00	850.90	311.15	391.00*	11778.75*
14780.49	0.00	120.00*	0.00	0.00	990.29	362.12	744.68	12803.39*
15800.00	0.00	120.00	0.00	0.00	1058.60	387.10	918.00*	13556.30*
18629.11	0.00	120.00*	0.00	0.00	1248.15	456.41	1427.24	15617.31*
18629.27	0.00	0.00*	0.00	0.00	1248.16	456.42	1427.27	15497.42*
19000.00	0.00	0.00	0.00	0.00	1273.00	465.50	1494.00*	15767.50*
22200.00	0.00	0.00	0.00	0.00	1487.40	543.90	2134.00*	18034.70*
27500.00	0.00	0.00	0.00	0.00	1842.50	673.75	3406.00*	21577.75*
32800.00	0.00	0.00	0.00	0.00	2197.60	803.60	4890.00*	24908.80*
37800.00	0.00	0.00	0.00	0.00	2532.60*	926.10	6490.00	27851.30*
38100.00	0.00	0.00	0.00	0.00	2532.60	933.45	6586.00*	28047.95*
40000.00	0.00	0.00	0.00	0.00	2532.60	980.00	7251.00	29236.40

Since Table 5.2 is constructed from the turning points of each of the included mappings, one could use the values in the table to find by interpolation any other value that might be wanted. (In practice, of course, one would seldom do interpolations by hand since it is faster and more accurate to have them generated by MAPSIT.) Conversely, interpolations based on Table 5.1 will be accurate only if the interval over which one is interpolating does not span a turning point for that mapping.

There are a couple of observations that might be made about the results in Table 5.2. First, the very gradual reduction in food stamp benefits may be surprising to some people, given the nominal tax back rate of 30 percent. Furthermore, when earned income is $6820.57, food stamps actually increase because of the end of eligibility for AFDC. Second, the loss of $2512 of estimated Medicaid benefits due to the additional few cents of earned income may be a strong incentive for families of this type to keep earned income below the point ($6820.57) that terminates AFDC, unless they can increase earned income more than enough to make up for that loss.

There are, of course, many other observations that one might make about Table 5.2, but our intent is simply to point out that Tables 5.1 and 5.2 contain a rich set of information about the combined effects of the various transfer programs. What these tables have to say may or may not be "surprising," but there is certainly a lot that is not obvious from the statement of the problem.

Since one of the fundamental characteristics of transfer programs that analysts and program designers want to know is the effective marginal tax rates, we also include such a table here. Similar to Table 5.2, Table 5.3 uses the calculated "turning points" for the various piecewise linear functions that constitute the program mappings. Consequently, the values within the body of the table are the true marginal tax rates.

The reader will notice that the values within the table occur between the abscissa values. This reflects the fact that the marginal tax rate applies over that specific interval. Thus, the marginal tax rate for AFDC is .6791 between earned income of $0 and $5000.00; for every hundred dollar increment of earned income, the family will lose $67.91 from AFDC. They will also lose $4.23 from food stamps, pay $6.70 more to FICA, and $2.45 more in state taxes. On the other hand, they will receive an extra $10 from EITC. The net result is effectively a marginal tax rate of 71.3%, a value dependent on our decisions about what to include in disposable income and what elements (such as child care expenditures) to ignore.

Table 5.3: Marginal Tax Rates for Benefit and Tax Programs

X	AFDC	FOODSTAMPS	MEDICAID	EITC	FICA	STATEINCTX	NETFEDTAX	DISPOSABLE
0.00								
	0.6791	0.0423	0	-0.1000	0.0670	0.0245	0	0.7129
5000.00								
	0.5791	0.0723	0	0	0.0670	0.0245	0	0.7429
6000.00								
	0.4541	0.1098	0	0.1250	0.0670	0.0245	0	0.7804
6700.00								
	0.8750	-0.0165	0	0.1250	0.0670	0.0245	0	1.0750
6820.50								
	> NOTCH <	> NOTCH <	> NOTCH <	0.1250	0.0670	0.0245	0	> NOTCH <
6820.57								
	0	0.2460	0	0.1250	0.0670	0.0245	0	0.4625
9808.33								
	0	0.2460	0	0.1250	0.0670	0.0245	0.1200	0.5825
10000.00								
	0	0.2460	0	0	0.0670	0.0245	0.1200	0.4575
10500.00								
	0	0.2460	0	0	0.0670	0.0245	0.1400	0.4775
12700.00								
	0	0.2460	0	0	0.0670	0.0245	0.1700	0.5075
14780.49								
	0	0	0	0	0.0670	0.0245	0.1700	0.2615
15800.00								
	0	0	0	0	0.0670	0.0245	0.1800	0.2715
18629.11								
	0	> NOTCH <	0	0	0.0670	0.0245	0.1800	> NOTCH <
18629.27								
	0	0	0	0	0.0670	0.0245	0.1800	0.2715
19000.00								
	0	0	0	0	0.0670	0.0245	0.2000	0.2915
22200.00								
	0	0	0	0	0.0670	0.0245	0.2400	0.3315
27500.00								
	0	0	0	0	0.0670	0.0245	0.2800	0.3715
32800.00								
	0	0	0	0	0.0670	0.0245	0.3200	0.4115
37800.00								
	0	0	0	0	0	0.0245	0.3200	0.3445
38100.00								
	0	0	0	0	0	0.0245	0.3500	0.3745
40000.00								

Like previous tables, this table contains a wealth of information for the analyst. One has at a glance the true marginal tax rates for each of the programs, the points where there are discontinuities in the marginal tax rates (noted by "NOTCH"), and the marginal tax rate for the entire system of programs. For incomes below the minimum wage (total earnings less than $6700) the marginal tax rate is over 70 percent. In the short interval between $6700 and $6820.50, the marginal tax rate hits a high of 107 percent. Beyond $14,780 AFDC, Medicaid, and EITC have terminated for this family and the food stamp allotment is a constant. Here, the marginal tax rates derive solely from the effect of FICA and taxes, initially falling back to a 27 percent rate and from there on reflecting the progressivity of the federal income tax schedule.

The principal surprise in this table for analysts familiar with the marginal tax rates faced by low income families is probably that such a table can be so easily generated. Similarly, one can easily generate tables of average tax rates, use a SOURCES command to identify the mapping that induces a particular turning point, specify the particular mappings to be included in the output, and specify the values of the independent variable at which one wishes to examine particular mappings. These and other features, which add greatly to the usefulness of MAPSIT, are discussed in more detail in Chapter 7.

The experienced analyst will recognize that what we have presented in this chapter is merely the beginning of an analysis. Our analysis has consisted of a single model and a single set of responses to the prompts of that model. In most analyses the problem being investigated requires that the analyst examine a wider set of alternatives, which in turn requires that the analyst generalize the model. The final section of this chapter addresses four different ways in which one can generalize analyses when using MAPSIT.

GENERALIZING A MODEL

Ordinarily, the analyst does not simply create a single model, solve it once, and then examine its output. Instead, a typical analysis involves comparisons among a number of fairly similar systems. The analyst draws his conclusions and policy implications from comparisons of the several systems. For example, in the present illustration the analyst may wish to examine the same system for a family with a different number of children. Alternatively he may wish to ascertain to what extent the results of his analysis are sensitive to changes in the state tax rate or the exclusion of child care expenses.

This section addresses several methods by which a given model can be generalized to examine the sensitivity of the model's results to various changes in the system. The capabilities designed into MAPSIT allow for at least four different types of generalization. Roughly in order of increasing complexity, these are: (1) changes in the values of numerical parameters, (2) changes in the postulated relationships among existing programs in the system, (3) changes involving the removal of mappings from the model and/or the addition of new mappings to the model, and (4) changes involving the creation of parallel systems within a single model. The remainder of this section takes up each of these methods in turn.

Changing Specific Parameters

The simplest form of model generalization involves changes in the values of the various numerical parameters. For example, the analyst may wish to examine the implications of a different number of children in the family, or a different nominal tax-back rate for the earned income credit. Thoughtful design of the original model can make such changes relatively simple. If the definition of the parameter has been localized in the model, the analyst may be able to effect the change by the use of a PROMPT operation or by altering only a single command in the model.

In the model developed in this chapter, for example, several of the mappings that determine the final mapping, disposable income, involve the number of children in the family. There are a number of ways in which the analyst can include the necessary information about the number of children in the family. First, the analyst can enter the number as a constant at each point where it was required (such as in the personal deduction for federal income taxes, the size of the assistance unit for AFDC benefits, the size of the household for the food stamp bonus and food stamp maximum income per month, and the number of persons covered under Medicaid). Second, the analyst can introduce mappings, such as CHLDN_GE_6, and CHLDN_LE_5, but give them a constant value via the CONSTANT operation. Third, the analyst can introduce those same two mappings, and instruct the solution module to prompt the analyst for the current value of those mappings (the method used here). These three approaches have quite different consequences if one wants to analyze a family unit with a different number of children or children of different ages. The first approach requires that one make a change in the model for every place where the values have been inserted in the previous construction of the model, and although possible, this is tedious and the analyst may forget to make a necessary change. The second method is considerably more efficient. One must edit the model, but only a single change, revision of the CONSTANT operation, need be made for each variable. The third method eliminates the necessity of editing the model. Notice, however, that the ease with which one can modify the model in this chapter is the result of careful thinking about the nature of the changes one is going to want to make. Clearly it is useful for the analyst to consider the changes he or she is likely to want to make in the model before beginning to construct it.

Changing Program Relationships

A second, slightly more complex form of change involves modifying the relationships among programs in the model. For example, some agency may suggest that the food stamp deduction for child care expenses is unreasonable if the family is also allowed to deduct child care expenses under AFDC. The analyst may wish to ascertain if the pattern of transfer levels and tax rates looks appreciably different if the family is not allowed to deduct child care expenses in food stamp income when the family is also receiving AFDC.

The analyst can easily alter the model of this chapter to reflect this new relationship among mappings in the model. Using the EDIT module, the analyst inserts a SELECTION operation after Operation 4900 that selects the previously computed value for child care deduction if AFDC is less than $.01, or zero if AFDC is greater than or equal to $.01.

Changing the Programs in the System

A third form of change involves the identity of the transfer programs appearing in the model. Where the second form of generalization involved modifications to existing mappings and programs, the third form permits the deletion of transfer programs from the system and/or the addition of new programs to the system. For example, the analyst may wish to examine the model constructed in this chapter, but with the addition of a federal income-conditioned energy tax credit. Alternatively, he or she may wish to see how the system performs if the family is disqualified for AFDC benefits on grounds not related to income, such as age of the head of the family, or the presence of two employable adults in the family.

To carry out this third form of generalization, the analyst uses the EDIT module to delete all operations that refer to the program(s) no longer wanted. The analyst can insert new mappings into the model as appropriate. In the example here, the analyst might add one new operation to define the nominal transfer schedule for the federal energy tax credit, add a second operation to define the income base for the tax credit program, and add a third operation to carry out the mapping-of-a-mapping operation combining the first and second new mappings. Finally, the analyst might revise the net federal income tax mapping and the disposable income mapping to include the tax credit. It is quite possible that the analyst would also have to modify other programs in the model. For example, one might postulate that under the new system the food stamp program would treat the energy tax credit as a substitute for the deduction of utility expenses in calculating food stamp available income. In this case, the analyst would also have to modify the operation that calculates the excess shelter deduction.

When making insertions in a model, the analyst must obey the same ordering restrictions imposed when the model was created: a mapping must be defined before it can be used in the definition of other mappings. For instance, if the energy tax credit is to be treated by the food stamp program as a substitute for part of the excess shelter cost deduction, then the energy tax credit mapping must be defined before calculating available income for food stamps.

Modeling Parallel Systems

The fourth form for generalizing a given model involves the creation of parallel systems within the model. In the first three types of generalization we have been treating a situation in which the analyst wishes to model a single system and then perhaps to make changes to it. Here we consider the possibility of modeling multiple systems simultaneously within a single model. For example, one may wish to measure the impact of a suggested change in AFDC. The analyst creates a model in which one set of mappings treats the elements of the system as it now operates. A second set treats the programs as they would operate under the proposed change. The summary table may include mappings from both sets.

One benefit of the simultaneous modeling may not be immediately obvious. The analyst can define mappings in the model that depend on multiple subsets of the model. For example, suppose that each subsystem includes a mapping that relates income taxes to earned income. The analyst is free to create a new mapping defined as the difference between the two income tax mappings, thereby ascertaining the effects of the change on income taxes payable. Alternatively, the analyst may choose to create a new mapping that is defined as the ratio of two disposable income mappings, with the numerator mapping corresponding to disposable income under a proposed system and the denominator mapping corresponds to disposable income under the current or baseline system. Ratios of less than one would indicate that the family is worse off over the relevant earned income values; ratios greater than one would indicate that the family benefits from the proposed change to the system.

The implementation of this fourth type of generalization parallels the creation of an original model. The analyst includes in the model the operations required to calculate all the mappings in the new (sub)system. Sometimes the new subsystem will be able to employ, without modification, a mapping from the original system. In such cases the mapping need not be included more than once. For example, FICA contributions as a function of earned income might be identical for both the baseline and hypothetical systems. Once again the analyst must ensure that the new operations obey the general ordering restrictions imposed by the MAPSIT solution module.

The example presented in this chapter used earned income as the independent variable and generated critical mappings as a function of earned income. The independent variable does not have to be earned income, however, as we shall see in Chapter 6. The only constraint on the independent variable is that one be able to define the other variables in terms of the independent variable. Chapter 6 presents a model in which the independent variable is the number of hours worked per week.

CHAPTER 6.
CETA AND WORK INCENTIVES, EXAMPLE 2

In Chapter 5 we discussed a problem in which the major motivation was to analyze the impact on a family of a whole system of welfare and tax programs. In that case, since most of the programs were contingent on income, it made sense to take income, or the major determinant of income for most people, earned income, as the independent variable. Earned income is the most frequent independent variable in MAPSIT models, but it is by no means the only variable one can employ. In this chapter we present a model in which the basic question concerns a work incentive problem for which we use "hours worked per week" as the independent variable.

The chapter has two major goals: first, to illustrate the use of a variable other than earned income as an independent variable for an analysis, and second, to illustrate the use of submodels. The second of these goals is as important as the first, for one of the major advantages of MAPSIT is that by using submodels one can often simplify analyses or reduce their costs.

In Chapter 5 we presented the model from the perspective of an analyst sitting at a terminal and interacting with the model-building module of MAPSIT. In the present chapter we present the model in segments as before, but use the output from the LIST version on the model. While the LIST version does not capture the model builder "at work," the output is more concise and easier to read.

The problem analyzed here arose from a concern with the issue of "skimming" under the Comprehensive Employment Training Act, CETA.[36] Since the early days of CETA there have been allegations that many of the people hired on CETA funds have been paid at salaries exceeding $10,000 per year, and that many of these workers

---

[36] The authors want to thank Joanne Hall and Christine Khan for their contributions to the work on which this chapter is based.

have been hired as computer programmers, "assistant lawyers," registered professional nurses, and administrative assistants (Adams, 1977; Cameron, 1979; Harstad, 1979).

Since CETA was initially established to assist the chronically unemployed, one might expect that the jobs provided would tend to go to people with fairly low skill levels, not to people with skills as computer programmers, nurses, or lawyers. As one might anticipate, there have been charges that local CETA administrators favored the employable at the expense of the chronically unemployed.

One can imagine several administrative reasons for this occurrence: cities have been tempted to use the CETA program to substitute for inadequate local funds (Adams, 1977), administrators may be inclined to select applicants "most likely to succeed" (Mirengoff, 1978), and it is undoubtedly easier to place people who are skilled than those who are unskilled. Granting this, the question remains whether there are other possible explanations that should also be examined. We began by exploring incentives for the low-skilled worker. What is the incentive to take a job through CETA and to leave the rolls of the chronically unemployed?

While we have cast this example in terms of CETA, the basic problem is a problem of incentives to seek or accept additional work. If one is not working, should he or she work? If so, how much? If one is already working, should he or she increase or decrease the number of hours per week? If so, how much?

For present purposes we conceptualize a job offer as consisting of a specific type of work, a number of hours (per week, per month), and a wage rate (per hour, per week, per month). Of these features we shall focus on the number of hours per week that the person might work, incorporate the wage rate as an input variable, but ignore the nature of the job offered. Furthermore, we shall ignore the fact that under certain circumstances welfare recipients are required to accept employment if it is offered. We ignore this since it seems likely that a worker who does not want a particular job can manage to avoid receiving a job offer in the first place, or can manage to be let go from a job that he or she is required to take but does not want. Our analysis, then, will take the number of hours that the person chooses to work at a given wage rate as the independent variable, with number of hours ranging from 0 to 80, which seems a reasonable upper limit.

Finally, since one of the original interests in this problem was whether there were alternative explanations for hiring higher paid workers and since CETA is currently being phased out, it seems appropriate to analyze the situation as it existed during the period when CETA was a more visible program. Consequently, we have chosen to do this analysis for 1980. Choosing a prior period for the analysis also allows us to demonstrate another feature of MAPSIT -- the possibility of modeling systems retrospectively as well as currently and prospectively.

THE MODEL

There are a number of principal effects that one would want the analysis to address. These include the effect of whether the employment offer is through public service employment (WIN) or not,[37] whether there is more than one parent in the family, the size of the family, the wage rate, and because it varies from state to state, the actual AFDC schedule that is relevant. Our model incorporates each of these elements.

CETA80, as we shall call the model, has five sections. Section 1 prompts for a number of necessary inputs, such as the number of parents in the household and the number of children age five or younger. These prompts are used in the same manner as the prompts in Section 1 of the model in Chapter 5, as a means of entering numerical values for variables in the analysis, particularly variables that differ from solution to solution. Section 2 calculates annual representations of mandatory withholdings, including FICA, federal income tax, state income tax, local wage tax, and mandatory pension contributions. The computation of the federal income tax is done by a submodel, the use of which is explained in that section. That same submodel also calculates the earned income tax credit.

Section 3 computes the welfare assistance benefits for AFDC, food stamps, and Medicaid. The computation of AFDC was substantially different prior to the Omnibus Budget Reconciliation Act of 1981. There was no cap on day care expenses, actual work-related expenses were deductible, the earned income exemption was not limited to the first four months, and there was no maximum on gross earned income. The computation of food stamps and Medicaid were basically the same then as now, but the food stamp program employed different parameter values.

---

[37] Knowing whether the job offer was through public service employment is important since it affected whether or not the person was eligible for the earned-income disregard in AFDC.

Section 4 computes the federal tax credit for dependent care expenses and adjusts federal income tax if needed. Finally, Section 5 computes disposable income and takes care of the final details of the model, which in this case include conversion of the annual disposable income to the weekly basis that will be needed for a special analysis, and the specification of the set of variables to be included in the solution set when the model is solved.

Before formally beginning with the model, we highlight several crucial assumptions. All of these are included in the detailed description that is part of the model (which can be seen in Appendix B):

1. All benefits and payments are determined on the basis of the legal and regulatory provisions for the state of Pennsylvania during 1980.

2. Hours worked per week is assumed constant over the year.

3. If there are two parents, only one is assumed to be working. In a two-parent, one-earner family, it is assumed that the other parent is not disabled and is therefore available to provide child care. Consequently, for this type of family, there are no allowable child care expenses either for AFDC and food stamp purposes or for the federal tax credit for dependent care.

4. For AFDC purposes it is assumed that any available assets are less than the maximum allowable.

5. As before, Medicaid is assumed to be a constant value per person per month and is available as long as one is eligible for AFDC.

6. For the present analysis we assume that there is no other income than wages and earnings, but to illustrate the incorporation of unearned income for future analyses we include it here as a variable with a value of zero.

7. The calculation of federal income taxes is done by means of a submodel. The construction of that submodel allows for all of the standard deductions taken on the 1040 long

form: excess medical expenses, interest, charitable deductions, casualty, and taxes. In the present case we shall default all of these deductions except the deduction of state and local taxes.

Each of these assumptions has been adopted as a convenience to the analyst; none of them is imposed by MAPSIT. The model could be modified to eliminate any or all of these restrictions. In the present case, however, we are less interested in creating the most general model possible than in illustrating the two aspects mentioned at the beginning of this chapter -- the use of an independent variable other than earnings and the use of submodels.

Section 1: The Initial Commands and Input Parameters.

The first nondocumentary operations (200 through 1100) establish several PROMPTS to allow for the input of important variables that will vary from solution to solution: number of parents, number of children age six or older, number of children age five or under, the cost of full-time day care, the hourly wage, whether the earnings are derived from public service employment under WIN, any local wage tax rate, any mandatory pension rate, annual shelter costs, and the geographical classification in Pennsylvania within which the family lives.[38]

```
200  N_PARENTS:  NUMBER OF PARENTS
       Operation: PROMPT
       Define N_PARENTS as a constant for all values of x, with the constant to be
       entered during the solution stage in response to the prompting message:
       HOW MANY PARENTS ARE IN THE ASSISTANCE UNIT?

300  CHLDN_GE_6: CHILDREN AGE 6 OR OLDER
       Operation: PROMPT
       Define CHLDN_GE_6 as a constant for all values of x, with the constant to be
       entered during the solution stage in response to the prompting message:
       CHILDREN AGE 6 OR OLDER?

400  CHLDN_LE_5: CHILDREN AGE 5 OR YOUNGER
       Operation: PROMPT
       Define CHLDN_LE_5 as a constant for all values of x, with the constant to be
       entered during the solution stage in response to the prompting message:
       CHILDREN AGE 5 OR YOUNGER?

500  CHLDCAREWK: FULL TIME DAY CARE COST PER CHILD PER WEEK
       Operation: PROMPT
       Define CHLDCAREWK as a constant for all values of x, with the constant to be
       entered during the solution stage in response to the prompting message:
       FULL TIME DAY CARE COST PER CHILD PER WEEK?
```

---

38 As explained in Chapter 5, Pennsylvania partitions the state into four divisions by cost of living and applies a different AFDC benefit schedule in each of those four divisions.

```
600  HRLYWAGE:   HOURLY WAGE
       Operation: PROMPT
       Define HRLYWAGE as a constant for all values of x, with the constant to be
       entered during the solution stage in response to the prompting message:
       HOURLY WAGE?

700  ERNDINCDED: EARNED INCOME DEDUCTION (1=YES,0=NO)
       Operation: PROMPT
       Define ERNDINCDED as a constant for all values of x, with the constant to be
       entered during the solution stage in response to the prompting message:
       IS THE FAMILY ELIGIBLE FOR EARNED INCOME DEDUCTION? (1=YES,0=NO)

800  LOCTAXRATE: LOCAL TAX RATE ON INCOME
       Operation: PROMPT
       Define LOCTAXRATE as a constant for all values of x, with the constant to be
       entered during the solution stage in response to the prompting message:
       LOCAL TAX RATE ON INCOME?

900  PENSIONRAT: MANDATORY PENSION RATE
       Operation: PROMPT
       Define PENSIONRAT as a constant for all values of x, with the constant to be
       entered during the solution stage in response to the prompting message:
       MANDATORY PENSION RATE?

1000 SHELTRCOST: ANNUAL SHELTER COST INCL. UTILITIES AND PHONE
       Operation: PROMPT
       Define SHELTRCOST as a constant for all values of x, with the constant to be
       entered during the solution stage in response to the prompting message:
       ANNUAL SHELTER COST INCL. UTILITIES AND PHONE?

1100 COUNTY_SET: THE SET OF COUNTIES FOR AFDC PURPOSES
       Operation: PROMPT
       Define COUNTY_SET as a constant for all values of x, with the constant to be
       entered during the solution stage in response to the prompting message:
       WHAT SET OF COUNTIES IS DESIRED (1,2,3 OR 4)?
```

With the previous inputs the analyst can now build some of the other constructs that will be needed. For example, family size is built from the number of parents and the number of children, and weekly and annual earned income are built as a function of hours worked per week and the hourly wage rate.

```
1200 N_CHILDREN: NUMBER OF CHILDREN IN THE FAMILY
       Operation: ADD
       Make N_CHILDREN equal to the sum of:
       CHLDN_GE_6
       CHLDN_LE_5

1300 FAMILYSIZE: FAMILY SIZE
       Operation: ADD
       Make FAMILYSIZE equal to the sum of:
       N_PARENTS
       N_CHILDREN

1400 HOURSWRKD:  HOURS WORKED PER WEEK
       Operation: COORDINATE
       Define HOURSWRKD using the following co-ordinate pairs as segment endpoints:
        X          Y
       ---        ---
       0          0
       80         80

1500 WK_ERNDINC: WEEKLY EARNINGS
       Operation: WEIGHT
       Make WK_ERNDINC equal to HOURSWRKD weighted by HRLYWAGE
```

```
1600  AN_ERNDINC: ANNUAL EARNED INCOME
        Operation: WEIGHT
        Make AN_ERNDINC equal to WK_ERNDINC weighted by 52

1700  ANTAXOTHER: ANNUAL TAXABLE INCOME OTHER THAN WAGE EARNINGS
        Operation: CONSTANT
        Define ANTAXOTHER as the constant, 0, for all values of x

1800  AN_TXBLINC: ANNUAL TAXABLE INCOME
        Operation: ADD
        Make AN_TXBLINC equal to the sum of:
        AN_ERNDINC
        ANTAXOTHER
```

Several of the mappings in the model are mappings of "annual" benefits or taxes. Since the purpose of the model is to look at the incentives for working another hour per week, one might wonder why we have taken this particular tack in introducing mappings that have an ordinate in annual terms. There are two reasons. First, the desire to look at hours worked per week as the independent variable does not dictate a clear preference for the nature of the dependent variable (disposable income per week, per month, or per year). The best choice would be the one most easily interpreted by the reader. Assuming that most people likely to read this book think about salaries in annual amounts, we have adopted basically an annual time frame for discussion of the dependent variable.

The second reason is that it is convenient to deal with annualized mappings since we shall be using a number of submodels that were created for general modeling purposes and that have been constructed using annualized mappings. Even if we had chosen to report our results in weekly or monthly disposable income, the efficiencies of using submodels is so great that it would have been worthwhile to compute major program benefits on an annualized basis and then convert them to weekly values than to do all of the modeling directly on the weekly basis. This is in fact what we do to obtain disposable income on a weekly basis.

This completes the initial operations. The next section begins with the computation of the various types of withholdings.

Section 2: Withholdings.

Ignoring a documentary comment, which merely announces that this is the beginning of Section 2 and outlines the mappings to be constructed, the first operation is a FETCH to establish 1980 FICA contributions.

```
2000  NOM_FICA:    FICA (1980)
        Operation: FETCH
        Fetch NOM_FICA from schedule file FICA80.SCH. Fetched pairs are:
               X              Y
              ---            ---
                0              0
          25905.38           1588
```

The reader may remember that in Chapter 5 FICA was established through a COORDINATE operation rather than a FETCH. Even though FICA is an extremely simple mapping, FETCH is useful since there is less to look up or remember and there are fewer opportunities for typographical mistakes.

In Operation 2000, nominal FICA is the annual contributions to FICA as a function of annual earnings. Since hours worked per week is the independent variable, it is necessary to compute annual FICA contributions as a function of hours worked per week. This is done easily using a MAPPING operation:

```
2100  FICA:        FICA AS FUNCTION OF HOURS WORKED PER WEEK
        Operation: MAPPING
        Make FICA [z(x)] from NOM_FICA [z(y)] and AN_ERNDINC [y(x)]
```

The next two variables, Pennsylvania state income tax and local wage tax, are constructed by weightings of annual taxable income or annual earned income, each of which is itself a function of hours worked per week.

```
2200  PSIT:        PENNSYLVANIA STATE INCOME TAX
        Operation: WEIGHT
        Make PSIT equal to AN_TXBLINC weighted by .022

2300  LOCAL_TAX:  LOCAL WAGE TAXES
        Operation: WEIGHT
        Make LOCAL_TAX equal to AN_ERNDINC weighted by LOCTAXRATE
```

To compute federal income tax we shall use FIT80.SUB, a submodel constructed for that purpose. The operation required to use a submodel is LINK and when FIT80 is linked to the main model, the submodel prompts for three mandatory inputs: earnings, the number of adults, and the number of children. If the analyst wants to include other taxable income or specific deductions, he or she is allowed to make additional optional inputs. In this case we take state and local taxes as deductions to taxable income.[39]

Since the use of the LINK operation was not demonstrated in Chapter 7, we depart from our pattern and show this operation as it was utilized by the analyst in the BUILD-module:

```
      2400  Operation  ? LINK
 Submodel name? FIT80.SUB

REQUIRED INPUT:
EARNINGS = AN_ERNDINC
N_ADULTS = N_PARENTS
N_CHILDREN = N_CHILDREN

Optional input:
1? YTXBLOTHER = ANTAXOTHER
2? TOTALTAXES = PSIT
3?

REQUIRED OUTPUT:
FEDINCTAX = FIT
MDESC ?
YE_CREDIT = EITC
MDESC ?

Optional output:
1?
```

In the LIST version. Operation 2400 appears as follows:

```
2400  FIT:          FEDERAL INCOME TAX FOR THE UNIT
      EITC:         EARNED INCOME CREDIT FOR THE UNIT
        Operation: LINK
        Make the above mapping(s) by linking to submodel FIT80.SUB using
        the CETA80.MOD = FIT80.SUB mapping linkages described below
             Name: FIT80.SUB[4,2705]
            Title: FEDERAL INCOME TAX CALCULATOR (1980)
      Submodel Linkages (Specified: 1980-04-22 15:17:13)
                     CETA80.MOD  FIT80.SUB   FIT80.SUB
                     mapping     mapping     mapping description
                     -------     -------     ------- -----------
      Input(s)
      --------
      required  AN_ERNDINC  EARNINGS    GROSS EARNED INCOME (WAGES AND SALARIES) (8)
                N_PARENTS   N_ADULTS    NUMBER OF ADULTS (1 IF HEAD ONLY, 2 IF HEAD
                                        AND SPOUSE)
                N_CHILDREN  N_CHILDREN  NUMBER OF DEPENDENT CHILDREN IN FAMILY
      optional  ANTAXOTHER  YTXBLOTHER  OTHER TAXABLE INCOME FOR THE FILING UNIT
                                        (9-21)
                PSIT        TOTALTAXES  STATE & LOC. INC., REAL EST., SALES & OTHER
                                        TAXES (A,16 & 34)
      Output(s)
      ---------
      required  FIT         FEDINCTAX   FEDERAL INCOME TAX FOR THE UNIT
                EITC        YE_CREDIT   EARNED INCOME CREDIT FOR THE UNIT
```

---

[39] The submodel FIT80 actually calculates federal taxes due rather than withholdings, but we shall use FIT as a surrogate for federal withholdings. FIT80 calculates the amount of tax due if one itemizes or if one takes the standard deduction and then selects the procedure that yields the smaller tax. Although in this example we have included the Pennsylvania state income tax as an itemized deduction on Schedule A, in fact these taxes alone will not make itemization preferable unless income is over $45,000.

The reader can see that the submodel automatically generates both the federal income tax and the earned income credit. A LIST version of FIT80.SUB is contained in Appendix B.

Finally, the computation of total withholdings can be computed as the sum of the several withholdings: FICA contributions, federal, state, and local taxes, and the pension contribution of Operation 2500.

```
2500  PENSIONCON: MANDATORY CONTRIBUTION TO COMPANY PENSION
        Operation: WEIGHT
        Make PENSIONCON equal to AN_ERNDINC weighted by PENSIONRAT

2600  WITHHOLDNG: SUM OF TAXES, FICA, AND MANDATORY PENSION
        Operation: ADD
        Make WITHHOLDNG equal to the sum of:
        FICA
        PSIT
        FIT
        LOCAL_TAX
        PENSIONCON
```

Section 3: Assistance Benefits.

Since AFDC, food stamps, and the federal tax credit for dependent care expenses all require information about child care expenses, we shall begin by making some initial calculations. In constructing child care expenses, the following conditions are imposed.

1. Full-time day care expenses are assumed to be $35 per child per week, based on a survey of day care centers in Pittsburgh in February 1981. Assuming a forty hour week for the previous value, average day care costs are $.88 per hour.

2. We shall assume that the parent can buy any fractional part of full-time day care and can purchase day care beyond forty hours per week at the same rate ($.88 per child per hour).

3. We assume that only preschool children, ages five or younger, receive day care. Additional assumptions about day care for older children could be added, but are not a part of the present model.

4. We assume that if there are two parents at most one is working and the other parent (unless disabled) is available to provide child care. Thus, in a two-parent, one-earner family, we assume that there are no allowable child care expenses.

Given these assumptions, the annual cost of child care can be found as follows:

1. Full-time cost per week per child is translated into an hourly rate, 1/40 (.025) of the weekly rate.

2. Cost per hour is multiplied by hours per week.

3. Actual cost per week is multiplied by 52 to obtain the annualized value for a single child.

4. Cost per year is weighted by the number of preschool age children.

5. Child care is eliminated if there is a second parent in the family.

The implementation of these steps occupies Operations 2800 through 3200.

```
2800  CHLDCAREHR: CHILD CARE COST PER HOUR
        Operation: WEIGHT
        Make CHLDCAREHR equal to CHLDCAREWK weighted by .025

2900  AKCHLDCARE: ACTUAL WEEKLY COST PER CHILD AFO HOURS WORKED
        Operation: WEIGHT
        Make AKCHLDCARE equal to HOURSWRKD weighted by CHLDCAREHR

3000  CHILDCRPER: ANNUAL COST PER CHILD AFO HOURS WORKED
        Operation: WEIGHT
        Make CHILDCRPER equal to AKCHLDCARE weighted by 52

3100  TOTCHILDCR: ANNUAL CHILD CARE EXPENSES (BEFORE TEST FOR NUM. OF PARENTS)
        Operation: WEIGHT
        Make TOTCHILDCR equal to CHILDCRPER weighted by CHLDN_LE_5

3200  CHILD_CARE: ANNUAL CHILD CARE EXPENSES
        Operation: SELECTION
        Make CHILD_CARE as follows:
             1. Select 0 where N_PARENTS is at least 2
             2. Select TOTCHILDCR where N_PARENTS is less than 2
```

The first assistance benefit calculated is AFDC. This is also done using a submodel, AFDC80.SUB, which is based on AFDC policy within the State of Pennsylvania in 1980:

```
3400  AFDC:        AFDC BENEFIT PAYABLE TO THE FAMILY, ANNUAL BASIS
      Operation: LINK
      Make the above mapping(s) by linking to submodel AFDC80.SUB using
      the CETA80.MOD = AFDC80.SUB mapping linkages described below
             Name: AFDC80.SUB[4,2705]
            Title: A SUBMODEL TO COMPUTE AFDC BENEFITS IN PENNSYLVANIA, 1980
      Submodel Linkages (Specified: 1980-04-05 17:53:26)
```

```
              CETA80.MOD  AFDC80.SUB  AFDC80.SUB
              mapping     mapping     mapping description
              -------     -------     ------- -----------
Input(s)
--------
required  COUNTY_SET   COUNTY_SET   COUNTY SET SELECTION VARIABLE
          N_PARENTS    N_PARENTS    NUMBER OF PARENTS IN ASSISTANCE UNIT
          N_CHILDREN   N_CHILDREN   NUMBER OF CHILDREN IN ASSISTANCE UNIT
          ERNDINCDED   ERNDINCDED   EARNED INCOME DEDUCTION (1=Y,0=N)
          AN_ERNDINC   EARNINGS     ANNUAL EARNED INCOME
          ANTAXOTHER   YTXBLOTHER   OTHER TAXABLE INCOME, ANNUAL BASIS
          WITHHOLDNG   WITHHOLDNG   TAXES AND OTHER MANDATORY WITHHOLDINGS,
                                    ANNUAL
          CHILD_CARE   CHILD_CARE   CHILD CARE EXPENSES
Output(s)
---------
required  AFDC         AFDC_BEN     AFDC BENEFIT PAYABLE TO FAMILY, ANNUAL BASIS
```

From the LINK operation one can see the inputs that are required. The input for "County Set" refers to the partitioning of counties within Pennsylvania according to their average costs of living. That variable provides the connection to a sub-submodel, ADCSCH.SUB, which locates the proper benefit schedule as a function of the county set for which the analysis is being done. Both of these submodels are contained in Appendix B. The output of AFDC80.SUB is the annual amount of the AFDC benefit as a function of hours worked.

Before linking to the food stamp submodel we shall express child care and AFDC as functions of earnings, since the food stamp submodel does some of its computations using mappings that are functions of annual earnings. The simplest way to do this is first to find the mapping of hours worked per week as a function of annual earnings by dividing INDEP, which is a straight line with a slope of 1 passing through the origin, by the hourly wage and the number of weeks per year. This gives the number of hours per week that one would have to work to generate the abscissa value of earnings per year. This is done in Operation 3600.

```
3600  HOURSAFOYE: HOURS WORKED PER WEEK AFO ANNUAL EARNINGS
        Operation: DIVIDE
        Make HOURSAFOYE equal to INDEP divided by 52
        and (by chain division)
        HRLYWAGE
```

Next, using the mapping HOURSAFOYE we employ the MAPPING operation to obtain child care as a function of earnings and AFDC as a function of earnings, CHLCRAFOYE and AFDCAFOYE.

```
3700  CHLCRAFOYE: CHILD CARE EXPENSES AFO GROSS EARNED INCOME
        Operation: MAPPING
        Make CHLCRAFOYE [z(x)] from CHILD_CARE [z(y)] and HOURSAFOYE [y(x)]
```

```
3800  AFDCAFOYE:  AFDC AFO ANNUAL GROSS EARNED INCOME
        Operation: MAPPING
        Make AFDCAFOYE [z(x)] from AFDC [z(y)] and HOURSAFOYE [y(x)]
```

The latter mapping is added to ANTAXOTHER to obtain unearned income as a function of earnings, UNERNAFOYE. (Since ANTAXOTHER is a constant valued function it can be thought of as a function of earnings, or almost any other variable for that matter.)

```
3900  UNERNAFOYE: UNEARNED INCOME AFO ANNUAL GROSS EARNED INCOME
        Operation: ADD
        Make UNERNAFOYE equal to the sum of:
        ANTAXOTHER
        AFDCAFOYE
```

These several variables are then used by the food stamp submodel:

```
4000  FS_AFO_YE:  FOOD STAMP BENEFITS ANNUALLY
        Operation: LINK
        Make the above mapping(s) by linking to submodel FS80.SUB using
        the CETA80.MOD = FS80.SUB mapping linkages described below
             Name: FS80.SUB[4,2705]
            Title: FOOD STAMP SUBMODEL (1980)
      Submodel Linkages (Specified: 1980-04-06 22:10:18)
                        CETA80.MOD  FS80.SUB    FS80.SUB
                        mapping     mapping     mapping description
                        -------     -------     ------- -----------
      Input(s)
      --------
      required  INDEP        EARNEDINC    ANNUAL EARNED INCOME
                UNERNAFOYE   UNEARNDINC   ANNUAL UNEARNED INCOME (INCLUDING PUBLIC
                                          ASSISTANCE)
                FAMILYSIZE   FAMILYSIZE   FAMILY SIZE
                CHLCRAFOYE   CHILD_CARE   CHILD CARE EXPENSES
                SHELTRCOST   SHELTRCOST   ANNUAL SHELTER COSTS INCL. HEAT, WATER,
                                          ELEC., & PHONE
      Output(s)
      ---------
      required  FS_AFO_YE    FS_BEN       FOOD STAMP BENEFITS ANNUALLY
```

Since the output of the submodel is expressed in annual earnings, it is necessary to convert this to a function of hours worked per week.

```
4100  FOODSTAMPS: ANNUAL FOOD STAMP BENEFIT AFO HOURS PER WEEK
        Operation: MAPPING
        Make FOODSTAMPS [z(x)] from FS_AFO_YE [z(y)] and AN_ERNDINC [y(x)]
```

The third benefit program is Medicaid. Although it is a program that merely reimburses medical expenses, we shall treat it as if it were a cash assistance program. Hausman (1975) reported that the average AFDC recipient in Illinois in 1971 used $222 of medical services. But medical costs have not remained static. In the period between March 1971 and April 1980, the consumer price index for medical services increased from 128 to 263. Correcting for growth in prices, the adjusted cost of Medicaid per AFDC recipient would be $455. This estimate is used in Operation 4300. Next, Operation 4400 ensures that persons are eligible for Medicare only as long as they receive AFDC.[40]

```
4300  PMEDICAID:  MEDICAID BENEFIT
        Operation: WEIGHT
        Make PMEDICAID equal to FAMILYSIZE weighted by 455

4400  MEDICAID:    MEDICAID BENEFITS PAYABLE
        Operation: SELECTION
        Make MEDICAID as follows:
              1. Select PMEDICAID where AFDC is at least .0000001
              2. Select 0 where AFDC is less than .0000001
```

Section 4: Federal Tax Credit for Dependent Care Expenses.

The final transfer to be computed is the federal tax credit for dependent care expenses. Unlike the earned income tax credit, the dependent care credit can be used only to reduce the amount of federal income tax due -- credit in excess of the federal income tax is not refundable. In CETA80 we modeled the dependent care tax credit under the following conditions:

1. We assumed that only one parent is employed. If there is a second parent that parent is assumed to be available to look after the child. In that case CHILD_CARE is set to zero and the tax credit is zero.

2. We assumed that there are no disabled dependents, and we limited relevant expenses to those for preschool children in a private day care center.

3. Although the child care credit is available when a parent is not working but is looking for a job, we ignored this provision and assumed that the parent receives a credit only for the portion of time that child care was required for actual employment.

4. The test of whether the parent has supplied more than 50 percent of the cost of running the home is approximated

---

40 Operation 4400 uses an extremely small value (.0000001) as the selection switch for Medicaid. This was done to avoid generating extraneous turning points in the solution to the model. Details of the implementation of MAPSIT are available upon request.

by testing whether the parent's total income (before transfers) is equal to or greater than the transfers, in this case AFDC.

5. Maximum allowable dependent care expenses are $2000 if there is only one dependent and $4000 if there are two or more dependents, and the actual allowable expenses can never be greater than the actual expenses or greater than earned income.

6. The credit is derived as 20 percent of the allowable dependent care expenses, but never more than the federal taxes to be paid.

7. The maximum credit, then, is $400 for one dependent and $800 for two or more dependents.

Using these conditions and assumptions we constructed a submodel to calculate the dependent care tax credit, DEPCDT.SUB. Here we shall show merely the link from the main model to the submodel, but the reader interested in the construction of the submodel will find it in Appendix B:

```
4600  CHLDCRCRDT: CHILD CARE TAX CREDIT
        Operation: LINK
        Make the above mapping(s) by linking to submodel DCTC80.SUB using
        the CETA80.MOD = DCTC80.SUB mapping linkages described below
             Name: DCTC80.SUB[4,2705]
            Title: DEPENDENT CARE EXPENSE FEDERAL TAX CREDIT
      Submodel Linkages (Specified: 1980-12-31 10:27:38)
                    CETA80.MOD  DCTC80.SUB  DCTC80.SUB
                    mapping     mapping     mapping description
                    -------     -------     ------- -----------
        Input(s)
        --------
          required  CHLDN_LE_5  CHLDN_LE_5  NUMBER OF CHILDREN AGE FIVE OR YOUNGER
                    AN_ERNDINC  EARNINGS    EARNED INCOME
                    AN_TXBLINC  TOTAL_INC   TOTAL TAXABLE INCOME
                    FIT         FEDINCTAX   FEDERAL INCOME TAX WITHHELD
                    AFDC        AFDC_BEN    AFDC BENEFITS TO THE FAMILY
                    CHILD_CARE  CHILD_CARE  CHILD CARE EXPENSES
        Output(s)
        ---------
          required  CHLDCRCRDT  CHLDCRCRDT  CHILD CARE TAX CREDIT
```

Section 5: Disposable Income.

The penultimate mapping is that for disposable income. We shall again adopt a fairly inclusive definition: earned and unearned income, plus transfers, including the coupon value of food stamps, the reimbursements for medical expenses, and the amount of the earned income credit, and minus taxes (state, federal, and local), FICA, any assumed pension contribution, and child care expenses. These are all reflected in the annual disposable income mapping, DISPOSABLE:

```
4800  DISPOSABLE: ANNUAL DISPOSABLE INCOME
        Combined operation: CADD
        Make DISPOSABLE the sum of the following weighted mappings, optionally
        imposing a floor on the result of each addition:
   addend mappings          weight factors       floor values
   ------ --------          ------ -------       ----- ------
        AN_ERNDINC            1
        ANTAXOTHER            1
        AFDC                  1
        FOODSTAMPS            1
        MEDICAID              1
        EITC                  1
        CHLDCRCRDT            1
        FICA                 -1
        FIT                  -1
        PSIT                 -1
        LOCAL_TAX            -1
        PENSIONCON           -1
        CHILD_CARE           -1
```

For reasons that will become clear when we turn to the analysis of the solution of this model, we shall also add a final mapping, WK_DISPINC, weekly disposable income.

```
4900  WK_DISPINC: WEEKLY DISPOSABLE INCOME
        Operation: WEIGHT
        Make WK_DISPINC equal to DISPOSABLE weighted by .01923
```

Finally, so that the results of the solution of the model will be accessible to the analyst, a SAVE operation is required.

```
5000  SAVE the following mappings:
        Mapping name   tax factor     description
        ------- ----   --- ------     -----------
        AN_ERNDINC     NO             ANNUAL EARNED INCOME
        AFDC           NO             AFDC BENEFIT PAYABLE TO FAMILY, ANNUAL BASIS
        FOODSTAMPS     NO             VALUE OF ANNUAL FOODSTAMP BENEFITS
        MEDICAID       NO             MEDICAID BENEFITS PAYABLE
        EITC           NO             EARNED INCOME CREDIT FOR THE UNIT
        CHLDCRCRDT     NO             CHILD CARE TAX CREDIT
        FICA           NO             FICA AS FUNCTION OF HOURS WORKED PER WEEK
        FIT            NO             FEDERAL INCOME TAX FOR THE UNIT
        PSIT           NO             PENNSYLVANIA STATE INCOME TAX
        CHILD_CARE     NO             ANNUAL ALLOWABLE CHILD CARE EXPENSES
        WITHHOLDNG     NO             SUM OF TAXES, FICA, AND MANDATORY PENSION
        DISPOSABLE     NO             ANNUAL DISPOSABLE INCOME
        WK_DISPINC     NO             WEEKLY DISPOSABLE INCOME
```

RESULTS

As in Chapter 5, the focus of this section will be on a few basic tables from the solution of the model. More extensive development of the types of secondary analyses that can be done with MAPSIT are shown in Chapter 7.

Before presenting any results, however, it is necessary to solve the model. We shall do that by informing MAPSIT, via the model's prompts, that this is to be a family with one parent and one child, who receives full time day care costing $35.00 per week. The parent earns the minimum wage ($3.35 per hour) on a job that is eligible for the earned income disregard. The local (Pittsburgh) tax rate is .0275. There is no mandatory pension contribution. The annual shelter cost including utilities and phone is $3600, and the family resides in county set number two, which includes Pittsburgh as well as Philadelphia. The actual set of prompts and responses appears as follows:

```
Model Prompts and Solution Stage Responses:
 HOW MANY PARENTS ARE IN THE ASSISTANCE UNIT?  1
 CHILDREN AGE 6 OR OLDER?  0
 CHILDREN AGE 5 OR YOUNGER?  1
 FULL TIME DAY CARE COST PER CHILD PER WEEK?  35
 HOURLY WAGE?  3.35
 IS THE FAMILY ELIGIBLE FOR EARNED INCOME DEDUCTION? (1=YES,0=NO)  1
 LOCAL TAX RATE ON INCOME?  0.0275
 MANDATORY PENSION RATE?  0
 ANNUAL SHELTER COST INCL. UTILITIES AND PHONE?  3600
 WHAT SET OF COUNTIES IS DESIRED (1,2,3 OR 4)?  2
```

The first table is again a summary table, although here the independent variable is, of course, hours worked per week and the entries in the table are the annualized results, the values that would result from working that number of hours per week for fifty-two weeks at the specified wage. As in Chapter 5 the independent variable in this first table is reported in integer values. In this case we have chosen increments of five hours per week.

If the parent worked forty hours per week, earning an annual income of $6968, the family would qualify for AFDC, Medicaid, and the earned income tax credit, but not for food stamps. After paying child care costs, but treating Medicaid benefits as cash transfers, the family would have had an effective income of $7719.67, roughly $750 more than earnings. If the parent were to work sixty hours per week, earning $10,452 for the year, in 1980 this family would still have qualified for AFDC and Medicaid.

Table 6.2 shows the comparable set of mappings where the abscissa values are the turning points for one or more of the mappings in the table. Thus, 5.87 hours per week appears in the column for the independent variable ("X") because it is the point at which AFDC benefits begin to be taxed back, and 24.68 hours appears in the table because it is the point at which the family begins to pay federal income tax, which affects AFDC and (through AFDC) food

Table 6.1: Earnings, Transfers, and Annual Disposable Income as a Function of Hours per Week at Minimum Wage

X	AN_ERNDINC	AFDC	FOODSTAMPS	MEDICAID	EITC	FIT	DISPOSABLE
0.00	0.00	3144.00	1030.80	910.0	00.00	0.00	5084.80
5.00	871.00	3144.00	821.76	910.00	87.10	0.00	5509.85
10.00	1742.00	2975.20	663.36	910.00	174.20	0.00	5816.75
15.00	2613.00	2770.80	515.64	910.00	261.30	0.00	6098.72
20.00	3484.00	2566.40	367.92	910.00	348.40	0.00	6380.69
25.00	4355.00	2369.70	217.89	910.00	435.50	7.70	6668.06
30.00	5226.00	2287.24	120.00	910.00	500.00	129.64	7099.20
35.00	6097.00	2198.96	0.00	910.00	487.88	251.58	7425.79
40.00	6968.00	2075.60	0.00	910.00	379.00	384.88	7719.67
45.00	7839.00	1958.30	0.00	910.00	270.12	524.24	7937.13
50.00	8710.00	1845.20	0.00	910.00	161.25	667.80	8118.58
55.00	9581.00	1745.32	0.00	910.00	52.37	824.58	8300.04
60.00	10452.00	1645.44	0.00	910.00	0.00	981.36	8538.00

Table 6.2: Earnings, Transfers, and Annual Disposable Income as a Function of Hours per Week at Minimum Wage, by Turning Points

X	AN_ERNDINC	AFDC	FOODSTAMPS	MEDICAID	EITC	FIT	DISPOSABLE
0.00	0.00*	3144.00	1030.80*	910.00	0.00*	0.00	5084.80*
5.87	1022.70	3144.00*	785.35*	910.00	102.27	0.00	5583.88*
24.68	4300.00	2374.91*	229.53*	910.00	430.00	0.00*	6644.86*
27.66	4817.62	2325.90	120.00*	910.00	481.76	72.47	6863.16*
28.70	5000.00	2308.64	120.00	910.00	500.00*	98.00	6978.67*
32.83	5719.26	2240.54	120.00*	910.00	500.00	198.70	7362.27*
32.83	5719.33	2240.54	0.00*	910.00	500.00	198.71	7242.31*
34.44	6000.00	2213.96*	0.00	910.00	500.00*	238.00	7392.00*
36.74	6400.00	2152.10*	0.00	910.00	450.00	294.00*	7531.33*
38.89	6774.24	2101.70	0.00	910.00	403.22	353.88	7669.18*
43.96	7657.14	1982.79	0.00	910.00	292.86	495.14	7899.24*
48.79	8500.00	1869.28*	0.00	910.00	187.50	630.00*	8074.83
57.41	10000.00	1697.27	0.00	910.00	0.00*	900.00	8387.33*
60.00	10452.00	1645.44	0.00	910.00	0.00	981.36	8538.00

stamps. As indicated in Chapter 5, an asterisk in a table constructed this way indicates a turning point for that mapping at the corresponding value of the independent variable.

Since we have shown a summary table for the CETA model done by turning points, it seems worthwhile to also display another of the output forms of secondary analysis that is so easy for MAPSIT, marginal analysis.Because Chapter 7 discusses secondary analysis at some length, we shall confine our attention to a single table with a single mapping, and since the purpose of the CETA model was to look at incentives for additional work, it is instructive to consider the marginal contribution to weekly pay resulting from an increase of a single hour per week in work effort. This is shown in Figure 6.1.

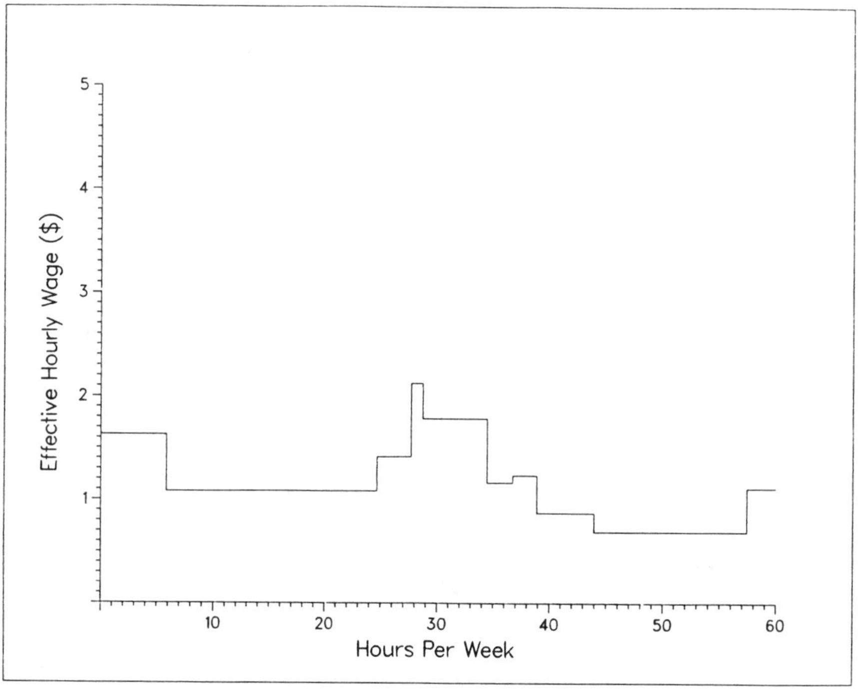

Figure 6.1: Effective Wage Rate at $3.35 per Hour

The marginal change in weekly disposable income as a function of hours worked per week can also, perhaps even more easily, be thought of as the effective wage rate and hence has been so labeled in that figure.

The results show that for the first six hours, if a parent with one child works at the minimum wage, after considering the various taxes (FICA, state income, local income), the costs of the necessary child care, the reduction in food stamps, and the increase in earned income tax credit, the effective hourly wage is $1.63. While the effective wage rate is a dollar or more during the first thirty-nine hours of work per week, if the person works between thirty-nine and fifty-seven hours, the effective wage drops to less than $.88 per hour.

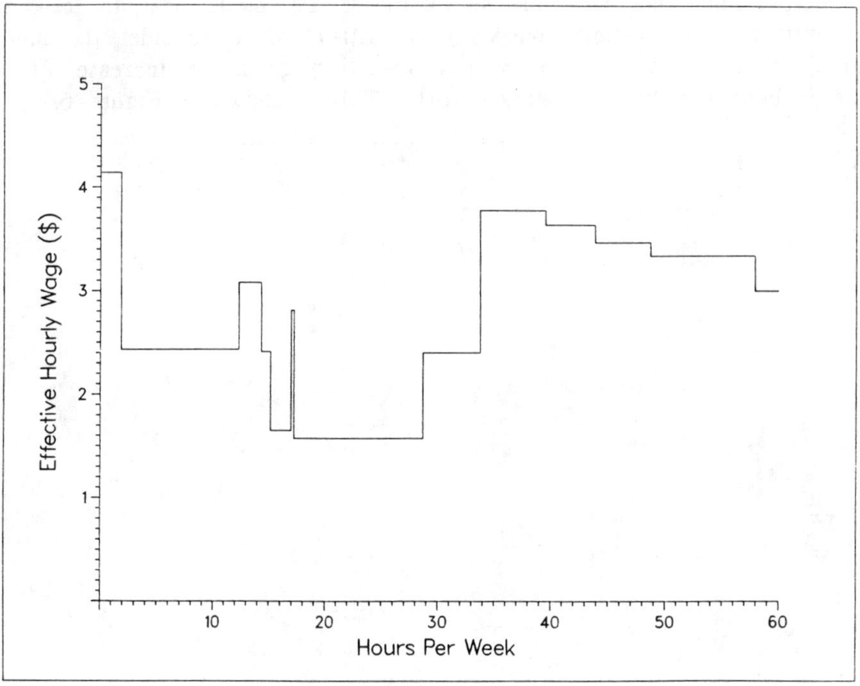

Figure 6.2: Effective Wage Rate at $6.70 per Hour

Figure 6.2 shows the effective wage when the nominal wage rate is raised to $6.70 (two times the minimum wage). During the first twelve hours per week the effective wage rate drops from $4.14 to $2.43. If the parent works seventeen to twenty-eight hours per week the effective wage rate for an additional hour falls to $1.57. Between twenty-eight and twenty-nine hours, the higher paid worker actually has a lower effective wage ($1.57) than the lower paid worker ($2.12). With the exception of this one brief period, however, the effective wage of the higher paid worker is above that of the lower paid worker, as is shown in Figure 6.3 where the effective wages for these two conditions are shown on the same graph. The shaded area in that figure shows the effective pay difference between these two nominal wages. The cross hatched area indicates the region in which the higher nominal wage actually generates less income per hour than the lower wage.

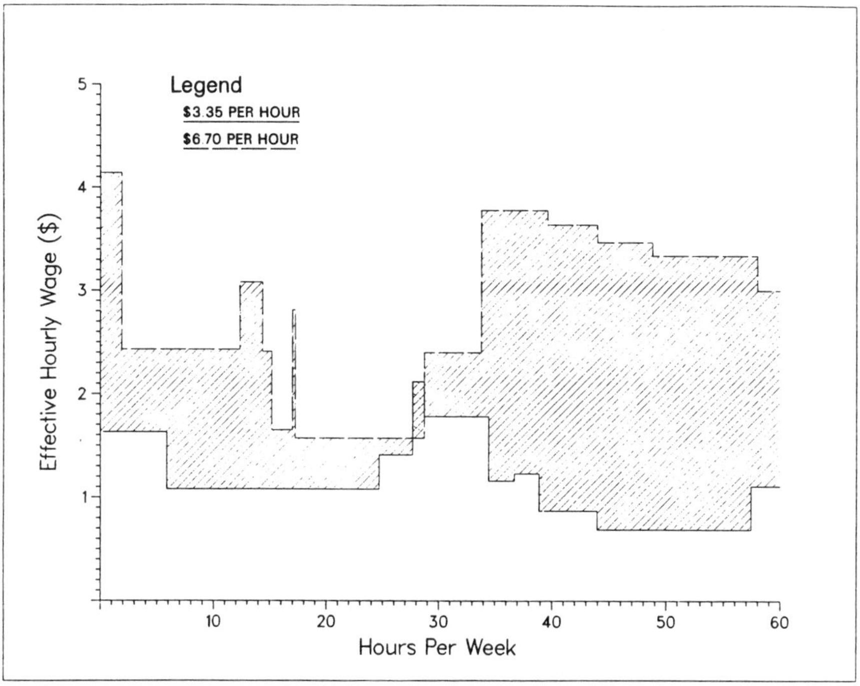

Figure 6.3: Effective Wage as a Function of Wages and Hours

The fact that a higher paid job can have a lower effective wage rate over a short interval does not mean that a worker in the higher paid job is necessarily receiving less in total income. Figure 6.4 shows the average wage per hour for a person who has worked a given number of hours at one of three nominal wage rates ($3.35, $6.70, and $10.05).[41] The wage of $6.70 makes the worker better off than if he or she had received only $3.35 per hour even though there was an interval where the effective wage was higher for the lower wage worker. But Figure 6.4 also shows that a person work-

---

[41] Average hourly wage here is calculated in a manner analogous to the average tax back rate, whereas the effective wage per hour is analogous to the marginal tax-back rate.

ing slightly more than twenty hours at a nominal wage of $10.05 per hour will have a lower average wage than someone working the same hours at a nominal wage of $6.70 per hour.

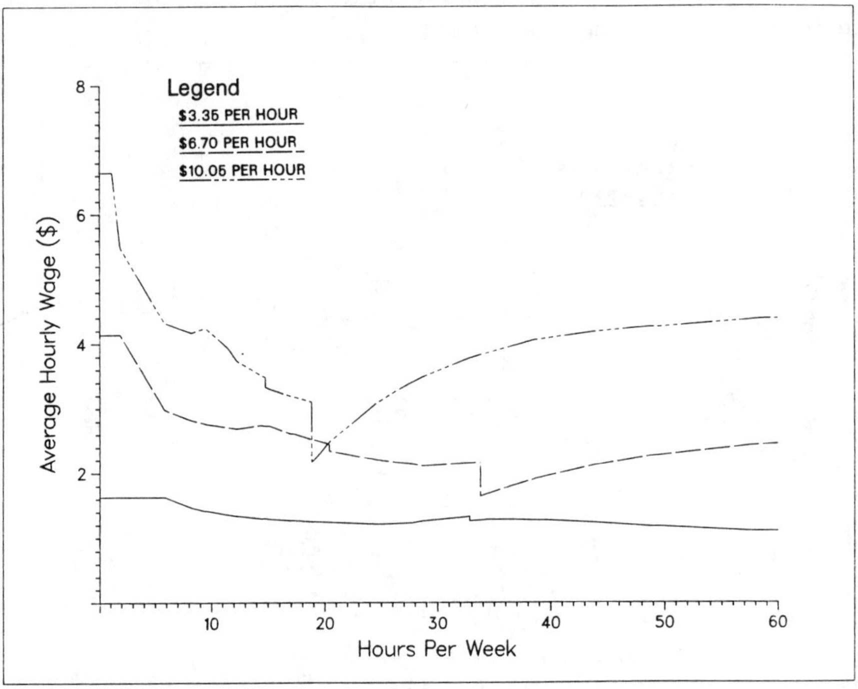

Figure 6.4: Average Hourly Wage as a Function of Wages and Hours

Figure 6.5 shows the effect in annual disposable income of working at the minimum wage, twice the minimum wage, and three times the minimum wage ($3.35, $6.70, $10.05) for different numbers of hours per week. One interesting characteristic of Figure 6.5 is how little difference there is between earning $3.35 per hour and earning $6.70 per hour. Although the latter nominal wage is twice as high, the disposable income at forty hours of work per week is only 19 percent greater.

Another feature of Figure 6.5 is the notches that appear in the curves for $6.70 and $10.05 per hour. These occur at the point at which the family loses AFDC and Medicaid. For the parent earning $6.70 per hour, this happens at thirty-four hours per week; for the parent earning $10.05 per hour, it occurs at nineteen hours per week.

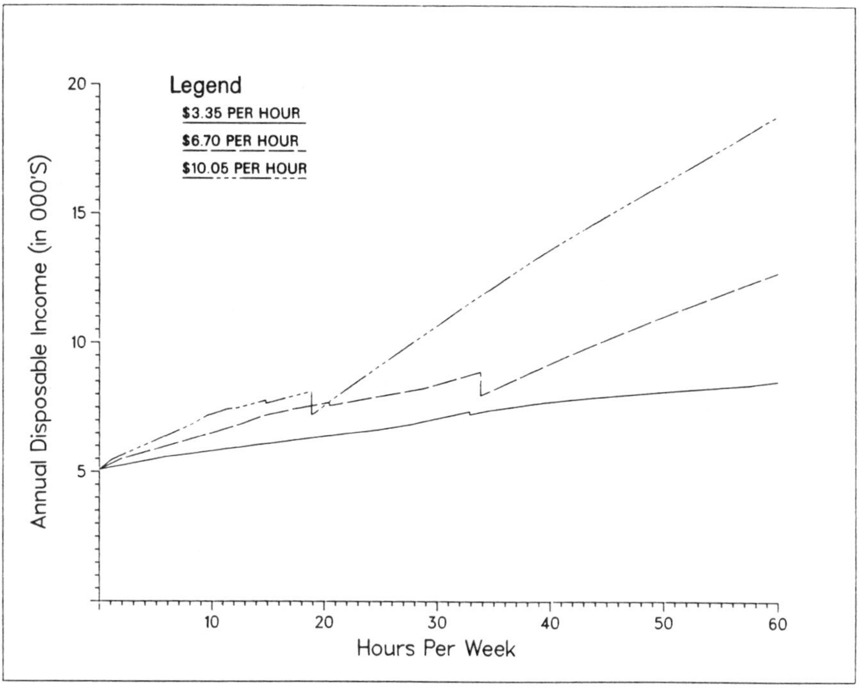

Figure 6.5: Annual Disposable Income as a Function of Wages and Hours

With regard to CETA, it appears from the analysis of effective wage rates that several conclusions might be drawn about the effect of nominal wage rates and incentives to accept employment. First, people who are offered employment at the minimum wage receive "effective wages" anywhere from $.87 to $2.12 per hour if they work forty hours or less per week, although the prevailing wage between five and twenty-five hours is $1.08. If they work overtime, however, their effective wage is in general worse, ranging from $.69 to $1.11 per hour.

Workers at $6.70 also show generally declining marginal wage rates for part-time work. If they work full time, however, the effective wage rate is roughly double that for half time. Workers who are offered employment at $10.05 per hour, however, are much better off when they work full time. If they were to work only half time they could make as much by receiving $6.70 as they would at $10.05. Beyond half time the differential between $10.05 and $6.70 increases steadily.

The implications for CETA appear to be that at the minimum wage there is relatively little incentive to work, either part time or full time. At wages twice and even three times the minimum wage there is still little incentive to work part time. At $10.05 per hour, however, full-time work holds out incentives 76 percent greater than work at the minimum wage and 168 percent greater than not working at all. The small advantage of $10.05/hour over $3.35/hour for part-time work suggests that nominal wage should not be a very important factor in whether people take a job, if the job is only half time. For full-time jobs, however, the low net wage at $3.35/hour and the much higher net wage at $10.05/hour are consistent with the hypothesis that employers and CETA administrators should find it much easier to induce a person to work at the higher wage rate.[42]

SUMMARY

One purpose of this model was to demonstrate that it is possible to use variables other than earned income as the independent variable for an analysis. In this chapter we used "hours per week," but we could have built a model that used the ratio of incomes in a two-earner family or the series of years and associated values that each of a set of variables would take on as a function of time. All that is required in a MAPSIT analysis is that it be possible to express the dependent variables as piecewise linear functions of the independent variable.

The second goal of this chapter was to demonstrate that the use of submodels can simplify the task of model building. This may not be as apparent to the reader as it might have been since the problem in this chapter includes more programs than the model in Chapter 5. Even so the number of operations used in Chapter 5 totaled eighty-seven including thirteen comments, while the number of operations used in this chapter was fifty, including eight comments. If the model of Chapter 5 had been written to make use of submodels, as many as fifty-two of the seventy-four functional operations could have been omitted.

---

[42]These comments are predicated on work that is reported to the relevant agencies (AFDC, IRS, and so forth). The incentives from participation in the underground economy are a different story entirely.

Using submodels, however, has advantages that go beyond the mere reduction in the number of operations required to model a system. First, it is faster, and second, there are advantages in knowing that the set of instructions has been debugged and works correctly. Both of these advantages, speed and accuracy, allow one to arrive sooner at the point of the modeling -- to be able to examine the results of the model. The examination of results is the topic of Chapter 7.

CHAPTER 7.
FORMATS FOR SECONDARY ANALYSIS

Because even the most sophisticated analysis is worthless if one cannot understand its results, we have emphasized the importance of presenting one's secondary analysis in an appropriate, understandable format. This admonition is even more critical when not all of the participants in policy discussions are technically skilled. For such persons, a clean format that is tailored to the problem at hand and resistant to misinterpretation can make the difference between an opportunity to bring their experiences to bear and a garbled exchange of confused misunderstanding.

To demonstrate how MAPSIT assists the analyst by providing results in appropriate formats, this chapter illustrates some of the output forms available in MAPSIT's secondary analysis module, EXAMINE. Although the formats presented here are by no means exhaustive, they do include most of the commonly used forms. Throughout the discussion, the focus lies rather more with reasons for each of the formats and less with an explanation of the formats' flexibility or technological intricacy. Many of the "bells and whistles" available are not even mentioned here.

The first section of this chapter illustrates the major MAPSIT output forms. Typically, for each form, the first portion of the presentation establishes the desirability of the form in terms of the substantive issues that an analyst might wish to address. Next a concrete example of the form is presented, drawing on the substance of the two example analyses of Chapters 5 and 6 for numerical values. Finally, a brief discussion shows how an analyst might interpret the output in terms of the substantive problem area. A final section of the chapter briefly highlights the major characteristics of some additional output forms.

MAJOR OUTPUT FORMS

Documentation Facilities

We have already stressed the importance of documenting the models one builds. Documenting the results of the analyses is equally important. Since more people tend to read the numerical results rather than the model, analytic results are much closer to being a direct policy input than are models, in the tributary structure of elements that affect policy.

Sound documentation serves as a necessary complement to the results proper and is crucial if the user of the analysis is to understand what the results mean. The documentation should convey to the reader the source of the results, the characteristics of the solution, the relevant assumptions, the nature of the several variables involved, and any appropriate warnings. The analyst himself may also require effective documentation, perhaps when dealing with several models simultaneously, or when reusing old models and analyses. Since the documentation must be produced before it can be used, it is important that the procedure for secondary analyses also includes a provision for creating the various items of documentation. Furthermore, it is important that the capacity be both convenient and inexpensive, lest time and resource pressures lead the analyst to forego the benefits derived from careful documentation.

The DOCUMENT command in MAPSIT provides the analyst with the capacity to include a variety of information that is useful in identifying and labeling results, in the secondary analysis. Three categories of relevant information are "available for the asking."[43] (1) The documentation can include the title of the model and the model description. Because these items typically summarize the nature of the model producing the results, they serve as a useful preface to the analytic results, providing a continuity across the several stages of analysis. (2) The documentation can include the text of any prompts in the model along with the analyst's responses to these prompts at the solution stage. Most MAPSIT models contain several prompts that allow the analyst to use a single model that is sufficiently general to permit a variety of parameter configurations. The analyst may, for example, wish to vary the number of children in the family

---

[43] The DOCUMENT command of the experimental version of MAPSIT provides additional information.

unit, or the numerical values of various policy parameters such as exemption levels and nominal tax back rates. Because the numerical results in the resulting solution depend on the particular responses that the analyst provides to the prompts, it is vital that this information be available to those who use the results. (3) The documentation can also include any warning or error messages generated during the course of the solution. For example, certain MAPSIT operations create mappings for which the piecewise linear representation is only an approximation, and output warning messages indicate that the approximation has been made. Since that information is available in EXAMINE, the user of the analytic results, as well as the solver of the model, can be aware of the approximation.

Generation of the documentation output is simple. The analyst merely enters the keywords for the categories to be included, and the secondary analysis module, EXAMINE, does the rest. Sometimes an analyst may generate the full set of documentation at the start of the secondary analysis session and subsequently include subsets along with the particular analyses for which they are relevant.

Table 7.1 displays a full set of documentation from the example developed in Chapter 5: description, prompts, and warnings. The several items remind the reader of the major assumptions in the analysis and the specific choice for the prompts that generated these results. They also indicate that there should be no problems with piecewise linear approximations to derived relationships.

Table 7.2 displays a subset of the documentation for the work incentive example of Chapter 6. It concentrates its attention on the parameter configuration as defined by the model prompts and the user's responses.

Legends

While the DOCUMENT command displays information pertaining primarily to a solution as a whole, the LEGEND command allows the analyst to obtain documentary information about individual mappings in isolation or in groups. Specifically, for any mapping or group of mappings chosen by the analyst, LEGEND prints a table showing the names of the mappings and the associated mapping descriptions assigned in the SAVE operations of the model that defined them. At a general level, the command conveys more information than can be packed into a name proper, even when considerable attention is devoted to good mnemonics. Within this general thrust, LEGEND

Table 7.1: Documentation for ILLUS4

Model Description:

WELFARE AND TAXES FOR THE SINGLE-PARENT FAMILY
AUTHORS: GORDON H. LEWIS AND RICHARD J. MORRISON
CREATED: JANUARY 1984

.

THE EXAMPLE ILLUSTRATES HOW MAPSIT CAN MODEL AN INCOME TRANSFER SYSTEM AS IT AFFECTS A FAMILY OVER A CONTINUUM OF GROSS EARNINGS. ALTHOUGH THE MODEL IS REASONABLY REALISTIC, ITS FOCUS LIES CONSIDERABLY MORE WITH ILLUSTRATING THE "FLAVOR" OF STACKING ANALYSIS THAN WITH THE CONSTRUCTION OF AN ABSOLUTELY PRECISE DESCRIPTION OF AN EXISTING SYSTEM. AS A GENERAL PRINCIPLE IN THIS MODEL, WHERE THE DETAILS NECESSARY FOR A PRECISE REPRESENTATION WOULD HAVE ENCUMBERED THE FLOW OF THE MODEL FOR ILLUSTRATIVE PURPOSES, WE HAVE UNHESITATINGLY EXCISED THE DETAIL AND SUBSTITUTED WHAT WE CONSIDER REASONABLE PROXIES. PARENTHETICALLY, IN ALL SUCH SUBSTITUTIONS, MAPSIT IS FULLY CAPABLE OF MODELING THE DETAILED FORM OF THE RELEVANT TRANSFER PROGRAM OR PROVISION.

.

THE MODEL INCLUDES THREE DIFFERENT WELFARE/SOCIAL ASSISTANCE PROGRAMS (AFDC, FOOD STAMPS, AND MEDICAID), THREE TAXES (FICA, FEDERAL INCOME TAX, AND A HYPOTHETICAL STATE INCOME TAX), THE DEPENDENT CARE TAX CREDIT, AND THE EARNED INCOME TAX CREDIT. IN CALCULATING THESE TRANSFERS THE MODEL ALSO GENERATES A NUMBER OF INTERVENING VARIABLES, E.G. PRESUMED CHILD CARE EXPENSES AND SHELTER COSTS.

.

THERE ARE A NUMBER OF SPECIAL ASSUMPTIONS AND CHARACTERISTICS IN THE MODEL:

(1) THE CALCULATIONS APPLY TO A SINGLE PARENT FAMILY, BUT THE MODEL PERMITS THE ANALYST TO SPECIFY ANY NUMBER OF CHILDREN.
(2) THE SIMULATION EMPLOYS A TIME PERIOD OF ONE YEAR. PROGRAMS ADMINISTERED ON A SHORTER PERIOD ARE THUS "SCALED UP" TO ANNUAL EQUIVALENTS.
(3) THE MODEL ASSUMES THAT THE WORKING PARENT RECEIVES WAGE AND SALARY INCOME AT A CONSTANT RATE THROUGHOUT THE YEAR.
(4) THE ANALYSIS IS LIMITED TO FAMILIES WITH GROSS EARNINGS (WAGES AND SALARIES) LESS THAN $100,000.
(5) WHEN A SINGLE PARENT IS WORKING, THE FAMILY MAY BE ELIGIBLE FOR A TAX CREDIT FOR CHILD CARE EXPENSES. SECTION 9 CONTAINS THE SPECIFIC ASSUMPTIONS ABOUT THAT CREDIT.
(6) THE MODEL ASKS WHETHER THE PARENT HAS BEEN EMPLOYED FOR MORE THAN FOUR MONTHS, SINCE THIS AFFECTS WHETHER THE ASSISTANCE UNIT IS ELIGIBLE FOR THE EARNED INCOME DEDUCTION IN AFDC.
(7) THE MODEL ASSUMES THAT ALL CHILDREN ARE (A) UNDER AGE 18 OR (B) UNDER AGE 19 AND A FULL TIME STUDENT IN SECONDARY SCHOOL OR AN EQUIVALENT LEVEL OF A VOCATIONAL OR TECHNICAL SCHOOL.
(8) THE VALUE OF FOOD STAMPS IS TREATED AS A CASH BENEFIT.
(9) THE VALUE OF THE MEDICAL EXPENSES REIMBURSED BY MEDICAID IS TREATED AS A CASH BENEFIT.
(10) THE FIXED PARAMETERS IN THE MODEL EMPLOY NUMERICAL VALUES APPROPRIATE FOR 1984.

Model Prompts and Solution Stage Responses:

HOW MANY CHILDREN ARE THERE AGE 5 OR YOUNGER? 1
HOW MANY CHILDREN ARE THERE AGE 6 OR OLDER? 2
HAS THE PARENT BEEN EMPLOYED FOR MORE THAN 4 MONTHS? (1=YES,0=NO) 1
DOLLAR VALUE OF TAXABLE INCOME (OTHER THAN EARNINGS) FOR THE FAMILY? 0
ANNUAL SHELTER COSTS INCLUDING HEAT, ELEC, WATER, & PHONE? 3600
DOLLAR VALUE OF TOTAL INCOME EXEMPT FROM STATE INCOME TAX? 0
STATE INCOME TAX RATE ON TOTAL INCOME LESS EXEMPTION? .0245

Warnings and Cautions:

None

Table 7.2: Partial Documentation for CETA80

```
Model Prompts and Solution Stage Responses:
 HOW MANY PARENTS ARE IN THE ASSISTANCE UNIT?  1
 CHILDREN AGE 6 OR OLDER?  0
 CHILDREN AGE 5 OR YOUNGER?  1
 FULL TIME DAY CARE COST PER CHILD PER WEEK?  35
 HOURLY WAGE?  3.35
 IS THE FAMILY ELIGIBLE FOR EARNED INCOME DEDUCTION? (1=YES,0=NO)  1
 LOCAL TAX RATE ON INCOME?  0.0275
 MANDATORY PENSION RATE?  0
 ANNUAL SHELTER COST INCL. UTILITIES AND PHONE?  3600
 WHAT SET OF COUNTIES IS DESIRED (1,2,3 OR 4)?  2
```

sees two specific applications. First, the analyst can generate legends to accompany the tables from EXAMINE. The tables, for reasons of appearance and formatting, contain only the mapping names as the relevant row or column headings. Provision of legends provides clearer, more completely labeled output. Second, the analyst can use the LEGEND command, upon entry to EXAMINE, for example, to recall the names of the available mappings that will later appear as arguments to the EXAMINE commands. This capsule summary will refresh the analyst's memory about the spelling of the mnemonic names as well as indicate the nature of the mappings.

Table 7.3 displays a LEGEND output consisting of the names and descriptions for all of the saved mappings from the model of Chapter 5. These names will appear in several of the illustrative tables in this chapter, making it useful to review the names and substance of these several mappings.

Table 7.3: Legends for ILLUS4

Mapping Name:	Description:
AFDC	AFDC BENEFIT PAYABLE TO THE FAMILY
FOODSTAMPS	FOOD STAMP BENEFIT PAYABLE TO THE FAMILY
MEDICAID	MEDICAID BENEFITS (REIMBURSEMENTS)
EITC	EARNED INCOME CREDIT FOR THE FAMILY
FICA	FICA PREMIUMS PAID BY THE EARNER
STATEINCTX	STATE INCOME TAXES PAYABLE BY THE HEAD
NETFEDTAX	FEDERAL INCOME TAX AFTER CHILD CARE EXPENSE CREDIT
DISPOSABLE	DISPOSABLE INCOME FOR THE FAMILY

Breakeven Analysis

Despite its importance, the documentation of results must inevitably be subordinate to the results themselves. One builds and solves models to ascertain the workings of the transfer system over the whole domain of the model's independent variable, for parameter configurations of interest. However, prior to addressing all of the values and inflections of the several mappings, it is often useful to characterize broadly the relationships in a solution.

To some extent one may highlight the behavior of a mapping in terms of particularly significant abscissa values. For a tax or contribution program, one significant point is the level of the independent variable at which the unit begins to pay the tax or contribution. For tax programs this point is often called the cut-in point. For a benefit program, with earnings as the independent variable, for example, the equivalent point is the level of earnings at which any additional income will cause a decrease from the maximum benefit level. For benefit programs this point is often called the turndown point. We shall refer to these two collectively as departure points.

Another significant point for benefit programs is the independent variable level at which the benefit payable is reduced to zero. Typically, one calls this point the breakeven level of income for the program. More generally, whenever the ordinate of any mapping reaches zero, after having been something other than zero, the mapping is said to have a breakeven. Sometimes a given mapping may have multiple breakevens.

The BREAKEVEN command in MAPSIT allows the analyst to generate the departure values and breakeven values for any of the mappings in the solution. A tabular presentation of this information gives a fairly good idea of where the various taxes and benefits start and stop. Often this information is relevant in addressing issues of program overlap, since in overlap analyses one is concerned about the number of programs simultaneously acting to tax back the unit's earnings. The greater the number of transfer programs that vary their transfers over a given income domain, the greater the need to make sure that the system of programs is well coordinated. Using just the information contained in the breakeven table, one can largely tell, for a given income domain, what transfer programs are "active" in the sense that they are increasing taxes or decreasing benefits in the domain. Information from the SUMMARY and MARGINAL commands can then add further detail as required.

Table 7.4 presents the departure and breakeven values for all of the mappings in the solution to the model described in Chapter 5, with a family assumed to consist of a single parent and three children. From the table we note that AFDC benefits begin to be reduced with the very first dollar of earnings and fall to zero when earned income reaches $6820.57. Food stamp benefits also begin to be reduced with the very first dollar of earned income, but don't reach a breakeven point until $18,629.27. (The alert reader will recall that there is a $85.00 per month standard deduction in the food stamp income definition and that various other deductions are available, but these deductions are more than offset at zero earnings by the AFDC benefit.)

Table 7.4: Departures and Breakevens for ILLUS4

Mapping	Departure	Breakevens
AFDC	0.00	6820.57
FOODSTAMPS	0.00	18629.27
MEDICAID	6820.50	6820.57
EITC	0.00	10000.00
FICA	0.00	- - -
STATEINCTX	0.00	- - -
NETFEDTAX	9808.33	- - -
DISPOSABLE	0.00	- - -

The Medicaid benefit does not have a departure point until it reaches essentially the breakeven point for AFDC. When this happens it drops very rapidly to its breakeven point. The earned income credit (EITC) has a departure at zero and a breakeven at $10,000. The rest of the mappings (FICA, taxes, and disposable income) have no breakevens and never attain an ordinate of zero after their departure. It is interesting to note that the net federal tax (tax after child care credit) does not depart from zero until earned income reaches $9808.33. It is also interesting to note that between $0, the departure point for AFDC and food stamps, and $6820.57, both of these benefits are being reduced as earnings increase. We shall examine shortly a table that allows us to look at the combined effect of simultaneous reduction in program benefits.

Table 7.5 displays breakevens and departures for the work incentive example of Chapter 6, but in it the analyst has selected only transfer programs that provide a benefit. Specifically, the table includes only AFDC, food stamps, Medicaid, the earned income tax credit, and the child care credit (CHLDCRCRDT). Recall that in this example the independent variable is hours worked per week and thus the breakevens and departures are expressed in terms of that variable.

Table 7.5: Departures and Breakevens for Selected Programs from CETA80

Mapping	Departure	Breakeven
AFDC	5.87	- - -
FOODSTAMPS	0.00	32.83
MEDICAID	- - -	- - -
EITC	0.00	57.41
CHLDCRCRDT	24.68	- - -

We see that the AFDC benefit does not begin to decline until the parent has worked approximately six hours per week at the minimum wage. The food stamp benefit begins to decline with the first minute of work and does not reach a breakeven point until the parent has worked over thirty-two hours and forty-eight minutes per week.[44] Since the Medicaid benefit is tied to the AFDC benefit, which did not reach a breakeven within the domain of analysis (a maximum of sixty hours per week), the Medicaid benefit has neither a departure nor a breakeven. The earned income credit, which as we know reaches a breakeven at annual earnings of $10,000, reaches a breakeven in hours worked per week at fifty-seven hours and twenty-five minutes (57.41 hours). Finally, the child care credit begins to be received when the parent worked more than twenty-four hours and forty minutes a week and continues to be received for any number of hours greater than that. Thus, at work levels near to full time, five of the six benefits are declining with additional work effort, indicating the importance of program coordination if work incentives are to be maintained.

Summary Analysis

Despite the utility of the DOCUMENT and BREAKEVEN commands, they typically serve largely as preliminaries. They indicate the general characteristics of mappings in a solution, but they omit information that is crucial to a full understanding of the mappings or the system: (1) they restrict themselves to a few abscissa values for each mapping, and (2) the departures say nothing about the ordinates of

---

[44] The values in the table are hours and hundredths of hours rather than hours and minutes.

the mappings, a very serious shortcoming should program or system adequacy be the analytic focus.

Generally, these isolated bits of information are far from sufficient for the analyst. Having built a model that derives the whole of each relationship, the analyst wants to look at the relationships, not just individually, with each mapping taken in isolation, but together so that the joint behavior of the programs can be ascertained. Thus, given the opportunity, an analyst will wish to look at the ordinates of several mappings at once, the ordinates appearing in conjunction with the corresponding values of the common independent variable.

The SUMMARY command, which was used to generate Tables 5.1 and 5.2 of Chapter 5 and Tables 6.1 and 6.2 of Chapter 6, gives the analyst the capacity to generate customized tables of this type. From an entire solution or from multiple solutions the analyst chooses those mappings to be included in the table. In addition, the analyst chooses the values of the independent variable at which the mappings are to be displayed, or defaults the choice to the system's turning points. MAPSIT then constructs a table showing the values of the several mappings' ordinates at those abscissa values. This natural presentation is by far the most commonly used form of secondary analysis.

The structure of the table's "direct form" is straightforward. The first column contains the abscissa values specified by the analyst and provides the row headings for the table. The remaining columns of the table correspond to the desired mappings, while the column entries are the mappings' ordinates. A table entry consists of the column mapping's ordinate evaluated at the abscissa value that serves as the row's heading.

There are two main ways that the analyst specifies the values of the independent variable at which the ordinates will appear for the table's mappings. One of these is simply to provide an explicit list of the desired abscissa values. For example, the analyst may want these to be round-numbered thousands of dollars, or may want them to be certain multiples of the prevailing minimum wage or of some relevant poverty line, or even mixtures of specifications. In general, using such a list, the analyst can provide any sequence of values felt appropriate.

Table 5.1 of Chapter 5 and Table 6.1 of Chapter 6 are examples of tables constructed with the analyst enumerating the specific values of the independent variable at which the ordinate values of the dependent variables are desired. Table 7.6, which contains the same

Table 7.6: Summary of Benefits and Tax Levels at Specified Values of Earned Income

X	AFDC	FOODSTAMPS	MEDICAID	EITC
0.00	4812.00*	2312.40*	2512.00	0.00*
1000.00	4132.90	2270.13	2512.00	100.00
2000.00	3453.79	2227.86	2512.00	200.00
3000.00	2774.69	2185.59	2512.00	300.00
4000.00	2095.58	2143.33	2512.00	400.00
5000.00	1416.48*	2101.06*	2512.00	500.00*
6000.00	837.37*	2028.79*	2512.00	500.00*
6700.00	519.50*	1951.95*	2512.00	412.50
7000.00	0.00	2034.00	0.00	375.00
8000.00	0.00	1788.00	0.00	250.00
9000.00	0.00	1542.00	0.00	125.00
10000.00	0.00	1296.00	0.00	0.00*
15000.00	0.00	120.00	0.00	0.00
20000.00	0.00	0.00	0.00	0.00
25000.00	0.00	0.00	0.00	0.00
30000.00	0.00	0.00	0.00	0.00
40000.00	0.00	0.00	0.00	0.00

X	FICA	STATEINCTX	NETFEDTAX	DISPOSABLE
0.00	0.00*	0.00*	0.00	9636.40*
1000.00	67.00	24.50	0.00	9923.53
2000.00	134.00	49.00	0.00	10210.65
3000.00	201.00	73.50	0.00	10497.78
4000.00	268.00	98.00	0.00	10784.90
5000.00	335.00	122.50	0.00	11072.03*
6000.00	402.00	147.00	0.00	11329.16*
6700.00	448.90	164.15	0.00	11482.90*
7000.00	469.00	171.50	0.00	8768.50
8000.00	536.00	196.00	0.00	9306.00
9000.00	603.00	220.50	0.00	9843.50
10000.00	670.00	245.00	23.00	10358.00*
15000.00	1005.00	367.50	782.00	12965.50
20000.00	1340.00	490.00	1694.00	16476.00
25000.00	1675.00	612.50	2806.00	19906.50
30000.00	2010.00	735.00	4106.00	23149.00
40000.00	2532.60	980.00	7251.00	29236.40

data as Table 5.1, shows a SUMMARY table where the analyst has selected as the critical values of the independent variable annual income from $0 to $10,000 in $1,000 increments, plus $5000 increments up to $30,000, and the values $6700 and $40,000.[45] Although this form of the SUMMARY table is often very valuable,

[45] Table 7.6 also illustrates some of the flexibility that MAPSIT allows the analyst in choice of format for table display.

especially where there are too many turning points for a compact presentation, it does have its faults. It tells the analyst what the mappings are doing at selected earnings values, but not much about what is happening between the values selected. In particular, note that it is not appropriate to interpolate for independent variable values between those in the first column. For example, the analyst cannot tell where the various tax brackets start and end. For a benefit program, if the effective tax-back rate changes somewhere between the departure and the breakeven, the analyst cannot identify the location of the change. Unless a breakeven table is available, the analyst cannot tell from this type of SUMMARY table (generated from an explicit list of abscissa values) where the mappings' departures and breakevens occur. Nevertheless, policymakers, as well as editors, sometimes insist on round-valued abscissa levels.

The second method of choosing row headings (abscissa values) overcomes these difficulties. Instead of specifying the numerical values directly, the analyst defaults the choice, letting MAPSIT choose them to be the natural turning points of the system under examination. That is, the table has a row heading for every independent variable value at which any of the table's mappings has an inflection point. Thus, independent variable values for things like tax bracket changes, departure points, breakeven points, and notches appear automatically in the table because mappings change slope at such values. This procedure regularly leads to row headings with uncommon numbers, a situation attributable to the system being modeled rather than MAPSIT's treatment of it. Furthermore, in contrast to row headings chosen by the analyst, the use of turning points permits linear interpolation anywhere within the table. For example, to obtain a mapping's ordinate halfway between two adjacent row headings, the analyst may appropriately average the mapping's ordinates for the two abscissas.

Table 7.7 contains the same data as Table 5.2 of Chapter 5, with the row headings defaulted to the natural turning points.[46] The

---

[46] The set of row headings for the top half of the table consists of the turning points for all mappings in the top half of the table, plus the specified upper limit of 40,000. The row headings in the bottom half of the table are more numerous since disposable income (DISPOSABLE) is one of the mappings, and it contains all of the turning points of the mappings in the top half of the table, plus those unique to the three tax mappings in the bottom half of the table. This table could also have been automatically generated using the same set of row headings in both halves of the table, another example of MAPSIT's flexibility.

Table 7.7: Summary of Benefits and Tax Levels at Earned Income Values Corresponding to Turning Points for the Mappings

X	AFDC	FOODSTAMPS	MEDICAID	EITC
0.00	4812.00*	2312.40*	2512.00	0.00*
5000.00	1416.48*	2101.06*	2512.00	500.00*
6000.00	837.37*	2028.79*	2512.00	500.00*
6700.00	519.50*	1951.95*	2512.00	412.50
6820.50	414.06*	1953.94*	2512.00*	397.44
6820.57	0.00*	2078.14*	0.00*	397.43
10000.00	0.00	1296.00	0.00	0.00*
14780.49	0.00	120.00*	0.00	0.00
18629.11	0.00	120.00*	0.00	0.00
18629.27	0.00	0.00*	0.00	0.00
40000.00	0.00	0.00	0.00	0.00

X	FICA	STATEINCTX	NETFEDTAX	DISPOSABLE
0.00	0.00*	0.00*	0.00	9636.40*
5000.00	335.00	122.50	0.00	11072.03*
6000.00	402.00	147.00	0.00	11329.16*
6700.00	448.90	164.15	0.00	11482.90*
6820.50	456.97	167.10	0.00	11473.86*
6820.57	456.98	167.10	0.00	8672.06*
9808.33	657.16	240.30	0.00*	10277.98*
10000.00	670.00	245.00	23.00	10358.00*
10500.00	703.50	257.25	83.00*	10629.25*
12700.00	850.90	311.15	391.00*	11778.75*
14780.49	990.29	362.12	744.68	12803.39*
15800.00	1058.60	387.10	918.00*	13556.30*
18629.11	1248.15	456.41	1427.24	15617.31*
18629.27	1248.16	456.42	1427.27	15497.42*
19000.00	1273.00	465.50	1494.00*	15767.50*
22200.00	1487.40	543.90	2134.00*	18034.70*
27500.00	1842.50	673.75	3406.00*	21577.75*
32800.00	2197.60	803.60	4890.00*	24908.80*
37800.00	2532.60*	926.10	6490.00	27851.30*
38100.00	2532.60	933.45	6586.00*	28047.95*
40000.00	2532.60	980.00	7251.00	29236.40

several mappings in the table show the transfers to and from the family and the resulting disposable income for the family. Note, for example, that AFDC benefits begin to decline with the very first penny of earned income and reach a breakeven at $6820.57. Food stamps also begin to decline with the first penny of earned income but they don't reach the breakeven point for this size family until earnings reach $18,629.27. Finally, the reader will notice that the departure and breakeven values for the several mappings, seen earlier in the BREAKEVEN table, appear as row headings in this summary table.

One notable contrast between Tables 7.7 and 7.6 is the appreciable number of asterisks in Table 7.7. The asterisks represent ordinates that are contained in turning points for the column mapping. For example, in the $5000.00 row of earned income, the $500 value of EITC corresponds to a turning point, in this case one that occurs because EITC reaches its maximum, where it remains until earned income reaches $6000. Each row of the table, with the exception of the row "40000" which was arbitrarily included as an upper limit for the table display, contains at least one asterisk, for if the abscissa value serving as the row heading were not a turning point for at least one of the table mappings, the row would not appear. Values not marked by an asterisk were computed for the table by interpolation between the mappings' turning points. Thus, for each involved mapping, the table indicates all abscissa values such that any mapping changes its slope. In appreciating the need for a systems orientation, it is particularly valuable to observe how the asterisks propagate. A turning point in one mapping will often induce a turning point, at the same abscissa, in another mapping whose calculation uses the first as a precedent. At $5000 there is a turning point in AFDC because EITC (which is part of the income base for AFDC) is no longer increasing. This change in rate of growth in gross income for AFDC also induces a turning point for food stamps because AFDC benefits are included in the income base there, and further induces a turning point at the same income level in the disposable income mapping.

Although analysts typically request a table presented in terms of the model's independent variable, the SUMMARY command also has the capacity to key its tables to other definitions of income, or more generally, to the ordinates of any of the mappings in the solution. Thus, instead of being forced to look at the world through "gross earnings glasses," the analyst may define tables in terms of disposable income, taxable income, or any other income measure contained in the solution. The analyst indicates what values of the income measure are considered relevant, and MAPSIT generates a table that displays the ordinates of desired mappings corresponding to the chosen income measure values. This capability is particularly valuable in a policy environment because it allows the analyst to customize presentations to officials who may be "wedded" to specific income measures, such as the one used in the program they administer. This alternative format, termed an "indirect" capability, is also useful in comparing alternate measures of income, and is available for most of the EXAMINE commands.

Of course there are some inherent difficulties in this more indirect approach. Specifically, because the chosen income measure may not be strictly monotonic in the model's independent variable, there may be some ambiguity about what value of the independent variable corresponds to a given value for the alternate income measure. Analogously, the values of the other mappings' ordinates may also be ambiguous. MAPSIT addresses this potential difficulty by including in the table all of the independent variable values that satisfy the condition. At the opposite end of the spectrum from the potential ambiguity problem, for a variety of reasons, the alternate income measure may never achieve some of the values that the analyst has specified for it. In such instances MAPSIT appends a "footnote" to the table to indicate that the values were never reached.

Table 7.8: Benefit Levels for Three Transfers as a Function of AFDC Benefit Levels

AFDC	X	FOODSTAMPS	EITC	STATEINCTX
0.00	6820.57 TO	2078.14	397.43	167.10
	+ INFINITY	0.00	0.00	2450.00
500.00	6722.29	1952.32	409.71	164.70
1000.00	5719.18	2049.08	500.00	140.12
1500.00	4877.01	2106.26	487.70	119.49
2000.00	4140.75	2137.38	414.07	101.45
2500.00	3404.48	2168.50	340.45	83.41
3000.00	2668.22	2199.62	266.82	65.37
3500.00	1931.96	2230.74	193.20	47.33
4000.00	1195.69	2261.86	119.57	29.29
4500.00	459.43	2292.98	45.94	11.26
5000.00	> N/A <			

Table 7.8 presents an indirect table from the first example. In it the analyst has chosen to look at the ordinates of food stamps, the earned income tax credit, and state income tax as a function of AFDC benefit levels, where the AFDC benefits are specified in five hundred dollar increments. The table contains no asterisks because these values of AFDC do not happen to correspond to any of the turning points in the transfer system. Even though the table is keyed to AFDC, as indicated by the first column, the model's independent variable, gross earnings, still appears in the table, but in this case in the second column. Its necessity can be seen in this example, at the zero level of AFDC, where multiple values for earned income correspond to the single value ($0) of AFDC. More specifically in this case, the continuous domain of earnings (from $6820.57 to plus infinity) implies zero AFDC benefits. Because there is potential ambiguity about which of the values in this domain the analyst really

wants, MAPSIT includes the domain endpoints in the table, as well as the transfer program values corresponding to the endpoints of the earnings domain identified. Thus, at the point where AFDC benefits are $3000, earned income is $2668.22 and the food stamp benefit is $2199.62. Finally, the table illustrates the manner in which MAPSIT responds if the analyst includes values which the key mapping does not attain: it prints out ">N/A<" for "not attained." This is illustrated in Table 7.8 where results for AFDC benefits of $5000 were requested.

Analysis of Marginals and Averages

Although examination of mappings per se is the analyst's major focus in secondary analysis, often one will want to look at the tax rates implicit in the mappings. Especially when concentrating on the work incentives that a transfer system provides for the families subject to it, one will be quite concerned with the slope of the mappings, either at given values of the independent variable, or averaged over appropriate domains of the independent variable. Such slopes indicate how fast taxes increase as income increases, or how fast benefits decrease as income increases. More generally, since the independent variable may be something other than earnings, the slopes indicate how fast the ordinates change with respect to changes in the independent variable.

The MARGINAL command allows the analyst to ascertain, along the entire continuum of the independent variable, the slope of one or more mappings. Here MAPSIT's focus on relationships rather than variables provides considerable power. One need not have an infinite number of slopes to cover the entire domain of the independent variable. Instead, because the mappings are piecewise linear, the slope of a mapping changes only at the mapping's turning points. Between turning points, the slope of a mapping is constant, and it is this slope that corresponds to the tax rate implicit in the mapping (the true marginal tax rate). If the analyst specifies arbitrary points between which the slopes are to be calculated, then the results correspond to cumulative marginal tax rates.

If the mapping describes a tax as a function of income, then the implicit tax rate, whether true marginal or cumulative marginal, is equal to the slope of the relevant segment. If the mapping describes a benefit as a function of income or another income measure as a function of income, then the formula for the tax rate is slightly different, but is still directly related to the slope of the mapping.

Table 7.9 shows a true marginal tax table for the example in ILLUS4.[47] It differs from a SUMMARY table, such as Table 7.7, in two main respects. The first and most important difference is that the table contains tax rates rather than just ordinate values. For example, the entry .067 that appears in the FICA column between earnings levels $0.00 and $5000 reflects the 6.7% FICA tax rate over that income domain in 1984. The second difference is that the table format is staggered. Tax rate entries appear between earnings levels (row headings) rather than at them, a format that reflects the applicability of the marginal tax rates over ranges of the independent variable.[48] One other difference deserves some comment. For four mappings in the table (AFDC, food stamps, Medicaid, and disposable income), the expression "NOTCH" appears in place of a numerical tax rate value. Looking back to Table 7.7 one observes that there are effective discontinuities in those mappings at these points ($6820.50 to $6820.57 and $18,629.11 to $18,629.27) because eligibility lapses in one program or another. MAPSIT recognizes that numerical computation of a tax rate would not be meaningful here, and indicates the existence of the discontinuities with the entry "NOTCH." The notches in disposable income reflect the notches in the AFDC, food stamp, and Medicaid components of disposable income.

The interpretation of the table is simple. For AFDC benefits between the values of $0 and $5000 the tax back rate as a function of earnings is 67.91 percent. Between $5000 and $6000 the tax back rate in the AFDC benefit is 57.91 percent. The difference of ten percentage points is a consequence of the ceiling on the earned income tax credit. Looking down the column for the earned income credit (EITC), one can see that the income credit has a negative tax back rate (-10 percent) for income between $0 and $5000 indicating that the credit increases with income over the range, a zero marginal tax between $5000 and $6000, and a positive 12.5 percent tax rate

---

[47] Table 7.9 is identical to Table 5.3. It is reproduced here to facilitate the discussion of marginal tax analyses.

[48] Table 7.9 could have been printed out in an alternative format that includes both the tax rates <u>and</u> the values of the dependent variables, thus combining all of the information of Tables 7.7 and 7.9. That format is initially harder to read, but the increased difficulty is often offset by the increased ease of accessing the desired information. This feature is another example of MAPSIT flexibility.

between $6000 and $10,000, which are in accord with the design of that program. Finally, since family disposable income is the sum of the various transfers to and from the family, along with earnings, the total of the tax or tax back rates for each of the included programs equals the net marginal tax-back rate. For earned income between $0 and $5000, the tax back rates are 67.91 percent for AFDC, 4.23 percent for food stamps, -10 percent for the earned income tax credit, 6.7 percent for FICA, and 2.45 percent for the Pennsylvania State Income Tax, yielding a sum or net marginal tax rate of 71.29 percent. This rate depends on our definition of disposable income; thus, for example, it would have been rather higher had we counted child care expenses as an involuntary outflow in the calculation of disposable income.

Turning to the substance of Table 7.9, it is interesting to note that for earned income less than $6700, full-time work at the minimum wage, the net marginal tax back rate is consistently high, varying between 71 percent and 78 percent. Between $6700 and $6820 the tax-back rate briefly hits a high of 107.5 percent, before falling to a rate of 46.25 when AFDC eligibility is terminated. The largest component of this 107.5 percent net marginal tax rate is AFDC itself, 87.5 percent. The jump from 45.41 percent to 87.5 percent in AFDC is caused by the ceilings on work expenses ($75 per month) and child care expenses ($160 per child per month.) Beyond $18,629.27 all of the welfare programs (AFDC, EITC, food stamps, and Medicaid) have been exhausted, and the aggregate tax rate on disposable income reflects only the several taxes: FICA, state income tax, and net federal income tax.

When we constructed the work incentive model in Chapter 6, we included at the end of the model a special mapping, weekly disposable income as a function of hours worked per week. By using MARGINAL, one can obtain directly the effective hourly wage rate, the amount that weekly disposable income increases because of one additional hour of work per week. These results are shown in Table 7.10.

For an earner working at the minimum wage in 1980 ($3.35), the effective wage rate between zero and 5.87 hours per week was $1.63. Between 5.87 and 24.68 hours per week, the effective wage rate was $1.08, and so on. Except for the brief interval between 27.66 and 28.70 hours per week, the effective net wage is less than half of the minimum wage. Finally, for those considering overtime, it is interesting to note that the first four hours had an effective wage rate of

Table 7.9: Marginal Tax Rates for the Mappings in ILLUS4

X	AFDC	FOODSTAMPS	MEDICAID	EITC	FICA	STATEINCTX	NETFEDTAX	DISPOSABLE
0.00	0.6791	0.0423	0	-0.1000	0.0670	0.0245	0	0.7129
5000.00	0.5791	0.0723	0	0	0.0670	0.0245	0	0.7429
6000.00	0.4541	0.1098	0	0.1250	0.0670	0.0245	0	0.7804
6700.00	0.8750	-0.0165	0	0.1250	0.0670	0.0245	0	1.0750
6820.50	> NOTCH <	> NOTCH <	> NOTCH <	0.1250	0.0670	0.0245	0	> NOTCH <
6820.57	0	0.2460	0	0.1250	0.0670	0.0245	0	0.4625
9808.33	0	0.2460	0	0.1250	0.0670	0.0245	0.1200	0.5825
10000.00	0	0.2460	0	0	0.0670	0.0245	0.1200	0.4575
10500.00	0	0.2460	0	0	0.0670	0.0245	0.1400	0.4775
12700.00	0	0.2460	0	0	0.0670	0.0245	0.1700	0.5075
14780.49	0	0	0	0	0.0670	0.0245	0.1700	0.2615
15800.00	0	0	0	0	0.0670	0.0245	0.1800	0.2715
18629.11	0	> NOTCH <	0	0	0.0670	0.0245	0.1800	> NOTCH <
18629.27	0	0	0	0	0.0670	0.0245	0.1800	0.2715
19000.00	0	0	0	0	0.0670	0.0245	0.2000	0.2915
22200.00	0	0	0	0	0.0670	0.0245	0.2400	0.3315
27500.00	0	0	0	0	0.0670	0.0245	0.2800	0.3715
32800.00	0	0	0	0	0.0670	0.0245	0.3200	0.4115
37800.00	0	0	0	0	0	0.0245	0.3200	0.3445
38100.00	0	0	0	0	0	0.0245	0.3500	0.3745
40000.00								

Table 7.10: Marginal Changes in Weekly Disposable Income as a Function of Hours Worked per Week

X	WK_DISPINC
0.00	
	1.63
5.87	
	1.08
24.68	
	1.41
27.66	
	2.12
28.70	
	1.79
32.83	
	> NOTCH <
32.83	
	1.79
34.44	
	1.17
36.74	
	1.23
38.89	
	0.87
43.96	
	0.70
57.41	
	1.12
60.00	

\$.87 per hour and the next thirteen hours (between forty-four and fifty-seven hours per week) had an effective wage rate of only \$.70, roughly one-fifth of the nominal wage rate.[49] One may infer that for those working at the minimum wage, working extra hours and reporting the resulting earnings does not provide an effective escape from poverty.

Sometimes the analyst is interested not so much in the marginal tax rate at a single value, or even over a domain of the independent variable, as in an average tax rate from a given starting point or base value to selected values of the independent variable. For example, the analyst might want to use the family head's present earnings level as a starting point and then ascertain the average fractions of additional earnings that would be taxed back in the form of changes in taxes and benefits. Such an analysis effectively averages

---

[49] In this example we are assuming that the person continues to work at the same nominal hourly wage and does not receive an increased wage rate for overtime work.

out the peaks, valleys, and notches that may occur in the marginal tax rate.

Table 7.11: Average Tax Rates (Base Value is 0.00)

X	AFDC	FOODSTAMPS	MEDICAID	EITC
0.00	- - -	- - -	- - -	- - -
1000.00	0.6791	0.0423	0	-0.1000
2000.00	0.6791	0.0423	0	-0.1000
3000.00	0.6791	0.0423	0	-0.1000
4000.00	0.6791	0.0423	0	-0.1000
5000.00	0.6791	0.0423	0	-0.1000
6000.00	0.6624	0.0473	0	-0.0833
6700.00	0.6407	0.0538	0	-0.0616
7000.00	0.6874	0.0398	0.3589	-0.0536
8000.00	0.6015	0.0656	0.3140	-0.0313
9000.00	0.5347	0.0856	0.2791	-0.0139
10000.00	0.4812	0.1016	0.2512	0
15000.00	0.3208	0.1462	0.1675	0
20000.00	0.2406	0.1156	0.1256	0
25000.00	0.1925	0.0925	0.1005	0
30000.00	0.1604	0.0771	0.0837	0
40000.00	0.1203	0.0578	0.0628	0

X	FICA	STATEINCTX	NETFEDTAX	DISPOSABLE
0.00	- - -	- - -	- - -	- - -
1000.00	0.0670	0.0245	0	0.7129
2000.00	0.0670	0.0245	0	0.7129
3000.00	0.0670	0.0245	0	0.7129
4000.00	0.0670	0.0245	0	0.7129
5000.00	0.0670	0.0245	0	0.7129
6000.00	0.0670	0.0245	0	0.7179
6700.00	0.0670	0.0245	0	0.7244
7000.00	0.0670	0.0245	0	1.1240
8000.00	0.0670	0.0245	0	1.0413
9000.00	0.0670	0.0245	0	0.9770
10000.00	0.0670	0.0245	0.0023	0.9278
15000.00	0.0670	0.0245	0.0521	0.7781
20000.00	0.0670	0.0245	0.0847	0.6580
25000.00	0.0670	0.0245	0.1122	0.5892
30000.00	0.0670	0.0245	0.1369	0.5496
40000.00	0.0633	0.0245	0.1813	0.5100

Table 7.11 displays an average tax table for the model in Chapter 5. The format, reflecting the substance of the relevant calculation, differs somewhat from that of the marginal tax table.[50] The rows are

[50] Note that, because average tax rates are not generally piecewise linear functions of the independent variable, linear interpolation is not appropriate in an average tax rate table, even when the row headings are the natural system turning points.

not staggered because the average tax rate calculation applies at the specified values of the independent variable. In the example shown, the values employ a base value of zero earned income, the no work situation, meaning that the average tax value for a given earnings level is the average over the range that extends from zero earned income to the row heading's earned income. Thus, for each of its mappings, the table shows the average amount of the earner's total income which is effectively taxed back in the form of reduced benefits or increased taxes.

In the case of FICA the average tax-back rate is a constant until earnings hit the maximum contributory earnings ($38,700), while in the case of the state income tax, which is a proportional tax, the average tax and the marginal tax are identical. For AFDC and food stamps, however, the picture that is created differs for average taxes and marginal taxes. In AFDC the average tax-back rate on benefits is 67.91% for incomes below $5000, and a declining percent as income exceeds $7000. For food stamps the average reduction rate is from four to five percent on income less than full-time work at the minimum wage. On income between ten and twenty thousand per year, however, the average reduction rate is between ten and eleven percent. For both AFDC and food stamps it is clear that the use of average tax back rates "smooths" the data.

The same is also true for DISPOSABLE. In this case, however, because the initial tax levels were substantial to begin with, smoothing them gives the impression of substantial average income reduction.

Sources of Turning Points

The various output forms discussed so far point have focused largely on "what happens" in the solution. For example, they tell one where breakevens occur, what the mapping ordinates are at various abscissas, and what the implicit tax rates are. The analyst may, however, also have some "why" questions in mind. A specific example of this type of question lies in identifying the sources or causes of the several turning points in a mapping or in the solution as a whole. By understanding why each of the turning points exists, the analyst can better understand how the system is operating, and perhaps better appreciate the consequences of any proposed changes to the system.

What are the causes of turning points in a mapping and how would one go about ascertaining such causes? Consider the following ways in which turning points might occur. Moving up to a higher tax bracket would create a turning point in an income tax mapping, and subsequently any income measure that included income taxes as a component. A benefit breaking even and then continuing at a zero level could cause a turning point, certainly in the mapping with the benefit as the dependent variable, and probably in any programs or income measures that use the benefit as a precedent. Reaching the upper income level for social security (FICA) contributions could also cause a turning point in, for example, a disposable income mapping. These examples seem to convey a sense of causality in the system. More generally, if program A has a particular abscissa value as one of its turning points (and no previous program in the sequence of calculations does), and if program A is used as a precedent in the calculation of benefits from program B, leading to the same abscissa value appearing as a turning point for program B, then program A has "caused" the turning point in program B. We have used the quotation marks to indicate that our notion of causality is not as rigorous as some might desire. Nonetheless, it has proved adequate for most analytic purposes and we shall employ it here, with the quotation marks omitted in subsequent uses.

Using a SUMMARY table containing all the mappings in a solution, the analyst could make the necessary inferences to ascertain the cause of each turning point in a mapping or in the solution as a whole, although this would be time-consuming and subject to errors through failing to recall what mappings were precedents to what other mappings. Fortunately, the SOURCES command in MAPSIT automates the search. For each of the turning points, SOURCES searches the mappings in the solution to find the first mapping (first in the sense of order of creation in the model) to contain the turning point. It then declares that mapping to be the cause of the turning point. If the analyst has used good mnemonics in naming the mappings, then such an identification typically gives a good idea why the turning point occurred. The mapping so identified is termed the "source" mapping for the turning point.[51] To aid the interpretation still further, MAPSIT also provides the ordinate of the source mapping at the abscissa under consideration. The value of this ordinate frequently makes the nature of the cause apparent. A departure, a

[51] Since EXAMINE has available only the mappings included in the SAVE operations of the model, the "source" will be the true source only if the true source was included in a SAVE operation.

breakeven, a ceiling value, or a shift from one tax bracket to another might be responsible.

There are two main applications for the SOURCES analysis. In the first, the analyst uses the capability when validating a model; in particular, the command assists in ascertaining the cause of any suspicious turning points in the solution mappings. In the second application, the analyst uses it in presenting the results to the relevant audiences to answer the inevitable questions about, for example, how there came to be a turning point at $6820.50 of gross earnings.

Table 7.12: The Primary Sources of the Turning Points for ILLUS4

X	SOURCE GROUP	Y-VALUE
0.00	FICA	0.00
5000.00	EITC	500.00
6000.00	EITC	500.00
6700.00	AFDC	519.50
6820.50	AFDC	414.06
6820.57	AFDC	0.00
9808.33	NETFEDTAX	0.00
10000.00	EITC	0.00
10500.00	NETFEDTAX	83.00
12700.00	NETFEDTAX	391.00
14780.49	FOODSTAMPS	120.00
15800.00	NETFEDTAX	918.00
18629.11	FOODSTAMPS	120.00
18629.27	FOODSTAMPS	0.00
19000.00	NETFEDTAX	1494.00
22200.00	NETFEDTAX	2134.00
27500.00	NETFEDTAX	3406.00
32800.00	NETFEDTAX	4890.00
37800.00	FICA	2532.60
38100.00	NETFEDTAX	6586.00

ORDER OF CREATION

SOURCE GROUP

FICA
STATEINCTX
EITC
AFDC
FOODSTAMPS
MEDICAID
NETFEDTAX
DISPOSABLE

Table 7.12 displays a SOURCES table for the turning points of the mapping DISPOSABLE from Chapter 5. The table tells the analyst which turning points stem from which transfer programs. For example, it shows that the fourth turning point ($6700) comes from AFDC. Looking back into the model, the analyst would find that that earnings' level corresponds to the point where work expenses and child care reach their ceiling values. If the analyst had included the mappings for these elements in a SAVE operation, then SOURCES would have attributed the causes still more explicitly. In Table 7.12 the food stamp program is indicated as the primary source of a turning point at three places, $14,780.49, $18,629.11 and $18,629.27. The first is the point at which the food stamp benefit reaches $10 per month ($120 per year), and the second and third points arise from the maximum income limit for the food stamp program, as can be seen from the ordinate value which changes from $120 to $0. The earned income credit is also indicated as the primary source of a turning point at three locations: $5000, $6000, and $10,000. Examination of the ordinates, or knowledge of the operations of the earned income tax credit, immediately confirms that these are in fact points at which there is a change in the slope of the function that relates the earned income credit to earned income. At the first value the credit reaches its maximum level, at the second it begins to decline, and at the third it breaks even. The later turning points in Table 7.12 stem primarily from tax bracket changes in the income tax system, and the y-values for these turning points help the analyst ascertain precisely which brackets are relevant.

Before turning to other output forms, a cautionary note regarding SOURCES is needed. The turning point at $0 of annual earnings is attributed to FICA and not attributed, as it could be, to the cut-in, or beginning, of EITC. This occurs because in the model FICA was calculated prior to EITC. Had EITC been calculated first, it, not FICA, would have been identified as the source of the turning point at $0 earnings. The reader will no doubt realize that there are several other mappings that might also have been identified as the source of that turning point if they had been first in the sequence of mappings created: the state income tax, the day care expense mapping, the work expense mapping, and so forth. In the case of the two expense mappings, however, they would not show up even if they were first unless they were included in the SAVE operation. This illustrates the sort of caution one must exercise when interpreting tables produced from the SOURCES command. Despite this need for caution, however, the capability to generate automatically the sources of turning points is of considerable analytical value.

OTHER OUTPUT FORMS

The several commands described thus far are sufficient for many analyses. However, MAPSIT produces other output forms for various special analyses. We present a few of them here, but in less detail and without illustrative tables and plots.

Partial Effects Analysis

Another task the analyst occasionally faces is finding the partial effects of simultaneous changes to a transfer system. For example, suppose that two parameters in the income tax system, exemptions and the standard deduction, change simultaneously. Obviously the total tax payable is likely to change along all or most of the independent variable, but the analyst may be interested in ascertaining how much of the total change can be attributed to the new exemption and how much to the new standard deduction. He or she may also want to know if there is an interaction effect between the two changes. Furthermore, the analyst may wish to ascertain the individual and interaction effects of the two changes for other programs in the system, such as a welfare program that permits the deduction of income taxes paid or withheld. Clearly the number of simultaneous changes may also be greater than two. In such cases, there may be not only the primary effects and interaction effects, but it may even be desirable to subdivide the interactions into dyadic interactions, triadic interactions, and so forth.

The MAPSIT command PARTIAL automates for the analyst analyses that disentangle the primary and interactive effects of simultaneous changes to a system. It presents these effects, along with the original and resultant systems, in an understandable, standard format.

Isoquants

Most of the time an analyst will wish to look at relationships between two variables at a time in the course of secondary analysis. This thrust is the formulation for MAPSIT's concern with mappings that relate exactly two variables. Sometimes, however, the paired variable format will unduly constrain the analyst. The MAPSIT command ISOQUANTS permits the analyst to take a step in the direction of looking at three variables simultaneously. Suppose that the analyst has several mappings that are identical except that the dependent variables depend also on a parameter that varies across the mappings, such as mappings that describe a family's disposable income as a function of earnings, but with the several mappings corresponding to the family with one, two, three, four, and five children. The ISOQUANTS command allows the analyst to address a variable space consisting of earnings (continuous) and number of children (discrete), and then to characterize this space in terms of the isoquants for various levels of disposable income. More generally, given several mappings with the same independent and dependent variables, but that differ with respect to a parameter used in their derivation, the ISOQUANTS command lets the analyst determine the independent variable/parameter value combinations that produce given values for the dependent variable. The analyst receives this information in the form of one or more tables and can easily plot the information if a graphic presentation is more suitable. Note that the ISOQUANTS capability is very similar in nature to the "indirect" version of the SUMMARY command. Thus, interpretation of its results is subject to the same sorts of restrictions concerning the possible lack of monotonicity between the independent and dependent variables in the mappings.

Graphics

Although a detailed discussion of graphics capabilities is not fundamental to this book's presentation of MAPSIT, graphics capabilities play a very important role in most MAPSIT applications. In this subsection we describe the highlights of these capabilities. For the most part the capabilities are unremarkable, but sufficient for the tasks required. Indeed, their major recommendation is that they have been formally integrated into MAPSIT. The analyst need not leave the MAPSIT package to use them, receiving prompts for all of the required information in a manner consistent with the man-machine interactions throughout MAPSIT.

The analyst has a choice of plotting devices, and within each device a choice of plot sizes. For large plots, or those where appearance or accuracy is particularly important, MAPSIT offers CALCOMP plotter facilities, creating as output a file that is processed in batch mode to yield the desired plots. For situations where obtaining a plot quickly is important and the plot need not be especially large, an electrostatic plotter is available which sits next to the analyst's terminal and produces plots in a matter of minutes. It thus permits the analyst to experiment with the plot characteristics until exactly the right product is obtained. Resolution from this source is good enough that photocopies of the output have gone directly into Cabinet documents in Canada. Finally, MAPSIT can produce plots on the analyst's terminal. Although these plots are severely limited in resolution, they can provide a quick, rough feel for the appearance of plots before they are produced on either of the other plotting devices.

The PLOT command offers a fair degree of control over just what is plotted. The analyst can include multiple mappings per plot, with either the mappings themselves or the implicit tax rates being plotted. Special lines, the forty-five degree line for mappings and a 100 percent line for tax rate plots, are available. The analyst chooses whether the points on the plot are to be drawn in isolation or joined. When points are joined, the analyst can control the line color and line type (solid, dashed, fenced, for example) for each line individually, or can default to a standard sequence for each plotting device. And, of course, the analyst can control the domain of the independent variable for the plot.

Consistent with the design emphasis on documentation of methods and results, PLOT offers the user several features to encourage well documented results resistant to misinterpretation. First among these is provision for a plot title and for axis labels for both the independent and dependent variables. Lest typographical errors mar the appearance of a graph, PLOT offers opportunities to review and edit these labels. Labeling can occur either at the ends of the lines or in a legend. If a legend is chosen, the analyst can have it placed in any corner of the plot or off the plot entirely. Taken together, these features allow the analyst to produce the desired plots and to document them precisely while paying attention to issues of appearance.

CONCLUSION

These comments conclude our description of the EXAMINE module per se. Although we have devoted an entire chapter to this topic, we have only begun to explain the features available in this rather sophisticated report generator module. Indeed, in the next chapter, where we describe several MAPSIT capabilities that cut across individual modules, we shall have more to say about EXAMINE and its role in income transfer analyses.

CHAPTER 8.
OTHER MAPSIT FEATURES

The preceding chapters have provided two illustrative MAPSIT models, and described the major outputs available through MAPSIT's secondary analysis module EXAMINE. Although we have chosen the examples and the outputs to illustrate the most important and most basic MAPSIT features, the limitations inherent in using relatively self-contained examples precluded description of other important MAPSIT features. Consequently, in this chapter we outline some of these other features. As before, the description focuses on the basic nature of the features and their place in policy analysis, and does not in any sense constitute a users' guide to the features. Specific topics in this chapter include:

- building general models,
- solving models with arbitrary independent variables,
- exploiting the multiple solutions capabilities, and
- utilizing the EXAMINE subsystems.

BUILDING GENERAL MODELS

Analysts building models with MAPSIT quickly find that it is desirable to create ones that are general. As analyses proceed, analysts often find it desirable to ask questions of a model that the model was not originally designed to answer. Furthermore, many, if not most, models eventually serve as starting points for other models, since it is often easier to adapt something that already exists and is similar to what is wanted than to build a new model from scratch. Analysts and supervisors come to recognize that, despite the constant pressures for immediate results, efficient use of resources in the longer run demands attention to the development of reasonably general models. Since MAPSIT is effectively a programming language for modeling systems of transfer programs, many of the principles for developing good general models are simply those of good programming and thus are readily available in the literature on program design. Here we illustrate two of the more important principles, the use of submodels and symbolic representation, concentrating on the applicability of these specific MAPSIT features.

MAPSIT submodels are effectively equivalent to subroutines or procedures in programming languages. They allow the analyst to build models that are more general, and at the same time they contribute to modeling speed, efficiency, and accuracy. Typically, a submodel mirrors the logic of a single tax or benefit program, like food stamps. In more complicated transfer programs, a submodel may reflect a major provision, such as the calculation of the earned income tax credit within the income tax system. For Canadian applications, Health and Welfare Canada maintains a large library of submodels covering major tax and benefit programs at the federal and provincial jurisdiction levels, and even some corresponding to municipal levels. In the United States the Food and Nutrition Service of the Department of Agriculture and the School of Urban and Public Affairs at Carnegie-Mellon University have initiated similar libraries.

Submodels contribute to generality through modularity. Analysts can construct models largely from existing submodels by picking and choosing relevant programs from the library, concentrating on the linkages between programs and on the provision of parameters to the programs rather than on the logic of the transfer programs. Analysts can alter existing models by deleting linkages to submodels no longer relevant to the questions at issue and by substituting linkages to new or existing submodels appropriate for the questions. The contribution to modeling speed comes about because submodels for individual transfer programs are often developed before they are actually needed. Submodels promote efficiency because of the economies of scale possible when a submodel is used in many models. The multiple usages in turn encourage greater attention to detail and thus accuracy during submodel construction.

MAPSIT's provision of optional input and output arguments for submodels also contributes to a potential for generality. Because an analyst can specify optional inputs for a submodel, with the submodel containing default definitions for those inputs should the eventual user of the submodel choose not to supply them, a single submodel can serve both users who wish to concern themselves with only "standard" inputs, and those wishing to model families with special characteristics. For example, an income tax submodel may include taxable capital gains as an optional input. A user modeling low income families can safely ignore it, the default definition being zero, but a user wishing to model after-tax savings incentives for higher income families will have the input available. Similarly, the availability of optional output arguments means that some users can get output mappings that would not be relevant for more typical users. Taken together, the optional input and output arguments enable a single submodel to serve very different kinds of users, while the typical users are free to ignore arguments that are of interest only to a more specialized audience.

MAPSIT's design also contributes to building more general models by permitting analysts to specify parameters and other values symbolically rather than explicitly. A major component in this capacity is MAPSIT's ability to accept a mapping name as input for any argument where a number would be reasonable or expected. During the solution stage MAPSIT extracts the necessary numerical value from the argument mapping. This feature enables an analyst to avoid "hard wiring" constants and parameters into a model or submodel, particularly those used in multiple locations. For example, even if an analyst expects to execute most of the solutions of a model with exactly two children in the family, it may still be useful to create a constant valued mapping, NCHILDREN, with value 2 early in the model. The analyst can then use this mapping wherever the 2 would otherwise have appeared, perhaps as an addend in calculating the number of persons for whom personal exemptions are to be claimed. Using this method, the analyst can quickly alter the model by redefining NCHILDREN if, at a later stage, the project supervisor decides that families with three children are now of interest. More likely, the analyst will define NCHILDREN via a PROMPT operation, making the logic still more general, but at the expense of having to specify the number of children each time MAPSIT solves the model.

MAPSIT's ability to accept a mapping name in place of a numeric parameter also makes it possible for the analyst to create generalized submodels. The analyst can create a general submodel for food stamps, for example, that represents the logic of the present program but that utilizes mapping names for each of the specific parameters, such as the "standard deduction." This is done by designating such parameters as "optional inputs" and also giving them current default values. In this way the analyst wishing to model an existing transfer program, but with new parameter values, need only link to the existing submodel, passing the desired parameter values to the submodel through the input arguments.

ARBITRARY INDEPENDENT VARIABLES

Typically, an analyst constructing a MAPSIT model has a specific independent variable in mind. In most cases this independent variable is some measure of income, like annual gross earned income. However, as seen in Chapter 6, other independent variables may be relevant for some analyses. More generally, a given transfer system usually is piecewise linear in many of its variables. Thus, in principle at least, any of these could be treated as an independent variable if desired, provided that the values of the other variables were held constant.

MAPSIT provides, in a rather straightforward way, a capability, termed its "arbitrary independent variable" (AIV) capacity, that lets an analyst build models without reference to a specific independent variable. Then, at the solution stage, the analyst chooses the specific independent variable desired. The SOLVE module carries out the indicated operations, and of the "saved" mappings, those that are piecewise linear functions of the chosen independent variable appear as such in the primary solution. In turn, the EXAMINE module contains special features so that all of the tabular output contains clear labels regarding the independent variables for the argument mappings.

A few examples will illustrate the potential applications of the AIV facility. An analyst wishing to compare a system's reactions to different sources of income might solve a model of the system using different income variables as the independent variables, in order to compare the penalties for honestly reporting unearned income relative to those for earnings, for example. Seeking to ascertain the extent to which program and system reactions to the presence of children in a family cover the costs of raising those children, another analyst might fix earnings for the family and let the number of children be the independent variable. Here the derived mappings will be functions of the number of children and should probably be examined only at integer values. Still another analyst might wish to gauge the sensitivity of taxes and benefits in a system to various numerical policy parameters and values in the system. This analyst might solve the relevant model several times, each time with a different policy parameter as the independent variable. The resulting mappings would show the sensitivity of transfers for the system to changes in the program parameters. Of particular interest would be the dependency of transfers for one program on the parameters of other programs.

Indeed, such analyses would be central to any meaningful study of program coordination.

The mechanics of employing the AIV capacity are simple. The analyst constructs a MAPSIT model with every variable potentially desirable as an independent variable defined in a PROMPT or CONSTANT operation that, when executed, would ordinarily yield a constant valued mapping. At the solution stage the analyst picks one of these variables as the independent variable, and SOLVE ignores the operation defining that variable, substituting, in place of the constant valued mapping that would have resulted from the operation, a segment of the forty-five degree line (representing that variable as a function of itself). Subsequently, during the course of executing the remaining operations in the model, any mapping that is a function of the chosen independent variable will be so derived. In the course of this execution MAPSIT checks to ensure that the requested calculations employ conformable arguments (that the analyst is not asking to have two mappings, functions of different independent variables, added together, for example) and that no multivalued mapping is used where a constant valued mapping is required. This automated check helps to guarantee the mathematical integrity of the model and its solutions. In the secondary analysis stage, the EXAMINE module labels each table with the relevant independent variable. Should the argument mappings for a table differ in their independent variables, EXAMINE notes this nonconformability and labels each column as to its independent variable.

In sum then, the AIV capacity permits analysts to execute calculations conveniently that would otherwise involve extensive mechanical editing of MAPSIT models. It enables them to ascertain quickly the sensitivity of systems to the various numerical parameters that help to define the systems, and to compute a variety of incentives that systems provide for the units they affect. In this sense, the AIV capacity provides "free" generalization of models along a number of lines useful for income transfer analysis.

MULTIPLE SOLUTIONS

After building a model, an analyst typically asks MAPSIT to solve it several times using different parameter configurations. The policy relevance is obvious. By using the same logic but different parameters, the analyst can compare the differences in transfers that depend on the parameters. Thus, for example, the analyst may generate two solutions from a given model, the first with a family containing two children and the second with a family containing three children. Examination of the output mappings that describe benefits or taxes as a function of some independent variable will indicate the reaction of the individual programs, and of the system as a whole, to the presence of the additional child. Similar comparisons reveal the impacts of other parameter changes or changes in groups of parameters.

Several of MAPSIT's features were provided primarily to make such comparisons convenient. For example, the NSOLVE option permits the analyst to generate several solutions to a model sequentially, without being automatically dumped into EXAMINE at the end of each solution. It also permits the placement of the solutions into several disk files so that successive solutions do not overwrite previous results. As an added bonus, under this option the analyst need not continually reenter SOLVE for successive solutions, nor respecify the name of the model to be solved. As a second example, we have already seen in Chapter 7 the availability of the DOCUMENT command in EXAMINE. Drawing on information carried in the solution file itself, the DOCUMENT command gives an analyst the ability to document the specific prompts and responses used to generate any solution.

However, the most prominent aspect of MAPSIT's attention to multiple solution capabilities lies with the EXAMINE module's ability to "load" several solutions at once and to generate tables and graphics that draw simultaneously on information from several solutions. For example, suppose that an analyst has generated and loaded several solutions, and that these solutions contain mappings showing the disposable income of families, one mapping from each solution. The analyst may wish to print a SUMMARY table with earnings levels as the row headings and parameter configurations as the column headings, with a typical table entry being the disposable income of the column configuration at the row earnings level. Because the syntax for interpreting mapping names includes an extension to denote the solution from which a mapping is to be taken, EXAMINE permits analysts to generate tables involving multiple solutions just as they would generate tables using mappings from only a single solution. The analyst need only provide the extensions when specifying the mappings that are arguments to the table. EXAMINE provides precise, automatic labeling of results with respect to the mapping solution combinations used as inputs. This capability is universal throughout EXAMINE; thus an analyst can mix and match mappings from multiple solutions in any EXAMINE command. This facility provides major assistance to analysts executing comparative or sensitivity analyses, and it reduces both the time needed to produce tables or graphics from multiple solution sources and the possibility of transcription error.

OTHER FEATURES IN EXAMINE

Beyond its ability to generate a wide array of tables and graphics and its ability to handle multiple solutions simultaneously, the EXAMINE module provides other features conducive to the responsive production of desired results. Here we describe two of them, the subsystems that permit users to define and reuse recurring constructs in the EXAMINE commands, and the ability to record sequences of EXAMINE commands so that they can be re-executed to provide parallel output for alternative solutions. Both act to enable the analyst to "fix" either data or instructions so that subsequent steps in secondary analyses can reuse the items rather than regenerate them.

The four subsystems reflect the four "packages" of information used most regularly as arguments to EXAMINE commands. First, Titles are blocks of text, consisting of one or more 70-character lines, used as headings on the various tables to provide documentation for the results that follow. Any table the analyst requests can be prefixed by such a heading. Groups are sets of mappings to be included in the construction of multiple tables. The name of each element appears as the column heading for that mapping. Sequences are lists of scalars in ascending order. Their major use is as row headings for EXAMINE tables. Finally, the Mappings subsystem allows the analyst to create, in EXAMINE, new mappings as weighted sums of existing ones. Usually the components of these new mappings are drawn from mappings present in the solution files. Since the weights can be negative, however, the analyst can generate difference mappings as well as sums.

Each subsystem makes available a series of commands for the manipulation of that subsystem's construct. For example, the GROUPS subsystem allows the analyst to define new groups using mappings and existing groups as arguments, to display the contents of any named group, to ascertain the names of available groups, and to delete groups no longer needed. The subsystem contributes to modeling speed because, in the course of a typical analysis, an analyst will often use the same group repeatedly in several tables. Instead of making the analyst define the sequence of mappings afresh each time, EXAMINE permits the analyst to place the sequence into a named group and then simply supply the name as an argument to the several commands.

Similar capabilities are available for the other three subsystems as well, in response to similar needs. For example, certain sequences may be repeated during analysis as row headings for multiple tables. The analyst need only define such a sequence once, and can subsequently refer to it by name. For the MAPPINGS subsystem, the major benefits lie in being able to define, in the secondary analysis stage, new income definitions from available income and transfer program taxes or benefits, and in being able to construct difference mappings. The difference mapping capacity is especially valuable when the minuend and subtrahend come from different solutions, since such mappings could not have been created directly in the model itself. EXAMINE extends the utility of these constructs by enabling analysts to write them out to disk files automatically, so that they can be restored and reused in subsequent secondary analysis sessions.

Although the subsystems contribute to analytic efficiency, they do so in a rather static sense. Specifically, a construct, once defined, is fixed; its utility lies in the possibility that the analyst may wish to use that same construct over again. However, EXAMINE also offers features contributing to a more dynamic sort of efficiency in usage. One command allows the analyst to record a series of EXAMINE commands to a disk file. The substance of these commands includes almost anything the analyst might do in EXAMINE. For example, the series might create several constructs via the relevant subsystems, generate several tables using the constructs as arguments, change the output device and then output some more tables. To produce a similar set of analyses for another solution or set of solutions, the analyst, using a single command, could instruct EXAMINE to execute the commands stored in the file. Where "mass production" analyses are necessary, this capacity can significantly reduce both the completion time and the potential for inconsistency across sets of analyses. As an added bonus EXAMINE permits the analyst to turn any of the commands and arguments in the recorded series into prompts, so that any detail in the package of instructions can be varied at execution, even though the major thrust remains constant. Both the subsystems and recorded command sequences reflect the MAPSIT philosophy of automating what can be automated, while at the same time giving the analyst who needs it interactive control over the instructions and output.

The description of these EXAMINE features completes our sketch of the MAPSIT software, and thus this second part of the book. Before turning to policy application issues, we shall take the opportunity to summarize the major thrusts of the five chapters in Part 2.

First, MAPSIT is a modeling package rather than a model. It provides a powerful, relationship-oriented language for modeling transfer programs and systems. This language permits, and indeed forces, users to specify all of the substance in the models constructed. After the analyst has specified the relevant logic, MAPSIT automatically derives the numerical implications of the models, and helps to provide sophisticated presentations of the results. The philosophy is that of a decision support system. MAPSIT's design seeks to automate the mechanics of complex simulation/interpretation tasks as much as possible without imposing in matters of substance.

Second, MAPSIT's design seeks to make analysts and policy planners more efficient in what they already do, not to force them into new views of the world. The several modules address major components of the overall simulation/interpretation tasks in divisions that are natural to both analysts and their supervisors. The BUILD and EDIT modules permit the construction of sophisticated, rigorous models of program regulations, with the substance and level of detail entirely at the discretion of the analyst. The LIST module provides precise, readable versions of these models, encouraging the active involvement of persons who are not technically skilled. The SOLVE and DEBUG modules contribute to model validation and enable virtually instantaneous derivation of models' numerical implications, while simultaneously ensuring computational accuracy. The EXAMINE module enables an analyst to display these implications quickly and in a wide variety of formats designed to resist misinterpretation, thereby supporting descriptive, comparative, and sensitivity analyses. Other modules attend to various support tasks, from providing on-line documentation on MAPSIT to retrieving information about the programs and systems modeled in the MAPSIT library.

Third, MAPSIT reflects the demands inherent in a working, policy-development environment. The pervasive concern for responsiveness mirrors the demands for analyses "needed yesterday" or ones that will be worthless if not available by tomorrow. The emphasis on submodels and modularity results from the requirement to model systems that are constantly changing for a variety of reasons, from new legislation, indexing provisions, or the reform of existing programs, to requirements to perform exploratory analyses or to evaluate proposed program or system changes. The extensive validation facilities and internal consistency checks recognize the importance of correctness when making recommendations with multi-billion dollar impacts. The attention to readily interpretable output formats and readable model listings acknowledges the need to involve policy actors who are not technically oriented. And, finally, the extensive provisions for both automatic and user-supplied documentation and its display reflect the importance of knowing just what one has done before drawing conclusions from the results.

In Chapters 5 and 6 of this part we have attempted to illustrate, by means of two sample applications, the extent to which MAPSIT successfully implements the several design considerations. The reader will recognize, however, that such examples, given their constraints on size and didactic content, can convey only part of the "flavor" of using MAPSIT for real applications. In the next part of this book we begin to remedy this shortcoming by describing more extensively the spectrum of analyses in which MAPSIT has seen use, as well as the procedural and human sides of this usage.

PART III

APPLICATIONS AND ISSUES

CHAPTER 9.
ELEMENTS OF MODELING PRACTICE

This third part of the book addresses the utility of MAPSIT in policy applications. Although the conceptual foundations and software described in the first segment certainly are relevant academically, from a pragmatic point of view the test of their utility rests with policy applications, and it was from this pragmatic viewpoint that the basic framework for income transfer analysis developed. Priorities for the development of MAPSIT, and for additions and enhancements to that foundation, stemmed from policy issues at hand and from those anticipated.

The chapters within Part III approach the issue of policy application from different perspectives. This chapter focuses on the general process of addressing interrelationship problems, or on turning problems into analyses; Chapter 10 presents a broad array of problems that have been analyzed using MAPSIT; and Chapter 11 describes the role of MAPSIT from the standpoint of the analyst, employing as its focus the interactions between the "policy shop" environment and the technology.

Any modeling package operates within an environment of viewpoints, expectations, and biases. To the extent that a package is able to reflect these ways of thinking and to meet these expectations, it will be successful with respect to that environment. Otherwise, whatever its credentials, it will be ignored, misunderstood, and/or abused. Thus we shall begin by describing the environment within which MAPSIT operates and MAPSIT's position in that environment, providing the context for our subsequent discussion of applications.

In this chapter we specify the environment by describing the stages of activity associated with a typical analysis: problem recognition, problem refinement, model development, model validation, production, and final report. The early sections of the chapter address the stages of the analysis and the role of MAPSIT in these stages. Later sections of the chapter take up topics that supplement the stage by stage description of a typical analysis: the important linkages that exist between pairs of stages, the characteristics that serve to distinguish longer and ongoing analyses from the one-shot variety, and the special part that documentation plays in analysis. This chapter, then, addresses the effect of MAPSIT on the policy environment, and Chapter 11 supplements this perspective by describing the policy environment's impact on MAPSIT.

STAGES IN ANALYSES

Problem Recognition

The first step in addressing a problem is inevitably that of recognizing that the problem exists. Recognition may stem from a variety of sources, several of which we discuss here. Whatever the source, there appear to be three main conditions that collectively identify the kind of problem for which MAPSIT may be appropriate. First, the focus rests on what happens to individuals or families, or classes of individuals or families. Second, the phenomenon of interest depends not on a single transfer program taken in isolation, but rather on several transfer programs taken together as a system or on a single program sufficiently complex that it qualifies as a complex system by itself. Third, the relevant calculations are complicated by the existence and interaction of multiple definitions of income and perhaps a nonobvious sequencing among the calculations. The analyst may, for example, require one result in order to compute an input necessary for another calculation which is in turn required for what he or she really wants. These are often called "stacking problems" because the calculations for later programs depend on the calculations for other programs lower down in the stack.

One common source of stacking problems is the literature on income transfers, especially that subset that is concerned with the receipt of multiple benefits. First, the problems often involve comparisons of two families. For horizontal equity problems, the same family is examined under alternate systems of transfer programs; for vertical equity problems, two differing families are examined for the same set of transfer programs. Second, in sophisticated analyses, several programs are usually relevant, and they typically interact to produce a net effect that cannot be anticipated from the individual programs. Third, the calculations are often inconvenient because the interactions and implications, especially those involving indirect effects, are often not readily apparent, and the computation of benefits and taxes for the several transfer programs must take place in an appropriate sequence to yield correct answers. As Chapter 1 indicates, many stacking problems have been documented in the income transfer literature, although that literature often fails to provide much in the way of resolution for those problems.

The adversarial nature of some policy analyses also contributes to the identification of stacking problems. In presenting their opposing viewpoints, the two sides will often seek to generate pertinent examples of the strengths and weaknesses of the various alternatives. For reasons of simplicity, these examples often focus on individuals or families. Furthermore, these examples often involve an indirect effect, such as a certain administration for one transfer program affecting the recipients of benefits from another program. Attention to such problems is consistent with traditional political concern for what happens to families interacting with transfer programs. Since most of the systems relevant for such problems involve multiple definitions of income and require sequenced calculations, the adversaries have a difficult problem on their hands. During the course of generating a series of pro and con examples, however, a fairly good understanding may develop of how the system works and what it is doing for or to client families.

A third common source of stacking problems is the tendency of analysts and policymakers to draw heavily on work done for past policies and policy proposals. As Braybrooke and Lindblom (1963) suggest, "new" policy is frequently a modification of last month's suggestion.[52] The observation seems particularly apropos for issues involving income transfers. Indeed, incrementalism is probably responsible for many of the problems with income transfer systems today. Individual program parameters may be revised, updated, or changed without attention to the implications for the interactions of those changes with the operation of other programs, especially when those other programs stem from different levels of government. Since income transfer programs, in both explanation and administration, inevitably involve individual families, the first criterion for the existence of a MAPSIT problem is satisfied. Because the present system usually involves the interaction of multiple programs, the second criterion is satisfied. And because the present system is complicated by the multitude of relevant programs and their interactions, definitions, and parameters, calculations are complex, and the third criterion is satisfied. Although problem complexity previously may have

---

[52] Bruno Stein carries this view even further and argues that in welfare there are few proposals that have not been around for centuries (Stein, 1971, Chapter 2, especially pp. 53-54).

precluded analyzing recognized problems, with large portions of an analysis automated, an analyst may be able to sort out enough of the tangled relationships to make reasoned policy recommendations.

The source hardest to characterize is the one involving spontaneous recognition of a "new" stacking problem. This source appears most frequently in the context of an ongoing analysis. Somewhat less frequently, the problem and a recognition that it involves stacking spring up independent of any previous analysis. These cases are more difficult to characterize than the sources previously described because they require a recognition and definition of the problem itself, as well as the discovery that the problem involves stacking.

At the end of this first stage, problem recognition, the analyst has discovered that a problem exists and has further ascertained that it is probably susceptible to MAPSIT analysis: (1) the problem involves microanalysis, (analysis at the level of the individual or family), (2) it addresses a system of transfer programs, and (3) the calculations required to analyze the system are sequenced and/or complicated. The next step is to refine the problem.

Problem Refinement

Typically a problem emerges from the recognition stage in an ill-specified form. The analyst may not have decided what a satisfactory answer to the problem involves. There may be little idea of the steps needed to calculate the answer or the components of the answer. There may even be uncertainty about whether it is possible to compute an acceptable answer. In this second stage the analyst takes as input the problem as it has been recognized and proceeds to fill in these and other details. At the conclusion of this stage there is, one hopes, a well-specified problem. On this basis one must then decide whether or not to analyze it.

The substance of problem refinement is largely a matter of common sense, and the factors involved are predictable. First, and most important, is the identification of the basic questions inherent in the problem. The way in which these questions are phrased will affect the entire remaining analysis. Next, the analyst must determine which particular relationships, tables, ratios, or plots are needed to answer the basic questions satisfactorily and what transfer programs are involved in the problem. The analyst must decide upon an appropriate level of generality for the model, avoiding the extremes of making it so specific that it is costly to build and limited in applicability and of making it so abstract that it is not useful for the problem at hand. The analyst must decide which parameters are to remain fixed across multiple solutions of the model and which ones will be allowed to vary from solution to solution. And of course, the analyst must decide whether it is reasonable to attempt to build a model that satisfies these specifications. At times, especially for complicated problems, this determination must rest more on judgment than on demonstrated feasibility.

Many of the items just mentioned may be "supplied" by the source of the problem. The literature or previous analyses may have identified the basic questions and the independent variable for the analysis. Furthermore, an appropriate format for answers may be obvious on the basis of past analyses or the necessity for comparability with the format of an "adversary" analysis. Similarly, the problem source may dictate the relevant transfer programs or program systems, possibly in abstract, if not in detail. Issues involving model generality and the identification of parameters to vary across model solutions are more likely to require judgments on the part of the analyst. However, even here concrete examples from past analyses may be available and thus constitute a conspicuous direction for development. And, of course, drawing on past analyses as a problem source provides a strong indication as to whether the analysis is feasible.

At the end of the problem refinement stage, after the basic structure of the problem is apparent, someone must make a decision about whether to proceed with an attempt to solve the problem. In some cases the analyst will have the authority to make this decision. Often the decision will be made at a higher level, and the analyst will receive that decision. In these latter cases the analyst is still likely to contribute to the decision, since the decision process is likely to employ the analyst's definition of the problem, estimates of the feasibility of solution, and estimates of the costs involved.

Many times it is a foregone conclusion that some analysis will occur. The real decision involves the level of investment in the problem area. Once again, while not making the actual decision, the analyst supplies major inputs in problem formulation and the feasibility and cost estimates. The "go/no-go" component of the refinement stage is an important one. High quality analysis is typically in short supply because it is expensive. Thus, it is desirable to choose carefully those problems that will receive further attention.

Often there is a tendency to shortchange this problem refinement stage of analysis and to move on to the actual modeling too quickly. One reason for this tendency is the unclear boundary between the two stages -- determination of the feasibility of problem solution inevitably shades into the actual model construction. Another reason is that many analysts enjoy modeling, since it allows the analyst to be creative, but within a structured environment. A third reason for the tendency is time pressure, since analyses are typically needed yesterday. Consequently there is a push to make do with the first acceptable formulation. Having discovered a few basic questions or identified a few desirable tables and relationships, the analyst ceases to search for others. This push is especially strong when the source of the problem is by analogy to past analyses. Proposing to do largely what was done before offers a ready-made, defensible "passage" through this stage. Our experience suggests that a little extra effort in this stage can save time overall by reducing the amount of backtracking and revision required later. A subsequent portion of this chapter takes up in greater detail various aspects of such backtracking behavior.

At the end of the problem refinement stage, then, the problem at hand is relatively well-defined. The analyst understands the basic questions involved and appreciates the output forms desirable for addressing these questions. The analyst knows the relevant transfer programs for the problem and the combinations in which these programs occur. The analyst has decided issues of model generality and which parameters are to be varied in alternate solutions of the model. On the basis of these specifications, the analyst and/or supervisors decide whether the analysis is to proceed.

Model Development

If analysis is to proceed, the third step in addressing a stacking problem is planning an appropriate model. This planning is a bit like providing a constructive proof for a theorem. The "givens" are the information available to the analyst in the library of schedules, programs, and models, plus the analyst's understanding of the logic of the relevant transfer programs and systems. The goal is the set of desired relationships specified in the problem refinement stage of analysis. The analyst's task is to construct a legal sequence of MAPSIT operations that will produce mappings directly or indirectly relevant to the desired relationships, while obeying whatever constraints the software imposes on the operations available and the arguments available within the operations. Subsequently, in other stages of the analysis, the analyst will solve the model and manipulate the resulting mappings, using the EXAMINE module to produce specific tables and plots.

At times the planning exercise is similar to backward induction. The analyst examines one of the desired goal relationships and realizes that it could be constructed using an available MAPSIT operation if certain arguments were available. For example, suppose the analyst wishes to determine a mapping that represents disposable income as a function of earned income. The analyst recognizes that if all of the components of disposable income were available, each expressed as a function of earned income, the ADD operation could be used to sum them and the result would be the desired disposable income mapping. In this example the analyst has pushed the task back a step by specifying subgoals relevant to the original goal. The determination of each of the component mappings is now one subgoal.

By working backward from the subgoals, the analyst can break the problem down into even smaller steps. To continue the example, suppose the analyst wishes to derive the mapping that represents income taxes as a function of earned income. This mapping is required because it is one of the component mappings for the disposable income mapping. The analyst considers two potentially useful mappings: (1) taxes as a function of taxable income and (2) taxable income as a function of earned income. With these two mappings as arguments the analyst could use the "mapping of a mapping" operation to achieve the subgoal mapping representing taxes as a function of earned income. Thus, these two mappings can be considered sub-subgoals. And, of course, the process can extend further back. In attempting to specify taxable income as a function of earned income, the analyst will typically require relationships and parameters involving components of taxable income, deductions, and personal exemptions. Eventually the analyst gets to the stage where the parameters and relationships required as sub-sub-...-subgoals are things that can be specified directly or fetched from the library.

By repeatedly applying this type of logic, the analyst may gradually discover the whole set of mappings relevant to the problem, and the MAPSIT operations necessary to produce them. The resulting version of the model resembles a tree. The trunk is the original goal, and each subgoal is a main branch of this trunk. In turn, sub-subgoals are secondary branches on the main branches, and so on.

The terminal nodes, or "leaves" on the tree, are the parameters and relationships that the analyst knows or can fetch from the library.

Once the tree is specified, the major part of the planning is complete, and the analyst only needs to convert the tree representation of the model into the "linear" sequence of operations that MAPSIT demands. This process is relatively straightforward. The analyst specifies as the first operations in the model those with only the "leaves" or terminal nodes as arguments (the order in which they are specified is arbitrary and irrelevant). The analyst knows what operations are necessary to combine these arguments properly, because that determination was the basis for developing the tree. Once these operations are specified one has worked forward from the lowest level goals to the next-to-lowest and can then treat these goal mappings as leaves, repeating the same procedure. Level by level the analyst works through the tree until finally the operation and arguments necessary to create the original goal mapping have been specified. At each level the appropriate operations and arguments to the model are added after the operations which have already been determined. When the original goal mapping is reached, the analyst adds its operation and arguments to the model and the planning and modeling stage of the analysis is complete.

Fortunately, the complicated, if logical, method just described is not the only way to plan a model. Usually the analyst can plan the model in its natural front to back sequence without resorting to the backward induction tree representation. In these cases, an appropriate sequence of transfer programs, one that defines the transfers from each program before they are needed in the calculations for any other program, may be obvious to the analyst from the start. When such is the case, the analyst can begin by specifying a set of operations to define the first transfer program in the sequence, then specify appropriate operations for the second program, and so on, until all the relevant transfer programs have been defined. When the analyst reaches the end of the sequence, he or she typically enters a few additional operations to group similar mappings together, construct appropriate difference or comparison mappings, and perform other such "cleanup" tasks. When the model is solved, these operations will serve to create the desired goal mappings. With a bit of experience, appropriate orderings of programs, orderings of operations within programs, and desirable "cleanup" mappings become second nature.

In practice the analyst tends to apply both the forward and backward methods for planning the model. The nature of the modeling task tends to reinforce this mixture. Often the early portions of different models are quite similar, and represent relatively fixed programs such as income taxes and social insurance contributions. The similarities among models permit the analyst to become familiar with relatively permanent "forward looking" sequences common to the models. In contrast, the final portions of different models tend to reflect the specific purposes of the models and the specific final mappings desired. Although similarities do exist among the final portions of models, they tend to be at a more abstract level. Thus, the end portions of models frequently require a greater use of backward induction planning than beginnings. The middle portions of models often contain the bulk of any "new" material, such as proposed new programs or modifications of existing programs. Here, the analyst uses a mixture of forward and backward planning to fill in the connections between the more structured beginning and end of the model.

Much of the "art" of modeling becomes apparent in making the connections in the middle of a model. The substance of the relevant calculations is probably the least clear to the analyst, because it involves most of the new material. There may exist several different ways to make the connections, some of which may be better than others. The analyst has to be concerned not only with the correctness of the computations, but also with their understandability, especially when less skilled persons will be reading or using the model. The creative, experienced analyst will discover efficient, understandable connections between the two ends of the model that others might not. In some ways this type of modeling is similar to solving differential equations or evaluating integrals. The analyst gradually develops a feel for what to do, though he or she may have difficulty explaining the appropriate actions and decisions to someone else.

Similarities among models simplify the actual modeling. Few programs are entirely new. Even when they are, the analyst probably receives their description couched in terms of analogies with existing programs. Typically, most transfer programs in a model already exist in a comparable level of detail in the library facility of other models. Provision for incorporating schedules, programs, and portions of other models permits the analyst to concentrate attention on those aspects of the problem that are new.

At the end of the planning stage the analyst has detailed, on paper, a MAPSIT model that consists of an appropriate sequence of MAPSIT operations. The sequence is ordered such that, before any mapping is used as an argument in an operation, it is defined in its own operation. Within each operation the analyst has specified all the relevant arguments and parameters. In short, during this stage the analyst has converted the problem statement of the refinement stage into a set of detailed plans for a MAPSIT model. This product is essentially a set of instructions which, when subsequently executed, will yield a desired set of relationships addressing the original problem.

Model Entry

The fourth step in addressing a stacking problem is entering the model. The analyst takes the paper version of the model as input and enters its contents into an appropriately formatted disk file. The model building module assists the analyst by prompting him or her for the necessary operations and for all the arguments within each operation. The disk version of the model that results is then acceptable as input into the LIST, CREF, SOLVE, and DEBUG modules. It is also suitable as input back into the EDIT module for revision, or as a starting point for another model.

The actual entry procedure is fairly simple. Since Chapter 5 illustrates it well, we limit ourselves here to a brief, general overview. When the analyst first enters the BUILD module, it prompts him or her for a textual description of the model. Now the analyst enters the main loop that serves to enter the remainder of the model. The module prompts for the appropriate keyword for the next operation. The analyst responds by entering the keyword for the operation to be entered next. Examples of such keywords include ADD, WEIGHT, SHIFT, SCALE, and COMMENT. After BUILD accepts the keyword response and checks it for legitimacy, it prompts the analyst for the arguments to the operation, one argument at a time. Sample arguments include the name of a mapping to be created in the operation, a description of that mapping, mappings required as inputs for the computations, and parameters required for the computations. Because BUILD prompts the analyst for these arguments, it helps to ensure that the analyst does not accidentally forget to enter one or more arguments to the operation. When the analyst has entered all the arguments for the operation, BUILD prompts for the keyword for the next operation. The process proceeds in this manner until the analyst has entered all the operations of the model and has indicated which of the many mappings that have been specified are to be transferred to the EXAMINE module when the model is solved.

During the course of entering the model, the analyst will probably make some errors. The MAPSIT package is designed to minimize the effort involved in discovering and correcting these errors. As would be expected, when the analyst notices an error before completing a response, MAPSIT lets the analyst backspace over the error and enter the correct response. But more importantly, BUILD and EDIT can diagnose some errors on-line and allow the analyst to correct individual arguments. Examples include mapping names or other text strings that are too long and argument mappings that have not yet been defined. When the analyst is using BUILD or EDIT to access elements of the library, he or she may accidentally enter a nonexistent file name. If this happens the module will point out that the file does not exist and permit reentry of the file name without disrupting the flow of model entry. In these and a number of other respects, the model building modules facilitate model entry by permitting graceful recovery from inevitable typing and substantive errors.

At the end of the model entry stage the analyst has created a disk file version of the model. By using the BUILD module to enter this model, one can ensure that the model contains only operations that MAPSIT recognizes. One can also ensure that all necessary arguments are complete in each operation. Because BUILD takes care of all the formatting requirements, the model will exist in a standardized format appropriate for the other relevant MAPSIT modules.

Model Validation

The fifth step, and most important, is validating the model. The model as entered in the preceding step quite possibly contains a variety of substantive errors that the BUILD and EDIT modules cannot, in principle, detect. The analyst may have mistyped numerical parameters in the model, may have omitted certain arguments in operations for which the number of arguments is variable, may have accidentally entered one legal mapping name where another was meant, or may have omitted crucial operations from the model, like neglecting to impose appropriate ceilings on certain deductions. If numerical results from the model are to be useful in policy applications, the analyst must identify and correct as many of these errors as is feasible. The validation stage of analysis represents a semiformalized mechanism for executing this task.

The validation process involves three phases, carried out in sequence. In the first of these the analyst examines a listing of the model. Because of the readable fashion in which MAPSIT lists models, many of the errors will be readily apparent. In the second phase of validation the analyst uses the SOLVE or DEBUG modules of MAPSIT to attempt to solve the model. Errors that are not apparent during examination of the model may trigger an error condition during the execution of the model; the resulting error messages indicate the nature of the error. The third phase takes place after the model has been sufficiently debugged so that MAPSIT can solve it. This last phase requires careful attention to the solution of the model to ensure that all of the mappings in the solution are correct as far as known. The succeeding discussion takes up each of the three phases in greater detail.

In phase one of validation, the analyst examines the model as it was entered. This is easily done by using the LIST module to produce a complete listing. The model listing displays all the operations and arguments in a format made readable by the addition of appropriate annotative text. The resulting sentences distinguish between the arguments of the model and the supporting explanatory text. Chapter 6 provides examples of these sentences, including the most frequently used MAPSIT operations. Because the sentences clearly indicate the sense of each operation, the analyst finds it relatively easy to identify many of the errors that may have been made. For example, reversed arguments, missing arguments, or inappropriate arguments are likely to stand out. Seeing the scalar parameters for the model printed out, the analyst is likely to notice typographical errors. Seeing the entire logic of the model presented in a consistent format, the analyst is likely to recognize omissions in the model. Furthermore, because the listing appears in such a readable format, the analyst can enlist the aid of others who, while familiar with the substance of the problem, need not be especially adept at using MAPSIT. The analyst may also find the cross-reference output from the CREF module useful in the first phase of validation.

The second phase of the validation stage is automated and requires little effort on the part of the analyst. After the first phase is complete, the analyst uses the SOLVE module to try to execute the instructions in the model. To borrow an analogy from computer science, the analyst is essentially trying to "compile" and "run" the model. The SOLVE module is designed to recognize a variety of conditions that might make the model insoluble and to print out clearly worded error messages that indicate the nature of the difficulty. For example, one of the operations in MAPSIT requires the calculation of the lowest abscissa value of a mapping such that the corresponding ordinate attains a specified value. If the analyst creates an otherwise perfectly acceptable model in which the relevant mapping never attains the specified value, the SOLVE module will print an appropriate error message and suspend calculations. Following the suspension, MAPSIT provides the user with access to "inspection" commands that permit summary presentations from the partial solution up to the point of the error.

The third phase, verifying sample results, completes the validation process. In this phase the analyst examines the solutions produced by one or more runs of the model and checks the correctness of sample points from mappings in the solution.[53] The basic purpose of this phase is elimination of nonapparent substantive errors. However, although the SOLVE or DEBUG module may be correctly solving the model as given, this does not mean that the analyst has correctly modeled the relevant situation. For a meaningful validation, the analyst checks to make sure that the results are reasonable. He or she does so by verifying that the mappings produced behave correctly in terms of general upward or downward slope, that they either have or do not have appropriate flat spots or notches, and that, when appropriate, they reach and hold relevant upper and lower limits. Beyond this examination of general tendencies, the analyst also checks the abscissa and ordinate values of selected segment endpoints for numerical accuracy.

The analyst begins the third phase by having the DEBUG or EXAMINE module produce summary tables containing all or most of the mappings in the model. The column headings in this table are the mapping names, appearing in the order in which the mappings are computed in the model. The row headings are the natural turning points for the income transfer system; they are the union, across the mappings in the table, of the abscissa values of the mappings' segment endpoints. Each table entry is the column mapping's ordinate at the row abscissa. The analyst works through the mappings in the table in order, checking a sample of the column entries of each mapping for correctness. Typically, the analyst concentrates on the ordinate for an abscissa of zero, checks the abscissas at which taxes begin or benefits begin to be reduced, examines breakevens, and chooses a few other points "at random." Some ordinates are more easily checked than others, and often the analyst will "oversample" these to increase the number of points verified. If all the checked points appear correct,

---

[53] These checks can be made using tables produced in EXAMINE from the model solution or from tables produced during the solution by the DEBUG module.

the analyst labels the mapping tentatively correct and goes on to the next mapping in the sequence. Once a mapping has tentatively been labeled correct, all the entries in that mapping are treated as correct for purposes of checking subsequent mappings. To do otherwise would essentially require redoing everything by hand, typically an infeasible undertaking. Gradually the analyst works through the whole set of mappings produced. Of course, when an incorrect result occurs, the analyst finds its cause in the model, fixes it, and reruns the model. The analyst then resumes checking at the point where the correction has been made, after verifying that the error correction does not necessitate revalidation of prior mappings.

An error discovered in any phase of validation must be corrected. The EDIT module provides a number of capabilities useful in accomplishing this task: the DELETE facility can be used to remove an unnecessary or unwanted operation, the INSERT facility can be used to add "missing" operations to the model, and the REPLACE facility can be used simultaneously to delete an incorrect version of an operation and to insert a correct one. Whenever the analyst is inserting or replacing material, he or she has access to the same defaults, error checking, and prompting as in the BUILD module. Additional editing commands are also available to type any part of the model, to help the analyst understand various prompts, or to write a version of the model onto disk. When the editing is complete, the analyst may wish to renumber the operations in the revised model and/or get an updated listing that reflects the revisions.

At the end of the model validation stage the analyst has, one hopes, eliminated all of the errors from the disk file version of the model. The situation is akin to that of a programmer debugging a computer program or someone trying to validate a simulation model. One learns, eventually, not to guarantee that something is bug free, but to assert only that aggressive error-checking has taken place. The distinction is particularly important insofar as it affects the analyst's attitude in proceeding to subsequent stages of the analysis.

Solution

The sixth step in a stacking analysis consists of generating solutions to the model. For the special case in which the analyst wants a solution for only a single parameter configuration, this phase is complete at the end of phase three of the validation steps, in which the analyst has a solution and has checked it thoroughly for errors.

In a typical analysis, however, the analyst wants to solve the model under multiple parameter configurations, producing a separate solution for each configuration. To permit convenient specification of the parameters, the analyst typically builds the necessary prompts into the model to eliminate the necessity of using the EDIT module to change portions of the model from one configuration to another.

In contrast to the extensive analyst/MAPSIT interaction during the model building and validation stage of analysis, the solution generation stage is trivially simple. The analyst simply tells MAPSIT to solve a model and supplies the name of the relevant model disk file. The SOLVE module immediately begins to execute the operations in the model. Usually some of these operations prompt the user for numeric values for various parameters. The analyst responds to these prompts, and the execution continues. Everything else is done for the analyst, right down to naming the output files so that previous results are not overwritten and all configurations are readily identifiable. For typical models the whole solution process, including the analyst's responses to the various prompts, may take less than two minutes elapsed time. The cost is often less than $20, even at prime time interactive rates.

Because the solution or production stage is so simple, the analyst can delegate the task to others. Knowledge of how to log on to the computer and five minutes of instruction are all that are required. The person solving the model needs to know only the proper sequence of responses for the parameter prompts for the first run, the second run, and so on. This simplicity and "delegatability" stands in stark contrast to hand calculations or models built without the benefit of a modeling package. In those cases, solution typically requires hours, days, or even weeks of calculation and a detailed knowledge of the model, including a variety of special flags, codes, and so forth. With MAPSIT the task is sufficiently simple to be delegated, but also so simple that it is often more convenient for the analyst to do it than to delegate it.

At the end of the production stage, the analyst has several "primary" solutions to the model, one for each parameter configuration. Each solution consists of a set of mappings calculated from the instructions in the model, and information about the model documentation and the parameter configuration used to produce the solution. In the form produced by the SOLVE module these solutions are seldom directly useful to the analyst. However, all the basic information is there, and needs only to be reformatted and/or recombined to the analyst's specifications.

Secondary Analysis

The seventh step in addressing a problem is secondary analysis. During the course of this stage the analyst uses the information contained in the primary solutions of the model to address the basic questions that motivated the entire analysis. To some extent the stage consists of two separate but related phases. In one of them the analyst uses the EXAMINE module in MAPSIT to convert the primary solutions into the particular tables and plots most relevant to the problem. In the other, the analyst uses the plots and tables to ascertain the answers to the basic questions.

The mechanics of the first phase are straightforward. The analyst decides what tables, plots, and documentation are needed and instructs the EXAMINE module to produce them from the primary solution. EXAMINE offers a wide variety of alternative presentational formats. Chapter 7 describes several of them in some detail. The important characteristic of this stage of analysis is that the analyst can generate the specific items that are desired and can do so quickly, accurately, and cheaply. If parallel tables are required for multiple solutions, MAPSIT even allows the analyst to record the instructions for their generation and then execute the instructions repeatedly and automatically for the different solutions. These capabilities allow the analyst to concentrate on the substance of the problem rather than wasting energy on technical, computational details.

Despite the importance and convenience of the presentational manipulation, the crucial portion of the secondary analysis stage is thinking about what the results mean. Useful as they may be, typically no one table or set of tables tells the whole story. Instead, the analyst spends most of his or her time on the interpretation of the various outputs. Especially when time is tight, there is a certain pressure to minimize the effort spent on this phase. Such pressure is reinforced because interpretation is largely an unstructured activity and produces little measurable output.

During the course of interpreting the various results, the analyst regularly observes an item that is not readily explicable. Unless the item falls totally outside the immediate problem, the analyst wants to discover the course of the anomaly. Such a situation highlights a major advantage of the primary solution -- the analyst can use the EXAMINE module to generate new or more detailed tables and plots to help track down the cause of the unexpected result. Furthermore, this can be done without having to re-solve the model. A typical analysis sees the analyst shuttling back and forth between the two phases of secondary analysis, generating results, interpreting them, generating new results suggested by the interpretation, and so on until the cause of the original anomaly is discovered.

The nature of the secondary analysis task affects the choice of personnel to execute it. The purely mechanical aspects can often be delegated to someone other than the analyst. The commands required to use the EXAMINE module are so simple that the most commonly used commands can be understood with only a few minutes instruction. Like the solution of a model, this aspect of analysis requires little understanding of the MAPSIT package as a whole, or of the particular model producing the results. The interpretation phase, however, generally requires the participation of the analyst, especially when it takes the form of the backtracking previously described.

The product or output from the secondary analysis phase thus consists of hard copy in the form of various pieces of documentation, tables, and plots, plus, most importantly, an understanding of what is happening in the model. MAPSIT provides the analyst with a great deal of flexibility in the specification of the hard copy portion. Many of the outputs appear in a form suitable for insertion into final reports. This feature saves time in producing an analysis, and it reduces the potential for transcription errors in the finished product. Most importantly however, the ability to interact with the solution allows the analyst to gain, rapidly and conveniently, an understanding of what is going on. It allows the analyst to appreciate how the modeled system functions with respect to the basic problem under consideration.

Report Generation

The eighth and final step in the analysis is writing up the results. The analyst puts the understanding gained during the course of the secondary analysis into a form that can be easily understood by others. This may require several different documents. Often, especially if the analysis is being performed on a consulting basis for another party, the output will consist of the desired tables and plots supplemented by a verbal or written summary of the model parameters and assumptions. Indeed, in such a case the requesting party has probably had extensive consultations with the MAPSIT analyst during the problem definition and refinement stages, and may even have supplied a number of table mockups as indications of the desired product. Another common form consists of multi-page report on the problem and its resolution. Often this main report will be supplemented by, or even replaced by, a short executive summary of the same material. At times, especially if the problem is important, the analyst will produce "archival" materials. These consist of materials not appropriate for inclusion in the main report, but likely to be useful if someone has to address the problem area again. Other aspects of the final stage include formalizing what has been learned in the course of the analysis and distribution of the results.

When a separate final report is appropriate, its substance is largely determined by the results from the secondary analysis. For the most part, the format for the report is standard. An introductory section describes the nature of the problem and provides appropriate references to the literature, or to past analyses. A second "procedure" section describes the basic approach taken to solve the problem. The third section provides a summary description of the model employed. The fourth and fifth sections describe the basic results of the analysis and provide summary and concluding material. In practice, the boundary between the write-up and secondary analysis stages is sometimes unclear. While trying to express the results clearly, the analyst often recognizes the need for additional items, or even recognizes problems with the model itself.

Depending on the type of report desired, several items produced by MAPSIT during the several stages of analysis may be included. The results portion of the report may of course contain appropriate tables or plots to communicate specific findings, and the analyst may wish to use material extracted from these items. Other items may be included in appendices. Listings of the model itself often provide readable documentation of the assumptions made in the analysis. Still other items may be useful in the archival material. Detailed listings of the model and more extensive tables are candidates for this level of reporting.

When time permits, formalization of what has been learned from the analysis is a useful component of the write-up stage. When such lessons address the substance of the problem, they are included in the final report. Often, however, important lessons may not be appropriate for a final report. The analyst may have discovered new methods of modeling particular programs or aspects of programs, may have recognized previously unnoticed analogies between programs or systems, or may have discovered new forms of output that are desirable, or novel uses for existing forms. When such findings are not formalized, they may well be forgotten; the analyst or other analysts may be forced to rediscover them in future efforts.

In a similar vein, because important problems are addressed repeatedly, the analyst may wish to put the model in "mothballs" at the conclusion of the analysis so that future analyses can take full advantage of the effort put into the present model and analysis. When this is done the analyst should double-check the model description and the comments contained in the model to ensure that they will be understandable at a later date. The disk version of the model may be relegated to magnetic tape with appropriate labels and references provided for it. If the substance of the model is sufficiently important and also not restricted, the analyst may add it to the library of models available to the public, together with specific programs or schedules from the model.

At the end of this stage the analysis is complete. The analyst has recognized and defined the problem, has constructed a model for the situation of interest, has entered this model in the standard MAPSIT format and validated it, has solved the model for all the parameter configurations of immediate interest, and has converted the solutions into the particular plots and tables desired. Finally, the analyst has written up the results and taken steps to ensure that future analyses can take full advantage of the work put into this project.

LINKAGES AMONG THE STAGES

For expositional convenience the preceding discussion treats the stages in analysis as if they were strictly sequential. However, in normal analytic practice, things do not happen this way. Often the process involves several loops among the various stages. The analyst may jump backwards one or more stages to fix some error that has been discovered. This section identifies linkages among the stages, describes typical causes of such backtracking, and indicates the effects on the flow of the analysis. Although there are linkages between almost every pair of stages, the discussion concentrates on the most common ones.

The most common linkage occurs between stages two and three, problem refinement and model planning. While trying to plan the model, the analyst recognizes that the goals developed during the problem refinement stage may not be sufficiently precise to guide the model building adequately. Perhaps several possible mappings may be relevant to the basic questions, and the analyst must choose among them. If the analyst recognizes that unconsidered variables, for example, family structure, affect the numerical solution, he or she must decide whether to incorporate those effects explicitly into the model or to ignore them. If the logic of component programs is not obvious, or the appropriate level of detail is not apparent, the analyst must determine the effect of alternate resolutions on the caliber of the analysis, or, if less ambitious, revise goals.

Another common linkage exists between the modeling and model entry stages. Compared to planning a model on paper, things often look different when one is sitting in front of a terminal and answering prompts while interacting with the software. For example, while the analyst is planning the model, he or she may forget about the existence of some of the arguments in certain operations and may fail to notice that certain library inputs to the model are not entirely suitable. At the terminal, however, the analyst faces a prompt to which a response must be supplied. The analyst can either guess at a response that may work, or abort the operation and go back to it after additional thought. Whichever approach is taken, there is some tendency for these missing items to occur in the murkier parts of the model. Often the analyst thinks that he or she has coped with the ambiguity by ignoring or suppressing it, only to discover later that the omission drives one back to the modeling stage of the analysis. Such an outcome is not always undesirable, since, having completed most of the modeling, the analyst has often attained a relatively good understanding of where the model is going. Relative to the level of understanding in the middle of the modeling stage, the analyst may be in a much better position to fill in the missing information.

Often during validation, there is a change in understanding of the model's purpose, forcing one back to the problem refinement stage. Seeing the model logic all together in a listing may trigger a better understanding of the system under consideration and the relationships among the pieces. The analyst may thus come to appreciate better the questions that should be asked. Seeing preliminary results and trying to interpret them in the course of checking them for reasonableness may spark a better comprehension of what is really wanted. On the basis of this new appreciation, the analyst may go back and redefine the underlying questions. In this linkage, the first one not involving adjacent stages in the sequence, the analyst has to redo the intervening stages. Before reaching the validation stage again, the analyst must modify the model and enter the changes into the disk version of the model.

Sometimes, from the validation stage, the analyst may not actually redefine his or her problem, but will still be forced back to an earlier stage, usually the modeling stage. While examining the model listing, the analyst may discover that the model includes typographical errors, or wrong or outdated constraints. The analyst may have omitted pieces of the model during data entry. After having corrected all such "obvious" errors, the analyst may notice from the listing or an attempted solution that the model is not doing what is wanted. That is, the instructions in the model may be illegal, or not substantively correct. However, the most common transition between the validation and modeling stages occurs when the analyst examines the results of test solutions and finds them incorrect. Breakevens may be too high or low, mappings may be unexpectedly constant-valued, or mapping ordinates may be unexpectedly negative or too large. Whatever the nature of the error, the analyst must ascertain the operations responsible for the anomalous results. The fault may lie with an operation creating an incorrect mapping, or with the operations that created the mappings that are the arguments to the mapping under consideration. The analyst must decide what is wrong with the model and how to fix it. Often the cause is an unnoticed ambiguity in logic not apparent during the construction and entry stages of the analysis. The analyst resolves the ambiguity, enters the correction into the disk file, and revalidates the modified model.

Similar anomalies often occur at the secondary analysis stage during the interpretation. The analyst will observe results that are clearly or possibly incorrect. The nature of these results may lead to the discovery of errors in the model. Such errors may have slipped through the validation stage because of inappropriate test cases, the analyst's casualness, or time pressures for completing the validation. The analyst must, of course, ascertain the cause of the results and, if time permits and the importance of the results demands, correct the model. Subsequently the analyst must revalidate the model, re-solve it, and begin again the secondary analysis stage. The likelihood of discovering errors at this stage is one reason to avoid delegating this stage to someone who does not understand the nature of the model being used.

Sometimes the secondary analysis may identify more fundamental issues. Specifically, discoveries during secondary analysis may involve the problem recognition and problem refinement stages at the beginning of the analytic sequence. The second of these sources is easier to deal with. An attempt to interpret results from a model may inspire a better recognition of what the analyst really wants to know, and sometimes may cast a much different light on the nature of the "real" problems. The analyst may revise the model to reflect the new understanding, revalidate it, re-solve it, and interpret the new results. In the more difficult case the analyst may discover, in the course of secondary analysis, that there are other, hitherto undiscovered, issues involved. In fact, thinking about the meaning of analyses seems to be one of the more fruitful sources of new problems. If time permits, the consequence of such discoveries may be extensive revisions of existing models, or the construction of new models to focus on the new issues.

In the final stage, report generation, the discipline imposed in communicating the results may send the analyst back to almost any of the preceding stages. Deliberations may lead to the discovery of new problems, in effect going back to the problem recognition stage. Difficulties in communicating the results may suggest new mappings or formats. Being forced to explain unexpected results may point to inappropriate assumptions or incorrect logic in the model. Or again, the analyst may elect to solve the model for additional parameter configurations to ensure that the conclusions are better founded. Most commonly, however, pressure to communicate the results effectively may lead the analyst to generate a variety of alternative secondary analyses and to interpret them more clearly in the context of the specific problem area.

In sum, a typical analysis does not involve "linear" progression from one analytic stage to the next, but rather a movement back and forth from one stage to another.

Figure 9.1 illustrates some of the more important of these linkages. The several linkages have in common that the nature of the "senior" portion permits a more reasoned evaluation of the success of the "junior" portion. These evaluations are often sufficient to identify errors made earlier in the analysis. For example, the analyst may not have defined the problem well, may have failed to resolve certain ambiguities in the model, may have been careless during the model entry, or may have been hasty in validating the model or interpreting the numerical results.

When the analyst makes the relevant corrections for these errors, they involve numerous loops and iterations through the various stages of the analysis. Although one would hope that careful attention to each stage would eliminate the necessity for such looping, such a hope appears unrealistic. The nature of the policy process often precludes the time even to attempt an error-free analysis. The involved nature of the questions and systems addressed seems to preclude the possibility of thinking of everything in advance. Rather,

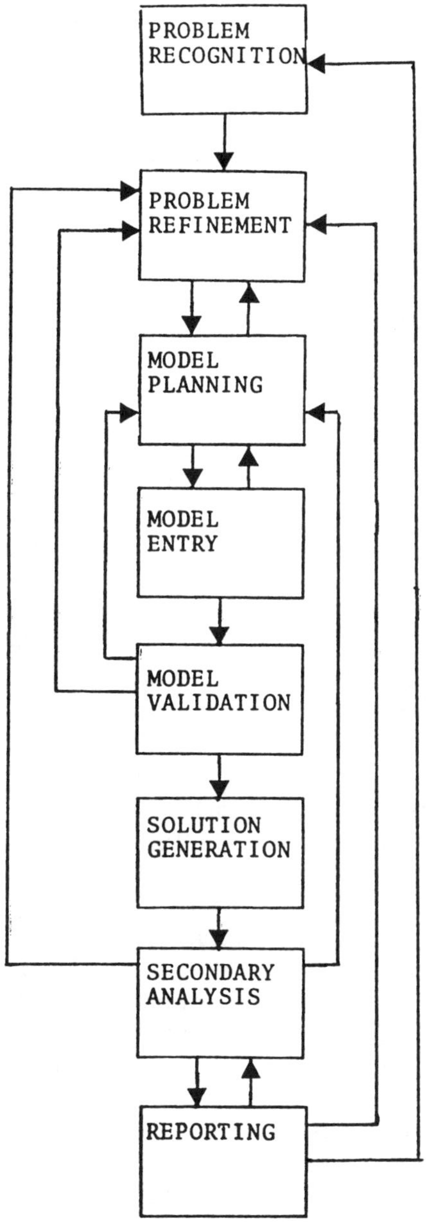

Figure 9.1: Linkages among Analytic Stages

errors and shortsightedness seem inevitably to occur. However, the analyst can take advantage of the perspective offered by the later stages of analysis to identify and correct many of the errors before they affect the final product. In many respects it is the rigor and efficiency of the MAPSIT approach that renders it feasible first to detect errors and second to correct them.

MORE AMBITIOUS ANALYSES

The preceding description of analytic stages and linkages is characteristic of analyses that are relatively short in duration; analyses that occupy a longer span of time follow the same general structure, but the details differ in predictable ways. The longer analyses are typically associated with a greater lead time and a relatively decreased pressure for quick results, often involve several participants, and may require the construction of several models. They usually warrant increased attention to documentation and to the reusability of the models constructed. Often the models will demonstrate a greater attention to detail and the ability to handle various special cases. Across the several analytic stages, the proportions of time allocated to the individual stages are likely to differ as compared to a typical short analysis. The remainder of this section addresses each of these topics in more detail.

More lengthy analyses often involve a greater number of participants, and a wider variety of participants as well. In the short analysis characterized earlier, a single analyst might execute all or nearly all of the analytic stages. In contrast, for longer analyses, multiple individuals may be employed in the execution of any one stage, with differing sets of individuals addressing different stages of the analysis. A senior staff committee may convene in order to define and refine the problem. Several analysts may plan, enter, and validate the models, perhaps with different analysts working on different models. Validation efforts may be supplemented by a formal, peer review procedure as part of a quality assurance effort. Clerical staff may handle the more repetitious aspects of the modeling, model entry, and secondary analysis. Those drafting the final report may not be the analysts who produced the results being described. Finally, once the analysis and write-up are complete, there may be a relatively large number of "outsiders" to whom the final report is circulated.

A long analysis is likely to involve more than one MAPSIT model, because there may be too many disparate questions to address conveniently in a single model. Although the structure of MAPSIT permits the analyst to address different transfer program systems and different system independent variables within a single model, the size of model listings and the cost of unwanted calculations encourages division. Often a longer analysis will require a sequence of progressively more sophisticated models as the project proceeds. The results from models early in the sequence may help to establish the feasibility of later models and determine their form. Or again, as described earlier, results from one model may spark the recognition of a new problem requiring a new model.

Furthermore, a long analysis is likely to involve greater formalization of analytic effort and greater attention to documentation than a short analysis. This tendency manifests itself in several ways. Because more resources are required, there is a greater degree of formalization in terms of problem recognition and/or refinement. Where a short analysis may begin immediately, a longer one may have to go through a cost estimation and formal approval phase, possibly involving a number of individuals. Because a longer analysis often employs several people, there is a greater need for effective coordination and consequently a greater emphasis on documentation internal to the model(s) and outside them. There may be a formalized work plan and periodic project reports to provide effective control of the effort. Because of the relatively wider audience for the final report, the final write-up stage of analysis may receive special attention. Also, because a longer analysis represents a major effort, it is more likely to result in models and solutions that are applicable to future efforts. Consequently, there is a tendency to worry more about model reusability and mothballing than in the case of a short analysis.

A long analysis is also likely to differ from a shorter one in its accuracy and attention to detail. The longer time horizon and reduced time pressure associated with long analyses may permit analysts to carry out the modeling in greater detail. For example, they may be able to obtain accurate descriptions of the logic for transfer programs rather than relying on make-do approximations. Similarly, the reduced time pressure may allow analysts the luxury of properly validating their models on a variety of carefully chosen test cases. Because more people are likely to be concerned with the modeling, incorrect assumptions and logic are more likely to be noticed and corrected. There may also be a tendency to build models that are more general. For example, analysts may be able to build models that handle one-parent families as well as two-parent families. They may also vary the age structure of the family, the number of earners, and various tax optimizing procedures available to the family. Such increased attention to detail in the modeling in turn justifies more effort in terms of mothballing the model. When a model is of high quality, it is cost effective to place it and its components in a library for access by others.

In addition to the changes in activities in the stages taken individually, the shift to a longer analysis is likely to affect the proportions of time spent on the several stages. Because of the greater attention to detail and the number of people involved, the problem recognition and refinement stages are likely to increase their proportions. The proportion spent on actual modeling is likely to decrease because the additional attention to detail may be overbalanced by economies of scale and reusable logic across models. For similar reasons, the proportion of resources devoted to model entry is likely to decrease for a longer analysis. The validation stage also benefits from economies of scale across models, but this effect may be counterbalanced by a more intensive validation effort. The production stage, or model solution phase will, of course, require a greater absolute effort, but probably a smaller proportional one. Because of the wider audience for the results, and the probable increased complexity of results, the secondary analysis and write-up/wrap-up stages are likely to require proportionally greater resources.

The differences in the characteristics of long and short analyses are largely predictable. For the most part they reflect rational responses to the nature of the two tasks. When there are more problems or bigger problems, analysis requires additional resources -- principally more time and more people. Because more resources are at stake, more formalized control mechanisms come into play. As a result, more effort goes into deciding what is wanted and into communicating the results of the analysis. The preceding discussion identifies many of the individual facets within this general tendency. In addition, the overall balance of resources across the several stages of the analysis shifts to reflect the greater attention to control and accountability.

DOCUMENTATION

Comments focusing on model documentation and its importance appear throughout this chapter. For the most part they address the issue of documentation as it relates to the particular points under discussion. Here, it is useful to examine documentation in its own right. The benefits of good documentation are fairly obvious. The act of producing documentation is conducive to thinking about what the model really means and thus to discovering and correcting errors, and hence to the creation of better models. In addition, when a model is well-documented, one can easily communicate its logic and assumptions to others. The analyst also will be able to determine quickly and conveniently the extent to which the model's logic may be applicable to other models under construction.

At the same time, there are often substantial costs involved. One of the major ones is in part psychological. Analysts and technicians who build models often immensely dislike documenting them. Perhaps their training has led them to focus more on the substance of the analysis rather than its communication; perhaps they are provided few rewards for producing good documentation. Whatever the reason, if the task is unpleasant or unrewarding, they will tend to put it off, and probably work at less than peak efficiency when doing it. Thus, a negative attitude can contribute to higher resource and manpower costs for documentation efforts and to an inferior product. Especially in an environment in which there are time pressures, and in which the benefits of documentation accrue in the future with the costs falling due in the present, documentation will often be slighted.

The design of MAPSIT acts directly to counteract this tendency. At the technical or mathematical level, MAPSIT automatically documents, in the form of a readable listing, all of the operations and arguments that make up a model. It cannot, of course, document the model's substance without help from the analyst. At the same time, MAPSIT contains a variety of features to make the substantive documentation as convenient as possible.

A facility for some of the most important documentation is inherent in the way in which MAPSIT treats its basic unit of analysis, the mapping. First, MAPSIT references mappings by names rather than code numbers or their positions in some sequence. Since mapping names have up to ten characters, the analyst has an excellent opportunity to use meaningful mnemonics. Still, even with a fair amount of creativity, it may be difficult to include all the relevant information in the name. Typically the analyst will want to communicate the dependent and possibly independent variables for the mapping, plus other information not so easily classified. The analyst may, for example, wish to specify that a mapping that has just been derived does not yet include a legislated floor or ceiling that will be applied in a future operation. Thus, a second device, the mapping description, is also available. With the exception of items fetched from the library, the analyst can supply this description for every mapping that is created in the model. The additional seventy characters available in the description are almost invariably sufficient to convey the sense of the mapping. The mapping names and descriptions just described are relevant to all the major MAPSIT modules: BUILD, EDIT, CREF, LIST, SOLVE, DEBUG and EXAMINE. The same names and descriptions entered during model construction are transmitted to model solutions and appear in model listings and in plots and tables specified during the secondary analysis.

As useful as the mapping names and descriptions are, they apply only to single mappings. MAPSIT also contains provisions for documenting whole models or parts of models. The comment capability lets the analyst insert explanatory text throughout the model. Typically, the analyst will use comments to describe the nature of a sequence of operations, or the nature of assumptions inherent in the model. One can insert comments wherever names, descriptions, or operations might not be clear. A second feature, the mandatory title and model description, if properly used, provides the reader with a summary of the entire model. A good model description includes information such as the basic purpose of the model, its creation or revision date, the system(s) modeled, the major assumptions, and perhaps an appropriate project designation. Such a description allows analysts to look quickly at a model and decide if it is relevant for their purposes.

MAPSIT includes a variety of other documentation related features as well. For the model construction stage the analyst has on-line access to the titles and descriptions of all the elements of the library: schedules, programs, and models. In the secondary analysis stage the analyst can generate an "instant" documentation of the primary solution being examined, which includes the model description, the prompts and the analyst's responses for all the parameters input at the solution stage, any warnings generated during the course of the solution, plus any subset of the relevant mapping names and descriptions. Also in the secondary analysis stage, the analyst can include a number of titles, axis labels, legends, and so forth to make sure that the output is clearly identified.

The preceding items apply only to the documentation of the models created and solved in MAPSIT and do not include the documentation for MAPSIT itself. Into this latter class fall a number of manuals and papers geared toward using MAPSIT. Also included are software features such as the HELP command, choice in level of detail for prompts and listings, and the ability to use a question mark in response to a prompt to obtain a list of legal responses.

In sum, because documentation is important, but often slighted, MAPSIT contains a variety of features that facilitate documentation throughout the entire analytic process. The automatic documentation of the technical aspects of a model provided by the LIST module facilitates model entry and validation. The provision for referencing mappings by name, and for including mapping descriptions, benefits several stages of the analysis. The major beneficiaries are planning, model entry, validation, and secondary analysis, because in these stages the analyst must refer to the mappings to carry out the tasks. The facility for optional comments and for the mandatory model description provides special help during the validation and secondary analysis phases. The facility for adding labels, titles, and legends is especially useful in the secondary analysis stage and for communicating the model's results to others. In general, the structure of MAPSIT automates much of the drudgery of documentation, even though it cannot reduce the substantive demands. By lowering these costs, it can increase the quantity and quality of documentation. In turn, it reduces the potential for confusion and improves the chances that modeling efforts will be properly interpreted, or reused rather than reinvented.

CONCLUSION

The usefulness of methodology and software as a policy tool is not something that one judges in isolation from the policy process. This chapter, the beginning of the section on policy applications, illustrates how the concepts and software operate in a policy analysis framework. The basic context is that of deriving relationships that are important inputs to the policymaking process. In this sense the focus of this chapter centers on the policy analytic aspects of the overall policy process rather than the actual policymaking. The chapter addresses answers to questions that either are or should be asked by those responsible for policy decisions. The first portion defines a sequence of analytic stages, from the initial problem recognition through to the final report, concentrating on what the analyst and policymaker do during these stages, and how MAPSIT can assist in doing these tasks well. The rest of the chapter addresses additional topics that supplement the discussion of the basic sequence. These topics include linkages among the stages of the basic sequence, comparative characteristics of long and short analyses, and issues in documenting models and analyses.

Within the broader context of the applications, this chapter describes one aspect of the environment in which the analyst and software operate. The next chapter describes a number of the problem areas in which MAPSIT has been used, although a mere listing of such problems does not adequately define the "field." When examining the set of problems displayed in Chapter 10, the reader should bear in mind the nature of the institutional processes that lead to the recognition, analysis, and resolution of stacking issues.

CHAPTER 10.
USES AND APPLICATIONS

No matter what desirable theoretical properties a policy-oriented tool possesses, no matter what elegant presentational formats it offers, the final test of its success is pragmatic. The technology is successful only to the extent that the policymakers use it in their deliberations. The initial authorization for the development of a new technology is especially important because it indicates both the seriousness of the problem area and the perceived inadequacy of existing techniques. Subsequent, continued use suggests that the technology is successful on three additional counts. First, the technology must be able to produce results that successfully address the issues posed, or at least do so better than alternative technologies. Second, it must be able to produce these results sufficiently quickly and inexpensively to meet the demands of an active policy environment. Third, given the alternative uses for analysts' time and the value placed on their time, it must be able either to produce a few results particularly well or many results competently in order to justify its continued usage.

MAPSIT has certainly met the test of usage. Since its inception, analysts have carried out a wide variety of analyses addressing a whole spectrum of substantive issues. This chapter attempts to illustrate the broad sweep of these applications by describing briefly several of the analyses done in Canada and the United States, focusing on the underlying problems and on the manner in which MAPSIT was able to address these problems. Indeed, the body of the chapter consists almost exclusively of brief descriptions that illustrate problems and the way in which MAPSIT has enabled analysts to address them.

This approach inevitably omits much of the detail relevant to those with strong substantive interests in the specific problem areas. Unfortunately, provision of such detail is incompatible with the presentation of a broad analytic spectrum. As can be seen from the development in Chapters 5 and 6, the description of even relatively simple problems and models can easily occupy an entire chapter. For some of the more involved problem areas, a book might be more in order. In addition to space limitations, however, there is the matter of confidentiality. While it is legitimate to describe the basic problem and approach for most issues, the presentation of analytic details, especially for intergovernmental analyses that involve prospective programs or revisions to politically sensitive programs, can be viewed as inappropriate. Fortunately, broad brush descriptions are sufficient to convey the essential picture without violating confidentiality.

Within this chapter we have grouped the applications roughly according to substance. The first section addresses analyses that were among the first for which MAPSIT saw use: day care and other social services. A second section examines a number of analyses dealing primarily with systems per se, rather than with particular portions of a system. Analyses focusing on the income tax system comprise a third substantive section. Because of the central role that income taxes play in many analyses, and because of their complexity, a variety of MAPSIT studies have addressed the workings of the tax system and the impacts of suggested changes. A fourth substantive section takes up issues of family size, family structure, and family splitting. Because of the high emotional content often present in analyses of such issues, we consider it extremely important to be able to conduct objective studies addressing the financial implications inherent in programs that affect these family decisions. The final three substantive sections address the use of MAPSIT in major policy development efforts, specifically relating to the federal support/supplementation proposals in Canada and some U.S. applications. A concluding section briefly describes some additional analyses and characterizes the type of support that MAPSIT can bring to income transfer analyses generally.

DAY CARE AND SOCIAL SERVICE ANALYSES

Among the first substantive applications of MAPSIT was the evaluation of provincial day care programs in Canada for their eligibility for cost-sharing by the federal government. The arrangements permitting the federal government to share the costs of provincially administered programs highlight several characteristics relevant for proposed programs. Among these were the income value at which a family ceases to receive a total subsidy (a subsidy equivalent to the full cost of service), the minimum benefit reduction rate (the tax-back rate applied to subsequent income), and the maximum income level at which a family can receive any subsidy. Provinces may submit program proposals to the federal government for an analysis of their eligibility for cost-sharing. The analysis for eligibility is by no means a pro forma concern. Indeed, the willingness of the federal government to share the program costs could be virtually a necessary condition for the program's implementation.

In essence then, this procedure creates an immediate demand for a micro-level, systems-oriented, analytic capability. It also serves to define the characteristics required of the capability. Since day care proposals need not, and typically did not, employ the same income definition as that used on the federal level, there is a demand for conversions between income definitions. Since the differences among income definitions typically consist of inclusions, exemptions, or offsets relating to other transfer programs in the system, there is a demand for modeling whole systems of programs. Since the federal criteria define an income measure net of taxes, it is necessary to model the behavior of the system over an entire range of incomes so that the effective tax rates can be accurately computed. Since various types of families might receive day care benefits, the modeling has to be sufficiently general to handle such things as different numbers of children in the family, different numbers of children enrolled in the day care program, different numbers of adults in the family, and different numbers of earners in the family.

A standard approach gradually evolved. One or two models were constructed for each province submitting a day care proposal. The models allowed a variety of parameters to be varied, such as the number of adults in the family, the numbers and ages of children in the family, and the number of children receiving the day care service. The models were used to derive the benefits that the province proposed to provide for the family, in the form of reduced day care costs, for all values of earned income. Similarly, the models were used to derive the envelope of permissible benefits for the family. This is a mapping showing, for each level of earned income, the maximum subsidy payable to the family within the federal criteria. Comparison of the proposed benefit relationship with the benefit envelope then revealed, for one family structure at a time, the extent to which the proposal implicitly contained costs that were not sharable. Looking at this type of result across several family compositions, the analyst ascertained the extent to which the proposal fell within the criteria. Sometimes the results of an analysis went a bit further, indicating that if the province were able to justify a certain figure for work-related expenses, for example, then the proposal would fall within the guidelines.

Even when a proposed day care program did fall within the guidelines, the analysis might reveal features that could complicate its administration or hinder its acceptance. For example, it might show that for particular family types the effective marginal tax rate that the system imposed on additional earnings was excessive over some income ranges. Alternatively, it might show that the day care programs or the systems as a whole generated undesirable notches at certain income values, thereby creating potential inequities and incentives to misrepresent incomes. Perhaps more importantly, with the system contained in a model, and specified parametrically, it was an easy matter to ascertain the consequences of varying the factors that served to define the day care program, such as reduction rates, exemptions, and income definitions. In this manner, it was sometimes possible to discover alterations that would eliminate or reduce specific trouble spots without altering the basic structure of the day care proposals.

Beyond testing for adherence to federal criteria, a number of other analyses have dealt with various aspects of day care. With the growing number of two-earner families, the availability and cost of day care have become much more important issues. Of special interest is the degree to which having a second earner makes a family better off once work-related expenses, taxes, and social insurance contributions are added to the direct cost of any necessary day care. A number of MAPSIT models have shown that the effective marginal tax rate on earnings by a second earner is often quite high. Consequently, the second earner may have to earn substantially more than the minimum wage in order for the family to be appreciably better off financially. A major contributor to this effect is the relatively high cost of private day care, and the extent to which many subsidized day care programs effectively charge the full cost of service by the time the second earner is earning any appreciable income.

To examine this situation, several models have been built along the following lines. A model fixes the nominal income of the primary earner and lets the earnings of the second earner be the independent variable. It calculates work-related expenses and social insurance contributions for both earners. It includes an assumption about the amount of day care needed at each level of the second earner's earnings and derives the gross cost of this amount to the family. If subsidized day care is available, the amount actually payable is also calculated. The model further calculates federal and provincial income taxes relevant for the family. This is a more difficult calculation for Canada than for the United States because income taxes in Canada are assessed individually rather than filed on a family basis. Consequently, due to linked eligibility conditions, transferable deductions, and a link between taxable Family Allowances and personal exemptions for dependent children, there is an inherent non-trivial optimization problem associated with deciding which adult claims which children as exemptions. The day care expenses also enter into the tax calculations because the second earner is allowed to deduct part of them. Of course, the models also include Family Allowances, federal and provincial tax reductions and credits, and other relevant programs such as Social Assistance.

The output from such a model then yields the impact of the second earner on the family's net income. The model includes all of the transfers to or from each of the earners, and to and from the family as a whole, expressed as a function of the second earner's earnings. Thus one can see the impact of the second earner on income taxes, tax reductions, tax credits, day care expenses, work-related expenses, Family Allowances, Social Assistance, and so forth. More importantly, knowing earnings and the amounts of all the transfers, it is a trivial matter to derive the family's disposable income after all these items have been taken into account and treated as a relationship with the second earner's earnings as the independent variable. Thus, the analyst ascertains, for the whole spectrum of the second earner's earnings, how much better off the family is financially as compared to the situation with no second earner. Similarly, by treating some point on the relationship as the status quo, the analyst can ascertain for the family the impact of both increases and decreases in earnings relative to that status quo level. More generally, the analyst can derive the effective marginal or average marginal tax rates on the second earner's earnings over the whole earnings spectrum.

For the policymaker an important facet of the model is that it can be used to derive the implications and incentives for institutions as well as those for families. For the different levels of government the analyst can ascertain the increases in social insurance contributions and taxes collected, balancing this against any possible subsidy given to the family through any subsidized day care, and considering as well the probable increase in taxes collected from the providers of any private sector day care. One can ascertain breakeven levels for the various levels of government, where the governments begin to be net beneficiaries from the participation of the second earner in the labor force, and can compare these with earnings levels typical for various occupations, including those likely as entry levels for a second earner. One can further ascertain whether there are situations in which the various governments, individually or collectively, are undergoing a relatively high net loss in order to provide the family with a relatively low net increase in disposable income. From the answers to these and other similar questions, the analyst and policymaker are better able to ascertain the rationality and merits of alternative day care policies and programs.

Day care has also been the focus for analysis within the United States. Lewis (1983) modeled the various ways in which day care is subsidized for families. These include payments to day care providers through the Title XX funds, treatment of day care expenses as deductions from income in the Aid to Families with Dependent Children (AFDC) and food stamp programs, and treatment of day care expenses for dependents as a tax credit on federal income taxes.

That analysis focused on the relative incentives for families to use private versus public (Title XX) day care centers. Among the findings was the discovery that prior to 1981 lower middle income families could be financially better off by using private day care centers even though such centers charged an average tuition of over $2000 per year. By paying for private day care, families would remain eligible for AFDC and because of their eligibility for AFDC they would also receive Medicaid. When the expected value of reimbursed medical services was treated as a cash benefit, the investment of $2000 for private day care could mean as much as $3000 in return.

In addition to calculating the financial incentives for families, however, Lewis also showed that it is possible to calculate the financial consequences for the state and for the federal government. Although private day care centers provided financial incentives for families, the state was financially better off if the family used public day care centers. The federal government, however, was much better off if the family used private day care. Following the changes to AFDC contained in the Omnibus Budget Reconciliation Act of 1981, there were dramatic changes in the incentives to use public rather than private day care. Families were almost always better off if they used public day care and the state was better off if the families used private day care. (It is important to remember of course, that it is basically the family that decides which kind of day care to use.)

The substantive findings (and the statement of limitations) of that analysis are spelled out elsewhere, but for our purposes here it is worth noting that the MAPSIT analysis made it possible to track separately the incentives to families, to the state, and to the federal government. In addition, MAPSIT analyses allowed the analyst to track the changes in that system over time and to identify the elements of the system that had produced the changes. Finally, although the changes made by the state of Pennsylvania were loudly decried by families who used public day care, the net effect of the state changes was of little effect on families relative to the effects produced by the federally enacted changes to AFDC.

Day care issues are only a special case of social services in general, and MAPSIT models have been constructed for a variety of these issues, from rehabilitation and counseling services to visiting homemaker services. Although one is not necessarily faced with multiple earner complications, it is still crucial to ascertain the benefits or subsidies for families with zero income and to derive the incentives to earn additional income. One must still ascertain the incentives for misrepresenting characteristics when eligibility is categorical.

There is an important set of issues that arises when a family is receiving multiple social services simultaneously. MAPSIT models have addressed the question of whether the services should reduce their benefits independently (and thus probably simultaneously), sequentially (with one service beginning to reduce its subsidy only after the subsidy of another service has fallen to zero), or whether there should be a joint user charge schedule based on the total value of the services that the family is receiving. For such models there has been a focus, of course, on the impact that the relevant systems hold for the families receiving the benefits, but also on the impacts that the systems produce for the institutions and governments that jointly make up the system. Furthermore, there is often a concern with the sensitivity of these impacts to program parameters and to alterations in the cost-sharing arrangements between governments.

SYSTEM SIMULATION

Although MAPSIT models have been very useful in looking at the implications of specific programs such as social services, with the rest of the system considered primarily to provide the precedents and successors for the program of interest, often the analytic focus rests with the system as a whole. Indeed, such systems-oriented simulations are the bread and butter of MAPSIT applications. The analyst models the entire set of programs relevant for a family, deriving the transfers to or from each program as a function of an appropriate independent variable, often earned income for a member of the subject family. From this basic information the analyst can then ascertain guaranteed subsidy levels, breakevens, departures, marginal and average tax rates, and other outputs as described in Chapter 7. Throughout such analyses, the thrust usually rests with the impact of a particular set of transfer programs, but specifically includes the contributions and impacts of the individual programs that comprise the set. One such analysis, regularly updated as a result of changes to the several programs involved, is a comparison across provinces of the several Social Assistance (welfare) programs. The analyst picks one or more family structures and then, using earnings as the model's independent variable, ascertains how that family would fare on Social Assistance across the ten provinces. Although the actual formulae for computing Social Assistance benefits differ across provinces, typically they will require inputs like earnings, family size and makeup, social insurance contributions, Family Allowances received, rents paid, and income tax withholdings. Tabulated or plotted side by side, the results allow the analyst to compare the incentives and generosity of the several provinces in terms of a common measure of income, despite the fact that the several programs may be calculated and administered in quite different fashions.

Other systems-oriented analyses have concentrated on the sets of programs that affect particular age groups, for example the elderly. For elderly families the relevant transfer systems may be quite different from those for younger families, containing transfers such as Canada Pension Plan benefits, Old Age Security benefits, Guaranteed Income Supplement benefits and provincial supplements to these benefits along with income sources such as private pension income and investment income. Even the operation of the income tax system differs, reflecting provisions for extra exemptions for the elderly, the deductibility of certain amounts of pension income, and the availability or transferability of certain reductions and credits not relevant for younger families. Although such models may involve earnings as the independent variable, more often the independent variable will be the investment income or private pension income for the family. The analyst may wish to examine the adequacy of the system in terms of the extent to which it provides the family with a disposable income at least equal to some of the accepted poverty lines or income standards. Alternatively, it may be useful to examine the effective marginal tax rates on the various sources of income that the family may have available, thus indicating the extent to which it is useful for the family to save for retirement by means of various investments or contributions to pension plans.

One analysis of recurring interest has been the calculation of replacement ratios when an earner retires. The focus here rests with the determination of the ratio of disposable income immediately after retirement to disposable income immediately before retirement. Usually the independent variable for the analysis is the earnings level before retirement, with the analyst specifying how post-retirement investment income and pension income vary as a function of earnings before retirement. With an assumption of this sort it is possible for the analyst to derive both pre-retirement and post-retirement disposable income as a function of pre-retirement earnings. Knowing these two functions it is then possible to derive the replacement ratio including adjustments for price changes, for any set of earnings values. Perhaps more importantly, it is also quite feasible to vary the parameters in the model, like those that occur in the formulae for computing Canada Pension Plan or Guaranteed Income Supplement benefits, and study their effects on the replacement ratio. In some of the models built by the Canadian government, the replacement ratio results turned out to be surprisingly insensitive to variations in what had been considered important policy parameters.

Many of the systems-oriented analyses are at least partially concerned with some form of sensitivity analysis. For these, the basic issues of concern are the reaction of the various programs in the system and the reaction of the system as a whole to changes in the parameters that serve to define a system. There is often a special concern for the extent to which a change in the benefit level for one program is amplified or attenuated by the reactions of other programs in the system. One such analysis addressed the impact of an increase in the Family Allowance paid per child per month. Because the Family Allowance benefit entered directly or indirectly into the computation of taxes and benefits for several other programs in the system, the family never saw its disposable income increase by the full amount of the Family Allowance increase. Indeed, due to a particular combination of effects, the lowest income families saw no increase at all in disposable income, lower middle income families saw the greatest increase, some middle income families suffered an actual decline in disposable income due to the Family Allowance increase, and higher income families achieved modest benefits. At several places along the income spectrum the sign, or cause of the effect, was quite unexpected.

Other models examined the incentives for seasonal or part time unemployment that may be created by Canada's unemployment insurance program. One of these models compared the situations between two earners, one of them working full time each year and the other working only part of the year, with the number of weeks worked being the independent variable for the model, and the seasonal worker being assumed to work the same number of weeks each year. Of course the seasonal worker, though working at the same pay rate, ended up with a lower disposable income over the year, since unemployment insurance benefits per week are less than the qualifying weekly earnings. However, the focus of the analysis lay with the proportion of full time disposable income foregone by working only seasonally. In one extreme case it was found that by working thirty-two weeks of the year the seasonal worker could achieve more than 90 percent of the disposable income that would result from fifty-two weeks of work, due primarily to the replacement contribution of unemployment insurance, the reduced marginal tax rate and reduced social insurance contributions payable. Equivalently, the worker could conceivably "vacation" for nearly 40 percent of the year foregoing less than 10 percent of the disposable income that would be available from full year work. In essence, the worker could use unemployment insurance income to increase substantially his effective "disposable income per week worked." Another model relaxed the assumption about working the same number of weeks each year and ascertained the "weeks-worked, weeks-unemployed" cycle that maximized the effective disposable income per week worked. For both of these analyses a variety of sensitivity runs ascertained the extent to which the strategies and their effectiveness depended on the values of the parameters in the system, such as the number of weeks waiting period before unemployment insurance benefits can be collected and the formula relating wage rate while employed to weekly unemployment insurance benefit. Subsequent to the analyses described, changes to both the Unemployment Insurance program and the Income Tax Act have reduced the incentives for seasonal employment.

Many other sets of analyses and models have also employed primarily a systems orientation. For example, the MAPSIT Library contains a "base model" for each province for each calendar year, with a typical base model employing the most common transfer programs (Family Allowances, social insurance contributions, Social Assistance,federal and provincial income taxes, tax reductions and tax credits) for a single earner family with one or two parents and arbitrary numbers of children of arbitrary ages. Although these models may hold some intrinsic interest for the analyst, they serve primarily as starting points for the construction of other more specialized models, getting out of the way material common to many models so that the analyst can concentrate on the aspects of particular interest. Various special provincial programs, for example the Quebec income supplement which is roughly comparable to the U.S. Earned Income Credit, were examined within the systems context of social insurance contributions, welfare, and federal and provincial income taxes, reductions, and credits.

MAPSIT has also been used to generate the fee schedules and tables used by field workers in the administration of various programs. Formerly a time-consuming, troublesome endeavor that had to be carried out periodically as costs of service for the programs changed, it has in some instances been completely automated in MAPSIT models so that new fee schedules, reflecting, for example, an increase in the wage rate for visiting homemakers that affects the cost of service, can be generated for the whole spectrum of incomes and family structures in a matter of minutes.

TAX FILING AND THE TAX SYSTEM

Because taxes are mandatory, they play a central role in any analysis other than those dealing with very low income families. Thus, most MAPSIT models will include operations modeling the logic of federal and state or provincial income taxes, complete with relevant reductions or credits. In several respects, due to its complexity and centrality, income tax is virtually a system by itself. Indeed, several MAPSIT analyses have concentrated on income taxes, deriving the implications they hold for particular types of families or particular types of transactions, and determining the sensitivity of these implications to the tax parameters.

One aspect of the income tax system, filing strategy, is considerably more troublesome in Canada than in the United States. Because tax filing is done on an individual rather than joint or family basis, multiple-earner families in Canada must decide which parent will claim which children as personal exemptions. The issue is made still more complicated by the fact that the value of the personal exemption for a child differs with the child's age, and that the individual who claims the exemption for a child must also claim as income the Family Allowances paid with respect to that child. The size of an exemption for a child also depends on the amount of income the child might have. The family must also recognize that the filing strategy chosen may also affect eligibility for provincial tax credits and/or reduced medical insurance premiums. The choice of a filing strategy is a nontrivial integer programming problem not at all closely linked to the usual form for stating such problems. Unfortunately, "obvious" rule of thumb approximations, such as assigning all child exemptions to the parent with the larger of the two preexemption incomes, do not always work well. Analysis of one case for a two-parent two-earner family with three children in Ontario in 1978 led to a completely unexpected result. The optimal filing strategy turned out to be that one parent earner, with $10,000 of earnings should claim all three children, while the other parent earner, with $20,000 of earnings and no unusual deductions, should claim no children as exemptions.

Another set of tax-oriented MAPSIT models has addressed tax expenditure analyses. In analyses of this sort it is recognized that the various exemptions in the tax system, serving as they do to reduce the amount of taxes paid, can in one sense be treated as benefits to the families who would otherwise have to pay more taxes. Typically, the amount of the tax savings to the family as a result of a given deduction, exemption, or credit is a function of the family's structure and its income. Accordingly, MAPSIT analyses have, for example, derived the size of the benefit as a function of income for the family, controlling for the family structure. Essentially, these analyses model the tax system both with and without the exemption, deduction, or credit and then compare the two tax mappings that result. They may also model other transfer programs that depend on the tax system to see if these other programs amplify or attenuate the tax effect. For example, one may find that a particular exemption provides a family with a tax benefit of $90 at a given earnings level, but that another transfer program, such as day care, permits taxes paid as a deduction from its income base, and with a 50 percent reduction rate of its own, effectively reduces the $90 benefit to $45. Other provisions of the tax system, the transferability of certain exemptions and deductions between members of a family, for example, can also be treated as tax expenditures.

Tax averaging has served as the focus for a number of other tax oriented MAPSIT models. Analysts have long recognized that because of the progressivity of the income tax system, someone whose income fluctuates appreciably from year to year will often pay considerably more tax than another person who has exactly the same amount of income over the same period, but who earns it at a more constant rate. To reduce some of this inequity, and to encourage entry into the labor force, the Canadian Income Tax Act has contained various tax averaging provisions that, when income is increasing, can allow a tax filer to pay less tax than if income tax had been computed independently over a series of years. (A similar provision exists for U.S. income taxes.) However, the amount of this tax relief depended heavily on the pattern and size of the fluctuation as well as the average income over the period and the sizes of the several tax brackets. Consequently, MAPSIT models were constructed to ascertain the degree of tax relief for particular situations, both absolutely and as a fraction of the extra tax payable because of the fluctuation. In most of these analyses the earnings history prior to the current year was taken as fixed and the independent variable was the earnings for the current year. In some cases sensitivity analyses were conducted for parameters that enter into the tax averaging formulae.

However, the most important tax-oriented MAPSIT analyses are probably those that ascertain the impact of the tax changes that occur, or are proposed, from time to time. The Canadian federal government and all of the provincial governments have the authority to change the parameters and elements of the tax system and do so frequently. In addition, other changes, such as the indexing of the tax schedule and the personal exemptions for inflation, occur at the beginning of each tax year. To ascertain the impact of these changes, it is necessary to develop a model of the new system and compare the system's impact with and without the changes. It is also necessary to consider the impact of the changes on the conclusions drawn from other analyses that were based on the prior tax system.

FAMILY SIZE AND FAMILY STRUCTURE

Throughout this book and this chapter, we have indicated the important roles that family size and structure play in analyzing program interactions. For some programs the nature of the family can affect eligibility or the applicability of particular program provisions. For even more programs the numbers of adults and children in the family affect the dollar amount of benefits received from the program or taxes paid to the program. Because family size and structure are not fixed aspects of a family (families are capable of altering these aspects either in fact or in representation), it is important to discover the existence and size of any incentives that programs and systems establish for marriages, for divorces, or for the conception of additional children. Given the frequency and vehemence of charges that "the system" or individual programs break up marriages, encourage marriages of convenience, discourage the raising of children, or promote baby mills, it is vital to consider objectively the financial rewards and penalties that transfer systems can impose on families as a result of their structures or changes to these structures. The importance exists whether the incentives arise as a matter of formal policy or as the result of capricious program interactions. Analysts must be able to ascertain "financial" family policy as applied, as well as family policy formally stated.

One of the major objections directed against transfer systems and against welfare programs in particular, is that they provide financial incentives for wage earners to desert their families. The logic underlying such charges is fairly clear. Two-parent families with one employed or employable member are often, by regulation or by practice, ineligible for welfare benefits. Even if a family with an earner is eligible for program benefits, the high marginal and average tax rates associated with such programs often mean that the family is little better off than if the earner were not working at all, and also has little financial incentive for greater work effort. However, if the earner should desert the family, the situation may be quite different. The deserted segment of the family, now a one-parent family, is a good deal more likely to be categorically eligible for welfare benefits. In addition, the earnings of the deserting earner no longer act to reduce benefits from the guarantee or zero earnings level. Thus, the deserted segment is likely to receive the full guarantee level, although this level will typically be smaller than it would have been for an intact, eligible family with zero earnings. The deserting member continues to receive the former earnings, although possibly with increased tax withholdings since there are no longer exemptions available for the deserted family members. Often however, for the family types under consideration, earnings are sufficiently low that no income taxes are payable either before or after the split. Even if the deserting member does pay taxes, the effective marginal tax rate on additional earnings would probably be relatively low.

Of course, the matter is not entirely one-sided. In addition to the possibility of an increased tax liability, there is also the likelihood that housing costs will increase to maintain two separate households after the split. All the same, the net financial benefit from the split can amount to multiple thousands of dollars a year, probably a substantial amount for a low income family.

A desire to ascertain and understand these incentives has led to the construction of several MAPSIT models for various periods and provinces in Canada. Several questions have received special attention. What is the size of the financial incentive for family splitting and on what does it depend? How sensitive is the incentive to variations in such variables as family size, province of residence, the presence and identity of other programs in the system, and the cost of maintaining a second household? How is the incentive to split attenuated if both parents in the family have some earnings? What particular programs and/or provisions of programs are responsible for what portions of the total incentive? (The tax system turns out to play an important role.) What are the implications of the system for children with meaningful earnings? Does the system provide incentives for such children to leave home, or for families to encourage them to leave, before the children might otherwise wish to do so? What are the implications of family splitting for the various levels of government concerned, particularly with respect to the extra financial support provided, the changes in tax revenues, and the extra social services that may be necessary? Depending on the particular cost-sharing formulae in effect, is it possible for one level of government to benefit from the split while another level pays the costs?

The reverse side of the question is also quite relevant. Given the number of single-parent families in existence, it is important to ascertain whether transfer systems are placing unintended financial obstacles in the way of possible marriages or remarriages. Indeed, the question of obstacles to marriage is not solely of concern to young families with children. There is a growing recognition that programs for the elderly may provide unintended financial disincentives for remarriage after the death of a spouse. Some MAPSIT modeling has been directed toward determining the net impact of systems including the Canada Pension Plan, the income tax system, Old Age Security benefits, and Guaranteed Income Supplement benefits for remarriage after the death of a spouse. Given the centrality of marriage and the family in U.S. and Canadian society, it is vital that programs of social security not provide capricious financial incentives to make the important personal and moral decisions involved even more difficult.

It has been established that the number of children enters into the eligibility and benefit calculations for many transfer programs. From welfare and survivors' benefits to the calculations of income taxes payable, transfer programs may explicitly include the number of children in their calculations. Thus, a change in the number of children in a family may alter a variety of the relevant taxes and benefits. In the case of taxes, an additional child typically reduces the amount of the tax or leaves it unchanged, presumably on the grounds that it is proper for some of the family's income to be spent for the benefit of the child. Similarly, in the case of transfer benefits, the presence an additional child typically causes the amount of the benefit to increase or remain unchanged, presumably on the grounds that failure to do so would unreasonably stretch the family's income and perhaps leave the child undersupported. The net effect of either a tax reduction or a benefit increase is to provide more spendable income for the family, in effect acting to cover part, or even all, of the additional cost of raising the child.

Several MAPSIT models focus on discovering the degree to which transfer systems react to the presence of a child to subsidize the costs of raising the child, at least for the first year, and additionally, how the size of the subsidy varies with the income and size of the family. Should the subsidy be too low, there is the concern, at least for low income families, that the resources will be stretched too tight, and that the child's physical and psychological development may be impaired. Should the subsidy turn out to be too high, or not to decline quickly, there is the concern that the government may be unintentionally providing financial incentives for the conception of children, or unnecessarily subsidizing the raising of children in middle and higher income families. In all of these cases it is important for the policymaker to be able to ascertain precisely what the various incentives are, how they affect specific families, and what features of the transfer system are causing the incentive. It has been our finding that the size of the subsidy for a given family and income can vary considerably across transfer systems, especially across different geographical locations. Furthermore, both the size of the subsidy and the rate at which it declines appear to depend heavily on the number of children already in the family. Specifically, governments appear often to underwrite a substantially larger proportion of the cost of raising the first child in a family as compared to a fifth child in a similar family. We believe it is important for policymakers and program administrators to appreciate the nature of these system effects so that effective financial family policy can correspond more closely to intended policy.

Beyond the decision to have an additional child, some MAPSIT analyses have addressed the question of raising children at all. In particular, attention lay with the much greater extent to which unmarried mothers have been choosing to keep their children rather than placing them for adoption. The concern was further aggravated by the increasing proportion of births attributable to unmarried mothers and the large unmarried mother caseload in provincial Social

Assistance programs. Within the analysis consideration was given to the fact that unattached single women without children are relatively unlikely to be able to receive Social Assistance benefits, while single mothers keeping their children are much more likely to be eligible for benefits. Strengthening the concern that short term incentives fall in the right direction, was the possibility that the mother might develop a longer term dependency because of child-induced difficulties in gaining relevant labor force experience, or in continuing educational pursuits.

SUPPORT/SUPPLEMENTATION PROPOSAL

In addition to its use on many substantive topics, MAPSIT has seen use in major policy initiatives. One of these, the development of a two tiered support/supplementation proposal came as an outgrowth of the 1973-1976 Federal-Provincial Social Security Review in Canada. The federal government proposed a support (welfare) program that, although admitting provincial variations, would be consistent across provinces, coupled with a supplementation program that would be identical across provinces and would provide benefits to the working poor as well as those with very low incomes. The two programs would be integrated with each other and designed to coordinate with the income tax system and the social insurance system.

MAPSIT models were used extensively in designing both the support and supplementation programs. Some of the many models built allowed the analyst to ascertain the implications of using various definitions of income for the programs, including or excluding other transfers as income or deductions. Other models permitted the analyst to vary the numerical parameters that acted to define the programs. The programs' guarantee levels, their tax back rates, and the amounts of exempted income were all addressed as variables in the design. Beyond deriving the implications of the support and supplementation programs per se, the models addressed the relationship and interaction of these programs with other programs, notably Family Allowances, Unemployment Insurance benefits, federal and provincial income taxes, and benefits for the elderly (primarily Old Age Security, Guaranteed Income Supplement, and provincial supplements to the Guaranteed Income Supplement). Furthermore, several of the models compared the overall transfer systems including the two proposed programs with the corresponding existing systems. Such analyses were done for all ten provinces to ascertain how the proposals compared to existing programs in terms of generosity and work incentives. Of course, throughout all of these analyses, the models permitted the analyst to vary the family structure from solution to solution.

Another aspect of the proposal receiving special attention was the possibility of using the income tax system to reconcile the effects from such income fluctuation as might occur throughout a year. Because of the necessity for the support program to be responsive to increases or decreases in income, it was understood that the accounting period for the support program would have to be something less than a year. Relative to a program administered using a longer accounting period, this could lead, if income fluctuated, to more benefits being paid out. For example, an earner employed during only the second half of the year might expect to receive benefits throughout the first half of the year, even though earnings in the second half might be sufficiently high that if the support program had employed an annual accounting period there would be no benefit entitlement. Similarly, income fluctuation tends to produce overwithholdings within the income tax system. Considering the two effects together, there is at least a potential for using the income tax system to carry out an end of year reconciliation of the overpayments and overwithholdings. Several models investigated possible reconciliations for a variety of family structures, for various patterns of income fluctuation, and for different hypothetical support and supplementation programs.[54]

When the federal proposal was accepted in principle, but not implemented due to financing and jurisdictional concerns, the federal government explored the feasibility of a single negative income tax program that would effectively replace the supplementation program and the income tax system. Several MAPSIT models contributed to this analysis, which was basically an exercise in "program fitting." Treating a variety of parameters in such an integrated program as variables, the models attempted to ascertain the parameter configuration that would best match the effect of the single integrated program to the sum of the effects of the proposed supplement program and the income tax system. Once again, the size and structure of families played an important part in the analyses; although the "optimal" parameter choice turned out to vary with family size, the various optimal choices were reasonably close.

---

[54] The general problem of accounting periods and their effect on welfare is discussed in the paper by Allen (1973) published as part of the work commissioned by the Joint Economic Committee.

CHILD BENEFIT SYSTEM/CHILD TAX CREDIT

In the later 1970s, the federal government of Canada began what has been the most extensive application of MAPSIT. Recognizing that for a variety of political and economic reasons, provincial support for its support supplementation proposals was not available, the federal government turned its attention to areas clearly lying in the federal jurisdiction. It concentrated further on families with children younger than eighteen, developing the notion of a "child benefit system" that consisted of programs and program provisions geared to the presence of such children, and possibly income, but lacking features such as needs tests or assets tests often associated with stigma and low participation rates. In the mid 1970s, the child benefit system (CBS) had two components, Family Allowances and personal exemptions on behalf of wholly dependent children. Except for a few details that are politically and administratively relevant but not germane to this discussion, Family Allowances at the time can be regarded as a demogrant paid to families as a given amount per child under eighteen. They were indexed annually to the consumer price index to keep the real value roughly constant, and they were taxable in the hands of the parent claiming a personal exemption for the support of the child. The personal exemption, claimable on behalf of a wholly dependent child, in turn exceeded the annual amount of Family Allowances received on behalf of the child.

A major objection to the CBS as it stood at that time was that the dollar value of benefits increased with income. This arose because the amount of the child exemption was greater than the annual Family Allowances received because of the child. In effect, the Family Allowances were tax free and there was a smaller exemption, equal to the difference between the nominal exemption and the amount of Family Allowances, whose value, in terms of tax savings, increased with taxable income. Thus, all across the income spectrum, the CBS provided higher benefits to families with higher incomes.

The federal government considered the possibility of retargeting these direct expenditures (Family Allowances) and tax expenditures (personal exemptions) to provide more benefits to low income families with children, and fewer benefits to high income families with children. In legislation passed in time to be effective for the 1978 tax year, the government rolled back indexing that had previously increased the amount of Family Allowances, and established a new child tax credit with the money thus released, along with additional new money. The new credit, in contrast to the income tax system, was administered on a family basis. It was income tested, with the algorithm for computing the amount of the credit as follows: the income base consisted of the sum of the net incomes for the parents in the family, using the income tax definition of net income. The credit permitted a large exemption, $18,000 for the 1978 tax year, against the sum. The credit for the family was then equal to a guarantee per child, $200, times the number of children receiving Family Allowances, less 5 percent of the amount by which the summed net incomes exceeded the exemption. For successive years, both the guarantee per child and the exemption against net income were indexed using the consumer price index to maintain the real value of the credit. A particularly notable feature is the refundability of the credit. If the credit exceeded taxes, the government sent a check for the excess to the family. Thus, in contrast to the situation with exemptions, low income families paying no income taxes could receive a benefit from the credit. Even coupled with the reduced Family Allowance benefits, the new CBS yielded much larger benefits for low income families, but smaller ones for higher income families, with more families "winning" from the change than losing.

In terms of general behavior across the income spectrum, the new system starts at a higher benefit level than the old system, increases slightly as the families begin to pay taxes (and the personal exemption for children begins to be valuable), declines substantially as the credit begins to reduce, and finally, well beyond the median income level, begins to increase again when the credit has been reduced to zero and the higher tax brackets make the exemptions for children more valuable. However, even with the upper end increases, the benefits provided to higher income families never approach those payable to lower income families.

Although the preceding description summarizes the policy output fairly well, it barely hints at the policy process that developed the output. Although a full description of this process would encompass a multitude of social, economic, political, and institutional factors, here we shall concentrate on the analytic role that MAPSIT played.

Early on, the requirement for an accurate picture of the then existing system became apparent. Models derived the effective child benefits as a function of earnings for many combinations of number of children, number of parents, and province of residence. More detailed runs yielded the tax savings resulting from the personal exemptions from children and the after tax value of the taxable Family Allowance benefits. Analysts constructed several models and initiated many solutions of the models for the different configurations of families.

Analysts then generalized or modified the models of the existing system to reflect proposals for changes. They added new logic for the child tax credit and parameterized parts of the models to permit the substitution of alternative values (such as new values for Family Allowance benefits, for the taxability of Family Allowances, the tax credits guarantee per child and for the exemption) and indicators for the choice of income definition for the credit.

Solutions of the generalized models then provided valuable policy inputs. Those developing the policy proposals could investigate new approaches, new logic, or new sets of parameter values, discovering in minutes or hours their impacts on families of interest. Understandably, many of the analyses dealt with the comparative impacts of the proposals relative to the existing system. A typical resultant mapping showed the difference between benefits in the new and old systems, with the breakeven for the mapping yielding the income value at which a family ceased to be better off under the proposed system. Such analyses, supplementing the mappings showing the new and old benefits proper, provided a micro-level illustration of the macro-derived distributions of winners and losers.

Other sets of MAPSIT analyses, more narrowly focused, also played an important role in the development of the CBS. Three examples illustrate the nature of this contribution. First, during the development of the proposal, concern arose that the new system might increase the incentives for families to split by inadvertently providing greater benefits to divided families than to intact ones. Consequently, for different possible forms of family splitting (head leaving, spouse leaving, older child leaving) analysts derived mappings that indicated the extent of family splitting incentives under the new and old systems. The measure employed was disposable income before and after the indicated split, either including or excluding additional housing costs attributable to the split. Comparisons showed that in general the incentives for splitting were less under the proposed system than under the existing one.

Second, because the child tax credit administration employed a family based income definition, drawing on an income definition from the individually based tax system, concern arose that two-earner families might cause difficulty with respect to equity. Two-earner analyses addressed the sensitivity of child benefits received to the proportion of income earned by a second earner in the family, holding constant either the income earned by the major earner, or the total earnings of the two earners.

In the third set of analyses, MAPSIT runs permitted the breaking out of the three major components of the CBS: the after tax value of Family Allowances, the value to the family of personal exemptions for wholly dependent children, and the amount of the child tax credit. Graphic presentations of this information from MAPSIT's PLOT command displayed clearly the relative contributions of the components and their interaction as a coordinated system. Such diagrams were a major aid to those seeking to understand the operation of the proposed system.

Throughout these extensive analyses, in which analysts developed several models and even more versions of models, and in which hundreds of solutions addressed the specific impacts occasioned by the interactions of particular parameter configurations and family structures, two characteristics of MAPSIT usage became especially apparent. First, MAPSIT's micro-oriented analyses provided an effective complement to the traditional cost and clientele macro results. They allowed policymakers to employ realistic examples to speed the development process. They indicated the sensitivity of system impacts on individual families with respect to changes in the logic or parameters of proposed systems. They indicated the nature of the system incentives for increases or decreases in labor force participation and permitted the calculation of true marginal tax rates where work incentives were an issue. MAPSIT tables and graphic displays saw extensive usage in briefing materials for those supervising the development of the proposals. In a highly unusual move, the Minister of Health and Welfare introduced graphics from MAPSIT analyses into Hansard, the Canadian equivalent to the U.S. Congressional Record, during the legislative debates on the proposal. As well, microlevel illustrations played an important part in materials communicating the new system to the public.

Second, with MAPSIT the examples generation that is an inevitable part of policy development was carried out in a very timely and responsive manner. With appropriate MAPSIT models available, and at times even when they were not, analyses that would have required days or weeks to perform by hand were generated in minutes or at most hours, coming complete with customized tabular presentations and automated graphics capabilities.

MAPSIT's contribution to CBS analyses did not terminate with the passage of the relevant legislation and the communication of the new provisions to the public. In 1981 a number of groups both in and outside the government made recommendations about possible reforms or extensions to the system. Proposals were made to eliminate the child tax credit and channel all of the revenues to increased Family Allowances, to end Family Allowances and use the funds to increase the child tax credit, to terminate personal exemptions on behalf of children and raise the child tax credit, and to make Family Allowances nontaxable. Common to several of the proposals was concern with the fact that the net child benefits increased with income over some income ranges, even though the overall trend was clearly a decreasing of benefits for increased incomes. For the most part, proposals sought to create a system whose benefits declined steadily with increases in income, possibly after an initial flat segment.

Health and Welfare Canada carried out an extensive series of analyses on a scale comparable to those undertaken prior to the 1978 reform of the CBS. Nearly all of the previous analyses were redone with updated parameters and a new status quo system, and with the proposals as the new systems being evaluated. As before, the MAPSIT analyses focused largely on ascertaining the comparative impacts of the existing and proposed systems for families across the spectrum of numbers of parents, numbers of children, numbers of earners, and provinces. In addition, however, a second use arose. MAPSIT analyses supplemented macroanalyses to generate an independent estimate of the proportions of families that would benefit by switching from the status quo to various proposed systems. Using a fairly representative set of family structures, analysts calculated changes in child benefits as a function of income. Then, applying exogenous information about the frequency of the family types and the relevant income distributions, they estimated the numbers and proportions of families of each type who would benefit financially from a change to one of the proposed systems. Reassuringly, the proportions of winners and losers closely matched those from the aggregate cost and clientele estimations.

TIMELINESS

One of the most important characteristics of MAPSIT has been the possibility of producing analyses in a timely fashion. In situation after situation MAPSIT analyses have been produced that were available when they were needed, not several months later. In part they are faster than traditional microsimulation analyses because MAPSIT analyses do not use traditional data bases. More importantly, however, MAPSIT analyses are fast because of the way in which MAPSIT is designed. The use of submodels, the ease of modifying submodels, the ability to store and fetch the various schedules needed for analyzing a new situation, and the use of extensive documentation have all contributed to the speed with which MAPSIT analyses can be performed. Three short examples will give some idea of what we mean by "timeliness."

The first example involves the request for information needed for a policy discussion at the top level of a federal department within the U.S. government. At issue was a proposal to change several parameters for a major assistance program. One of the participants called Carnegie-Mellon to ask whether an analysis could be made of the effects of those changes for each of several family types and for a number of states, differing in the level of support they provided for families. Within three working hours of the request the results were available. In this case it was possible to provide results for a variety of states because models already existed for the status quo in those states. The answer to the request involved copying the existing models, making the changes corresponding to the proposed parameter changes, solving the models and comparing the results after the changes to the results before the changes.

The second example involves even quicker response. During a short break in a federal policy deliberation in Canada, a cabinet member phoned in a request for a simulation based on different assumptions and received the results before the end of the phone call, the necessary solutions and tables having been generated while the cabinet member was·talking with the analyst. In this case the cabinet member wanted to know the breakeven point if the program were changed in each of several ways. That such a request was even made, to say nothing of being met, says a great deal about MAPSIT's reputation for responsiveness.

In both of these examples the timeliness of the response of MAPSIT was due in part to the fact that the necessary models and submodels existed that allowed the analyst to proceed almost immediately to the solution of alternative outcomes. But MAPSIT has proved itself to be fast in another way as well. In more than one instance people with no prior training in how to model with MAPSIT have learned to model and have created useful models after short periods of training. As an example, two analysts from the Congressional Budget Office were sent to Carnegie-Mellon to learn how to use MAPSIT. They arrived with a problem to model and with the understanding that they were to learn how to use MAPSIT and then return to Washington where they would spend the next two months finishing their modeling work and preparing their results. When they arrived they had read through some of the material describing MAPSIT, but they had had no experience in modeling in MAPSIT or in using MAPSIT models. Their task involved designing a model to address a problem involving the interaction of social security, federal income taxes, and a set of other federal programs. Within twenty-four hours of the time they arrived at the university they had designed and built the model, run the model, obtained results for every parameter configuration of apparent relevance, and were on their way back to Washington with answers two months ahead of schedule.

COMMENT

These applications complete our descriptions of illustrative MAPSIT analyses. The particular examples given represent, of course, only a fraction of analyses performed, but they do serve to indicate the broad spectrum of demonstrated applicability.

Having discussed MAPSIT's contributions to specific problems and analyses, we now turn to issues of procedure. The next chapter addresses MAPSIT's role in the policy development process, including the demands and rewards it brings to analysts and policymakers, and its impact on the process itself.

CHAPTER 11.
POLICY USAGE :
PROBLEMS AND PROMISE

A technology such as MAPSIT does not stand on its own; rather, it exists and operates within an environment of people, institutions, practices and issues. Thus, in understanding the technology and what it can or cannot do, one must examine it within that environment. One must examine the interactions that occur among the actors, technology, standard practices, and the issues that arise. This chapter describes in overview the ways in which MAPSIT's development and applications have interacted with its policy environment. Although we make no claim to have constructed an exhaustive list of these issues nor to have solutions for the several problems raised, we believe that their identification permits a more realistic application of the technology than would otherwise be possible. With respect to the problem areas cited, we hope that this rough map of potential pitfalls will enable others to avoid those pitfalls, or at least to minimize their impacts.

Classified on functional grounds, the major topics in this chapter fall into three groupings. Its first section describes a number of issues that arise when one uses the technology to analyze income transfer systems, such application being, of course, the raison d'etre for the technology. The second section of this chapter describes the issues that arise as analysts and policymakers are trained in the use of the technology. Section 3 describes similar issues encountered in developing and extending the technology.

The contents of this chapter stem largely from our experience in the course of developing MAPSIT, training people in its use, and applying it to policy problems. Most of this experience has occurred in the Policy, Planning, and Information Branch in the Department of National Health and Welfare, Canada, and in the School of Urban and Public Affairs at Carnegie-Mellon University. Although there is no guarantee that our conclusions will be applicable to the use of MAPSIT in other policy-oriented organizations or to the development of analogous methodologies in other areas, we can see no obvious reasons why the experience should not prove a useful guide outside its specific source. To the contrary, our conversations with other analysts and our reading of policy and organizational literature lead us to believe that pressures and problems elsewhere are often quite similar.

APPLICATION ISSUES

Our discussion in the previous chapter characterizes the application of MAPSIT in terms of several analytic phases. In this section, for purposes of describing the interactions between the environment and the technology, we shall collapse the sequence described there into four steps. First, there is the decision whether or not to analyze a particular issue. Assuming that the answer is positive, there is the question of analytic style, an issue that determines the basic thrust of the analysis. Third, there is a decision that affects analytic intensity, involving the choice of an appropriate balance among speed, resources, and generality. Finally, there are several decisions concerning the manner in which one uses the analytic results. The several portions of this section address these topics in sequence.

The Decision to Analyze

Before one can begin to analyze a problem, one must recognize it. Examined more closely, the decision to analyze resolves into three components. First, one must recognize at the substantive level that a potential problem exists. For example, an analyst may observe that program regulations permit individuals to make artificial transactions that serve to increase the amount of benefits they receive. The analyst realizes that this possibility may provide unintended incentives that are inconsistent with the program goals and that there is thus a potential problem. Second, the analyst must recognize that a microanalysis could be useful in addressing the problem. Basically, the analyst is asking (1) "What might an answer to the problem look like?" (2) "Would such an answer be micro-oriented?" and (3), "If I knew the answer, would it make any difference?" In the example just given, the analyst would have to recognize the potential utility of a model that showed the increase in benefits received and matched them against such other costs as might stem from the artificial transaction. Third, assuming that the problem has survived these questions, the analyst must recognize that microanalysis is possible and achieve a rough notion of what the model would look like. The importance of this third step should not be underestimated, because it reflects the operation of the "What I think I want depends on what I think I can get" line of reasoning. Thus, analysts who are not sufficiently clever to imagine the form of a model for a problem may decide they are not interested in the answers obtained. Since MAPSIT has made new problem areas potentially tractable, historically based notions of feasibility can interfere with effective analysis.

All three of these components demand some minimum of insight and effort. In effect, these components act as sequential screening devices that serve to reduce the number of problems that are eventually subject to microanalysis, and before an analysis can begin, a problem must pass through all three screens. The "mesh size" or rejection rate for each screen is neither objectively measurable nor constant over time. Rather, the problems that pass through are determined in part by a variety of environmental pressures. Institutional and personnel factors, like time pressures, the demands of other problems, the availability of resources, and the skills and conceptual biases of analysts, will all affect the number and nature of the problems that eventually see analysis.

Even after an analyst has recognized that a problem exists and is susceptible to microanalytically oriented solution, he or she may choose to ignore it. A prime reason for such a choice is the impact of organizational boundaries. Different agencies have different responsibilities, such as income tax collection, subsidized housing, social insurance, or welfare. Associated with the different responsibilities are different views of the world, different goals, and different, if overlapping, clientele. When coordination problems inevitably arise, the response is likely to be, "Well, coordination is certainly important, but it's a complex matter, and anyway, it's not part of my mandate." In many cases such an answer is not only accurate, but also organizationally rational. Agency one's suggestion that agency two should alter some policy parameters so that agency one can improve its performance, even if it is obviously the "right" thing to do, is typically an act of war. Although there may be some positive incentives for invading another agency's domain, major dangers are involved as well. When coordination activities do receive a mandate, it is often in the form of awkward cross-departmental committees, with participants far removed from line responsibilities and often in no position to implement recommendations.

Assuming that one does not simply choose to ignore an issue, perhaps due to the influence of extraorganizational factors, there is still the problem of relative priorities. Resources for an analysis must be justifiable in terms of both other stacking analyses and analytic demands for efforts that do not address stacking. In essence the supervisor who allocates analytic resources must weigh the relevant costs and benefits of the analysis against these for other projects. Benefits are difficult to discuss at an abstract level because they are likely to reflect the pressures of the day. Costs, however, typically have a number of factors in common. First, there is the expected cost of the modeling proper. Subcomponents here include previous experience in addressing similar problems, the complexity of the systems and component transfer programs, and the extent to which one can borrow directly from models that already exist. Second, there is the extent to which the problem requires additional conceptual work. Such work typically constitutes research rather than analysis and demands an unacceptably long time frame. As well, personnel skills may be stronger on analytic fronts than on methodological fronts. Third, there is a very important concern about the extent to which one can present the analytic results in a clean, interpretable format. Overall, if one decides that the costs are acceptable relative to expected benefits from analysis, both absolutely and when compared to other investments of analytic resources, then the problem has survived the screening process.

Analytic Style

After one has decided to analyze a problem, there is still the major issue of analytic style or the flavor of the analysis to be produced. One important dimension within this issue can be characterized in terms of an analysis/example axis. At the example end of this axis one is trying to illustrate some particular effect or interaction, or the operation of a given program. At the other end of the axis one is trying to characterize the main features of the subject system. As one moves along the axis from the examples end to the analysis end, the following changes will take place in the style of analysis. There will be more attention to varying system parameters and observing the effect on the component transfers. There will be a greater concern with the generality of the model(s), and more attention to the characteristics of the subject unit. There will be a greater propensity to draw conclusions and to summarize tendencies. In addition, analysis will typically become more expensive. Where the example end of the axis focuses on the "what" aspect of the system, the analysis end focuses more on the "how," and perhaps the "why."

On a related dimension, analytic style involves the extent to which analysis is active rather than passive, and policy-oriented rather than descriptive. The MAPSIT technology in its present state is largely neutral, and it gives the analyst the capability of conveniently performing a large variety of manipulations involving parameters and relationships. At the same time, in contrast to many optimization oriented technologies, it is a passive technology; it does not possess an innate tendency to drive an analysis in a particular direction. Thus the analyst must supply the analytic drive. He or she must initiate any sensitivity analyses, must set up and compare any relevant alternatives. The analyst must choose the transfer programs in the systems and must choose an appropriate level of detail for each system component. The analyst must decide what relationships to adapt from legislation, what relationships to extract from empirical studies, and what relationships to impose by assumption. If the overall purpose of the analysis is to optimize some parameter configuration, the analyst must develop an algorithm whereby the optimization can be carried out. The overall combination of these decisions will determine the position that the resulting analysis takes on the active/passive dimension. If the model falls at one end of the axis, it will serve primarily to describe how a given system operates, and may be useful in describing, for example, the strong and weak points of the status quo. At the other end of the axis, the model may be useful in addressing the nature of the effects of a changed system, emphasizing the individual, interaction, and net impacts of altering system components. The more active end of the axis will tend to be more relevant to policy decisions, but also a good deal more expensive to execute.

A third aspect of analytic style involves the interaction between the analyst and the analyst's supervisor as the work proceeds. In the typical order of affairs, the individual who decides that an analysis is to be done is not the same individual who actually executes the analysis. This separation, when combined with the nature of the activities in modeling, means that the character of the supervisor/analyst interaction can appreciably affect the outcome of the analysis. Our experience has been that, no matter how carefully the initial specifications are laid out, a variety of additional decisions become necessary as the analysis proceeds. There are questions about what parameters should be variable from solution to solution. There are questions about the appropriate level of detail for the various transfer programs. There are previously unnoticed and undiscussed factors that turn out to affect the results in a non-negligible way. As the analyst works with the problem, a different and possibly better approach may become apparent. In resolving these problems, the analyst may either make the choices, or go back to the supervisor. The situation may well be an awkward one. The analyst juggles the cost of potentially appearing indecisive, or of not having understood the initial directions, against the possibility of making a decision that weakens the results of the analysis. The situation is complicated by the fact that at times the supervisor may not be able to recognize the implications of the choice unless they are pointed out by the analyst. It is awkward for the analyst to have to fill simultaneously the multiple, somewhat incompatible roles of employee, colleague, and teacher.

The situation may be equally awkward from the supervisor's point of view. The supervisor begins with a major relative advantage in terms of knowing what form of analysis is needed and why it is important. However, as the analysis proceeds, the analyst actually executing the effort will come to achieve a much more detailed appreciation of the detailed aspects of the problem, quite possibly including ramifications that the supervisor "should have" considered earlier. The situation may also be awkward for the supervisor because the analyst retains much of the initiative in the process, from a major input into the initial estimation of the likely costs of the analysis, to the decisions about whether the supervisor should be involved in the unexpected choices that arise during the course of the analysis. A supervisor who has become used to relying on "judgment" for resolving systems issues, or one who is not technically oriented, may perceive the ongoing interaction with the analyst, even when necessary for a responsive analysis, as threatening.

Analytic Intensity

In addition to the choice of analytic style, there is another major choice involving analytic intensity. It is something of a truism that no model can ever be completely accurate and that one must gear the model to the problem. At the same time, such lore does little to guide the analyst in the choice of detail for any given problem. The decision that the analyst makes can have, at least potentially, a great impact on the utility of the resulting analysis. In particular, if those using the results are uncomfortable with the level chosen by the analyst, then the results will carry less weight as decision inputs. The general question of modeling intensity can be divided into four subtopics: systems, programs, family structures, and parameters. For the first three of these the basic issue is one of speed versus completeness. For the fourth, it is what things are to be taken as given.

One of the more important decisions the analyst will make involves the system or systems to be modeled, including the number and identities of the component transfer programs. Sometimes, of course, the nature of the analysis may dictate the component programs. At other times the choice is likely to be largely judgmental. There is a strong tendency to include relatively common programs at the expense of those with smaller clientele. Although this practice has the advantage of improving the general applicability of the results, it may obscure or ignore the awkward or perverse situations created by programs that are less common. Often too, the analyst will tend to include the programs that he or she has modeled before or that are available from a "premodeled" library of transfer programs. Such a procedure may be responsive to pressures to complete analyses quickly, but it reduces the likelihood of discovering new trouble areas in program coordination.

In addition to the decisions about the programs to be included in the system, the analyst is faced with decisions about the appropriate level of detail for each of the component programs. Often these decisions will be influenced by what is available already, but the choice is not simply a matter of picking the most detailed version of the program readily available, assuming such a version exists. The more complete and detailed versions of a program typically demand a good deal more in the way of input parameters and values. Such attention to detail may be inconsistent with the way in which other programs in the system are modeled. However, at times the analyst knows that most of the action in the model is taking place in a given subset of the model, and he or she can afford to be less picky about the less important inputs. The analyst's ability to use elements of the library of transfer programs may be further affected by how recently the programs, and the library, have been updated. At times, the convenience in modeling a given transfer program may influence the analyst's decision to include that program in the system.

A third place where analytic intensity becomes important concerns the generality of the family structure for the model. In many cases the nature of the intended subject family will affect the choice of transfer programs in the system. For example, subsidized day care programs will be irrelevant for families without children or elderly dependents, and benefits for the elderly will be irrelevant for young working families. Even after the component programs are fixed, family structure remains important. For some transfer programs the logic of program benefits or taxes depends on the family structure. The case of U.S. income taxes provides a familiar example. The Internal Revenue Service regulations provide for a number of distinct tax schedules, since family structure characteristics such as widowhood, presence of a spouse, and the eligibility for filing jointly affect the particular schedule that may or must be used. The analyst wishing to apply a given system to a variety of family structures will have to decide whether to build multiple models for the structures or a single more general model. Although it is almost always possible to build a single general model, the overhead involved in generating a special set of "switches" to activate the appropriate logic may not be worthwhile unless large sections of the model are identical across family structures. Once again, the nature of the problem to be addressed may suggest the structure or structures that are relevant, but a great deal will depend on the analyst's judgment.

The fourth category within the topic of analytic intensity deals with the choice of those parameters and items to be fixed during the course of an analysis. Often an agency will be forced to take everything outside its own boundaries as fixed despite the relevance of the rest of the system for the success of the agency's goals. This forces the policy decisions that result from the analysis to be in the nature of "constrained optimizations." Although such restrained approaches may be useful in avoiding interorganizational feuding, they do little to advance the overall coordination of income transfer programs. The adoption of such constraints sometimes precludes any meaningful reform. Even some of the agency's own programs may have to be regarded as fixed. One common reason is that a program may have been revised too recently for another change to be politically acceptable. It is, of course, inevitable that a given analysis cannot allow everything to vary and that consequently some things will have to be taken as fixed for purposes of the analysis. However, the kinds of "blinders" often inherent in policy development appear to obscure the recognition that conditions in one transfer program can have a strong effect on what happens in other programs. It is our hope that a policy tool such as MAPSIT will allow governments to address issues of local and global rationality for income transfer programs.

To summarize, once one has decided to execute a particular analysis, there are four major choices with respect to analytic intensity. The analyst must (1) decide on an appropriate level of detail for the analysis, (2) choose the particular transfer programs for inclusion in the system, (3) determine the appropriate degree of flexibility with respect to family structure, and (4) decide which system parameters are to be fixed and which allowed to vary from solution to solution. At the low end of the analytic intensity spectrum the analyses will be cheap to construct and to explain, but are less likely to yield profound insights. At the high end of the spectrum the models constructed may be richer, but at considerable expense in terms of construction and ease in explaining, or even obtaining, useful results. The analyst must use judgment in choosing an appropriate level of intensity for a particular problem.

Using the Results

Having addressed issues of problem recognition, analytic style, and analytic intensity, we turn our attention now to the way in which decisionmakers use the analytic results.[55] One major topic in this area is the conflict between the completeness of the model and the ambiguity of the analytic results. On the basis of our experience, the more complete and detailed the model, the harder it is to summarize its implications.[56] As the model becomes more complex, the solutions become bigger and involve more relationships, thus requiring additional tables and graphs. One becomes less able to state summary relationships without qualifications about where those relationships do and do not hold. It is important to recognize that the complexity results from the system being modeled or from the level of detail in which it is modeled, and not from the technology used to model the system. Nevertheless, the resulting ambiguity and complexity are not typically considered desirable by those who wish to use the results of the analysis. Thus, the analyst and the supervisor must take care not to generate so much detail that the broad picture is lost. At the same time they must avoid simplifying the world so much that the conclusions reached simply are not realistic for the families of concern.

A second topic, closely related to one just discussed, concerns the communication of the analytic results. The results will be useful in-

---

[55] For an alternative view of the relation between modeling and the decision-making process, see Greenberger et al., 1976, Chapter 10.

[56] Of course, in one sense the model itself is a summary of the subject system, but it is not a form in which the implications are typically apparent. From this difficulty arises the focus on deriving the implications of the model and presenting the results clearly.

puts to policymakers only to the extent that they understand the results. Because of differing backgrounds and skills, different individuals will want to see results displayed in different formats. Although MAPSIT's attention to secondary analysis and to the presentation of results began with an attempt to allow analysts to avoid repetitive work, and to reduce the likelihood of transcription errors, the major payoffs have come in the ease with which the results can be communicated and used. Three distinct factors seem to be relevant. First, since the same formats are used across analyses, economies of scale appear, making it possible to give greater attention to generating a carefully designed consistent format for each form of output. Second, analysts become more likely to see the world in the same way; there seem to be fewer instances in which individuals who really agree find themselves arguing with each other. Third, the consistency of terminology and form appears to simplify the enhancement of technical skills for both analysts and supervisors. Despite the general ease in communicating results, however, some difficulties have arisen. While the forms of secondary analysis seem particularly suited to the passive description of existing or proposed systems, they are less effective at presenting cross system effects, the sensitivity of a system to changes in its parameters and relationships, and multivariable effects. It seems possible that part of the difficulty may stem from the fact that these latter concepts are simply more abstract or more difficult, or perhaps just less attuned to traditional ways of approaching transfer program analysis.

The third topic in using analytic results involves documenting the models and the results so that one can better use them at a later date. We have several times referred to earlier analyses as desirable starting points for subsequent analyses. When the earlier work has been well documented, the analyst can use it either explicitly or by analogy to make subsequent modeling and analysis more efficient. Given the time pressures relevant for many analyses then, documentation is potentially very important as a capital stock base for subsequent analyses. There are, however, countervailing pressures that discourage high quality documentation of models and their results. First, there is the same time pressure that serves to make good documentation desirable. Even with the documentation aids inherent in MAPSIT, documentation can be fairly time consuming. It is often easier to achieve an answer you need than to document the logic that led you to the approach used. Consequently, there will be a distinct tendency to push on to the next "fire" rather than tying up loose ends on an analysis just completed. In addition, analysts often find documentation boring and avoid it when possible. Second, documentation highlights any shortcuts or omissions made in the course of analysis; since one constructs a model in order to abstract certain features of transfer systems, such omissions are inevitable. However, when one conducts an analysis in the course of an adversary proceeding, good documentation can provide free ammunition to the opposition, and can cast doubt on the competence of the analyst. (See Moynihan, 1973:470-484.) Third, many of the benefits of good documentation will accrue to those outside the shop where the analysis is done. Especially within governments, mechanisms do not exist to charge the users of the documentation with any of the costs of its production. Even where cost recovery is attempted, receipts go to general revenues rather than the producers of the documentation. This "free rider" situation serves to ensure that documentation is undersupplied. The situation is aggravated by the fact that any costs are borne immediately, and benefits accrue in the future, if at all.

TRAINING ISSUES

Although our primary emphasis has been on the effect of environmental factors when applying MAPSIT to policy problems, the policy environment also affects analysts as they are trained in the use of MAPSIT. The particular aspects discussed in this section stem from our experience in teaching MAPSIT, and stacking analysis in general, to a fairly large number of analysts in the Canadian federal government, the several provinces, and to graduate students and government officials in the United States. As might be expected for a tool of this sort, the teaching has taken place in a variety of formats, from formal presentations to the Canadian Privy Council Office, to casual terminal demonstrations. It has involved executive overviews, formal three and four day workshops, and one-on-one instruction and consulting. These experiences have identified several issues.

Although MAPSIT was designed largely to automate analyses formerly carried out by hand, or that would have been carried out by hand had they been tractable, its application does require some training. Often analysts, especially those not technically skilled, will be unfamiliar with symbolically manipulating relationships rather than numeric values. Furthermore, the MAPSIT technology draws on a relatively large body of analytic techniques. Although the individual techniques are relatively simple, even experienced analysts may have some gaps in their training. But the largest necessity for training stems from the fact that MAPSIT is a piece of software. No matter how well designed a package is, most people cannot simply sit down at a terminal and start using the package. No amount of purely conceptual training prepares one for the specific prompts, keywords, commands, error messages, and output formats in the package. For users with no computer background, there may even be the necessity to explain, for example, log-on procedures, the nature of a disk file, and elementary programming techniques. In short, despite the careful attention given to consistent terminology, parallel structures, and integrated conceptual foundations in MAPSIT, one must allocate some resources to training analysts.

The diverse group of individuals for whom MAPSIT is relevant affects the nature of the training provided. Individuals across the user spectrum (policymakers, analysts, economists, statisticians, programmers, research assistants, and clerks) require different presentations of the basic concepts, different emphases on MAPSIT's capabilities, and different levels of proficiency to carry out their duties. Policymakers or senior analysts must know only enough to recognize problems, determine their general feasibility, and assign them to others; they do not require the capacity to build models themselves. For some policymakers, only the ability to understand the analytic results is necessary. For the analysts who will actually build models, training at both the conceptual and software levels is necessary. For junior personnel working under fairly explicit direction, knowledge of only one or two modules in MAPSIT may be sufficient for them to carry out relevant support activities, like the execution of specified secondary analyses using the EXAMINE module. And, of course, persons participating in the development of the package need a reasonable competence in several facets of conceptual understanding, experience with applications, and software design.

To some extent proper documentation materials can serve as a partial substitute for training, but the substitutability is far from complete. Much of the emphasis on documenting software lies in the production of reference materials. Because such materials place a premium on completeness, they typically contain information far beyond the minimum needed to use the program. The mass of material already produced in support of MAPSIT quite exceeds what a given individual needs. Second, even when documentation is written with a teaching purpose in mind, say in the form of an introductory user's guide, it cannot anticipate all of the questions that the student might have. Thus, some formal training or at least an opportunity to ask questions, is typically necessary. Furthermore, one cannot write special training documents for the multitude of backgrounds and desired learning sets. In contrast, the feedback-oriented aspect of training gives the instructor ample opportunity to respond to the needs of a particular class or individual. A curriculum with exercises is also desirable because it tends to prevent students from unintentionally convincing themselves that they have mastered a given piece of material when in fact they have not, a possibility to which learning from documentation materials is especially susceptible. The possibility of using a classroom training situation to avoid the problems inherent in learning from documentation materials should not obscure the difficulties that can arise. For example, although the classroom situation permits feedback and custom tailoring of the presentation to a given class, the different backgrounds and interests in a diverse group can make the choice of appropriate presentations and feedback problematic.

Training difficulties have been aggravated because MAPSIT has not been a static piece of software. One of the problems in being on a frontier is that one keeps discovering new applications and wanting to alter the software to address them in an integrated fashion. In many cases the provision of new capabilities has required both the development of new software and the revision of earlier software to yield a coordinated package. Such changes complicate the training procedure in two ways. First, one must inform the existing user community of the improvements, particularly where their requests instigated the change. Second, one must incorporate the improvements into the documentation and the training curriculum. This incorporation may demand reordering existing presentations so that concepts again appear in a logical order and/or dropping parts of the existing presentation due to constraints on the total amount of material that one can present in a given period.

The physical distance separating some MAPSIT users from the shop that carries out the development and training presents additional problems. When the users are in the same building as the developers and trainers, additional updating can be provided on an informal or consulting basis. This procedure is especially convenient when a change is useful but not sufficient by itself to warrant a complete new "version" of the software. However, the situation is somewhat more complicated for a user some hundreds of miles away. Although transmission of documents by mail, communication by phone and letter, automatic messages from MAPSIT printed on entry to the package, and "permitted" or shared datasets ease the difficulties somewhat, there is often no real substitute for face to face contact. High fixed costs for transportation and accommodation thus serve to decrease the frequency with which distant users become informed of changes and new capabilities.

The mass of material to be communicated also presents some difficulties. As MAPSIT has expanded to achieve the capacity for addressing new kinds of problems, the software has become more sophisticated. Correspondingly, additional conceptual and documentation material must be taught. Also, some of the more sophisticated features are difficult for many analysts to appreciate until they have gained a certain level of experience using MAPSIT. If one tries to present everything in one course, even a rather leisurely one, a wasteful overloading occurs. Consequently there is a need for some of the training, especially that relating to advanced topics, to occur in stages. Such staging is somewhat harder to achieve for users not close to the central office.

DEVELOPMENT ISSUES

Because MAPSIT has been a developing tool, and because that development has taken place in the same shop as the training and applications, the policy environment has also affected the form of the development. This section addresses a number of these effects, but does not address the substance of past or planned changes. In many respects, development of the technology takes second place to applications of the technology. Compared to such applications, problems encountered in development are thus typically less immediate, though in the longer run equally important in providing meaningful inputs toward the creation and reform of income transfer programs.

A treatment of the impact of the policy environment on the development of MAPSIT can best begin with a characterization of a typical enhancement. The process begins with recognition that some relevant substantive problem is not handled conveniently, or at all, by the existing version of MAPSIT. If the shortcoming is sufficiently serious, resources may be devoted to ascertaining both the sort of analysis that is really wanted and the feasibility of enhancing MAPSIT to generate those results.[57] Next there is an evaluation stage

---

[57] The determination of feasibility is necessarily affected by one's understanding at the time. On several occasions, enhancements that had appeared not to be feasible have in fact become feasible, as the result of conceptual advances.

in which one generates cost estimates for the enhancement and polls the user community to ascertain the expected utility of the enhancement. Assuming that a favorable balance between costs and benefits appears, actual "construction" commences. During this construction stage there is a substantial effort to coordinate the new enhancement with the previous package. For example, software changes, which make the software easier to use, may take up as many resources as the substance of the enhancement. At the conclusion of the construction stage, one proceeds to the testing stage of construction, which often overlaps with the first use of the enhancement in real applications. In the final stage, the enhancement is documented and incorporated into the training materials. Resources are needed for each of these several stages, the enhancement being forced to compete with other enhancements, applications, and training demands.

Despite efforts to look ahead, most of the development has proceeded on an item by item basis. Decisions are made for each enhancement alone by comparing the marginal costs and benefits for the package of adding the enhancement. This way of allocating resources for development does not facilitate the examination of interactions among enhancements. The difficulty is heightened by the fact that potential candidates for simultaneous development may be at different stages in the development sequence. Item by item justification and development undoubtedly impose some cost. In particular, enhancements often require changes in the previous terminology, software, and documentation. It is unclear to what extent more coordinated planning would cut the net effective cost by substituting more planning and less revision.

The policy environment has its greatest impact on package development through its effects on the expected benefits for the various enhancements. Specifically, the day to day pressures for one analysis or another can cause the relative priorities among alternate enhancements to fluctuate, at times rather drastically. Because some enhancements build on others, the resulting priorities may be awkward or illogical. Sometimes one enhancement suddenly given a high priority may drag along with it other "antecedent" enhancements that were not sufficient to stand on their own merits.

The development process is further affected by the fact that it operates with a longer time horizon than is typically relevant for applications and training. Thus, the firefighting aspect of some day to day operations can lead to uneasy combinations of applications and development. One may be forced, as a result of a high priority project, to develop a quick patchwork version of an enhancement. As is the nature of such efforts, the product may be substantially less user oriented than is desirable. However, there is always a certain reluctance to then rewrite and then redocument something that works and that a part of the user community has grown accustomed to using.

One of the major difficulties in developing a software package is forecasting the expected benefits from the various enhancements. The benefits for a particular analyst or analysis may be clear, but it is often hard to anticipate the usefulness of an enhancement to the larger user community. Since many of the enhancements rest on the frontiers of income transfer analysis, at least as we have seen it practiced, there may be times when potential users of a specific enhancement have not yet recognized the relevant problems that the enhancement would address. Indeed, the availability of the technology for dealing with a particular type of problem area is often a spur towards recognizing and analyzing the problem. Furthermore, major uncertainties often exist about the costs of various enhancements. Experience in developing MAPSIT has shown instances in which a new concept drastically simplified the achievement of a given capacity, and other instances in which an apparently straightforward enhancement turned out to be extraordinarily complex.

The policy environment also creates a tendency for the package to become dependent on a particular installation or computer. Despite professional norms that call for the avoidance of nonstandard features in software, the pressures for getting something working because it is needed can lead to the incorporation of nonstandard approaches simply because they may be faster or easier. Subsequently, one tends not to be willing to devote resources for eliminating the nonstandard aspects from something that works, especially if it works well and there are other enhancements needed. Furthermore, this tendency is cumulative. If one has used a nonstandard feature ten times already, avoidance of the eleventh has little value. Although installation dependence may be a necessary evil in the initial development stages of a package, it increases the investment required for someone else to become involved in the process, and can severely limit the transportability of the package.

SUMMARY AND CONCLUSION

The main point of this chapter is that one can understand a technology like MAPSIT only in relation to the policy environment in which it exists, including the actors, their incentive structures, and traditional practices. A failure to appreciate the importance of this point will result in a distorted view of what technological inputs to the policy process can and cannot achieve. In addressing this topic, we have focused on the interaction between the policy environment and the technology in three major areas: the application of the package to the policy problems, the training of analysts to use the package, and the development of the package itself. Within each of these areas the environment provides the relevant actors with incentives that in large measure determine the organizational practice. From the preceding description of the policy environment we think it is possible to derive the nature of the ultimate impact that a technology like MAPSIT is likely to have on income transfer policy.

The policy environment simultaneously creates the awareness that transfer programs need to be coordinated and restricts attempts to coordinate them. This situation occurs because agency specialization and limited organizational mandates serve to ensure that portions of the total transfer system will inevitably be working at cross-purposes and providing perverse incentives. The resulting confusion, inefficiencies, and ineffectiveness in turn create demands for coordination, but these demands stem from the clientele rather than from the agencies themselves and are usually ineffectual. Agencies naturally view outside attempts at coordination as attempts to reduce their autonomy and fight to defend their programs. Conflicting pressures for and against coordination result in a balance whereby the worst practices may be eventually weeded out, but without the establishment of a system that is coordinated in any meaningful sense. We believe that MAPSIT's main contribution will be to reduce analytic and coordination costs so that fewer problem areas are ignored. It will do this by making mismatches easier to detect, document and resolve, and by making the exploration of alternatives and compromises easier. From a dynamic point of view the cutting point will depend in part on the sophistication of the coordination technology. In turn, the resources allocated to improve this technology will depend on the success that is achieved in using early versions of the technology to detect and resolve coordination problems.

PART IV

CONCLUSION

CHAPTER 12.
CONCLUSION

The first portion of this chapter recapitulates the major themes of the first eleven chapters, concentrating on just what was done, and on the contributions that these chapters make to the literature. It also notes that our enthusiasm for MAPSIT centers on the vitality of the approach rather than the mechanics of the software proper. In the second portion our attention shifts from what has been done to what can be done, from recapitulation to prospectus. In it we project the nature of usage for packages such as MAPSIT, focusing on both the amount and location of such usage and its impact on policy processes and outcomes.

REVIEW

In this section we summarize what we have done in this book, linking our comments to the three main parts of the book: income transfer analysis, MAPSIT, and applications. In each area we describe not only the major themes developed, but also the unique contributions that they offer. The section concludes with a few remarks about the limitations embodied in our approach, at least insofar as it is implemented through MAPSIT.

Part I is primarily an introduction. It reviews the importance of income transfers as a part of the American economy, as well as the growing numbers and complexity of income transfer programs. Drawing on the literature, it establishes the necessity of examining program impacts on individual families, and of performing such analyses in terms of program systems. It also notes some of the obstacles to competent analysis. In all of these respects the major points represent largely a synthesis of the existing literature. The unique contributions of this part of the book begin with the recognition that it is possible to develop a decision support system that can generate the kinds of examples and analyses required. Two aspects of this recognition deserve special emphasis. First, on a theoretical level, we note that an approach oriented to the derivation of mappings or relationships is not only consistent with the characteristics of current analyses, but also provides a particularly useful way to address vital issues of equity, incentives, and sensitivity analysis. Second, on a more pragmatic level, Part I provides a rather extensive, constructive checklist of desirable features for such a decision support system.

Part II describes the MAPSIT software and its capabilities for generating examples and analyses. The existence of the package constructively demonstrates the feasibility of software that incorporates the features of the checklist. It is this feasibility, much more so than the MAPSIT software per se, that is the main theme of Part II. Subthemes include the implementation of characteristics permitting speed, reproducibility of results, comprehensiveness, a systems focus, the concentration on producing the output forms that analysts need, the support of several levels of documentation, and the correspondence to current simulation and analytic practices. These features also demonstrate the need for decision support systems and underscore our concern with MAPSIT as one implementation of such a system.

Although Part II includes illustrative applications to two relatively simple stacking problems, it is Part III that takes up applications in earnest. Portions of Part III describe the wide array of applications in which MAPSIT has already seen use. Nevertheless, such applications, as important and extensive as they may be, are only one part of the applications theme. The second major theme in Part III is the interaction of MAPSIT with the policy environment in which it operates, along with the recognition that the success of a decision support system must rest in large part with its accommodation to the manner in which things are actually done, as opposed to rigid proclamations of how things ought to be done. In this respect, the opportunity to develop MAPSIT in an active environment regularly carrying out policy development has contributed immensely to the package's utility.

Despite our enthusiasm for MAPSIT, we make no claims for it as an "ultimate tool" for income transfer analyses. Indeed, during the course of our descriptions, we have noted several respects in which MAPSIT is inadequate or awkward. Many more instances were omitted because they were irrelevant to the issues at hand. Here, we recall, by way of illustration, three particularly important shortcomings.

First, MAPSIT is weak in handling multiperiod issues, and many of the really interesting problems, many of the ones most vital to the performance of income transfer systems, inevitably span multiple time periods. From fundamental taxation issues such as depreciation schedules, through income fluctuation analyses such as those described by Allen (1973), to issues of incentives for pension plan participation and retirement savings, the analyst cannot avoid modeling systems of tax and benefit programs as they affect individuals, and particularly cannot avoid modeling them for multiple, usually consecutive, periods in time. Although MAPSIT can help analysts to do some of this, the result is usually a brute force analysis, one in which new mappings must be derived for each period in the analysis. In practice MAPSIT sees use in this area only when the number of periods is relatively small and when the problem itself is especially important.

Second, the design of MAPSIT did not anticipate the desirability of integrating mapping-oriented simulation capabilities with the more traditional cost and clientele estimation analyses. Thus, MAPSIT's implementation as an example generator did not foresee the possibility of generating an exhaustive set of examples keyed to available distributional data in order to obtain cost estimates more naturally while at the same time drawing on MAPSIT's facility for sensitivity incentive and equity analyses. Although MAPSIT has been used in conjunction with Canadian cost estimation technology, the analyses have been in large part parallel and distinct, with the integration coming, after the fact, in an inelegant, ad hoc, nonautomated fashion that barely met the demands of a vigorous policy development initiative.

Third, given MAPSIT's implementation as a primarily passive technology, focused on answering "what if?" questions, the package provides little active assistance in identifying "worst cases," in deriving optimal parameter configurations, or even in simulating families' optimal responses to decisions under their control. Although analysts can, and do, use MAPSIT in addressing such issues, the optimizations themselves typically take place outside MAPSIT, and with attendant negative consequences for speed, domain of tractable problems and documentability.

To place things in their proper perspective, we are encouraged that MAPSIT is able to make a meaningful contribution in any of these areas, particularly since none of them was important in the design stages. However, our discussion does begin to indicate directions in which improvement is both possible and desirable. Independent of the substance of such improvements, we believe there are three major categories into which improvements will fall. First, through experience, analysts will better learn how to use the existing technology. They will share useful techniques, improve standards for models and submodels, systematize naming and documentation conventions, improve validation techniques, and better recognize commonalities across issues and problems. Second, the MAPSIT software itself may continue to evolve, with new features being integrated into those already available, thereby offering new opportunities for faster, cheaper, or more elegant modeling. The ease with which many of the present features were grafted into a framework not designed to support them suggests the realism of this expectation. Many of the now central features were add-ons, from the general interchangeability of mappings and numbers, through the existence of submodels and the arbitrary independent variable capacity, to new modeling operations and new EXAMINE commands. Third, we expect the construction of new, improved packages that essentially will treat MAPSIT as a feasibility demonstration. In constructing such packages, implementers would attempt to draw on the strengths that MAPSIT exhibits, while reworking features that are awkward, and incorporating new capabilities whose utility has become apparent.

In addition to these developments with regard to MAPSIT and to other programs likely to incorporate MAPSIT-type concepts on mainframe computers, there will undoubtedly be developments in the minicomputer and microcomputer area. One such program, *VolksMap*, already exists.[58] That system, written in Advanced BASIC (BASICA), embodies the core MAPSIT capabilities in a format that permits convenient, low-cost analyses in a microcomputer (IBM-PC) environment.

Our main themes, then, are as follows: Systems of income-tested transfer programs, through their impacts on the economy, and through the incentives they provide and the decisions they induce, are central to our economic well-being, our social security, and our lifestyle. However, because of the increasing proliferation of such programs, their increasing complexity, and their extensive interactions as part of income transfer systems, the programs are regularly failing to meet their objectives, despite their sometimes massive clientele and budgets. Indeed, analyses often reveal system effects that are capricious or perverse, programs that are working at cross-purposes, and "holes" in supposedly coordinated social security and taxation systems. While some of these problems and costs are undoubtedly due to different programs with different purposes, others may be laid at the door of

---

[58] VolksMap (New York and Philadelphia: Immergut and Siolek, 1987).

analytic difficulties that prevent program administrators, creators, and reformers from appreciating how systems of transfer programs affect the individuals and families they are designed to serve. A decision support system, MAPSIT, serves as an analytically oriented example generator that eliminates many of the difficulties otherwise encountered during income transfer analyses, and substantially reduces others. Drawing on nine years of experience with MAPSIT, including personal involvement in major policy initiatives, we are confident that MAPSIT, as a tool for analysis and coordination, warrants special attention by policy actors in the income transfers field, for what the package can already do, and for the potential it demonstrates.

PROSPECTUS

Having completed our answer to the question "what?" with our statement of major themes, we turn now to the issue of "what does it all mean?" Our answer is twofold. First we attempt to describe the amount and pattern of usage that one can reasonably expect for MAPSIT and for income transfer analyses generally. Second, we anticipate the probable impacts of such usage, on the procedures by which policy is developed, and on the resulting policies.

We predict confidently that the number of systems-oriented, micro-level analyses will increase substantially. The foundation for this growth lies in the adage "What I want depends on what I think I can get." The existence of MAPSIT means that policy actors are now able to "get" more than ever before, and in a cheaper and more comprehensive framework. Thus, the analytic community is now able to respond to underlying demands for analyses and examples at a microlevel as a way of understanding, designing, and managing complex systems of transfer programs. The unique mapping oriented approach permits convenient derivation, not only of basic descriptive representations of systems, but also of analyses involving the whole spectrum of traditional concerns, from issues of adequacy and incentives, to topics of equity, sensitivity analysis, and the design or reform of transfer programs. The very act of using these kinds of analysis tends to develop a more knowledgeable policy actor and thus engender an increased demand for more analyses and more sophisticated analyses.

We believe that the increased use of this kind will be spread across the entire spectrum of policy actors. Policy analysts and critics of the existing programs and systems will make use of the descriptive facilities to document the existence of system deficiencies and the mechanisms by which they arise. Policy developers will employ the analytic and comparative capabilities to explore ways in which new programs or changes to existing programs can address perceived needs. In particular they will take advantage of MAPSIT's speed and economy to explore alternatives more fully and to compare them more rigorously. Legislators and regulators will use all three of the capabilities in choosing among alternative policies and programs. Implementers and administrators will use the descriptive capabilities to supply case workers, clients, and the public with more realistic, more comprehensible illustrations of their programs, thereby increasing public knowledge of the programs and probably reducing administration costs.

Although resting on a foundation of usage, the question of impact expands into other dimensions, and is ultimately the test by which the value of income transfer analysis must be measured. Two kinds of impacts are particularly important, impacts on the process by which transfer programs are designed or reformed, and impacts on the outputs from that process. Here, based on our experience with MAPSIT, we indicate our beliefs about the impacts of MAPSIT-like technology in both of these areas.

There seems little doubt that there has been, and will continue to be, a major procedural impact, primarily due to the improved speed and economy of analysis. Proficiency in generating examples means that more examples and more comprehensive analyses become feasible. Analysts are able to document more clearly the effects of transfer systems, and more precisely ascertain the causes of perverse or unintended effects. A standardized technology means that analyses become less idiosyncratic and that analysts, even when they are adversaries, can concentrate more on the substance of their disagreements and less on the mechanics of their simulation methods. Program design and reform become more ambitious because the economies of analysis permit actors to address more cases more fully, and because feedback is available more quickly. Also, the number of actors increases because the costs of participating in the review and design processes are no longer prohibitive. Taken together, these consequences effectively constitute a revolution when viewed in the light of procedures prior to the advent of MAPSIT.

Turning to the issue of impacts on the output of the policy process, we argue that the major effect of MAPSIT-like technologies will be better coordinated transfer systems, regardless of governmental tendencies to expand or contract those systems. In large part this coordination will occur through improved design of new programs and reforms to existing transfer programs, both of these being a result of the more comprehensive analyses made possible by improvements in speed and economy. In part coordination will occur because of larger numbers of better informed policy actors. Proponents of changes to the system will be required to demonstrate that the proposals work well, not only in isolation, but also in conjunction with the rest of the transfer programs in the overall transfer system. The ability to provide better program coordination will stem from the improved technology, while the requirement to provide better program coordination will stem from the availability of that same technology to others. Whether governments or agencies are attempting to expand an existing system, to economize by passing costs off to another jurisdiction, or to reduce or eliminate programs, they have incentives to avoid being seen to create or accentuate inequities and perverse incentives.

Obviously, both the impact and ability will be amplified to the extent that the technology for performing sophisticated MAPSIT-style analyses is economical and widely available. It is in this sense that we are enthusiastic about the VolksMap computer program that offers much of the power of MAPSIT to anyone with an IBM Personal Computer or compatible, and a rudimentary programming capability in BASIC. Although VolksMap uses algorithms very different from MAPSIT's, and many of the special features of MAPSIT are absent, VolksMap's analytic results are effectively identical. Indeed, part of the testing process for VolksMap involved replication of the results presented in this book's examples.

However, despite our expectation that transfer systems will become more coordinated over time as a consequence of income transfer analysis, we do not expect that they will become coordinated in an absolute sense. The real issue is more one of the balance between pressures for greater coordination and for less coordination. The growing numbers of agencies and transfer programs, combined with the increasing complexity of individual transfer programs, the numbers of jurisdictions involved, and the heterogeneous clientele, serve to ensure that at least portions of the total transfer system will be working at cross-purposes for some clients. The resulting confusion, inefficiencies, ineffectiveness, and capricious incentives will create a demand for coordination, but this demand will come from the affected clientele rather than from the agencies themselves, and will be thus partially blunted. Individual agencies will understandably be reluctant to sacrifice autonomy in search of increased coordination, and will defend their perspectives and practices.

The conflicting pressures for and against coordination attempts should eventually result in elimination of particularly objectionable programs and features, but without establishment of a transfer system that is coordinated in any absolute sense. We believe that a technology such as MAPSIT can contribute to this process by reducing the costs of detecting and documenting particularly bad programs and features, and by improving the potential for discovering better alternatives and compromises. Taken together, these capabilities will lead, over time, to a system that is more rational, and more coordinated, than that presently in existence.

APPENDICES

APPENDIX A. FOUNDATIONS FOR ANALYSIS

The purpose of this appendix is to present the conceptual foundations for MAPSIT. The first section, system specification, provides a more explicit treatment of what we mean by mappings and describes the ways in which they are commonly defined. It begins with a definition of a system and a statement of the restrictions that are imposed on the class of transfer programs that will be considered. It describes the typical difference between the ways in which nominal transfer schedules and income bases are specified. Furthermore, it illustrates a number of tasks performed by program administrators and shows how MAPSIT operations perform analogous tasks.

The second section, system analysis, provides additional restrictions that must be met if the system as a whole is to be analyzed. In doing that it defines the concept of precedence for transfer programs and presents two results implied by the restrictions. Finally, this second section defines what is meant by a "solution" to a problem of transfer analysis and suggests in what manner a sequence of operations in MAPSIT can be reasonably thought of as a "model."

SYSTEM SPECIFICATION

Definitions and Assumptions.

Let a system, S, be defined as a finite set of (typically) interrelated mappings. For example:

$$S = \{X_\alpha, X_\beta, \ldots, X_\omega\}$$

Variables in the system include a single independent variable, the dependent variables of interest, and such intervening variables as may be convenient for the analysis.[59] Each of the mappings, x, is a real, single-valued function of a single variable. Furthermore, not all of the mappings are necessarily functions of the same variable. However, for at least one of the mappings in the set, the single variable will be the independent variable for the system. Mappings in the system are further assumed to be continuous.[60] Referents for the mappings may include relationships such as (1) taxes payable as a function of taxable income, or (2) taxable income as a function of earnings. Associated with each mapping in the system is a single definition for that mapping.

MAPSIT employs two categories of definitions for the mappings that make up a system. One category treats a mapping as a primitive; it consists of mappings that are expressed directly. In this category, the definition of a mapping consists of a list of sequential coordinate pairs that are the segment endpoints for a continuous piecewise linear function. (Only functions that are piecewise linear and continuous are acceptable as primitives in the system.) Mappings of this sort are regularly established by legislation to relate taxes or program benefits to taxable income or available income, or other variables. Table 2.1 in Chapter 2 presents an example of a mapping of this type, taxes payable as a function of taxable income. Additional examples can be found in ILLUS4 (cf., Appendix B) in the construction of mappings for EITC (Operation 1800), the AFDC guarantee as a function of family size (Operation 3000), and the food stamp maximum bonus by family size (Operation 5100), although the last two are meaningful only at integer values.

The second category of mapping definition specifies the mapping

---

[59] The assumption of a single independent variable appears to be unnecessarily restrictive. The model's logic appears to generalize to n-dimensions with the substitution of a "piecewise hyperplanarity" property in place of the piecewise linearity actually assumed. An example of the application of multiple independent variables would be the calculation of disposable income as a function of both earned income and family assets. However, for many purposes, a single independent variable, with the other parameters in the analysis held constant, should prove sufficient.

[60] In a technical sense, the assumption of continuity is not justified in many analyses because the units of the monetary system are indivisible beyond a certain point. In practice, the restriction is a rather innocuous one. The analyst is usually content to treat income as continuous and to model sharp jumps or notches in transfer programs using appropriately steep linear segments.

indirectly, in terms of other mappings and mathematical operators. For example, the analyst may wish to define a mapping that describes the relationship between taxable income and earned income. Often mappings that describe each of the relevant components of taxable income as a function of earned income are already available. Such components might include taxable benefits as a function of earnings, allowable deductions as a function of earnings, and exemptions as a function of earnings. Similar to the construction of withholdings in Chapter 6 (Operation 2600), the analyst can simply specify the desired mapping as the sum of the relevant component mappings. In general, the indirect specification can be represented as:

$$X_i = f_i(X_\alpha, X_\beta, \ldots, X_\gamma)$$

In this expression the various arguments to $f_i(\cdot)$ are the elements of S used to compute X_i.

Nominal transfer schedules, which specify benefits (or taxes) as a function of some income base, are typically expressed as primitive mappings. They define a set of points through a set of coordinate pairs (or the equivalent), the level of the transfer being a function of the level of the income base. State welfare manuals do precisely this (see the Pennsylvania Public Assistance Eligibility Manual). Four aspects of these mappings are of interest: (1) the schedule corresponds to a relationship between two variables, (2) the relationship is piecewise linear, (3) information about just the segment endpoints is sufficient to determine by linear interpolation transfers anywhere along the schedule, and (4) the slopes on the diagrams, when the information is expressed graphically, correspond to the implicit tax rates.

Income bases, on the other hand, are usually not expressed as primitive mappings. Commonly, an income base may include a number of components, including transfers from one or more other transfer programs. One example is the income base for income taxes, which includes a number of separate deductions. Several other examples of this type of income base with multiple components were given in ILLUS4 (Operations 3800, 4300, 6000, and 6200).

When doing calculations involving income transfer programs, it is important to keep differences in the income bases in mind. One cannot, for example, always make inferences about the relative breakevens for two nominal schedules if they are stated in terms of different income bases. Often some sort of "common denominator" (typically gross earnings) is needed for meaningful analysis. Given a common denominator, however, it is possible to "add" the programs, as was illustrated in the examples in Chapters 5 and 6 (for example, CETA80. Operation 3900).

If the functions are continuous and piecewise linear, one can do much more than merely add them, as can be seen in this next section on operators.

Operators for Mappings.

The model imposes an important restriction on the class of operators permitted. Specifically it admits only those operators such that, if the arguments to the operator are piecewise linear mappings, then the result is a piecewise linear mapping. The following examples illustrate some of the more important operators:

1. The WEIGHT operator produces a new mapping by multiplying each ordinate of an existing mapping by a non-zero scalar.

2. The ADD operator produces a new mapping by adding together existing mappings, under the assumption that all the argument mappings are functions of the same variable.

3. The MAXIMUM (MINIMUM) operator produces a new mapping whose ordinate at any given abscissa is the maximum (minimum) of the argument mappings at that abscissa.

4. The MAPPING OF A MAPPING operator combines two argument mappings, Z(Y), and Y(X), to produce a new mapping, Z(X).

5. The SELECTION operator produces a new mapping whose ordinate at any given abscissa is the ordinate of either of two argument mappings, and the choice between the two is conditioned on the ordinate of a third argument mapping at that same abscissa.

Many additional operators are included in MAPSIT. The list of simple operations, including the five just described, consists of:

ABSOLUTE	IVALUE	SHIFT
ADD	LARGEST	SLOPE
CEILING	LINK	SLOPEINT
CONSTANT	MAPPING	SMALLEST
COORDINATE	MAXIMUM	STEP
DIVIDE	MINIMUM	SUBTRACT
DUPLICATE	MULTIPLY	VALUE
FETCH	PROMPT	WEIGHT
FLOOR	SCALE	
INVERSE	SELECTION	

In addition to these operations there is another set of operations, "Combined Operations," prefixed with the letter "C," that lets the analyst perform multiple operations within the same basic instruction. Some of these were illustrated in the construction of ILLUS4 and CETA80:

CABSOLUTE	CIVALUE	CSHIFT
CADD	CMAXIMUM	CSLOPE
CCEILING	CMINIMUM	CSUBTRACT
CDIVIDE	CMULTIPLY	
CFLOOR	CSCALE	

Finally, in addition to these two sets of operations there is still a third set of "utility" operations that allows the analyst to insert comments, delete mappings, and so on. Morrison et al. (1985) provide a thorough description of each of the operations in these three sets.

In actual transfer analyses, the limitations on allowable operators are not particularly restrictive. All of the operators used in typical income transfer calculations satisfy the restrictions. In each of the examples just cited the operator performs for mappings the analog of the calculations that an administrator of transfer programs carries out using scalars. For example, a person calculating income tax usually does some or all of the following types of tasks:

1. WEIGHT - The calculation of taxes or benefits regularly involves taking some fraction of a previously calculated value. "Enter on line 5 3% of line 4."

2. ADD - The income measure employed by a transfer program is typically the sum of several components. "Enter on line 24 the sum of lines 8 through 23."

3. MAXIMUM (MINIMUM) - This operator is useful in modeling many of the legislated bounds on variables in the system. "Claim as a deduction the least of Total Payments, or Limitation A, Limitation B, or Limitation C."

4. MAPPING OF A MAPPING - This operator is the equivalent of a computational formula or a table "lookup." "Determine the required contribution from the Contribution Table in the Tax Guide."

5. SELECTION - Often the method for calculating a value depends on the value of another variable. "The tax table may be used to calculate your tax only if taxable income is less than $24,000; otherwise use Schedule 1."

In each case, the mapping operator is used to do a task analogous to the task performed in the standard evaluation of benefits or net transfers computed by the program administrator(s). The only difference is that whereas program administrators are usually interested in finding the single point corresponding to the net benefits for the individual filing unit we are interested in finding the net benefits across the entire domain of the independent variable. This is, of course, the point illustrated at the beginning of Chapter 5.

The preceding description of operators characterizes an income transfer system as a set of mappings. It imposes restrictions both on the types of mappings admissible as primitives in the system and on the class of mathematical operators admissible for defining system mappings indirectly. The section illustrates some of the admissible operators and their counterparts in the calculation used to administer income transfer programs. The restrictions already considered apply only to mappings taken in isolation. It still remains to consider additional restrictions imposed on groups of mapping definitions and to derive the system properties implied by the assumptions.

SYSTEM ANALYSIS

System Properties.

Practical administration of transfer systems seems to require that the various transfer programs be arranged in hierarchies. We shall first formalize the concept of a precedence relationship between two transfer programs and define the system hierarchy in terms of that relation. Finally, we shall address the implications of the hierarchy for the system. Specific results include: (1) the extent to which the mappings in the system are orderable, and (2) the piecewise linearity of all mappings in the system.

For convenience in computing mappings that are defined indirectly, it is useful to have the definition's argument mappings already determined. Thus a mapping, X_i, in some sense precedes another mapping, X_j, if mapping X_i occurs in the definition of mapping X_j. More formally,

> X_i is defined as a direct precedent to X_j if and only if X_i is an argument in the definition of X_j.

Let $\{P_j^d\}$ represent the set of all direct precedents to a mapping X_j. For example, suppose that X_j is a mapping that describes taxable income as a function of some variable. X_j would typically be constructed as the sum of several mappings, each of which describes one component of taxable income as a function of the variable. If one of these component mappings is self-employment income, then self-employment income is a direct precedent of taxable income. Thus, in this example, the set $\{P_j^d\}$ consists of all the mappings that are components of taxable income.

One mapping may also affect another mapping indirectly. Such an effect can arise through chains of direct precedence relationships. For example, if $X_i \in \{P_j^d\}$, $X_j \in \{P_k^d\}$, and $X_k \in \{P_l^d\}$, then X_i affects X_l indirectly through the X_i, X_j, X_k, X_l chain. A more comprehensive definition of precedence must thus include both indirect and direct effects. Mapping X_i is a precedent of mapping X_j if there exists a sequence of direct precedence relationships leading from X_i to X_j. More formally,

> X_i is a precedent of X_j if and only if there exists a sequence of mappings X_i, X_a, X_b, ... , X_k, X_j such that $X_i \in \{P^d_a\}$, $X_a \in \{P^d_b\}$, ... , $X_k \in \{P^d_j\}$.[61]

Let $\{P_j\}$ be the set of all precedents to a mapping X_j. As an example, suppose that earned income is a direct precedent of taxable income and that taxable income is a direct precedent of income taxes. Then earned income is an indirect precedent to income taxes. It is quite common for a given mapping to be a precedent of another mapping through several different chains of mappings.

The model assumes that, consistent with typical administrative practice, no mapping is its own precedent. Equivalently, the model does not permit closed sequences of mappings connected by the direct precedence relation. Formally, for all $X_i \in S$, $X_i \notin \{P_i\}$. The assumption is intended to prevent problems of simultaneity and circularity that might arise in its absence. For example, without the assumption, a system or subsystem might consist of a closed chain of mappings, each mapping in the chain defined in terms of the two preceding mappings in the chain. Although it is possible that such a system could have a solution, there is no convenient starting point for the calculation of the solution.

It is useful to examine the problems of administration that could arise in the absence of the assumption about closed sequences. Allen (1972) describes one such possibility:

> A simultaneous solution of cumulative tax and transfer programs might be attractive theoretically but since, in the real world, it could only be simulated by shuttling recipients back and forth between program offices until compensating benefits adjustments converge to zero, such a solution does not seem very practical (p. 13).

---

61 A direct precedent is a special case of the more general precedence relation, one in which the relevant sequence has length two.

An alternative might require every program in the closed sequence to model the reactions of the other programs in determining benefits. However, this would require such close coordination that the several programs would effectively be a single program administered by a joint agency. Equivalently, the programs in the closed sequence could be viewed as "really" operating on income definitions and transfer schedules other than those nominally proclaimed. The assumption also precludes incompatible definitions such as two mappings, each defined as the greater of the identity mapping and twice the other. Allen (1972, pp. 13-14) suggests that simultaneity is rare in the United States. Thus far, there appear to be no examples of it in Canada.[62]

The input data for the computer implementations of both the Allen package and the present package require that the analyst order the mappings in the system such that the precedents to a given mapping occur before the mapping itself. The preceding assumptions are sufficient to guarantee that there exists an ordering of mappings that permits the calculations to be performed sequentially. More formally,

Theorem A:

> Given $X_i \in S$, $X_i \notin \{P_i\}$, there exists a sequence of mappings, say $X_1, X_2, \ldots, X_n$ such that for all pairs of mappings
>
> $X_i, X_j \in S, \; j \geq i \Rightarrow X_j \notin \{P_i\}$.

An outline of a proof by construction proceeds as follows. Define the relation ${}_iR_j$ to hold between two elements of S, X_i and X_j, if and only if $X_i \notin \{P_j\}$. Under the definitions in Sen (1970), the

---

[62] In the event that the analyst wishes to model a system with simultaneity, this can be accomplished in the model using successive approximations. Rough guesses are put into the system as primitives for a first approximation of the programs in the closed sequence. The mappings in the loop are recomputed several times, each time using the mappings from the previous iteration of the loop. It is possible that the successive versions of a mapping will not converge. However, for the few simple examples examined, where convergence was possible, it occurred rather quickly, even from bad first approximations.

relation R is (1) reflexive, (2) complete, and (3) acyclical. Sen shows that these three conditions guarantee that a <u>choice set</u> exists for any finite collection of elements. In the context of this problem, a choice set is a subset of mappings such that no other mappings in the collection have the choice set elements as precedents. The required sequence of mappings can be derived by the repeated application of the choice set operation to successively smaller subsets of S resulting from the removal of previous choice sets. The successive choice sets, in reverse order, generate all possible legitimate sequences (once the permutations within each choice set are taken into account).

The assumptions of the model are also sufficient to guarantee that all the mappings in the system are piecewise linear. More formally,

Theorem B:

For all $X_i \in S$, X_i is a piecewise linear mapping.

This property results from the assumption that all primitive mappings are piecewise linear and the assumption that only operators yielding piecewise linear mappings as outputs are admissible for defining mappings indirectly. This result is important from the point of view of an analyst building a computer model to carry out the calculations for a system, because it defines the demands to be placed on his data structures.

There are two remaining concepts that are needed: the definition of the "solution" to a system of income transfer programs and the way in which a sequence of operations on mappings can be thought of as a "model." These are taken up in the following sections.

Definition of a Solution

A numerical analysis of a transfer system is considered complete when all the system mappings have been reduced to the form of the system primitives. Systems of simultaneous linear equations provide a useful analogy. There, assuming that the system can be triangularized, the system elements, scalar quantities, are defined in terms of other system elements using a restricted class of operators, linear transformations. Once triangularization of the matrix occurs, the elements have been sequenced such that the definition of any given element employs only the values of elements earlier in the sequence. The system is considered solved when values are obtained for all the elements. The present case of transfer systems is roughly similar, but more complex. The system elements are mappings rather than scalar values. The class of permissible operators is more general than linear transformations. Also, the ordering of computation is more restricted than that permitted by the algorithm for triangularizing systems of linear equations. The concept of a system solution is, however, nearly identical. A system of linear equations is solved by determining the scalar associated with each system element. A transfer system is solved by determining the mapping associated with each system element.

Models as Sequences of Operations

We are now able to provide a more rigorous definition of a MAPSIT model and its relationship to the system of mappings. A MAPSIT model is a sequence of operations, an ordered list of instructions, most of which serve to define mappings, either by specifying them directly, or by specifying how they are to be computed from other mappings.[63] Collectively, the mappings, once they have been computed (when the operations are executed), comprise the system of relationships that the analyst has specified for analysis of the problem under consideration.

The actual computation of the mappings, either as primitives or as functions of other mappings, is accomplished by the execution of the relevant operations and is termed the solution stage of the analysis. This computation starts at the beginning of the sequence of operations and proceeds operation by operation through the sequence until the end is reached. Upon completion of the computations for all the operations in the sequence the system is complete.

SUMMARY

In this approach to income transfer analysis, a system of transfer programs is characterized as a set of interrelated mappings. Certain assumptions, such as continuity and piecewise linearity, restrict the

---

[63] Earlier we noted that some operations when executed do not serve to create mappings. Instead, they perform other functions relating to modeling systems of transfer programs: documentation of models, allocation of storage space, or control of output, and so forth.

primitives in the system. An assumption about permissible operators restricts the mappings that can be constructed from the primitives. Finally, an assumption about permissible relationships among sets of mappings imposes a partial ordering on the entire set of mappings. These conditions define a system that can be subjected to rigorous analysis.

APPENDIX B.
MODEL/SUBMODEL LISTINGS

ILLUS4.MOD

```
       Name: ILLUS4.MOD[4,2705] (Last updated 1986-06-27 10:04:14)

-100   Title: WELFARE AND TAXES FOR THE SINGLE-PARENT FAMILY

Description: AUTHORS: GORDON H. LEWIS AND RICHARD J. MORRISON
             .
             CREATED: JANUARY 1984
             .
             THE EXAMPLE ILLUSTRATES HOW MAPSIT CAN  MODEL AN  INCOME TRANSFER
             SYSTEM AS IT AFFECTS A FAMILY OVER A CONTINUUM OF GROSS EARNINGS.
             ALTHOUGH  THE  MODEL IS  REASONABLY  REALISTIC,  ITS  FOCUS  LIES
             CONSIDERABLY  MORE  WITH  ILLUSTRATING  THE  "FLAVOR" OF STACKING
             ANALYSIS  THAN WITH  THE  CONSTRUCTION  OF  AN ABSOLUTELY PRECISE
             DESCRIPTION OF  AN  EXISTING  SYSTEM.  AS A GENERAL PRINCIPLE IN
             THIS MODEL, WHERE THE DETAILS  NECESSARY FOR A PRECISE  REPRESEN-
             TATION WOULD HAVE  ENCUMBERED THE FLOW OF THE MODEL FOR ILLUSTRA-
             TIVE PURPOSES,  WE HAVE  UNHESITATINGLY  EXCISED  THE  DETAIL AND
             SUBSTITUTED WHAT WE CONSIDER REASONABLE PROXIES. PARENTHETICALLY,
             IN ALL SUCH  SUBSTITUTIONS, MAPSIT IS FULLY  CAPABLE  OF MODELING
             THE DETAILED FORM OF THE  RELEVANT TRANSFER PROGRAM OR PROVISION.
             .
             THE  MODEL  INCLUDES THREE  DIFFERENT  WELFARE/SOCIAL  ASSISTANCE
             PROGRAMS (AFDC, FOOD STAMPS, AND  MEDICAID),  THREE  TAXES (FICA,
             FEDERAL  INCOME  TAX, AND A  HYPOTHETICAL STATE INCOME TAX),  THE
             DEPENDENT CARE TAX CREDIT, AND THE EARNED INCOME  TAX CREDIT.  IN
             CALCULATING THESE TRANSFERS THE MODEL ALSO  GENERATES A NUMBER OF
             INTERVENING  VARIABLES,  E.G. PRESUMED  CHILD  CARE  EXPENSES AND
             SHELTER COSTS.
             .
             THERE ARE A NUMBER OF SPECIAL ASSUMPTIONS  AND CHARACTERISTICS IN
             THE MODEL:
                (1) THE CALCULATIONS APPLY TO A SINGLE PARENT FAMILY, BUT
                    THE MODEL PERMITS THE ANALYST TO SPECIFY ANY NUMBER OF
                    CHILDREN.
                (2) THE SIMULATION EMPLOYS A TIME PERIOD OF ONE YEAR.
                    PROGRAMS ADMINISTERED ON A SHORTER PERIOD ARE THUS
                    "SCALED UP" TO ANNUAL EQUIVALENTS.
                (3) THE MODEL ASSUMES THAT THE WORKING PARENT RECEIVES WAGE
                    AND SALARY INCOME AT A CONSTANT RATE THROUGHOUT THE YEAR.
                (4) THE ANALYSIS IS LIMITED TO FAMILIES WITH GROSS EARNINGS
                    (WAGES AND SALARIES) LESS THAN $100,000.
                (5) WHEN A SINGLE PARENT IS WORKING, THE FAMILY MAY BE
                    ELIGIBLE FOR A TAX CREDIT FOR CHILD CARE EXPENSES.
                    SECTION 9 CONTAINS THE SPECIFIC ASSUMPTIONS ABOUT THAT
                    CREDIT.
                (6) THE MODEL ASKS WHETHER THE PARENT HAS BEEN EMPLOYED
                    FOR MORE THAN FOUR MONTHS, SINCE THIS AFFECTS
                    WHETHER THE ASSISTANCE UNIT IS ELIGIBLE FOR THE EARNED
                    INCOME DEDUCTION IN AFDC.
                (7) THE MODEL ASSUMES THAT ALL CHILDREN ARE (A) UNDER AGE
                    18 OR (B) UNDER AGE 19 AND A FULL TIME STUDENT IN
                    SECONDARY SCHOOL OR AN EQUIVALENT LEVEL OF A VOCATIONAL
                    OR TECHNICAL SCHOOL.
                (8) THE VALUE OF FOOD STAMPS IS TREATED AS A CASH BENEFIT.
                (9) THE VALUE OF THE MEDICAL EXPENSES REIMBURSED BY MEDICAID
                    IS TREATED AS A CASH BENEFIT.
               (10) THE FIXED PARAMETERS IN THE MODEL EMPLOY NUMERICAL VALUES
                    APPROPRIATE FOR 1984.
 100  COMMENT:   SECTION 1: PROVISION OF VARIABLES THAT MAY CHANGE FROM SOLUTION TO
                 SOLUTION, AND DEFINITION OF THE MODEL'S INDEPENDENT VARIABLE.

 200  CHLDN_LE_5: NUMBER OF CHILDREN AGE 5 OR YOUNGER
        Operation: PROMPT
        Define CHLDN_LE_5 as a constant for all values of x, with the constant to be
        entered during the solution stage in response to the prompting message:
        HOW MANY CHILDREN ARE THERE AGE 5 OR YOUNGER?
```

```
300  CHLDN_GE_6: NUMBER OF CHILDREN AGE 6 OR OLDER
       Operation: PROMPT
       Define CHLDN_GE_6 as a constant for all values of x, with the constant to be
       entered during the solution stage in response to the prompting message:
       HOW MANY CHILDREN ARE THERE AGE 6 OR OLDER?

400  N_CHILDREN: NUMBER OF CHILDREN IN THE FAMILY
       Operation: ADD
       Make N_CHILDREN equal to the sum of:
       CHLDN_LE_5
       CHLDN_GE_6

500  FAMILYSIZE: NUMBER OF PERSONS IN THE FAMILY
       Operation: ADD
       Make FAMILYSIZE equal to the sum of:
       N_CHILDREN
       1

600  AFDCINCEXM: AFDC INCOME EXEMPTION (30 AND 1/3)
       Operation: PROMPT
       Define AFDCINCEXM as a constant for all values of x, with the constant to be
       entered during the solution stage in response to the prompting message:
       HAS THE PARENT BEEN EMPLOYED FOR MORE THAN 4 MONTHS? (1=YES,0=NO)

700  YTXBLOTHER: DOLLAR VALUE OF TAXABLE INCOME (OTHER THAN EARNINGS) FOR THE FAMILY
       Operation: PROMPT
       Define YTXBLOTHER as a constant for all values of x, with the constant to be
       entered during the solution stage in response to the prompting message:
       DOLLAR VALUE OF TAXABLE INCOME (OTHER THAN EARNINGS) FOR THE FAMILY?

800  SHELTRCOST: ANNUAL SHELTER COSTS INCLUDING HEAT, ELEC, WATER, & PHONE?
       Operation: PROMPT
       Define SHELTRCOST as a constant for all values of x, with the constant to be
       entered during the solution stage in response to the prompting message:
       ANNUAL SHELTER COSTS INCLUDING HEAT, ELEC, WATER, & PHONE?

900  STATE_EXEM: DOLLAR VALUE OF TOTAL INCOME EXEMPT FROM STATE INCOME TAX
       Operation: PROMPT
       Define STATE_EXEM as a constant for all values of x, with the constant to be
       entered during the solution stage in response to the prompting message:
       DOLLAR VALUE OF TOTAL INCOME EXEMPT FROM STATE INCOME TAX?

1000 STATE_RATE: STATE INCOME TAX RATE ON TOTAL INCOME LESS EXEMPTION
       Operation: PROMPT
       Define STATE_RATE as a constant for all values of x, with the constant to be
       entered during the solution stage in response to the prompting message:
       STATE INCOME TAX RATE ON TOTAL INCOME LESS EXEMPTION?

1100 EARNINGS:   GROSS EARNED INCOME (WAGES AND SALARIES) FOR THE FAMILY'S EARNER
       Operation: COORDINATE
       Define EARNINGS using the following co-ordinate pairs as segment endpoints:
        X            Y
       ---          ---
       0            0
       100000       100000

1200 COMMENT:    SECTION 2:  CALCULATION OF TRANSFERS FOR PROGRAMS THAT HAVE NO
                 OTHER PROGRAMS AS INPUTS
                    (1) FICA CONTRIBUTIONS ARE CALCULATED USING 1984
                        PARAMETERS AS 6.7% OF EARNINGS UP TO A MAXIMUM CONTRI-
                        BUTION OF $2532.60 (OCCURRING AT AN EARNINGS LEVEL OF
                        $37,800).
                    (2) STATE INCOME TAXES ARE CALCULATED AS THE GIVEN PROPOR-
                        TION TIMES THE QUANTITY "TOTAL INCOME (EARNINGS PLUS OTHER
                        TAXABLE INCOME) LESS THE GIVEN EXEMPTION."
1300 FICA:         FICA PREMIUMS PAID BY THE EARNER
       Combined operation: CCEILING
       Make FICA equal to the lesser of [EARNINGS weighted by .067] and the ceiling
       value 2532.60

1400 TOTAL_INC:  TOTAL INCOME (GROSS EARNED INCOME PLUS OTHER TAXABLE INCOME)
       Operation: ADD
       Make TOTAL_INC equal to the sum of:
       EARNINGS
       YTXBLOTHER
```

```
1500  YTXBLSTATE: TAXABLE INCOME FOR STATE INCOME TAX CALCULATIONS
        Combined operation: CSUBTRACT
        Make YTXBLSTATE equal [TOTAL_INC weighted by 1] minus the following weighted
        mappings, optionally imposing a floor on the result of each subtraction
   subtrahend mappings       weight factors       floor values
   ---------- --------       ------ -------       ----- ------
        STATE_EXEM            1                    0

1600  STATEINCTX: STATE INCOME TAXES PAYABLE BY THE HEAD
        Operation: WEIGHT
        Make STATEINCTX equal to YTXBLSTATE weighted by STATE_RATE

1700  COMMENT:    SECTION 3:  CALCULATION OF THE EARNED INCOME CREDIT.
                  .
                  AFTER DEFINING THE EARNED INCOME CREDIT SCHEDULE, THE MODEL
                  COMPUTES THE CREDIT ON TWO BASES:
                     (1) USING EARNINGS AS THE INCOME BASE, AND
                     (2) USING ADJUSTED GROSS INCOME (TOTAL_INC) AS THE INCOME BASE.
                  .
                  IT THEN SELECTS (1) OR (2) RESPECTIVELY AS ADJUSTED GROSS INCOME
                  IS LESS THAN OR GREATER THAN $6000 (CF. THE EARNED INCOME CREDIT
                  WORKSHEET IN THE IRS DOCUMENT, "INSTRUCTIONS FOR PREPARING
                  FORM 1040").
                  .
                  THE PRESENT MODEL USES TOTAL_INC AS A SURROGATE FOR ADJUSTED GROSS
                  INCOME.  (IF THE MODEL WERE TO BE USED FOR MORE THAN ILLUSTRATIVE
                  PURPOSES ONE MIGHT WANT TO INCLUDE MORE DETAIL IN THE CALCULATION OF
                  ADJUSTED GROSS INCOME, E.G. INCLUSION OF THE DEDUCTION FOR A MARRIED
                  COUPLE WHEN BOTH WORK.)   FINALLY, THE CREDIT IS "DISALLOWED", I.E.
                  SET TO 0, IF THERE ARE NO CHILDREN IN THE FAMILY.

1800  EICTABLE:   EARNED INCOME CREDIT TABLE
        Operation: COORDINATE
        Define EICTABLE using the following co-ordinate pairs as segment endpoints:
         X            Y
        ---          ---
        0            0
        5000         500
        6000         500
        10000        0

1900  ADJGROSS:   ADJUSTED GROSS INCOME
        Operation: DUPLICATE
        Make ADJGROSS a duplicate of TOTAL_INC

2000  EICEARNNGS: EARNED INCOME CREDIT USING INCOME BASE OF EARNINGS
        Operation: MAPPING
        Make EICEARNNGS [z(x)] from mappings EICTABLE [z(y)] and EARNINGS [y(x)]

2100  EICTOTAL:   EARNED INCOME CREDIT USING INCOME BASE OF ADJUSTED GROSS INCOME
        Operation: MAPPING
        Make EICTOTAL [z(x)] from mappings EICTABLE [z(y)] and ADJGROSS [y(x)]

2200  LESSER:     LESSER OF EICTOTAL AND EICEARNINGS (CF. WORKSHEET 6C)
        Operation: MINIMUM
        Make LESSER equal to the minimum of:
        EICTOTAL
        EICEARNNGS

2300  EITC:       EARNED INCOME CREDIT FOR THE FAMILY (BEFORE CONSIDERING CHILDREN)
        Operation: SELECTION
        Make EITC as follows:
              1. Select LESSER where ADJGROSS is at least 6000
              2. Select EICEARNNGS where ADJGROSS is less than 6000

2400  EITC:       EARNED INCOME CREDIT FOR THE FAMILY
        Operation: SELECTION
        Make EITC as follows:
              1. Select EITC where N_CHILDREN is at least 1
              2. Select 0 where N_CHILDREN is less than 1
```

```
2500  COMMENT:    SECTION 4:  CHILD CARE EXPENSES
                  SINCE SEVERAL PROGRAMS (AFDC, FOOD STAMPS, AND THE DEPENDENT CARE
                  TAX CREDIT)  USE  INFORMATION  ABOUT  CHILD  CARE  EXPENSES, THIS
                  SECTION MAKES THE INITIAL CALCULATIONS.  THE FOLLOWING ASSUMPTIONS
                  ARE RELEVANT:
                     (1) DAY CARE USE IS PROPORTIONAL TO WORK EFFORT AND THAT AT
                         $3.35/HR (MINIMUM WAGE IN JANUARY 1984) EARNINGS OF $6700
                         CORRESPOND TO FULL TIME EMPLOYMENT.  THUS, EARNINGS OF $1675,
                         $3350, $5025, AND $6700 IMPLY 25%, 50%, 75%, AND 100% EMPLOY-
                         MENT, RESPECTIVELY.  INCOME ABOVE $6700 IS ASSUMED TO BE THE
                         RESULT OF FULL TIME EMPLOYMENT AT A HIGHER WAGE RATE.
                     (2) FULL TIME DAY CARE EXPENSES ARE ASSUMED TO BE $54.70 PER
                         CHILD PER WEEK, OR $2735 FOR 50 WEEKS, BASED ON A SURVEY
                         OF DAY CARE CENTERS IN PITTSBURGH IN MAY 1980 AND UPDATED
                         BY AN AVERAGE OF 5% PER YEAR FOR ASSUMED INCREASES IN DAY
                         CARE COSTS FROM 1980 TO 1984.
                     (3) THE MODEL ASSUMES THAT DAY CARE IS NEEDED ONLY IF THE CHILD
                         IS PRE-SCHOOL AGE (FIVE OR YOUNGER).

2600  PROP_FULL:  PROPORTION OF FULL TIME EMPLOYMENT
        Operation: COORDINATE
        Define PROP_FULL using the following co-ordinate pairs as segment endpoints:
         X           Y
        ---         ---
        0           0
        6700        1

2700  COSTPERCHD: DAY CARE COSTS PER CHILD
        Operation: WEIGHT
        Make COSTPERCHD equal to PROP_FULL weighted by 2735

2800  CHLDCAREEX: TOTAL CHILD CARE EXPENSES
        Operation: WEIGHT
        Make CHLDCAREEX equal to COSTPERCHD weighted by CHLDN_LE_5

2900  COMMENT:    SECTION 5:  CALCULATION OF AFDC BENEFITS
                     (1) THE SCHEDULE OF MONTHLY MAXIMA (AS A FUNCTION OF FAMILY
                         SIZE) FOR PHILADELPHIA OR PITTSBURGH, PENNSYLVANIA, JANUARY
                         1984, IS CONVERTED TO AN ANNUAL BASIS.
                     (2) AVAILABLE INCOME FOR AFDC PURPOSES IS EQUAL TO EARNINGS PLUS
                         EITC AND OTHER TAXABLE INCOME, LESS DEDUCTIONS FOR WORK
                         EXPENSES, CHILD CARE EXPENSES, AND THE EARNED INCOME
                         EXCLUSION, IF APPLICABLE.
                     (3) THE WORK EXPENSE DEDUCTION IS $75 PER MONTH, PRORATED FOR
                         LESS THAN FULL TIME WORK.
                     (4) CHILD CARE EXPENSES ARE DEDUCTIBLE IF NECESSARY TO WORK,
                         WITH A MAXIMUM DEDUCTION PER CHILD PER MONTH OF $160.
                         WE SHALL ASSUME THAT DAY CARE IS ALLOWED PROPORTIONAL TO
                         WORK EXPERIENCE UP TO MAXIMUM OF 40 HOURS PER WEEK.
                     (5) THE EARNED INCOME EXCLUSION IS $30 PER MONTH PLUS ONE THIRD
                         OF THE NET EARNED INCOME (NET EARNED INCOME IS EARNED INCOME
                         MINUS THE DEDUCTIONS FOR WORK EXPENSES, CHILD CARE EXPENSES,
                         AND THE FIRST $30 PER MONTH), BUT THIS EXCLUSION IS NOT
                         ALLOWED IF THE PARENT HAS BEEN WORKING FOR FOUR CONSECUTIVE
                         MONTHS WHILE RECEIVING AFDC.
                     (6) BENEFITS PAYABLE TO THE FAMILY ARE THEN EQUAL TO THE
                         GUARANTEE LESS AVAILABLE INCOME, SUBJECT OF COURSE TO
                         THE CONDITION THAT THE BENEFIT NOT BE NEGATIVE.
                     (7) FINALLY, IF THE AVAILABLE INCOME (EARNINGS, EITC, AND
                         OTHER INCOME) IS GREATER THAN 150% OF THE PAYMENT STANDARD
                         (IN THIS CASE THE AFDC ANNUAL GUARANTEE) THE FAMILY IS
                         INELIGIBLE FOR ANY AFDC BENEFIT.
3000  AFDCMOGUAR: AFDC MONTHLY GUARANTEE AS A FUNCTON OF FAMILY SIZE
        Operation: COORDINATE
        Define AFDCMOGUAR using the following co-ordinate pairs as segment endpoints:
         X           Y
        ---         ---
        1           172
        2           262
        3           335
        4           401
        5           460
        6           501
        20          1313
```

```
3100  AFDCYRGUAR: AFDC ANNUAL GUARANTEE AS A FUNCTION OF FAMILY SIZE
        Operation: WEIGHT
        Make AFDCYRGUAR equal to AFDCMOGUAR weighted by 12

3200  AFDC_GUAR:  AFDC ANNUAL GUARANTEE FOR THIS FAMILY
        Operation: VALUE
        Make AFDC_GUAR the value of AFDCYRGUAR where x equals FAMILYSIZE

3300  WORKEXPDED: ANNUAL WORK EXPENSE DEDUCTION ($75 PER MONTH)
        Operation: WEIGHT
        Make WORKEXPDED equal to PROP_FULL weighted by 900

3400  MAXDCPERC:  MAXIMUM DAY CARE PER CHILD PER YEAR ($160 X 12)
        Operation: WEIGHT
        Make MAXDCPERC equal to PROP_FULL weighted by 1920

3500  MAXDAYCARE: MAXIMUM DAY CARE CONSIDERING ALL CHILDREN AGE 5 OR YOUNGER
        Operation: WEIGHT
        Make MAXDAYCARE equal to MAXDCPERC weighted by CHLDN_LE_5


3600  ADCDAYCARE: DAY CARE EXPENSES ALLOWABLE IN COMPUTING AFDC
        Operation: MINIMUM
        Make ADCDAYCARE equal to the minimum of:
        CHLDCAREEX
        MAXDAYCARE

3700  AFGROSSINC: GROSS INCOME FOR AFDC
        Operation: ADD
        Make AFGROSSINC equal to the sum of:
        TOTAL_INC
        EITC

3800  AFDCNETINC: NET INCOME FOR AFDC
        Combined operation: CADD
        Make AFDCNETINC the sum of the following weighted mappings, optionally
        imposing a floor on the result of each addition:
  addend mappings         weight factors      floor values
  ------ --------         ------ -------      ----- ------
        EARNINGS          1.
        EITC              1.
        WORKEXPDED        -1
        ADCDAYCARE        -1                  0


3900  EXEMPT_VAL: EARNED INCOME EXEMPTION IF APPLICABLE (30 PER MONTH)
        Operation: SELECTION
        Make EXEMPT_VAL as follows:
             1. Select 0 where AFDCINCEXM is at least 1
             2. Select 360 where AFDCINCEXM is less than 1

4000  EXEMPTPROP: EARNED INCOME EXEMPTION: PROPORTION EXCLUDED
        Operation: SELECTION
        Make EXEMPTPROP as follows:
             1. Select 0 where AFDCINCEXM is at least 1
             2. Select .333333333 where AFDCINCEXM is less than 1

4100  YELESSEXM1: AFDC NET INCOME LESS FIXED VALUE EXEMPTED
        Combined operation: CSUBTRACT
        Make YELESSEXM1 equal [AFDCNETINC weighted by 1.] minus the following
        weighted mappings, optionally imposing a floor on the result of each
        subtraction
  subtrahend mappings     weight factors      floor values
  ---------- --------     ------ -------      ----- ------
        EXEMPT_VAL        1                   0

4200  YELESSEXEM: EARNINGS LESS APPLICABLE EARNED INCOME EXEMPTION
        Combined operation: CSUBTRACT
        Make YELESSEXEM equal [YELESSEXM1 weighted by 1] minus the following weighted
        mappings, optionally imposing a floor on the result of each subtraction
  subtrahend mappings     weight factors      floor values
  ---------- --------     ------ -------      ----- ------
        YELESSEXM1        EXEMPTPROP
```

```
4300  YAVAILAFDC: INCOME DEEMED AVAILABLE BY AFDC
        Operation: ADD
        Make YAVAILAFDC equal to the sum of:
        YELESSEXEM
        YTXBLOTHER

4400 ·AFDC1:        AFDC BEFORE ELIMINATING BENEFITS UNDER $10 PER MONTH
        Combined operation: CSUBTRACT
        Make AFDC1 equal [AFDC_GUAR weighted by 1.] minus the following weighted
        mappings, optionally imposing a floor on the result of each subtraction
   subtrahend mappings      weight factors      floor values
   ---------- --------      ------ -------      ----- ------
        YAVAILAFDC          1                   0

4500  AFDC2:        AFDC AFTER ELIMINATING BENEFITS UNDER $10 PER MONTH
        Operation: SELECTION
        Make AFDC2 as follows:
              1. Select AFDC1 where AFDC1 is at least 120
              2. Select 0 where AFDC1 is less than 120


4600  AFDCMAXINC: MAXIMUM INCOME FOR AFDC ELIGIBILITY
        Operation: WEIGHT
        Make AFDCMAXINC equal to AFDC_GUAR weighted by 1.5

4700  AFDC3:        AFDC BENEFIT BEFORE TESTING FOR PRESENCE OF CHILDREN
        Operation: SELECTION
        Make AFDC3 as follows:
              1. Select 0 where AFGROSSINC is at least AFDCMAXINC
              2. Select AFDC2 where AFGROSSINC is less than AFDCMAXINC

4800  AFDC:         AFDC BENEFIT
        Operation: SELECTION
        Make AFDC as follows:
              1. Select AFDC3 where N_CHILDREN is at least 1
              2. Select 0 where N_CHILDREN is less than 1

4900  COMMENT:      SECTION 6: CALCULATION OF FOOD STAMP BENEFITS FOR THE FAMILY.
                    THIS CALCULATION IS DIVIDED INTO TWO PARTS.  SECTION 6A DERIVES
                    THE NOMINAL BENEFIT SCHEDULE (BENEFITS AS A FUNCTION OF THE
                    FOOD STAMP INCOME BASE); SECTION 6B DERIVES THE INCOME BASE
                    AS A FUNCTION OF EARNINGS.


5000  COMMENT:      SECTION 6A:  DERIVATION OF NOMINAL BENEFIT SCHEDULE FOR FOOD
                    STAMPS.
                        (1) THE SCHEDULES OF MAXIMUM BONUS AND MAXIMUM ALLOWABLE
                            INCOME BY FAMILY SIZE ARE CONVERTED TO AN ANNUAL BASIS
                            AND THE ANNUAL LEVELS FOR THE PARTICULAR FAMILY EXTRACTED.
                        (2) WE DERIVE THE NOMINAL SCHEDULE FOR FOOD STAMP BENEFITS
                            BY APPLYING A 30% REDUCTION RATE (WITH RESPECT TO THE
                            FOOD STAMP INCOME BASE) ON THE MAXIMUM BONUS FOR THE
                            FAMILY, BY IMPOSING A $10/MONTH ($120/YEAR) MINIMUM
                            ON BENEFITS PAYABLE, AND BY ENSURING THAT NO BENEFITS
                            ARE PAYABLE FOR INCOMES EXCEEDING THE MAXIMUM ALLOWABLE
                            INCOME FOR THE FAMILY.

5100  MAXBONUSCH:   MONTHLY MAXIMUM FOOD STAMP BONUS BY FAMILY SIZE (JAN 1984)
        Operation: COORDINATE
        Define MAXBONUSCH using the following co-ordinate pairs as segment endpoints:
         X            Y
        ---          ---
        1            75
        2            139
        3            199
        4            253
        5            300
        6            360
        7            398
        8            455
        9            512
        10           569
        20           1139
```

```
5200  MAXBONUSMO: MONTHLY MAXIMUM FOOD STAMP BONUS FOR THE FAMILY
        Operation: VALUE
        Make MAXBONUSMO the value of MAXBONUSCH where x equals FAMILYSIZE

5300  MAXBONUSYR: ANNUAL MAXIMUM FOOD STAMP BONUS FOR THE FAMILY
        Operation: WEIGHT
        Make MAXBONUSYR equal to MAXBONUSMO weighted by 12

5400  MAXINCSCH:  MONTHLY MAXIMUM ALLOWABLE INCOME BY FAMILY SIZE (JAN 1984)
        Operation: COORDINATE
        Define MAXINCSCH using the following co-ordinate pairs as segment endpoints:
         X           Y
        ---         ---
        1           527
        2           709
        3           891
        4           1073
        5           1255
        6           1437
        7           1619
        8           1801
        9           1983
        10          2165
        20          3985


5500  FSMAXINCMO: FOOD STAMP MAXIMUM ALLOWABLE INCOME FOR THE FAMILY (MONTHLY)
        Operation: VALUE
        Make FSMAXINCMO the value of MAXINCSCH where x equals FAMILYSIZE

5600  FSMAXINCYR: FOOD STAMP MAXIMUM ALLOWABLE INCOME FOR THE FAMILY (ANNUALLY)
        Operation: WEIGHT
        Make FSMAXINCYR equal to FSMAXINCMO weighted by 12

5700  TENTNOMFS:  NOMINAL FOOD STAMP BENEFIT SCHEDULE (BEFORE MAX INC PROVISION)
        Combined operation: CSUBTRACT
        Make TENTNOMFS equal [MAXBONUSYR weighted by 1] minus the following weighted
        mappings, optionally imposing a floor on the result of each subtraction
   subtrahend mappings     weight factors      floor values
   ---------- --------     ------ -------     ----- ------
        INDEP               .30                 120

5800  NOMFSSCH:   NOMINAL FOOD STAMPS BENEFIT SCHEDULE FOR THE FAMILY
        Operation: SELECTION
        Make NOMFSSCH as follows:
             1. Select 0 where INDEP is at least FSMAXINCYR
             2. Select TENTNOMFS where INDEP is less than FSMAXINCYR

5900  COMMENT:    SECTION 6B:   DERIVATION OF THE INCOME BASE FOR FOOD STAMPS
                  (1) "NET FOOD STAMP INCOME" IS CALCULATED AS THE SUM OF
                      EARNED AND UNEARNED INCOME (INCLUDING IN THE LATTER
                      CATEGORY AID FROM FEDERAL OR FEDERALLY AIDED PUBLIC
                      ASSISTANCE PROGRAMS, E.G. SSI AND AFDC), LESS A
                      SERIES OF DEDUCTIONS:
                         * AN EARNED INCOME DEDUCTION, 18% OF EARNED INCOME
                         * A STANDARD DEDUCTION, $1020 PER YEAR ($85 PER MO.)
                         * A DEPENDENT CARE DEDUCTION
                         * A DEDUCTION FOR MEDICAL COSTS IN EXCESS OF $35
                           A MONTH (FOR PERSONS AGE 60 AND OVER)
                         * AN EXCESS SHELTER COSTS DEDUCTION
                  (2) THE MAXIMUM DEPENDENT CARE DEDUCTION IS $1380 PER YEAR
                      ($115 PER MONTH) OR ACTUAL EXPENSES WHICHEVER IS LESS.
                      WE ASSUME THAT THE ACTUAL EXPENSES ARE EQUAL TO
                      THE CHILD CARE EXPENSES PREVIOUSLY DEFINED IN THIS
                      MODEL AND THAT THERE ARE NO OTHER DEPENDENT CARE
                      EXPENSES.
                  (3) EXCESS SHELTER COSTS ARE DEFINED AS SHELTER COSTS IN
                      EXCESS OF 50% OF THE NET INCOME (INCOME AFTER THE
                      EARNED INCOME DEDUCTION, THE STANDARD DEDUCTION, THE
                      MEDICAL EXPENSE DEDUCTION, AND THE DEPENDENT CARE
                      DEDUCTION).  THESE EXCESS EXPENSES ARE DEDUCTIBLE UP
                      TO A MAXIMUM OF $1380 PER YEAR ($115 PER MONTH), BUT
                      THE COMBINED DEDUCTION FOR DEPENDENT CARE EXPENSES AND
                      EXCESS SHELTER COSTS CANNOT EXCEED $1380 PER YEAR.
```

```
6000  FSTOTALINC: TOTAL INCOME COUNTED BY FOOD STAMPS
        Operation: ADD
        Make FSTOTALINC equal to the sum of:
        TOTAL_INC
        AFDC

6100  CHDCAREDED: FOOD STAMP CHILD CARE DEDUCTION
        Operation: MINIMUM
        Make CHDCAREDED equal to the minimum of:
        CHLDCAREEX
        1380

6200  FSNETINC:    NET FOOD STAMP INCOME
        Combined operation: CSUBTRACT
        Make FSNETINC equal [FSTOTALINC weighted by 1] minus the following weighted
        mappings, optionally imposing a floor on the result of each subtraction
   subtrahend mappings       weight factors       floor values
   ---------- --------       ------ -------       ----- ------
        EARNINGS             .18
        1020                 1
        CHDCAREDED           1                    0

6300  TSHELALLW:  TENTATIVE SHELTER ALLOWANCE, BEFORE MAX ALLOWABLE DEDUCTION
        Combined operation: CSUBTRACT
        Make TSHELALLW equal [SHELTRCOST weighted by 1] minus the following weighted
        mappings, optionally imposing a floor on the result of each subtraction
   subtrahend mappings       weight factors       floor values
   ---------- --------       ------ -------       ----- ------
        FSNETINC             .5                   0


6400  MAXSHLTDED: FOOD STAMP MAXIMUM SHELTER DEDUCTION
        Combined operation: CSUBTRACT
        Make MAXSHLTDED equal [1380 weighted by 1] minus the following weighted
        mappings, optionally imposing a floor on the result of each subtraction
   subtrahend mappings       weight factors       floor values
   ---------- --------       ------ -------       ----- ------
        CHDCAREDED           1                    0

6500  FSSHELALLW: FOOD STAMP SHELTER ALLOWANCE
        Operation: MINIMUM
        Make FSSHELALLW equal to the minimum of:
        TSHELALLW
        MAXSHLTDED

6600  FSINCBASE:  FOOD STAMPS INCOME BASE FOR THE FAMILY
        Combined operation: CSUBTRACT
        Make FSINCBASE equal [FSNETINC weighted by 1] minus the following weighted
        mappings, optionally imposing a floor on the result of each subtraction
   subtrahend mappings       weight factors       floor values
   ---------- --------       ------ -------       ----- ------
        FSSHELALLW           1                    0

6700  FOODSTAMPS: FOOD STAMPS BENEFIT PAYABLE TO THE FAMILY
        Operation: MAPPING
        Make FOODSTAMPS [z(x)] from mappings NOMFSSCH [z(y)] and FSINCBASE [y(x)]


6800  COMMENT:    SECTION 7:  CALCULATION OF MEDICAID BENEFITS
                     (1) FOR EARNINGS LEVELS AT WHICH THE FAMILY RECEIVES A
                         POSITIVE BENEFIT FROM AFDC, MEDICAID IS ASSUMED TO
                         REIMBURSE THE FAMILY'S MEDICAL EXPENSES; OTHERWISE
                         THE FAMILY IS ASSUMED TO PAY THE MEDICAL EXPENSES
                         ITSELF.
                     (2) L. HAUSMAN (1975, P. 45) REPORTED AVERAGE EXPENDITURES
                         FOR AFDC RECIPIENTS IN ILLINOIS IN 1971 AS $222 PER
                         PERSON PER YEAR.  BETWEEN 1971 AND 1980 THE CONSUMER
                         PRICE INDEX FOR MEDICAL CARE INCREASED FROM 128 TO 263,
                         A COMPOUND RATE OF 8.33% PER YEAR.  EXTRAPOLATED TO
                         1984 THE AVERAGE EXPENDITURES PER PERSON WOULD BE $628
                         PER YEAR.
                     (3) FAMILIES ARE ELIGIBLE FOR MEDICAID IF THEY RECEIVE A
                         A PAYMENT FROM AFDC OR IF THEY WOULD HAVE RECEIVED A
                         PAYMENT EXCEPT FOR THE $10 MINIMUM PAYMENT REGULATION.
```

```
6900  MEDICALEXP: MEDICAL EXPENSES INCURRED BY THE FAMILY
        Operation: WEIGHT
        Make MEDICALEXP equal to FAMILYSIZE weighted by 628

7000  PMEDICAID:  PRELIMINARY MEDICAID CALCULATION
        Operation: SELECTION
        Make PMEDICAID as follows:
             1. Select MEDICALEXP where AFDC1 is at least 0
             2. Select 0 where AFDC1 is less than 0

7100  MEDICAID:   MEDICAID BENEFIT
        Operation: SELECTION
        Make MEDICAID as follows:
             1. Select 0 where AFGROSSINC is at least AFDCMAXINC
             2. Select PMEDICAID where AFGROSSINC is less than AFDCMAXINC

7200  COMMENT:    SECTION 8: CALCULATION OF FEDERAL INCOME TAX
                    (1) THE TAX CALCULATION USES SCHEDULE  Z EVEN THOUGH LOW INCOME
                        FILERS WOULD NORMALLY USE THE TAX TABLES.
                    (2) SCHEDULE Z IS USED BECAUSE THERE IS A SINGLE PARENT FAMILY
                    (3) TAXABLE INCOME IS CALCULATED AS TOTAL INCOME LESS $1000
                        PER PERSON.

7300  SCHEDULE_Z: U.S. FEDERAL INCOME TAX RATE SCHEDULE Z, HEAD HOUSEHOLD, 1984
        Operation: FETCH
        Fetch SCHEDULE_Z from schedule file USZ84.SCH[4,4206]. Fetched coordinate pairs are:
              X           Y
             ---         ---
               0           0
            2300           0
            4400         231
            6500         483
            8700         791
           11800        1318
           15000        1894
           18200        2534
           23500        3806
           28800        5290
           34100        6986
           44700       10696
           60600       17374
           81800       26914
          108300       39634

7400  TAXABLEINC: TAXABLE INCOME FOR THE FAMILY
        Combined operation: CSUBTRACT
        Make TAXABLEINC equal [TOTAL_INC weighted by 1] minus the following weighted
        mappings, optionally imposing a floor on the result of each subtraction
   subtrahend mappings      weight factors      floor values
   ---------- --------      ------ -------      ----- ------
       FAMILYSIZE           1000                0

7500  FEDINCTAX:  FEDERAL INCOME TAX
        Operation: MAPPING
        Make FEDINCTAX [z(x)] from mappings SCHEDULE_Z [z(y)] and TAXABLEINC [y(x)]

7600  COMMENT:    SECTION 9:  TAX CREDIT FOR CHILD CARE EXPENSES
                  THIS SECTION COMPUTES THE DEPENDENT CARE TAX CREDIT UNDER THE FOLLOW-
                  ING CONDITIONS:
                     (1) SINCE THERE IS ONLY A SINGLE PARENT THE CONDITIONS
                         RELATED TO TWO-PARENT FAMILIES CAN BE IGNORED.
                     (2) WE ASSUME THERE ARE NO DISABLED DEPENDENTS, AND WE SHALL
                         LIMIT RELEVANT EXPENSES TO THOSE FOR PRESCHOOL CHILDREN
                         IN A DAY CARE FACILITY.
                     (3) ALTHOUGH THE CHILD CARE CREDIT IS AVAILABLE WHEN A PARENT IS
                         NOT WORKING BUT IS LOOKING FOR A JOB, WE HAVE IGNORED THIS
                         PROVISION AND ASSUMED THAT THE PARENT RECEIVES CREDIT ONLY
                         FOR THE PORTION OF TIME THAT CHILD CARE WAS REQUIRED FOR
                         ACTUAL EMPLOYMENT.
                     (4) THE TEST OF WHETHER THE PARENT HAS SUPPLIED MORE THAN
                         50% OF THE COST OF RUNNING A HOME IS APPROXIMATED BY TEST-
                         ING WHETHER THE PARENT'S TOTAL INCOME (BEFORE TRANSFERS) IS
                         EQUAL TO OR GREATER THAN THE TRANSFERS, IN THIS CASE AFDC.
                     (5) MAXIMUM ALLOWABLE DEPENDENT CARE EXPENSES ARE $2000 IF THERE
                         IS ONLY ONE DEPENDENT AND $4000 IF THERE ARE TWO OR MORE
```

```
                    DEPENDENTS, BUT THE MAXIMUM ALLOWABLE EXPENSES CAN NEVER
                    BE GREATER THAN THE ACTUAL EXPENSES OR GREATER THAN EARNED
                    INCOME.
                (6) THE CREDIT IS DERIVED AS 20% OF THE MAXIMUM ALLOWABLE
                    DEPENDENT CARE EXPENSES, BUT NEVER MORE THAN THE FEDERAL
                    TAXES TO BE PAID.
                (7) THE MAXIMUM CREDIT, THEN, IS $400 FOR ONE DEPENDENT AND
                    $800 FOR TWO OR MORE DEPENDENTS.

7700  HOMEMAINT:  PARENTAL CONTRIBUTION TO RUNNING HOME IN EXCESS OF BENEFITS RECEIVED
      Combined operation: CADD
      Make HOMEMAINT the sum of the following weighted mappings, optionally
      imposing a floor on the result of each addition:
   addend mappings          weight factors      floor values
   ------ --------          ------ -------      ----- ------
      TOTAL_INC             1.
      EITC                  1.
      AFDC                  -1

7800  LIMIT:      MAXIMUM ALLOWABLE CHILD CARE EXPENSE (2441, LINE 4)
      Operation: SELECTION
      Make LIMIT as follows:
           1. Select 4000 where CHLDN_LE_5 is at least 2
           2. Select 2000 where CHLDN_LE_5 is less than 2

7900  MAXALLWEXP: MAXIMUM ALLOWABLE CHILD CARE EXPENSE
      Operation: MINIMUM
      Make MAXALLWEXP equal to the minimum of:
      LIMIT
      CHLDCAREEX
      EARNINGS

8000  PCREDIT:    PRELIMINARY CHILD CARE CREDIT
      Operation: WEIGHT
      Make PCREDIT equal to MAXALLWEXP weighted by .2


8100  CHLDCRCRDT: CHILD CARE CREDIT
      Operation: SELECTION
      Make CHLDCRCRDT as follows:
           1. Select PCREDIT where HOMEMAINT is at least 0
           2. Select 0 where HOMEMAINT is less than 0

8200  COMMENT:    SECTION 10: CALCULATION OF FEDERAL TAXES AFTER CHILD CARE EXPENSE
                  CREDIT AND CALCULATION OF DISPOSABLE INCOME

8300  NETFEDTAX:  FEDERAL INCOME TAX AFTER CHILD CARE EXPENSE CREDIT
      Combined operation: CSUBTRACT
      Make NETFEDTAX equal [FEDINCTAX weighted by 1] minus the following weighted
      mappings, optionally imposing a floor on the result of each subtraction
   subtrahend mappings      weight factors      floor values
   ---------- --------      ------ -------      ----- ------
      CHLDCRCRDT            1                   0

8400  COMMENT:    DIFFERENT ANALYSTS USE DIFFERENT DEFINITIONS OF DISPOSABLE INCOME.
                  THE ONE WE EMPLOY HERE IS RATHER COMPREHENSIVE.  IT INCLUDES
                  ALL INCOME SOURCES FOR THE FAMILY (EARNINGS, OTHER TAXABLE
                  INCOME, AND ALL PROGRAM BENEFITS) AND THEN DEDUCTS INVOLUNTARY
                  OUTFLOWS (FICA PREMIUMS, STATE INCOME TAXES, AND FEDERAL
                  INCOME TAXES). IN ADDITION IT TREATS FOOD STAMPS AND MEDICAID AS
                  IF THEY WERE CASH BENEFITS.
8500  DISPOSABLE: DISPOSABLE INCOME FOR THE FAMILY
      Combined operation: CADD
      Make DISPOSABLE the sum of the following weighted mappings, optionally
      imposing a floor on the result of each addition:
   addend mappings          weight factors      floor values
   ------ --------          ------ -------      ----- ------
      EARNINGS              1
      YTXBLOTHER            1
      AFDC                  1
      FOODSTAMPS            1
      MEDICAID              1
      EITC                  1
      FICA                  -1
      STATEINCTX            -1
      NETFEDTAX             -1
```

```
8600  COMMENT:   SECTION 11: SPECIFICATION OF MAPPINGS TO BE PLACED IN THE
                 PRIMARY SOLUTION:
                    (1) ALL BENEFITS AS FUNCTIONS OF EARNINGS
                    (2) ALL TAXES OR CONTRIBUTIONS AS FUNCTIONS OF EARNINGS
                    (3) DISPOSABLE INCOME AS A FUNCTION OF EARNINGS

8700  SAVE the following mappings:
        Mapping name    tax factor     description
        ------- ----    --- ------     -----------
        AFDC            NO             AFDC BENEFIT PAYABLE TO THE FAMILY
        FOODSTAMPS      NO             FOOD STAMP BENEFIT PAYABLE TO THE FAMILY
        MEDICAID        NO             MEDICAID BENEFITS (REIMBURSEMENTS)
        EITC            NO             EARNED INCOME CREDIT FOR THE FAMILY
        FICA            NO             FICA PREMIUMS PAID BY THE EARNER
        STATEINCTX      NO             STATE INCOME TAXES PAYABLE BY THE HEAD
        FEDINCTAX       NO             FEDERAL INCOME TAX FOR WITHHOLDINGS PURPOSES
        CHLDCRCRDT      NO             CHILD CARE CREDIT
        NETFEDTAX       NO             FEDERAL INCOME TAX AFTER CHILD CARE EXPENSE CREDIT
        DISPOSABLE      YES            DISPOSABLE INCOME FOR THE FAMILY
```

```
----------+-----------------------------------------------------------------------
MAPPING   !       OPERATION NUMBERS      (???=UNDEFINED)
NAMES     +-----------+-----------------------------------------------------------
          !  CREATED ! USED      S=SAVED, D=DELETED, P=SCALAR
----------+-----------+-----------------------------------------------------------
ADCDAYCARE!    3600 !     3800
ADJGROSS  !    1900 !     2100     2300
AFDC      !    4800 !     6000     7700     8500     8700S
AFDC1     !    4400 !     4500     4500     7000
AFDC2     !    4500 !     4700
AFDC3     !    4700 !     4800
AFDCINCEXM!     600 !     3900     4000
AFDCMAXINC!    4600 !     4700P    7100P
AFDCMOGUAR!    3000 !     3100
AFDCNETINC!    3800 !     4100
AFDCYRGUAR!    3100 !     3200
AFDC_GUAR !    3200 !     4400     4600
AFGROSSINC!    3700 !     4700     7100
CHDCAREDED!    6100 !     6200     6400
CHLDCAREEX!    2800 !     3600     6100     7900
CHLDCRCRDT!    8100 !     8300     8700S
CHLDN_GE_6!     300 !      400
CHLDN_LE_5!     200 !      400     2800P    3500P    7800
COSTPERCHD!    2700 !     2800
DISPOSABLE!    8500 !     8700S
EARNINGS  !    1100 !     1300     1400     2000     3800     6200     7900
          !         !     8500
EICEARNNGS!    2000 !     2200     2300
EICTABLE  !    1800 !     2000     2100
EICTOTAL  !    2100 !     2200
EITC      !    2300 !     2400
          !    2400 !     3700     3800     7700     8500     8700S
EXEMPTPROP!    4000 !     4200P
EXEMPT_VAL!    3900 !     4100
FAMILYSIZE!     500 !     3200P    5200P    5500P    6900     7400
FEDINCTAX !    7500 !     8300     8700S
FICA      !    1300 !     8500     8700S
FOODSTAMPS!    6700 !     8500     8700S
FSINCBASE !    6600 !     6700
FSMAXINCMO!    5500 !     5600
FSMAXINCYR!    5600 !     5800P
FSNETINC  !    6200 !     6300     6600
FSSHELALLW!    6500 !     6600
FSTOTALINC!    6000 !     6200
HOMEMAINT !    7700 !     8100
INDEP     !PREDEFINED!    5700     5800
LESSER    !    2200 !     2300
LIMIT     !    7800 !     7900
MAXALLWEXP!    7900 !     8000
MAXBONUSCH!    5100 !     5200
MAXBONUSMO!    5200 !     5300
MAXBONUSYR!    5300 !     5700
MAXDAYCARE!    3500 !     3600
MAXDCPERC !    3400 !     3500
MAXINCSCH !    5400 !     5500
MAXSHLTDED!    6400 !     6500
```

```
MEDICAID   !     7100 !     8500      8700S
MEDICALEXP!      6900 !     7000
NETFEDTAX  !     8300 !     8500      8700S
NOMFSSCH   !     5800 !     6700
N_CHILDREN!       400 !      500      2400      4800
PCREDIT    !     8000 !     8100
PMEDICAID  !     7000 !     7100
PROP_FULL  !     2600 !     2700      3300      3400
SCHEDULE_Z!      7300 !     7500
SHELTRCOST!       800 !     6300
STATEINCTX!      1600 !     8500      8700S
STATE_EXEM!       900 !     1500
STATE_RATE!      1000 !     1600P
TAXABLEINC!      7400 !     7500
TENTNOMFS  !     5700 !     5800
TOTAL_INC  !     1400 !     1500      1900      3700      6000      7400      7700
TSHELALLW  !     6300 !     6500
WORKEXPDED!      3300 !     3800
YAVAILAFDC!      4300 !     4400
YELESSEXEM!      4200 !     4300
YELESSEXM1!      4100 !     4200      4200
YTXBLOTHER!       700 !     1400      4300      8500
YTXBLSTATE!      1500 !     1600
```

CETA80.MOD

Name: CETA80.MOD[4,2705]

-100 Title: CETA AND HOURLY WORK INCENTIVES (PENNSYLVANIA, 1980)

Description: .

CETA80 IS A MODEL WHICH CALCULATES THE ANNUAL DISPOSABLE INCOME FOR SPECIFIC FAMILY TYPES AS A FUNCTION OF THE NUMBER OF HOURS WORKED PER WEEK BY THE HEAD OF HOUSEHOLD. THE PRIMARY PURPOSE OF THE MODEL IS TO ASSESS FINANCIAL INCENTIVES TO WORK AN ADDITIONAL HOUR. MULTIPLE SOLUTIONS OF THE MODEL MAY BE USED TO COMPARE THE DIFFERENT INCOME EFFECTS OF HOURS WORKED DUE TO PUBLIC SERVICE EMPLOYMENT VS. NON-PUBLIC SERVICE EMPLOYMENT, SIZE OF FAMILY, NUMBER OF PARENTS, THE LEVEL OF AFDC BENEFITS, AND THE HOURLY WAGE RATE. THE MODEL USES 1980 PARAMETERS.

.

IN THE DETERMINATION OF DISPOSABLE INCOME, THE MODEL TAKES INTO ACCOUNT THE THREE MAJOR WELFARE/SOCIAL ASSISTANCE PROGRAMS FOR WHICH THE FAMILY MAY BE ELIGIBLE (AFDC, FOOD STAMPS, AND MEDICAID). ANNUAL ASSISTANCE BENEFITS ARE ADDED TO ANNUAL EARNED INCOME. PAYMENTS TO FICA, MANDATORY PENSION CONTRIBUTIONS (IF ANY), AND FEDERAL, STATE, AND LOCAL TAXES ARE DEDUCTED. THE FEDERAL EARNED INCOME TAX CREDIT AND THE FEDERAL TAX CREDIT FOR DEPENDENT CARE EXPENSES ARE ALSO INCLUDED IN THE ANALYSIS. EACH OF THESE COMPONENTS IS DETERMINED, AS A FUNCTION OF THE INDEPENDENT VARIABLE, HOURS WORKED PER WEEK.

.

THE MODEL HAS FIVE SECTIONS. SECTION 1 PROMPTS FOR THE FOLLOWING NECESSARY INPUTS: 1) NUMBER OF PARENTS IN HOUSEHOLD, 2) NUMBER OF CHILDREN AGE 6 OR OLDER, 3) NUMBER OF CHILDREN AGE 5 OR YOUNGER, 4) THE HOURLY WAGE RATE, 5) WHETHER OR NOT THE INDIVIDUAL IS ON PUBLIC SERVICE EMPLOYMENT IN WIN, 6) ANNUAL SHELTER COSTS, 7) THE SET OF PENNSYLVANIA COUNTIES FOR WHICH AFDC BENEFITS ARE TO BE CALCULATED (CF. PENNSYLVANIA'S "PUBLIC ASSISTANCE ELIGIBILITY MANUAL" PP. 174-5 FOR A LISTING OF THE SET OF COUNTIES), 8) DAY CARE COSTS, 9) THE LOCAL TAX RATE (IF ANY), AND ANY MANDATORY PENSION RATE. AN ADDITIONAL PROMPT MAY BE ADDED FOR AMOUNT OF TAXABLE INCOME OTHER THAN WAGE EARNINGS AN INDIVIDUAL FAMILY HAS, BUT CURRENTLY THIS VARIABLE IS SET AT ZERO.

.

IN SECTION 2 ANNUAL MANDATORY WITHHOLDINGS ARE CALCULATED. THE WITHHOLDINGS INCLUDE FICA, FEDERAL INCOME TAX, PENNSYLVANIA STATE INCOME TAX, LOCAL WAGE TAX, AND MANDATORY PENSION CONTRIBUTIONS. THIS SECTION ALSO INCLUDES COMPUTATION OF THE FEDERAL EARNED INCOME TAX CREDIT AS PART OF THE SUBMODEL THAT CALCULATES FEDERAL TAXES. SECTION 3 COMPUTES THE WELFARE ASSISTANCE BENEFIT FOR AFDC, FOODSTAMPS, AND MEDICAID. SECTION 4 CALCULATES THE FEDERAL TAX CREDIT FOR DEPENDENT CARE EXPENSES, AND SECTION 5 ESTABLISHES DISPOSABLE INCOME.

THE FOLLOWING ASSUMPTIONS AND/OR PARAMETERS WERE USED IN THE CONSTRUCTION OF THIS MODEL:

1) ALL BENEFITS AND PAYMENTS ARE DETERMINED ON THE BASIS OF THE LEGAL AND REGULATORY PROVISIONS FOR THE COMMONWEALTH OF PENNSYLVANIA IN THE FIRST HALF OF 1980.

2) HOURS WORKED PER WEEK IS ASSUMED CONSTANT OVER THE YEAR.

3) IF THERE ARE TWO PARENTS, AT MOST ONE IS ASSUMED TO BE WORKING. IN A SINGLE PARENT FAMILY, CHILD CARE EXPENSE IS CALCULATED ONLY FOR THE HOURS OF EMPLOYMENT AND ONLY FOR PRESCHOOL AGE CHILDREN. IN A MAY 1980 SURVEY OF PRIVATE DAY CARE CENTERS IN PITTSBURGH, THE AVERAGE COST OF FULL TIME DAY CARE WAS $35 PER CHILD PER WEEK.

4) MEDICAID IS ASSUMED TO BE A CONSTANT VALUE PER PERSON PER MONTH AND IS AVAILABLE AS LONG AS ONE IS ELIGIBLE FOR AFDC. THE MODEL DOES NOT AT PRESENT CALCULATE MEDICAID FOR THE "MEDICALLY INDIGENT".

5) FOR AFDC PURPOSES IT IS ASSUMED THAT AVAILABLE ASSETS ARE LESS THAN THE MAXIMUM ALLOWABLE.
6) AS STATED ABOVE, TAXABLE INCOME OTHER THAN WAGE EARNINGS IS CURRENTLY SET AT ZERO.
7) ALL TAX DEDUCTIONS HAVE DEFAULTS OF ZERO. THE ASSUMPTIONS MADE IN THE FEDERAL INCOME TAX SUBMODEL ARE LISTED AT THE BEGINNING OF THAT SUBMODEL.

```
100  COMMENT:  SECTION 1:

200  N_PARENTS: NUMBER OF PARENTS
      Operation: PROMPT
      Define N_PARENTS as a constant for all values of x, with the constant to be
      entered during the solution stage in response to the prompting message:
      HOW MANY PARENTS ARE IN THE ASSISTANCE UNIT?

300  CHLDN_GE_6: CHILDREN AGE 6 OR OLDER
      Operation: PROMPT
      Define CHLDN_GE_6 as a constant for all values of x, with the constant to be
      entered during the solution stage in response to the prompting message:
      CHILDREN AGE 6 OR OLDER?

400  CHLDN_LE_5: CHILDREN AGE 5 OR YOUNGER
      Operation: PROMPT
      Define CHLDN_LE_5 as a constant for all values of x, with the constant to be
      entered during the solution stage in response to the prompting message:
      CHILDREN AGE 5 OR YOUNGER?

500  CHLDCAREWK: FULL TIME DAY CARE COST PER CHILD PER WEEK
      Operation: PROMPT
      Define CHLDCAREWK as a constant for all values of x, with the constant to be
      entered during the solution stage in response to the prompting message:
      FULL TIME DAY CARE COST PER CHILD PER WEEK?

600  HRLYWAGE:  HOURLY WAGE
      Operation: PROMPT
      Define HRLYWAGE as a constant for all values of x, with the constant to be
      entered during the solution stage in response to the prompting message:
      HOURLY WAGE?

700  ERNDINCDED: EARNED INCOME DEDUCTION (1=YES,0=NO)
      Operation: PROMPT
      Define ERNDINCDED as a constant for all values of x, with the constant to be
      entered during the solution stage in response to the prompting message:
      IS THE FAMILY ELIGIBLE FOR EARNED INCOME DEDUCTION? (1=YES,0=NO)

800  LOCTAXRATE: LOCAL TAX RATE ON INCOME
      Operation: PROMPT
      Define LOCTAXRATE as a constant for all values of x, with the constant to be
      entered during the solution stage in response to the prompting message:
      LOCAL TAX RATE ON INCOME?

900  PENSIONRAT: MANDATORY PENSION RATE
      Operation: PROMPT
      Define PENSIONRAT as a constant for all values of x, with the constant to be
      entered during the solution stage in response to the prompting message:
      MANDATORY PENSION RATE?

1000 SHELTRCOST: ANNUAL SHELTER COST INCL. UTILITIES AND PHONE
      Operation: PROMPT
      Define SHELTRCOST as a constant for all values of x, with the constant to be
      entered during the solution stage in response to the prompting message:
      ANNUAL SHELTER COST INCL. UTILITIES AND PHONE?

1100 COUNTY_SET: THE SET OF COUNTIES FOR AFDC PURPOSES
      Operation: PROMPT
      Define COUNTY_SET as a constant for all values of x, with the constant to be
      entered during the solution stage in response to the prompting message:
      WHAT SET OF COUNTIES IS DESIRED (1,2,3 OR 4)?

1200 N_CHILDREN: NUMBER OF CHILDREN IN THE FAMILY
      Operation: ADD
      Make N_CHILDREN equal to the sum of:
      CHLDN_GE_6
      CHLDN_LE_5
```

```
1300  FAMILYSIZE: FAMILY SIZE
        Operation: ADD
        Make FAMILYSIZE equal to the sum of:
        N_PARENTS
        N_CHILDREN

1400  HOURSWRKD:  HOURS WORKED PER WEEK
        Operation: COORDINATE
        Define HOURSWRKD using the following co-ordinate pairs as segment endpoints:
         X           Y
        ---         ---
        0           0
        80          80

1500  WK_ERNDINC: WEEKLY EARNINGS
        Operation: WEIGHT
        Make WK_ERNDINC equal to HOURSWRKD weighted by HRLYWAGE

1600  AN_ERNDINC: ANNUAL EARNED INCOME
        Operation: WEIGHT
        Make AN_ERNDINC equal to WK_ERNDINC weighted by 52

1700  ANTAXOTHER: ANNUAL TAXABLE INCOME OTHER THAN WAGE EARNINGS
        Operation: CONSTANT
        Define ANTAXOTHER as the constant, 0, for all values of x

1800  AN_TXBLINC: ANNUAL TAXABLE INCOME
        Operation: ADD
        Make AN_TXBLINC equal to the sum of:
        AN_ERNDINC
        ANTAXOTHER

1900  COMMENT:    SECTION 2:
                        COMPUTATION OF ANNUAL WITHHOLDINGS (FICA, PENNSYLVANIA STATE
                        INCOME TAX, FEDERAL INCOME TAX, LOCAL WAGE TAX, AND MANDATORY
                        PENSION CONTRIBUTIONS) AND THE EARNED INCOME TAX CREDIT (EITC).

2000  NOM_FICA:   FICA (1980)
        Operation: FETCH
        Fetch NOM_FICA from schedule file FICA80.SCH.  Fetched pairs are:
              X           Y
             ---         ---
               0           0
          25905.38        1588

2100  FICA:       FICA AS FUNCTION OF HOURS WORKED PER WEEK
        Operation: MAPPING
        Make FICA [z(x)] from NOM_FICA [z(y)] and AN_ERNDINC [y(x)]

2200  PSIT:       PENNSYLVANIA STATE INCOME TAX
        Operation: WEIGHT
        Make PSIT equal to AN_TXBLINC weighted by .022

2300  LOCAL_TAX:  LOCAL WAGE TAXES
        Operation: WEIGHT
        Make LOCAL_TAX equal to AN_ERNDINC weighted by LOCTAXRATE

2400  FIT:        FEDERAL INCOME TAX FOR THE UNIT
      EITC:       EARNED INCOME CREDIT FOR THE UNIT
        Operation: LINK
        Make the above mapping(s) by linking to submodel FIT80.SUB using
        the CETA80.MOD = FIT80.SUB mapping linkages described below
             Name: FIT80.SUB[4,2705]
            Title: FEDERAL INCOME TAX CALCULATOR (1980)
      Submodel Linkages (Specified: 1980-04-22 15:17:13)
                     CETA80.MOD  FIT80.SUB   FIT80.SUB
                     mapping     mapping     mapping description
                     -------     -------     ------- -----------
      Input(s)
      --------
      required  AN_ERNDINC  EARNINGS    GROSS EARNED INCOME (WAGES AND SALARIES) (8)
                N_PARENTS   N_ADULTS    NUMBER OF ADULTS (1 IF HEAD ONLY, 2 IF HEAD
                                        AND SPOUSE)
                N_CHILDREN  N_CHILDREN  NUMBER OF DEPENDENT CHILDREN IN FAMILY
      optional  ANTAXOTHER  YTXBLOTHER  OTHER TAXABLE INCOME FOR THE FILING UNIT
                                        (9-21)
                PSIT        TOTALTAXES  STATE & LOC. INC., REAL EST., SALES & OTHER
                                        TAXES (A,16 & 34)
```

```
      Output(s)
      ---------
      required  FIT        FEDINCTAX   FEDERAL INCOME TAX FOR THE UNIT
                EITC       YE_CREDIT   EARNED INCOME CREDIT FOR THE UNIT

2500  PENSIONCON: MANDATORY CONTRIBUTION TO COMPANY PENSION
        Operation: WEIGHT
        Make PENSIONCON equal to AN_ERNDINC weighted by PENSIONRAT

2600  WITHHOLDNG: SUM OF TAXES, FICA, AND MANDATORY PENSION
        Operation: ADD
        Make WITHHOLDNG equal to the sum of:
        FICA
        PSIT
        FIT
        LOCAL_TAX
        PENSIONCON

2700  COMMENT:    SECTION 3A:  CHILD CARE EXPENSES
                       SINCE SEVERAL PROGRAMS (AFDC, FOOD STAMPS, AND THE FEDERAL TAX
                  CREDIT FOR DEPENDENT CARE EXPENSES) REQUIRE INFORMATION ABOUT CHILD
                  CARE EXPENSES, THIS SECTION MAKES THE INITIAL CALCULATIONS.  THE
                  FOLLOWING ASSUMPTIONS ARE MADE:
                      (1) FULL TIME DAY CARE EXPENSES ARE ASSUMED TO BE $35 PER CHILD
                          PER WEEK, BASED ON A SURVEY OF DAY CARE CENTERS IN PITTSBURGH
                          IN MAY 1980.  ASSUMING A 40 HOUR WEEK FOR THE PREVIOUS VALUE,
                          AVERAGE DAY CARE COSTS ARE $.875 PER HOUR.
                      (2) WE SHALL ASSUME THAT THE PARENT CAN BUY ANY FRACTIONAL PART
                          OF FULL TIME DAY CARE AND CAN PURCHASE DAY CARE BEYOND FORTY
                          HOURS PER WEEK AT THE SAME RATE ($.875 PER CHILD PER HOUR).
                      (3) WE ASSUME THAT ONLY CHILDREN OF PRESCHOOL AGE (5 OR YOUNGER)
                          RECEIVE DAY CARE.  ADDITIONAL ASSUMPTIONS ABOUT DAY CARE FOR
                          OLDER CHILDREN COULD BE ADDED, BUT ARE NOT A PART OF THE
                          PRESENT MODEL.
                      (4) WE ASSUME THAT IF THERE ARE TWO PARENTS AT MOST ONE IS WORK-
                          ING AND THE OTHER PARENT (UNLESS DISABLED) IS AVAILABLE TO
                          PROVIDE CHILD CARE.  THUS, IN A TWO-PARENT, ONE-EARNER
                          FAMILY WE ASSUME THAT THERE ARE NO ALLOWABLE CHILD CARE
                          EXPENSES.
                  THE ANNUAL COST OF CHILD CARE IS FOUND IN FIVE STEPS:
                      (1) FULL TIME COST PER WEEK PER CHILD IS TRANSLATED INTO AN
                          HOURLY RATE,  1/40  OF THE WEEKLY RATE (.025)
                      (2) COST PER HOUR IS MULTIPLIED BY HOURS PER WEEK
                      (3) ACTUAL COST PER WEEK IS MULTIPLIED BY 52 WEEKS PER YEAR
                      (4) COST PER YEAR IS WEIGHTED BY NUMBER OF PRESCHOOL CHILDREN
                      (5) COSTS ARE DISALLOWED IF THERE ARE TWO PARENTS IN THE FAMILY.

2800  CHLDCAREHR: CHILD CARE COST PER HOUR
        Operation: WEIGHT
        Make CHLDCAREHR equal to CHLDCAREWK weighted by .025

2900  AKCHLDCARE: ACTUAL WEEKLY COST PER CHILD AFO HOURS WORKED
        Operation: WEIGHT
        Make AKCHLDCARE equal to HOURSWRKD weighted by CHLDCAREHR

3000  CHILDCRPER: ANNUAL COST PER CHILD AFO HOURS WORKED
        Operation: WEIGHT
        Make CHILDCRPER equal to AKCHLDCARE weighted by 52

3100  TOTCHILDCR: ANNUAL CHILD CARE EXPENSES (BEFORE TEST FOR NUM. OF PARENTS)
        Operation: WEIGHT
        Make TOTCHILDCR equal to CHILDCRPER weighted by CHLDN_LE_5

3200  CHILD_CARE: ANNUAL CHILD CARE EXPENSES
        Operation: SELECTION
        Make CHILD_CARE as follows:
              1. Select 0 where N_PARENTS is at least 2
              2. Select TOTCHILDCR where N_PARENTS is less than 2

3300  COMMENT:    SECTION 3B:
                       COMPUTATION OF WELFARE ASSISTANCE BENEFITS (AFDC, FOOD STAMPS
                  AND MEDICAID).  IN THE AFDC SUBMODEL TRANSPORTATION EXPENSES ARE
                  ASSUMED TO BE 6% OF EARNINGS UP TO A MAXIMUM OF $360 PER YEAR.
                  ADDITIONAL ASSUMPTIONS AND DETAILS ARE AVAILABLE IN THE DESCRIPTIONS
                  OF THE SUBMODELS.
```

```
3400  AFDC:        AFDC BENEFIT PAYABLE TO THE FAMILY, ANNUAL BASIS
      Operation: LINK
      Make the above mapping(s) by linking to submodel AFDC80.SUB using
      the CETA80.MOD = AFDC80.SUB mapping linkages described below
             Name: AFDC80.SUB[4,2705]
            Title: A SUBMODEL TO COMPUTE AFDC BENEFITS IN PENNSYLVANIA, 1980
      Submodel Linkages (Specified: 1980-04-05 17:53:26)
                    CETA80.MOD  AFDC80.SUB  AFDC80.SUB
                    mapping     mapping     mapping description
                    -------     -------     ------- -----------
      Input(s)
      --------
      required  COUNTY_SET  COUNTY_SET  COUNTY SET SELECTION VARIABLE
                N_PARENTS   N_PARENTS   NUMBER OF PARENTS IN ASSISTANCE UNIT
                N_CHILDREN  N_CHILDREN  NUMBER OF CHILDREN IN ASSISTANCE UNIT
                ERNDINCDED  ERNDINCDED  EARNED INCOME DEDUCTION (1=Y,0=N)
                AN_ERNDINC  EARNINGS    ANNUAL EARNED INCOME
                ANTAXOTHER  YTXBLOTHER  OTHER TAXABLE INCOME, ANNUAL BASIS
                WITHHOLDNG  WITHHOLDNG  TAXES AND OTHER MANDATORY WITHHOLDINGS,
                                        ANNUAL
                CHILD_CARE  CHILD_CARE  CHILD CARE EXPENSES
      Output(s)
      ---------
      required  AFDC        AFDC_BEN    AFDC BENEFIT PAYABLE TO FAMILY, ANNUAL BASIS

3500  COMMENT:    BEFORE LINKING TO THE FOOD STAMP SUBMODEL WE SHALL NEED TO
                  CONSTRUCT MAPPINGS FOR UNEARNED INCOME AND FOR CHILD CARE
                  EXPENSES THAT ARE A FUNCTION OF ANNUAL GROSS EARNED INCOME
                  RATHER THAN AS A FUNCTION OF HOURS WORKED PER WEEK.  WHILE
                  THIS IS A MINOR INCONVENIENCE, IT IS NECESSITATED BY THE FACT
                  THAT THE FOOD STAMP SUBMODEL IS CONSTRUCTED ON AN ANNUAL EARNINGS
                  BASIS AND THAT IT DOES SOME OF ITS COMPUTATIONS USING
                  MAPPINGS THAT ARE BASED ON ANNUAL EARNINGS.

3600  HOURSAFOYE: HOURS WORKED PER WEEK AFO ANNUAL EARNINGS
        Operation: DIVIDE
        Make HOURSAFOYE equal to INDEP divided by 52
        and (by chain division)
        HRLYWAGE

3700  CHLCRAFOYE: CHILD CARE EXPENSES AFO GROSS EARNED INCOME
        Operation: MAPPING
        Make CHLCRAFOYE [z(x)] from CHILD_CARE [z(y)] and HOURSAFOYE [y(x)]

3800  AFDCAFOYE:  AFDC AFO ANNUAL GROSS EARNED INCOME
        Operation: MAPPING
        Make AFDCAFOYE [z(x)] from AFDC [z(y)] and HOURSAFOYE [y(x)]

3900  UNERNAFOYE: UNEARNED INCOME AFO ANNUAL GROSS EARNED INCOME
        Operation: ADD
        Make UNERNAFOYE equal to the sum of:
        ANTAXOTHER
        AFDCAFOYE

4000  FS_AFO_YE:  FOOD STAMP BENEFITS ANNUALLY
        Operation: LINK
        Make the above mapping(s) by linking to submodel FS80.SUB using
        the CETA80.MOD = FS80.SUB mapping linkages described below
             Name: FS80.SUB[4,2705]
            Title: FOOD STAMP SUBMODEL (1980)
      Submodel Linkages (Specified: 1980-04-06 22:10:18)
                    CETA80.MOD  FS80.SUB    FS80.SUB
                    mapping     mapping     mapping description
                    -------     -------     ------- -----------
      Input(s)
      --------
      required  INDEP       EARNEDINC   ANNUAL EARNED INCOME
                UNERNAFOYE  UNEARNDINC  ANNUAL UNEARNED INCOME (INCLUDING PUBLIC
                                        ASSISTANCE)
                FAMILYSIZE  FAMILYSIZE  FAMILY SIZE
                CHLCRAFOYE  CHILD_CARE  CHILD CARE EXPENSES
                SHELTRCOST  SHELTRCOST  ANNUAL SHELTER COSTS INCL. HEAT, WATER,
                                        ELEC., & PHONE
      Output(s)
      ---------
      required  FS_AFO_YE   FS_BEN      FOOD STAMP BENEFITS ANNUALLY
```

```
4100  FOODSTAMPS: ANNUAL FOOD STAMP BENEFIT AFO HOURS PER WEEK
        Operation: MAPPING
        Make FOODSTAMPS [z(x)] from FS_AFO_YE [z(y)] and AN_ERNDINC [y(x)]

4200  COMMENT:    THE MEDICAID CALCULATION IS AN APPROXIMATION.  HAUSMAN (1975,
                  P. 45) REPORTED AVERAGE EXPENDITURES FOR AFDC RECIPIENTS IN
                  ILLINOIS IN 1971 AS $222 PER PERSON PER YEAR.  WE HAVE ADJUSTED
                  THE 1971 VALUE BY THE RATIO OF THE APRIL 1980 CONSUMER PRICE INDEX
                  FOR MEDICAL CARE (263) TO THE MARCH 1971 CPI FOR MEDICAL CARE
                  (128).  THUS THE ADJUSTED ESTIMATE OF THE AMOUNT OF MEDICAL
                  EXPENSES REIMBURSED BY MEDICAID IS $222(263/128) OR $455 PER
                  PERSON PER YEAR IN 1980.  FOR EARNINGS LEVELS AT WHICH THE FAMILY
                  RECEIVES A POSITIVE BENEFIT FROM AFDC, WE ASSUME THAT THE MEDICAL
                  EXPENSES ARE REIMBURSED BY MEDICAID; OTHERWISE WE ASSUME THAT THE
                  FAMILY PAYS THE MEDICAL EXPENSES ITSELF.  FINALLY, WE ASSUME THAT
                  THE VALUE OF THE REIMBURSEMENT CAN BE TREATED AS A BENEFIT OF
                  EQUAL CASH VALUE.

4300  PMEDICAID:  MEDICAID BENEFIT
        Operation: WEIGHT
        Make PMEDICAID equal to FAMILYSIZE weighted by 455


4400  MEDICAID:   MEDICAID BENEFITS PAYABLE
        Operation: SELECTION
        Make MEDICAID as follows:
           1. Select PMEDICAID where AFDC is at least .0000001
           2. Select 0 where AFDC is less than .0000001

4500  COMMENT:    SECTION 4:
                       THE DEPENDENT CARE EXPENSE FEDERAL TAX CREDIT COMPUTES CHILD
                  CARE TAX CREDITS UNDER THE FOLLOWING CONDITIONS:
                       (1) IT ASSUMES THAT THERE ARE NO DISABLED DEPENDENTS AND
                           LIMITS RELEVANT EXPENSES TO THOSE FOR PRESCHOOL CHILDREN
                           IN A PRIVATE DAY CARE CENTER
                       (2) ALTHOUGH THE CHILD CARE CREDIT IS AVAILABLE WHEN A PARENT
                           IS NOT WORKING BUT IS LOOKING FOR A JOB, THIS SUBMODEL
                           IGNORES THIS PROVISION AND ASSUMES THAT THE PARENT RECEIVES
                           CREDIT ONLY FOR THE PORTION OF TIME THAT CHILD CARE WAS
                           REQUIRED FOR ACTUAL EMPLOYMENT
                       (3) THE TEST OF WHETHER THE PARENT HAS SUPPLIED MORE THAN
                           50% OF THE COST OF RUNNING A HOME IS APPROXIMATED BY
                           TESTING WHETHER THE PARENT'S TOTAL INCOME (BEFORE
                           TRANSFERS) IS EQUAL TO OR GREATER THAN THE TRANSFERS,
                           IN THIS CASE AFDC.
                       (4) MAXIMUM ALLOWABLE DEPENDENT CARE EXPENSES ARE $2000
                           IF THERE IS ONLY ONE DEPENDENT AND $4000 IF THERE ARE TWO
                           OR MORE DEPENDENTS.  BUT THE MAXIMUM ALLOWABLE EXPENSES
                           CAN NEVER BE GREATER THAN THE ACTUAL EXPENSES OR GREATER
                           THAN EARNED INCOME
                       (5) THE CREDIT IS DERIVED AS 20% OF THE MAXIMUM ALLOWABLE
                           DEPENDENT CARE EXPENSES, BUT NEVER MORE THAN THE FEDERAL
                           TAXES TO BE PAID.
                       (6) THE MAXIMUM CREDIT, THEN, IS $400 FOR ONE DEPENDENT AND
                           $800 FOR TWO OR MORE DEPENDENTS.

4600  CHLDCRCRDT: CHILD CARE TAX CREDIT
        Operation: LINK
        Make the above mapping(s) by linking to submodel DCTC80.SUB using
        the CETA80.MOD = DCTC80.SUB mapping linkages described below
             Name: DCTC80.SUB[4,2705]
            Title: DEPENDENT CARE EXPENSE FEDERAL TAX CREDIT
      Submodel Linkages (Specified: 1980-12-31 10:27:38)
                     CETA80.MOD  DCTC80.SUB  DCTC80.SUB
                     mapping     mapping     mapping description
                     -------     -------     ------- -----------
        Input(s)
        --------
          required   CHLDN_LE_5  CHLDN_LE_5  NUMBER OF CHILDREN AGE FIVE OR YOUNGER
                     AN_ERNDINC  EARNINGS    EARNED INCOME
                     AN_TXBLINC  TOTAL_INC   TOTAL TAXABLE INCOME
                     FIT         FEDINCTAX   FEDERAL INCOME TAX WITHHELD
                     AFDC        AFDC_BEN    AFDC BENEFITS TO THE FAMILY
                     CHILD_CARE  CHILD_CARE  CHILD CARE EXPENSES
        Output(s)
        ---------
          required   CHLDCRCRDT  CHLDCRCRDT  CHILD CARE TAX CREDIT
```

```
4700  COMMENT:   SECTION 5:

4800  DISPOSABLE: ANNUAL DISPOSABLE INCOME
        Combined operation: CADD
        Make DISPOSABLE the sum of the following weighted mappings, optionally
        imposing a floor on the result of each addition:
   addend mappings          weight factors      floor values
   ------ --------          ------ -------      ----- ------
        AN_ERNDINC          1
        ANTAXOTHER          1
        AFDC                1
        FOODSTAMPS          1
        MEDICAID            1
        EITC                1
        CHLDCRCRDT          1
        FICA                -1
        FIT                 -1
        PSIT                -1
        LOCAL_TAX           -1
        PENSIONCON          -1
        CHILD_CARE          -1

4900  WK_DISPINC: WEEKLY DISPOSABLE INCOME
        Operation: WEIGHT
        Make WK_DISPINC equal to DISPOSABLE weighted by .01923

5000  SAVE the following mappings:
        Mapping name   tax factor     description
        ------- ----   --- ------     -----------
        AN_ERNDINC     NO             ANNUAL EARNED INCOME
        AFDC           NO             AFDC BENEFIT PAYABLE TO FAMILY, ANNUAL BASIS
        FOODSTAMPS     NO             VALUE OF ANNUAL FOODSTAMP BENEFITS
        MEDICAID       NO             MEDICAID BENEFITS PAYABLE
        EITC           NO             EARNED INCOME CREDIT FOR THE UNIT
        CHLDCRCRDT     NO             CHILD CARE TAX CREDIT
        FICA           NO             FICA AS FUNCTION OF HOURS WORKED PER WEEK
        FIT            NO             FEDERAL INCOME TAX FOR THE UNIT
        PSIT           NO             PENNSYLVANIA STATE INCOME TAX
        CHILD_CARE     NO             ANNUAL ALLOWABLE CHILD CARE EXPENSES
        WITHHOLDNG     NO             SUM OF TAXES, FICA, AND MANDATORY PENSION
        DISPOSABLE     NO             ANNUAL DISPOSABLE INCOME
        WK_DISPINC     NO             WEEKLY DISPOSABLE INCOME

----------+-------------------------------------------------------------------------
MAPPING   !       OPERATION NUMBERS       (???=UNDEFINED)
NAMES     +-----------+-------------------------------------------------------------
          !  CREATED ! USED      S=SAVED, D=DELETED, P=SCALAR
----------+-----------+-------------------------------------------------------------
AFDC      !     3400 !     3800       4400      4600      4800      5000S
AFDCAFOYE !     3800 !     3900
AKCHLDCARE!     2900 !     3000
ANTAXOTHER!     1700 !     1800       2400      3400      3900      4800
AN_ERNDINC!     1600 !     1800       2100      2300      2400      2500      3400
          !          !     4100       4600      4800      5000S
AN_TXBLINC!     1800 !     2200       4600
CHILDCRPER!     3000 !     3100
CHILD_CARE!     3200 !     3400       3700      4600      4800      5000S
CHLCRAFOYE!     3700 !     4000
CHLDCAREHR!     2800 !     2900P
CHLDCAREWK!      500 !     2800
CHLDCRCRDT!     4600 !     4800       5000S
CHLDN_GE_6!      300 !     1200
CHLDN_LE_5!      400 !     1200       3100P     4600
COUNTY_SET!     1100 !     3400
DISPOSABLE!     4800 !     4900       5000S
EITC      !     2400 !     4800       5000S
ERNDINCDED!      700 !     3400
FAMILYSIZE!     1300 !     4000       4300
FICA      !     2100 !     2600       4800      5000S
FIT       !     2400 !     2600       4600      4800      5000S
FOODSTAMPS!     4100 !     4800       5000S
FS_AFO_YE !     4000 !     4100
HOURSAFOYE!     3600 !     3700       3800
HOURSWRKD !     1400 !     1500       2900
HRLYWAGE  !      600 !     1500P      3600
INDEP     !PREDEFINED !    3600       4000
```

```
LOCAL_TAX !     2300 !     2600      4800
LOCTAXRATE!      800 !     2300P
MEDICAID  !     4400 !     4800      5000S
NOM_FICA  !     2000 !     2100
N_CHILDREN!     1200 !     1300      2400      3400
N_PARENTS !      200 !     1300      2400      3200      3400
PENSIONCON!     2500 !     2600      4800
PENSIONRAT!      900 !     2500P
PMEDICAID !     4300 !     4400
PSIT      !     2200 !     2400      2600      4800      5000S
SHELTRCOST!     1000 !     4000
TOTCHILDCR!     3100 !     3200
UNERNAFOYE!     3900 !     4000
WITHHOLDNG!     2600 !     3400      5000S
WK_DISPINC!     4900 !     5000S
WK_ERNDINC!     1500 !     1600
```

ADCSCH.SUB

```
            Name: ADCSCH.SUB[4,2705] (Last updated 1982-06-15 22:38:26)

-100       Title: AFDC SCHEDULE SELECTION

     Description: THIS SUBMODEL SELECTS THE APPROPRIATE SET OF AFDC SCHEDULES
                  DEPENDING ON THE SET OF COUNTIES INCLUDED IN THE ANALYSIS.
                  FOR DETAILS ON THE COUNTIES CF. PENNSYLVANIA DPW PUBLIC
                  ASSISTANCE ELIGIBILITY MANUAL, SECTION 175.23(A).
                  THE SCHEDULES ARE MONTHLY GUARANTEES AS A FUNCTION OF FAMILY
                  SIZE AND MONTHLY MAXIMUM INCOME LIMITS AS A FUNCTION OF
                  FAMILY SIZE.  DEFAULT (COUNTY_SET = 0) WOULD PRODUCE THE
                  HIGHEST GUARANTEES AND MAXIMUM INCOME LIMITS, THE SAME
                  AS COUNTY_SET = 1.

-50        Submodel Linkage Mappings (Specified 1980-04-05 17:14:35)
                  Mapping Name  Mapping Description
                  ------------- -------------------
       Input(s)
       --------
         required COUNTY_SET    COUNTY_SET SELECTION VARIABLE
       Output(s)
       ---------
         required AFDCGUARMO    AFDC MONTHLY GUARANTEE BY FAMILY SIZE

100  AFDC_CNTY1: GUARANTEE PER MO. BY FAMILY SIZE FOR COUNTY SET 1
       Operation:FETCH
       Fetch AFDC_CNTY1 from schedule file ADCPA1.SCH. Fetched coordinate pairs are:
              X           Y
             ---         ---
               1          181
               2          273
               3          332
               4          395
               5          451
               6          490
              20         1302

200  AFDC_CNTY2: PA COUNTY SET 2 AFDC BENEFITS (INCREASES ALA O'BEIRNE)
       Operation: FETCH
       Fetch AFDC_CNTY2 from schedule file PAAF22.SCH. Fetched coordinate pairs are:
              X           Y
             ---         ---
               1          172
               2          262
               3          335
               4          401
               5          460
               6          501

300  AFDC_CNTY3: GUARANTEE PER MO. BY FAMILY SIZE FOR COUNTY SET 3
       Operation: FETCH
       Fetch AFDC_CNTY3 from schedule file ADCPA3.SCH. Fetched coordinate pairs are:
              X           Y
             ---         ---
               1          164
               2          253
               3          311
               4          369
               5          424
               6          463
              20         1276
```

```
400  AFDC_CNTY4: GUARANTEE PER MO. BY FAMILY SIZE FOR COUNTY SET 4
       Operation: FETCH
       Fetch AFDC_CNTY4 from schedule file ADCPA4.SCH. Fetched coordinate pairs are:
            X           Y
           ---         ---
             1         147
             2         232
             3         290
             4         350
             5         405
             6         440
            20        1252

500  AFDCGUARMO: AFDC MONTHLY GUARANTEE BY FAMILY SIZE
       Operation: SELECTION
       Make AFDCGUARMO as follows:
            1. Select AFDC_CNTY2 where COUNTY_SET is at least 2
            2. Select AFDC_CNTY1 where COUNTY_SET is less than 2

600  AFDCGUARMO: AFDC MONTHLY GUARANTEE BY FAMILY SIZE
       Operation: SELECTION
       Make AFDCGUARMO as follows:
            1. Select AFDC_CNTY3 where COUNTY_SET is at least 3
            2. Select AFDCGUARMO where COUNTY_SET is less than 3

700  AFDCGUARMO: AFDC MONTHLY GUARANTEE BY FAMILY SIZE
       Operation: SELECTION
       Make AFDCGUARMO as follows:
            1. Select AFDC_CNTY4 where COUNTY_SET is at least 4
            2. Select AFDCGUARMO where COUNTY_SET is less than 4
```

```
-----------+-----------------------------------------------------------------
MAPPING    !        OPERATION NUMBERS        (???=UNDEFINED)
NAMES      +-----------+-----------------------------------------------------
           !  CREATED ! USED        S=SAVED, D=DELETED, P=SCALAR
-----------+-----------+-----------------------------------------------------
AFDCGUARMO!       500 !        600
          !       600 !        700
          !       700 ! MANDATORY
AFDC_CNTY1!       100 !        500
AFDC_CNTY2!       200 !        500
AFDC_CNTY3!       300 !        600
AFDC_CNTY4!       400 !        700
COUNTY_SET! MANDATORY !        500         600          700
```

AFDC80.SUB

```
           Name: AFDC80.SUB[4,2705] (Last updated 1984-03-20 03:07:30)

-100      Title: A SUBMODEL TO COMPUTE AFDC BENEFITS IN PENNSYLVANIA, 1980

    Description:     THE OUTPUT OF THIS SUBMODEL IS AFDC BENEFITS ON AN
                 ANNUAL BASIS.  TO COMPUTE THESE BENEFITS SEVERAL STEPS
                 ARE INVOLVED:
                    (1) USE ADCSCH.SUB TO FETCH THE APPROPRIATE SCHEDULE
                        AS A FUNCTION OF THE SET OF COUNTIES WITHIN PENNSYL-
                        VANIA UNDER EXAMINATION.
                    (2) CHANGE THE MONTHLY AFDC TO AN ANNUAL BASIS
                    (3) COMPUTE ANNUAL TRANSPORTATION EXPENSES:  ASSUMED TO
                        BE 6% OF GROSS EARNINGS UP TO A MAXIMUM DEDUCTION
                        OF $360 (AT AN EARNINGS LEVEL OF $6000 PER YEAR.
                        THUS AN EARNER WORKING AT $3/HR, 8 HRS/DAY, 20
                        DAYS/MONTH FOR 12 MONTHS WOULD JUST QUALIFY FOR
                        MAXIMUM TRANSPORTATION EXPENSE DEDUCTION, $30
                        PER MONTH.  THE MAXIMUM ALSO CORRESPONDS TO $1.50
                        PER DAY WORKED.
                    (4) THE EARNED INCOME INCENTIVE DEDUCTION (30 AND 1/3) IS
                        AVAILABLE ONLY FOR JOBS THAT ARE NOT PUBLIC SERVICE
                        EMPLOYMENT UNDER WIN.  SUCH EARNINGS DO NOT QUALIFY
                        FOR THIS DEDUCTION (CF. CFR 233.20(4)).
                    (5) AVAILABLE INCOME FOR AFDC PURPOSES INCLUDES EARNINGS
                        LESS EARNED INCOME INCENTIVE DEDUCTION, IF ANY, AND
                        OTHER TAXABLE INCOME REDUCED BY PERSONAL
                        EXPENSES (TRANSPORTATION AND CHILD CARE) AND
                        WORK EXPENSES (WITHHOLDINGS).
                    (6) THE BENEFIT IS THE GUARANTEE REDUCED BY AVAILABLE
                        INCOME.

-50       Submodel Linkage Mappings (Specified 1980-04-05 17:53:26)
                 Mapping Name  Mapping Description
                 ------------  -------------------
      Input(s)
      --------
        required COUNTY_SET    COUNTY SET SELECTION VARIABLE
                 N_PARENTS     NUMBER OF PARENTS IN THE ASSISTANCE UNIT
                 N_CHILDREN    NUMBER OF CHILDREN IN THE ASSISTANCE UNIT
                 ERNDINCDED    EARNED INCOME DEDUCTION (1=Y,0=N)
                 EARNINGS      ANNUAL EARNED INCOME
                 YTXBLOTHER    OTHER TAXABLE INCOME, ANNUAL BASIS
                 WITHHOLDNG    TAXES AND OTHER MANDATORY WITHHOLDINGS, ANNUAL
                 CHILD_CARE    CHILD CARE EXPENSES
      Output(s)
      ---------
        required AFDC_BEN      AFDC BENEFIT PAYABLE TO THE FAMILY, ANNUAL BASIS

100  N_AFDCUNIT: NUMBER OF PERSONS IN THE ASSISTANCE UNIT
      Operation: ADD
      Make N_AFDCUNIT equal to the sum of:
      N_PARENTS
      N_CHILDREN
```

```
 200  AFDCGUARMO: AFDC MONTHLY GUARANTEE BY FAMILY SIZE
        Operation: LINK
        Make the above mapping(s) by linking to submodel ADCSCH.SUB using
        the AFDC80.SUB = ADCSCH.SUB mapping linkages described below
             Name: ADCSCH.SUB[4,2705]
            Title: AFDC SCHEDULE SELECTION
      Submodel Linkages (Specified: 1980-04-05 17:14:35)
                    AFDC80.SUB  ADCSCH.SUB  ADCSCH.SUB
                    mapping     mapping     mapping description
                    -------     -------     ------- -----------
        Input(s)
        --------
          required  COUNTY_SET  COUNTY_SET  COUNTY_SET SELECTION VARIABLE
        Output(s)
        ---------
          required  AFDCGUARMO  AFDCGUARMO  AFDC MONTHLY GUARANTEE BY FAMILY SIZE

 300  AFDCGUARYR: AFDC ANNUAL GUARANTEE BY FAMILY SIZE
        Operation: WEIGHT
        Make AFDCGUARYR equal to AFDCGUARMO weighted by 12

 400  AFDC_GUAR:  AFDC ANNUAL GUARANTEE FOR THIS SIZE FAMILY
        Operation: VALUE
        Make AFDC_GUAR the value of AFDCGUARYR where x equals N_AFDCUNIT

 500  TRANSPORT:  TRANSPORTATION EXPENSES
        Combined operation: CCEILING
        Make TRANSPORT equal to the lesser of [EARNINGS weighted by .06] and the
        ceiling value 360

 600  PROPEXCLUD: PROPORTION OF EARNINGS EXCLUDED FROM AFDC AVAILABLE INC
        Operation: SELECTION
        Make PROPEXCLUD as follows:
             1. Select .333333333 where ERNDINCDED is at least 1
             2. Select 0 where ERNDINCDED is less than 1

 700  EXEMPTION:  AFDC EXEMPTION
        Operation: SELECTION
        Make EXEMPTION as follows:
             1. Select 360 where ERNDINCDED is at least 1
             2. Select 0 where ERNDINCDED is less than 1

 800  YELESSEXEM: EARNINGS LESS AFDC EXEMPTION
        Combined operation: CSUBTRACT
        Make YELESSEXEM equal to [EARNINGS weighted by 1] minus the following weighted
        mappings, optionally imposing a floor on the result of each subtraction
   subtrahend mappings      weight factors      floor values
   ---------- --------      ------ -------      ----- ------
        EXEMPTION           1                   0

 900  AVAIL_INC:  INCOME DEEMED AVAILABLE BY AFDC
        Combined operation: CSUBTRACT
        Make AVAIL_INC equal to [YELESSEXEM weighted by 1] minus the following weighted
        mappings, optionally imposing a floor on the result of each subtraction
   subtrahend mappings      weight factors      floor values
   ---------- --------      ------ -------      ----- ------
        YTXBLOTHER          -1
        YELESSEXEM          PROPEXCLUD
        TRANSPORT           1
        CHILD_CARE          1
        WITHHOLDNG          1                   0

1000  AFDC_BEN:   AFDC BENEFITS PAYABLE TO THE FAMILY
        Combined operation: CSUBTRACT
        Make AFDC_BEN equal to [AFDC_GUAR weighted by 1] minus the following weighted
        mappings, optionally imposing a floor on the result of each subtraction
   subtrahend mappings      weight factors      floor values
   ---------- --------      ------ -------      ----- ------
        AVAIL_INC           1                   0

1100  AFDC_BEN:   AFDC BENEFITS PAYABLE TO THE FAMILY
        Operation: SELECTION
        Make AFDC_BEN as follows:
             1. Select AFDC_BEN where N_CHILDREN is at least 1
             2. Select ZERO where N_CHILDREN is less than 1
```

```
----------+-----------------------------------------------------------------------------
MAPPING   !       OPERATION NUMBERS       (???=UNDEFINED)
NAMES     +-----------+-----------------------------------------------------------------
          !   CREATED ! USED       S=SAVED, D=DELETED, P=SCALAR
----------+-----------+-----------------------------------------------------------------
AFDCGUARMO!       200 !       300
AFDCGUARYR!       300 !       400
AFDC_BEN  !      1000 !      1100
          !      1100 ! MANDATORY
AFDC_GUAR !       400 !      1000
AVAIL_INC !       900 !      1000
CHILD_CARE! MANDATORY !       900
COUNTY_SET! MANDATORY !       200
EARNINGS  ! MANDATORY !       500         800
ERNDINCDED! MANDATORY !       600         700
EXEMPTION !       700 !       800
N_AFDCUNIT!       100 !       400P
N_CHILDREN! MANDATORY !       100        1100
N_PARENTS ! MANDATORY !       100
PROPEXCLUD!       600 !       900P
TRANSPORT !       500 !       900
WITHHOLDNG! MANDATORY !       900
YELESSEXEM!       800 !       900         900
YTXBLOTHER! MANDATORY !       900
ZERO      !PREDEFINED !      1100
```

DCTC80.SUB

```
             Name: DCTC80.SUB[4,4206] (Last updated 1981-11-20 00:35:56)

-100        Title: DEPENDENT CARE EXPENSE FEDERAL TAX CREDIT

      Description: THIS SUBMODEL COMPUTES THE CHILD CARE TAX CREDIT UNDER THE
                   FOLLOWING CONDITIONS:
                       (1) IT ASSUMES THAT THERE IS A SINGLE PARENT AND HENCE
                           THE CONDITIONS RELATED TO TWO-PARENT FAMILIES ARE
                           IGNORED
                       (2) IT ASSUMES THAT THERE ARE NO DISABLED DEPENDENTS, AND
                           LIMITS RELEVANT EXPENSES TO THOSE FOR PRESCHOOL CHILDREN
                           IN A PUBLIC OR PRIVATE DAY CARE CENTER
                       (3) ALTHOUGH THE CHILD CARE CREDIT IS AVAILABLE WHEN A PARENT
                           IS NOT WORKING BUT IS LOOKING FOR A JOB, THIS SUBMODEL
                           IGNORES THIS PROVISION AND ASSUMES THAT THE PARENT RECEIVES
                           CREDIT ONLY FOR THE PORTION OF TIME THAT CHILD CARE WAS
                           REQUIRED FOR ACTUAL EMPLOYMENT
                       (4) THE TEST OF WHETHER THE PARENT HAS SUPPLIED MORE THAN
                           50% OF THE COST OF RUNNING A HOME IS APPROXIMATED BY
                           TESTING WHETHER THE PARENT'S TOTAL INCOME (BEFORE
                           TRANSFERS) IS EQUAL TO OR GREATER THAN THE TRANSFERS,
                           IN THIS CASE AFDC.
                       (5) MAXIMUM ALLOWABLE DEPENDENT CARE EXPENSES ARE $2000
                           IF THERE IS ONLY ONE DEPENDENT AND $4000 IF THERE ARE TWO
                           OR MORE DEPENDENTS.  BUT THE MAXIMUM ALLOWABLE EXPENSES
                           CAN NEVER BE GREATER THAN THE ACTUAL EXPENSES OR GREATER
                           THAN EARNED INCOME.
                       (6) THE CREDIT IS DERIVED AS 20% OF THE MAXIMUM ALLOWABLE
                           DEPENDENT CARE EXPENSES, BUT NEVER MORE THAN THE FEDERAL
                           TAXES TO BE PAID.
                       (7) THE MAXIMUM CREDIT, THEN, IS $400 FOR ONE DEPENDENT AND
                           $800 FOR TWO OR MORE DEPENDENTS.

-50          Submodel Linkage Mappings (Specified 1980-12-31 10:27:38)
                     Mapping Name  Mapping Description
                     ------------  -------------------
       Input(s)
       --------
         required    CHLDN_LE_5    NUMBER OF CHILDREN AGE FIVE OR YOUNGER
                     EARNINGS      EARNED INCOME
                     TOTAL_INC     TOTAL TAXABLE INCOME
                     FEDINCTAX     FEDERAL INCOME TAX WITHHELD
                     AFDC_BEN      AFDC BENEFITS TO THE FAMILY
                     CHILD_CARE    CHILD CARE EXPENSES
       Output(s)
       ---------
         required    CHLDCRCRDT    CHILD CARE TAX CREDIT

100  LIMIT:       MAXIMUM ALLOWABLE CHILD CARE EXPENSE (2441, LINE 4)
       Operation: SELECTION
       Make LIMIT as follows:
            1. Select 4000 where CHLDN_LE_5 is at least 2
            2. Select 2000 where CHLDN_LE_5 is less than 2


200  MAXALLWEXP: MAXIMUM ALLOWABLE CHILD CARE EXPENSE
       Operation: MINIMUM
       Make MAXALLWEXP equal to the minimum of:
       LIMIT
       CHILD_CARE
       EARNINGS

300  PCREDIT:     PRELIMINARY CHILD CARE CREDIT
       Operation: WEIGHT
       Make PCREDIT equal to MAXALLWEXP weighted by .2
```

```
400  HOMEMAINT:  PARENTAL CONTRIBUTION TO RUNNING HOME IN EXCESS OF BENEFITS RECEIVED
       Operation: SUBTRACT
       Make HOMEMAINT equal to TOTAL_INC minus:
       AFDC_BEN

500  CHLDCRCRDT: CHILD CARE CREDIT
       Operation: SELECTION
       Make CHLDCRCRDT as follows:
            1. Select PCREDIT where HOMEMAINT is at least 0
            2. Select 0 where HOMEMAINT is less than 0

600  CHLDCRCRDT: CHILD CARE CREDIT
       Operation: MINIMUM
       Make CHLDCRCRDT equal to the minimum of:
       CHLDCRCRDT
       FEDINCTAX
```

MAPPING NAMES	OPERATION NUMBERS (???=UNDEFINED)	
	CREATED	USED S=SAVED, D=DELETED, P=SCALAR
AFDC_BEN	MANDATORY	400
CHILD_CARE	MANDATORY	200
CHLDCRCRDT	500	600
	600	MANDATORY
CHLDN_LE_5	MANDATORY	100
EARNINGS	MANDATORY	200
FEDINCTAX	MANDATORY	600
HOMEMAINT	400	500
LIMIT	100	200
MAXALLWEXP	200	300
PCREDIT	300	500
TOTAL_INC	MANDATORY	400

FIT80.SUB

```
            Name: FIT80.SUB[4,2705] (Last updated 1984-03-20 02:52:03)

-100       Title: FEDERAL INCOME TAX CALCULATOR (1980)

     Description: PURPOSE:  THIS SUBMODEL CALCULATES FORM 1040 INCOME TAX AND THE
                            EARNED INCOME CREDIT FOR 1980 (USING LATEST SCHEDULES
                            AVAILABLE, I.E. THOSE FOR 1979)
                  ASSUMPTIONS:
                        (1) FORM 1040 RATHER THAN 1040A IS AN ACCEPTABLE BASIS FOR TAX
                            MODELING.
                        (2) FILING UNIT CONSISTS ONLY OF HEAD, POSSIBLY A SPOUSE, AND
                            AN ARBITRARY NUMBER OF CHILDREN.
                        (3) FILING STATUS IS 1, 2, OR 4  (CF. 1040).
                        (4) INCOME SOURCES CONSIST ONLY OF EARNINGS AND OTHER TAXABLE
                            INCOME.
                        (5) COMPUTATION OF TAXES FROM SCHEDULES (X, Y, OR Z) IS
                            ACCEPTABLE.
                        (6) AUTOMATICALLY ADOPT ITEMIZED DEDUCTIONS IF BENEFICIAL TO
                            THE FAMILY.
                        (7) 50% OF TAXABLE INCOME IS SOMEWHAT ARBITRARILY TAKEN AS
                            UPPER LIMIT FOR FEDERAL INCOME TAX PAYABLE.
                        (8) ASSUMES THAT FIFTY PERCENT OF THE SUPPORT OF EACH
                            DEPENDENT IS PAID BY THE PARENT(S).
                  REFERENCES:
                   FORM 1040, DEPARTMENT OF THE TREASURY/INTERNAL REVENUE SERVICE.
                   INSTRUCTIONS FOR PREPARING FORM 1040 (AND CERTAIN SCHEDULES),
                   DECEMBER 1979, DEPARTMENT OF THE TREASURY/INTERNAL REVENUE SERVICE


-50         Submodel Linkage Mappings (Specified 1980-04-22 15:17:13)
                    Mapping Name  Mapping Description
                    ------------  -------------------
        Input(s)
        --------
          required  EARNINGS      GROSS EARNED INCOME (WAGES AND SALARIES) (8)
                    N_ADULTS      NUMBER OF ADULTS (1=HEAD ONLY;2=HEAD & SPOUSE)
                    N_CHILDREN    NUMBER OF DEPENDENT CHILDREN IN THE FAMILY
          optional  OTHERBOXES    NUMBER AGE/BLINDNESS EXEMPTIONS FOR HEAD/SPOUSE
                    YTXBLOTHER    OTHER TAXABLE INCOME FOR THE FILING UNIT (9-21)
                    ADJUSTMNTS    TOTAL ADJUSTMENTS (TO TOTAL INCOME) (30)
                    MEDINSPREM    MEDICAL INSURANCE PREMIUMS, FOR (A,1) AND (A,5)
                    MEDICINE      MEDICINE AND DRUG EXPENSES (A,2)
                    OTHRMEDEXP    OTHER MEDICAL EXPENSES (A,6A - 6C)
                    TOTALTAXES    STATE/LOCAL, PROP, SALES & OTHER (A,16 & 34)
                    INTERSTEXP    TOTAL INTEREST EXPENSE (A,20 & 35)
                    CHARITYCON    TOTAL CHARITABLE CONTRIBUTIONS (A,24 & 36)
                    CASUALTY      TOTAL CASUALTY OR THEFT LOSS(ES) (A,29 & 37)
                    UNIONDUES     UNION DUES (A,30)
                    OTHERDED      OTHER MISCELLANEOUS DEDUCTIONS (A, 31)
        Output(s)
        ---------
          required  FEDINCTAX     FEDERAL INCOME TAX FOR THE UNIT
                    YE_CREDIT     EARNED INCOME CREDIT FOR THE UNIT
          optional  TOTAL_INC     TOTAL INCOME FOR THE FILING UNIT (22)
                    EXEMPTIONS    TOTAL NUMBER OF EXEMPTIONS CLAIMED (7)
                    ADJYGROSS     ADJUSTED GROSS INCOME FOR THE FILING UNIT (31)
                    TAXABLEINC    TAXABLE INCOME FOR THE FILING UNIT (34)
                    XCSITEMDED    EXCESS ITEMIZED DEDUCTIONS OVER ZERO BRACKET (33)
                    ZEROBRACKT    ZERO BRACKET AMOUNT FOR THE FILING UNIT (33,40)
```

```
 100  COMMENT:    SECTION 1:
                         SPECIFICATION OF DEFAULT VALUES FOR ALL OPTIONAL ARGUMENTS
                         (ALL ZERO)

 200  OTHERBOXES: DEFAULT FOR HEAD AND SPOUSE AGE/BLINDNESS BOXES CHECKED
        Operation: CONSTANT
        Define OTHERBOXES as the constant, 0, for all values of x

 300  YTXBLOTHER: TAXABLE INCOME OTHER THAN WAGES
        Operation: CONSTANT
        Define YTXBLOTHER as the constant, 0, for all values of x

 400  ADJUSTMNTS: DEFAULT FOR TOTAL ADJUSTMENTS (TO TOTAL INCOME) (30)
        Operation: CONSTANT
        Define ADJUSTMNTS as the constant, 0, for all values of x

 500  MEDINSPREM: DEFAULT FOR MEDICAL INSURANCE PREMIUMS DEDUCTIBLE
        Operation: CONSTANT
        Define MEDINSPREM as the constant, 0, for all values of x

 600  MEDICINE:   DEFAULT FOR MEDICINE AND DRUG EXPENSES DEDUCTIBLE
        Operation: CONSTANT
        Define MEDICINE as the constant, 0, for all values of x

 700  OTHRMEDEXP: DEFAULT FOR OTHER MEDICAL EXPENSES DEDUCTIBLE
        Operation: CONSTANT
        Define OTHRMEDEXP as the constant, 0, for all values of x

 800  TOTALTAXES: STATE AND LOCAL INCOME, REAL ESTATE,SALES AND OTHER TAXES
        Operation: CONSTANT
        Define TOTALTAXES as the constant, 0, for all values of x

 900  INTERSTEXP: DEFAULT FOR TOTAL INTEREST EXPENSES DEDUCTIBLE
        Operation: CONSTANT
        Define INTERSTEXP as the constant, 0, for all values of x

1000  CHARITYCON: DEFAULT FOR CHARITABLE CONTRIBUTIONS DEDUCTIBLE
        Operation: CONSTANT
        Define CHARITYCON as the constant, 0, for all values of x

1100  CASUALTY:   DEFAULT FOR CASUALTY AND THEFT LOSS(ES) DEDUCTIBLE
        Operation: CONSTANT
        Define CASUALTY as the constant, 0, for all values of x

1200  UNIONDUES:  DEFAULT FOR UNION DUES DEDUCTIBLE
        Operation: CONSTANT
        Define UNIONDUES as the constant, 0, for all values of x

1300  OTHERDED:   DEFAULT FOR OTHER (MISCELLANEOUS) DEDUCTIONS
        Operation: CONSTANT
        Define OTHERDED as the constant, 0, for all values of x

1400  COMMENT:    SECTION 2:
                         CALCULATION OF TOTAL EXEMPTIONS

1500  EXEMPTIONS: TOTAL VALUE OF EXEMPTIONS CLAIMED
        Combined operation: CADD
        Make EXEMPTIONS the sum of the following weighted mappings, optionally
        imposing a floor on the result of each addition:
   addend mappings          weight factors      floor values
   ------ --------          ------ -------      ----- ------
        N_ADULTS            1000
        N_CHILDREN          1000
        OTHERBOXES          1000

1600  COMMENT:    SECTION 3:
                         CALCULATION OF TOTAL INCOME, ADJUSTED GROSS INCOME
                         AND DEDUCTIONS

1700  TOTAL_INC:  TOTAL INCOME FOR THE FILING UNIT (22)
        Operation: ADD
        Make TOTAL_INC equal to the sum of:
        EARNINGS
        YTXBLOTHER
```

```
1800  ADJYGROSS:  ADJUSTED GROSS INCOME FOR THE FILING UNIT (31)
        Combined operation: CSUBTRACT
        Make ADJYGROSS equal [TOTAL_INC weighted by 1] minus the following weighted
        mappings, optionally imposing a floor on the result of each subtraction
   subtrahend mappings       weight factors      floor values
   ---------- --------       ------ -------      ----- ------
        ADJUSTMNTS            1                   0

1850  COMMENT:    THE NEXT OPERATION, THE LINK TO SCHA79.SUB, CALCULATES THE
                  EXCESS OF ITEMIZED DEDUCTIONS OVER ZERO BRACKET AMOUNT.
                  USE ALL INPUTS AND OUTPUTS (REQUIRED AND OPTIONAL) WITH SOME
                  NAMES, THEREBY GENERATING  XCSITEMDED  AND  ZEROBRACKT , AND
                  USING DESCRIPTIONS FROM THE SUBMODEL ENTRY OPERATION.

1900  XCSITEMDED: EXCESS OF ITEMIZ. DEDUCT. OVER ZERO BRACK. AMOUNT (A,41) (33)
      ZEROBRACKT: ZERO BRACKET AMOUNT FOR THE FILING UNIT (A,40)
        Operation: LINK
        Make the above mapping(s) by linking to submodel SCHA79.SUB using
        the FIT80.SUB = SCHA79.SUB mapping linkages described below
             Name: SCHA79.SUB[4,2705]
            Title: SCHEDULE A CALCULATIONS FOR FORM 1040 (1979)
      Submodel Linkages (Specified: 1980-04-29 21:59:14)
                  FIT80.SUB   SCHA79.SUB  SCHA79.SUB
                  mapping     mapping     mapping description
                  -------     -------     ------- -----------
        Input(s)
        --------
          required N_ADULTS   N_ADULTS    NUMBER OF ADULTS IN THE FILING UNIT
                  ADJYGROSS   ADJYGROSS   ADJUSTED GROSS INCOME FOR THE FILING
                                          UNIT, LINE 31, FORM 1040
        Output(s)
        ---------
          required XCSITEMDED XCSITEMDED  EXCESS ITEMIZ. DEDUCT. OVER ZERO
                                          BRACKET AMOUNT (A,41) (33)
                  ZEROBRACKT  ZEROBRACKT  ZERO BRACKET AMOUNT FOR UNIT (A,40)

2000  COMMENT:    SECTION 4:
                          TAX COMPUTATION, FOLLOWING THE TAX COMPUTATION SECTION
                          OF FORM 1040 AND SCHEDULE TC (TAX COMPUTATION SCHEDULE).
                          THE SEVERAL OPERATIONS THAT FOLLOW THE DEFINITION OF
                          TAXABLE INCOME SPECIFY THE TAX SCHEDULES X, Y, AND Z
                          AND SELECT THE ONE THAT APPLIES TO THE SUBJECT FAMILY.
                          A FINAL OPERATION CALCULATES FEDERAL TAXES PROPER.

2100  TAXABLEINC: TAXABLE INC. (ADJ. GROSS-EXEMPTIONS-EXCESS DEDUC.) (TC,3)
        Combined operation: CSUBTRACT
        Make TAXABLEINC equal [ADJYGROSS weighted by 1] minus the following weighted
        mappings, optionally imposing a floor on the result of each subtraction
   subtrahend mappings       weight factors      floor values
   ---------- --------       ------ -------      ----- ------
        XCSITEMDED            1
        EXEMPTIONS            1                   0

2200  SCHEDULE_X: U.S. FEDERAL INCOME TAX SCHEDULE X 1979
        Operation: FETCH
        Fetch SCHEDULE_X from schedule file USX79.SCH. Fetched coordinate pairs are:
              X             Y
             ---           ---
               0             0
            2300             0
            3400           154
            4400           314
            6500           692
            8500          1072
           10800          1555
           12900          2059
           15000          2605
           18200          3565
           23500          5367
           28800          7434
           34100          9766
           41500         13392
           55300         20982
           81800         37677
          108300         55697
         1000000        679887
```

```
2300  SCHEDULE_Y: U.S. FEDERAL INCOME TAX SCHEDULE Y (JOINT RETURN) 1979
        Operation: FETCH
        Fetch SCHEDULE_Y from schedule file USYJ79.SCH. Fetched coordinate pairs are:
              X          Y
             ---        ---
               0          0
            3400          0
            5500        294
            7600        630
           11900       1404
           16000       2265
           20200       3273
           24600       4505
           29900       6201
           35200       8162
           45800      12720
           60000      19678
           85600      33502
          109400      47544
          162400      81464
          215400     117504
         1000000     666724


2400  SCHEDULE_Z: U.S. FEDERAL INCOME TAX SCHEDULE Z 1979
        Operation: FETCH
        Fetch SCHEDULE_Z from schedule file USZ79.SCH. Fetched coordinate pairs are:
              X          Y
             ---        ---
               0          0
            2300          0
            4400        294
            6500        630
            8700       1026
           11800       1708
           15000       2476
           18200       3308
           23500       4951
           28800       6859
           34100       9085
           44700      13961
           60600      22547
           81800      35055
          108300      51750
          161300      87790
         1000000     674880


2500  ONEPARSCHD: RELEVANT TAX SCHEDULE ASSUMING ONLY ONE ADULT IS PRESENT
        Operation: SELECTION
        Make ONEPARSCHD as follows:
              1. Select SCHEDULE_Z where N_CHILDREN is at least 1
              2. Select SCHEDULE_X where N_CHILDREN is less than 1

2600  RIGHTSCHED: APPROPRIATE TAX SCHEDULE FOR THE FILING UNIT
        Operation: SELECTION
        Make RIGHTSCHED as follows:
              1. Select SCHEDULE_Y where N_ADULTS is at least 2
              2. Select ONEPARSCHD where N_ADULTS is less than 2

2700  FEDINCTAX:  FEDERAL INCOME TAX (BEFORE MAXIMUM TAX)
        Operation: MAPPING

        Make FEDINCTAX [z(x)] from mappings RIGHTSCHED [z(y)] and TAXABLEINC [y(x)]

2800  FEDINCTAX:  FEDERAL INCOME TAX FOR THE FILING UNIT
        Combined operation: CMINIMUM
        Make FEDINCTAX equal to the minimum of the following weighted mappings,
        optionally imposing a floor on the result of the minimization:
   argument mappings        weight factors      floor values
   -------- --------        ------ -------      ----- ------
        FEDINCTAX           1
        TAXABLEINC          .5
```

```
2900  YE_CREDIT:  EARNED INCOME CREDIT
        Operation: LINK
        Make the above mapping(s) by linking to submodel EIC80.SUB using
        the FIT80.SUB = EIC80.SUB mapping linkages described below
             Name: EIC80.SUB[4,2705]
            Title: EARNED INCOME CREDIT, 1979, FAMILY BASIS
      Submodel Linkages (Specified: 1980-04-30 10:34:19)
                   FIT80.SUB   EIC80.SUB   EIC80.SUB
                   mapping     mapping     mapping description
                   -------     -------     ------- -----------
        Input(s)
        --------
          required EARNINGS    EARNINGS    EARNED INCOME (ANNUAL)
                   YTXBLOTHER  YTXBLOTHER  OTHER TAXABLE INCOME
                   N_CHILDREN  N_CHILDREN  NUMBER OF CHILDREN ("0"= NO CREDIT)
        Output(s)
        ---------
          required YE_CREDIT   YE_CREDIT   EARNED INCOME CREDIT
```

```
----------+-------------------------------------------------------------------------
MAPPING   !        OPERATION NUMBERS      (???=UNDEFINED)
NAMES     +-----------+-------------------------------------------------------------
          !   CREATED ! USED       S=SAVED, D=DELETED, P=SCALAR
----------+-----------+-------------------------------------------------------------
ADJUSTMNTS!  OPTIONAL !
          !       400 !       1800
ADJYGROSS !      1800 !       1900          2100      OPTIONAL
CASUALTY  !  OPTIONAL !
          !      1100 !
CHARITYCON!  OPTIONAL !
          !      1000 !
EARNINGS  ! MANDATORY !       1700          2900
EXEMPTIONS!      1500 !       2100      CPTIONAL
FEDINCTAX !      2700 !       2800
          !      2800 ! MANDATORY
INTERSTEXP!  OPTIONAL !
          !       900 !
MEDICINE  !  OPTIONAL !
          !       600 !
MEDINSPREM!  OPTIONAL !
          !       500 !
N_ADULTS  ! MANDATORY !       1500          1900          2600
N_CHILDREN! MANDATORY !       1500          2500          2900
ONEPARSCHD!      2500 !       2600
OTHERBOXES!  OPTIONAL !
          !       200 !       1500
OTHERDED  !  OPTIONAL !
          !      1300 !
OTHRMEDEXP!  OPTIONAL !
          !       700 !
RIGHTSCHED!      2600 !  2700
SCHEDULE_X!      2200 !  2500
SCHEDULE_Y!      2300 !  2600
SCHEDULE_Z!      2400 !  2500
TAXABLEINC!      2100 !  2700               2800      OPTIONAL
TOTALTAXES!  OPTIONAL !
          !       800 !
TOTAL_INC !      1700 !  1800           OPTIONAL
UNIONDUES !  OPTIONAL !
          !      1200 !
XCSITEMDED!      1900 !  2100           OPTIONAL
YE_CREDIT !      2900 ! MANDATORY
YTXBLOTHER!  OPTIONAL !
          !       300 !       1700          2900
ZEROBRACKT!      1900 !  OPTIONAL
```

FS80.SUB

```
             Name: FS80.SUB[4,2705] (Last updated 1984-02-11 16:21:25)

-100        Title: FOOD STAMP SUBMODEL (1980)

      Description: FS80.SUB ESTABLISHES THE ANNUAL FOOD STAMP BENEFITS IN TWO MAJOR
                   STEPS:
                      (1) IT OBTAINS THE MAXIMUM BONUS VALUE (GUARANTEE) AND THE
                          MAXIMUM INCOME LEVEL (BREAKEVEN) IN GENERAL AND THEN
                          FOR THIS PARTICULAR FAMILY SIZE
                      (2) IT COMPUTES THE FOOD STAMP INCOME BASE.
                       WE DERIVE THE NOMINAL SCHEDULE FOR FOOD STAMP BENEFITS
                   BY APPLYING A 30% REDUCTION RATE (WITH RESPECT TO THE
                   FOOD STAMP INCOME BASE) ON THE MAXIMUM BONUS FOR THE
                   FAMILY, BY IMPOSING A $10/MONTH ($120/YEAR) MINIMUM
                   ON BENEFITS PAYABLE, AND BY ENSURING THAT NO BENEFITS
                   ARE PAYABLE FOR INCOMES EXCEEDING THE MAXIMUM ALLOWABLE
                   INCOME FOR THE FAMILY.
                       INCOME IS CALCULATED AS FOLLOWS:  FIRST, "NET FOOD
                   STAMP INCOME" IS CALCULATED AS THE SUM OF EARNINGS, OTHER
                   TAXABLE INCOME, AND AFDC BENEFITS, LESS DEDUCTIONS OF
                   20% OF EARNINGS, AN ANNUAL STANDARD EXEMPTION OF $900
                   PER YEAR ($75/MONTH), CHILD CARE EXPENSES UP TO A MAXIMUM
                   OF $1080 PER YEAR, AND THE SHELTER DEDUCTION.  THE SHELTER
                   DEDUCTION IS EQUAL TO ACTUAL SHELTER COSTS MINUS 50% OF
                   THE NET INCOME (TOTAL INCOME LESS THREE PRIOR DEDUCTIONS)
                   UP TO A MAXIMUM OF $90 PER MONTH MINUS THE CHILD CARE DEDUCTION.
                      THE BASIC PARAMETERS USED IN THESE CALCULATIONS ARE:
                      (1) THE MINIMUM (NON-ZERO) FOOD STAMP BENEFIT: 10/MO.
                      (2) THE STANDARD DEDUCTION                   : 75/MO.
                      (3) THE MAXIMUM DEDUCTION FOR CHILD CARE     : 90/MO
                      (4) THE MAXIMUM EXCESS SHELTER COST DEDUCT.  : 90/MO

-50         Submodel Linkage Mappings (Specified 1980-04-06 22:10:18)
                     Mapping Name  Mapping Description
                     ------------  -------------------
     Input(s)
     --------
       required      EARNEDINC     ANNUAL EARNED INCOME
                     UNEARNDINC    ANNUAL UNEARNED INCOME (INCLUD. PUBLIC ASSISTANCE)
                     FAMILYSIZE    FAMILY SIZE
                     CHILD_CARE    CHILD CARE EXPENSES
                     SHELTRCOST    ANNUAL SHELTER COSTS INCL. HEAT, WATER, ELEC., &
                                   PHONE
     Output(s)
     ---------
       required      FS_BEN        FOOD STAMP BENEFITS ANNUALLY


 100  FS_BONUSMO: FOOD STAMP GUARANTEE AFO FAMILY SIZE
       Operation: FETCH
       Fetch FS_BONUSMO from schedule file FSG80A.SCH. Fetched coordinate pairs are:
              X          Y
             ---        ---
               1          63
               2         115
               3         165
               4         209
               5         248
               6         298
               7         329
               8         376
               9         423
              10         470
              20         940

 200  FS_GUARMO:  MONTHLY FOODSTAMP GUARANTEE LEVEL FOR THIS FAMILY SIZE
       Operation: VALUE
       Make FS_GUARMO the value of FS_BONUSMO where x equals FAMILYSIZE
```

```
300  FS_GUAR:     ANNUAL FOODSTAMP GUARANTEE
       Operation: WEIGHT
       Make FS_GUAR equal to FS_GUARMO weighted by 12

400  YEMAXMOSCH: FOOD STAMP BREAKEVEN AFO FAMILY SIZE
       Operation: FETCH
       Fetch YEMAXMOSCH from schedule file FSB80A.SCH. Fetched coordinate pairs are:
              X            Y
             ---          ---
               1          306
               2          403
               3          500
               4          596
               5          693
               6          790
               7          886
               8          983
               9         1080
              10         1177
              20         2147

500  YEMAXMO:    MAXIMUM MONTHLY INCOME FOR FOODSTAMP ELIGIBILITY THIS FAMILY
       Operation: VALUE
       Make YEMAXMO the value of YEMAXMOSCH where x equals FAMILYSIZE

600  FSMAXINC:   ANNUAL MAXIMUM INCOME FOR THIS SIZE FAMILY
       Operation: WEIGHT
       Make FSMAXINC equal to YEMAXMO weighted by 12

700  PRE_FS_SCH: PRELIMINARY FOOD STAMP SCHEDULE
       Combined operation: CSUBTRACT
       Make PRE_FS_SCH equal [FS_GUAR weighted by 1] minus the following weighted
       mappings, optionally imposing a floor on the result of each subtraction
  subtrahend mappings      weight factors       floor values
  ---------- --------      ------ -------      ----- ------
       INDEP               .3                   120

800  FS_SCHED:    NOMINAL FOOD STAMP SCHEDULE
       Operation: SELECTION
       Make FS_SCHED as follows:
            1. Select 0 where INDEP is at least FSMAXINC
            2. Select PRE_FS_SCH where INDEP is less than FSMAXINC

900  CHLCAREDED: ANNUAL CHILD CARE DEDUCTION
       Operation: MINIMUM
       Make CHLCAREDED equal to the minimum of:
       CHILD_CARE
       1080

1000  YELESSEXEM: INCOME LESS STANDARD EXEMPTION AND CHILD CARE DEDUCTION
       Combined operation: CSUBTRACT
       Make YELESSEXEM equal [EARNEDINC weighted by .8] minus the following weighted
       mappings, optionally imposing a floor on the result of each subtraction
  subtrahend mappings      weight factors       floor values
  ---------- --------      ------ -------      ----- ------
       UNEARNDINC          -1
       75                  12
       CHLCAREDED          1                    0

1100  TSHELALLW:  TENTATIVE SHELTER ALLOWANCES, BEFORE CEILING
       Combined operation: CSUBTRACT
       Make TSHELALLW equal [SHELTRCOST weighted by 1] minus the following weighted
       mappings, optionally imposing a floor on the result of each subtraction
  subtrahend mappings      weight factors       floor values
  ---------- --------      ------ -------      ----- ------
       YELESSEXEM          .5                   0

1200  MAXSHLTDED: MAXIMUM ALLOWABLE SHELTER DEDUCTION
       Combined operation: CSUBTRACT
       Make MAXSHLTDED equal [1080 weighted by 1] minus the following weighted
       mappings, optionally imposing a floor on the result of each subtraction
  subtrahend mappings      weight factors       floor values
  ---------- --------      ------ -------      ----- ------
       CHLCAREDED          1
```

```
1300  FSSHELALLW: FOOD STAMP SHELTER ALLOWANCE
        Operation: MINIMUM
        Make FSSHELALLW equal to the minimum of:
        TSHELALLW
        MAXSHLTDED

1400  FSINCBASE:  ANNUAL FOOD STAMP INCOME BASE
        Combined operation: CSUBTRACT
        Make FSINCBASE equal [YELESSEXEM weighted by 1] minus the following weighted
        mappings, optionally imposing a floor on the result of each subtraction
   subtrahend mappings       weight factors       floor values
   ---------- --------       ------ -------       ----- ------
        FSSHELALLW            1                    0

1500  FS_BEN:      FOOD STAMP BENEFIT (ANNUAL BASIS)
        Operation: MAPPING
        Make FS_BEN [z(x)] from mappings FS_SCHED [z(y)] and FSINCBASE [y(x)]
```

MAPPING NAMES	OPERATION NUMBERS (???=UNDEFINED) CREATED	USED S=SAVED, D=DELETED, P=SCALAR	
CHILD_CARE	MANDATORY	900	
CHLCAREDED	900	1000	1200
EARNEDINC	MANDATORY	1000	
FAMILYSIZE	MANDATORY	200P	500P
FSINCBASE	1400	1500	
FSMAXINC	600	800P	
FSSHELALLW	1300	1400	
FS_BEN	1500	MANDATORY	
FS_BONUSMO	100	200	
FS_GUAR	300	700	
FS_GUARMO	200	300	
FS_SCHED	800	1500	
INDEP	PREDEFINED	700	800
MAXSHLTDED	1200	1300	
PRE_FS_SCH	700	800	
SHELTRCOST	MANDATORY	1100	
TSHELALLW	1100	1300	
UNEARNDINC	MANDATORY	1000	
YELESSEXEM	1000	1100	1400
YEMAXMO	500	600	
YEMAXMOSCH	400	500	

REFERENCES

Aaron, Henry J. 1973. *Why is Welfare So Hard to Reform?* Washington, DC: The Brookings Institution.

Aaron, Henry J. 1980. *On Social Welfare.* Cambridge, MA: Abt Books.

Adams, J. R. 1977. "The Unskilled Need Not Apply." *Wall Street Journal*, November 5, p. 20.

Allen, Jodie T. 1972. *The Cumulative Tax Rate Model.* Working Paper 505-2. Washington, DC: The Urban Institute.

Allen, Jodie T. 1973. "Designing Income Maintenance Systems: The Income Accounting Problem." In U.S. Congress, Joint Economic Committee, Subcommittee on Fiscal Policy, *Studies in Public Welfare.* Washington, DC: U.S. Government Printing Office.

Anderson, Joseph. 1980. *Modeling Analysis for Retirement Income Policy: Background and Overview.* Washington, DC: Employee Benefit Research Institute.

Anderson, Martin. 1978. *Welfare: The Political Economy of Welfare Reform in the United States.* Palo Alto, CA: Hoover Institute.

Angel, Ronald and Marta Tienda. 1982. "Determinants of Extended Household Structure: Cultural Pattern or Economic Need?" *American Journal of Sociology*, 87:1360-1383.

Appel, Gary Louis. 1972. *Effects of a Financial Incentive on AFDC Employment: Michigan's Experience Between July 1969 and July 1970.* Minneapolis, MN: Institute for Interdisciplinary Studies.

Beebout, Harold and Margaret Sulvetta. 1974. *TRIM: A Microsimulation Model for Evaluating Transfer Income Policies.* Working Paper 971-04. Washington, DC: Urban Institute.

Bennett, Carole T. F. 1979. "The Social Security Benefit Structure: Equity Considerations of the Family as its Basis." *American Economic Review*, 69(2):227-231.

Bergmann, Barbara R., Judith Radlinski Devine, Patrice Gordon, Diane Reedy, Lewis Sage, and Christina Wise. 1980. "The Effect of Wives' Labor Force Participation on Inequality in the Distribution of Family Income." *Journal of Human Resources*, 15:452-455.

Blinder, Alan and Harvey Rosen. 1985. "Notches." *American Economic Review*, 75(4):736-747.

Boland, Barbara. 1973. "Participation in the Aid to Families with Dependent Children (AFDC)." In U.S. Congress, Joint Economic Committee, Subcommittee on Fiscal Policy, *The Family, Poverty, and Welfare Programs: Household Patterns and Government Policies*, Washington, DC: U.S. Government Printing Office.

Braybrooke, David and Charles E. Lindblom. 1963. *A Strategy of Decision.* New York: The Free Press.

Brazer, Harvey. 1968. "Tax Policy and Children's Allowances." In Eveline M. Burns (Ed.), *Children's Allowances and the Economic Welfare of Children.* New York: Citizens Committee for Children of New York.

Burkhauser, Richard and Joseph Quinn. 1981. *The Effect of Changes in Mandatory Retirement Rules on the Labor Supply of Older Workers.* Vanderbilt University and Boston College. Processed.

Cameron, J. 1979. "How CETA Came to be a 4-Letter Word." *Fortune*, 99 (7):112ff.

Committee on Ways and Means, U.S. House of Representatives. February 18, 1982. *Background Material and Data on Major Programs Within the Jurisdiction of the Committee on Ways and Means.* Washington, DC: U.S. Government Printing Office.

Congressional Budget Office. 1977. *Poverty Status of Families Under Alternative Definitions of Income.* Background Paper No. 17, revised. Washington, DC: U.S. Government Printing Office.

Congressional Budget Office. 1982. *Financing Social Security: Issues and Options for the Long Run.* Washington, DC: U.S. Government Printing Office.

Cutright, Phillips and John Scanzoni. 1973. "Income Supplements and the American Family." In U.S. Congress, Joint Economic

Committee, Subcommittee on Fiscal Policy, *Studies in Public Welfare*, Paper no. 12, pp. 54-89. Washington, DC: U. S. Government Printing Office.

Danziger, Sheldon. 1980. "Do Working Wives Increase Family Income Inequality?" *Journal of Human Resources*, 15:444-51.

Danziger, Sheldon and Robert Plotnick. 1981. "Income Maintenance Programs and the Pursuit of Income Security." *ANNALS of the American Association of Political and Social Science*, January:130-145.

Danziger, Sheldon, Robert Haveman, and Robert Plotnick. 1981. "How Income Transfer Programs Affect Work, Savings, and the Income Distribution: A Critical Review." *Journal of Economic Literature*, 19:975-1028.

Danziger, Sheldon and Plotnick, Robert. 1982. "The War on Income Poverty: Achievements and Failures." Pp. 31-52 in Paul Sommers (Ed.), *Welfare Reform in America: Perspectives and Prospects.* Boston, MA: Kluwer-Nijhoff.

Dickinson, Paul and Donald MacDonald. 1974. *The Integration of Income Supplementation and In-kind Subsidy Programmes.* Discussion Paper Document 243. Ottawa, Canada: Department of National Health and Welfare.

Employee Benefit Research Institute. 1981. *Employee Benefit Programs and Policy: Modeling Research.* Washington, DC: Employee Benefit Research Institute.

Federal Council on the Aging. 1975. *The Interrelationships of Benefit Programs for the Elderly*, and *The Interrelationships of Benefit Programs for the Elderly, Appendix III, The Combined Impact of Selected Benefit Programs on Older Americans: A TRIM Analysis.* Washington, DC: U.S. Government Printing Office.

Feldstein, Martin S. 1973. "Unemployment Compensation: Adverse Incentives and Distributional Anomalies." *National Tax Journal*, 27:231-244.

Feldstein, Martin S. 1975. "Unemployment Insurance: Time for Reform" *Harvard Business Review*, March/April: 51-61.

Golladay, Frederick L. and Robert H. Haveman. 1976. *The Economic Impacts of Tax Transfer Policy.* New York: Academic Press.

Goodwin, Leonard. 1983. *Causes and Cures of Welfare: New Evidence on the Social Psychology of the Poor.* Lexington, MA: Lexington Books.

Green, Christopher. 1966. *Negative Taxes and the Poverty Problem.* Washington, DC: The Brookings Institution.

Greenberger, Martin, Matthew Crenson, and Brian Crissey. 1976. *Models in the Policy Process: Public Decision Making in the Computer Era.* New York: Russell Sage.

Gueron, Judith M. and Richard P. Nathan. 1983. "The MDRC Work/Welfare Project: Objectives, Status, Significance." New York: Manpower Development Research Corporation. Paper presented at the Association for Policy Analysis and Management, Philadelphia, Pennsylvania, October 20-22.

Hannon, Michael, Nancy Brandon Tuma, and Lyle P. Groeneveld. 1977. "Income and Marital Events: Evidence from an Income-maintenance Experiment." *American Journal of Sociology*, 82:1186-1211.

Harris, Robert. 1978. *Microanalytic Simulation Models for Analysis of Public Welfare Policies.* Washington, DC: Urban Institute.

Harstad, C. L. 1979. "CETA's Problems." *Fortune*, 99(9):324.

Hausman, Leonard. 1975. "Cumulative Tax Rates in Alternative Income Maintenance Systems." In I. Lurie (Ed.), *Integrating Income Maintenance Programs.* New York: Academic Press.

Haveman, Robert H. (Ed.). 1977. *A Decade of Federal Antipoverty Programs: Achievements, Failures, and Lessons.* New York: Academic Press.

Haveman, Robert H., Irene Lurie, and Thad Mirer. 1973. *Earnings Supplementation Plans for 'Working Poor' Families: An Evaluation of Alternatives.* Discussion Paper 175-73. Madison, WI: Institute for Research on Poverty.

Hoagland, G. William. 1984. "Perception and Reality in Nutrition Programs." Pp. 43-71 in John C. Weicher (Ed.), *Maintaining the Safety Net: Income Redistribution Programs in the Reagan Administration.* Washington, DC: American Enterprise Institute.

Honig, Marjorie. 1974. "AFDC Income, Recipient Rates, and Family Dissolution," *Journal of Human Resources*, 9:303-322.

Jencks, Christopher. 1974. "The Poverty of Welfare: Alternative Approaches to Income Maintenance." *Working Paper for a New Society*, 2(4):5-74.

Joe, Tom. 1982. *Profiles of Families in Poverty: Effects of the FY1983 Budget Proposals on the Poor*. Working Paper. Washington, D.C.: Center for the Study of Social Policy.

Lalonde, Marc. 1973. *Working Paper on Social Security in Canada*. Technical Report. Ottawa, Canada: Department of National Health and Welfare.

Lampman, Robert J. 1971. *The Welfare Reform Provisions in H.R. 1*. Discussion Paper 105-71. Madison, WI: Institute for Research on Poverty.

Lawrence, William J., and Stephen Leeds. 1978. *An Inventory of Federal Income Transfer Programs*. White Plains, NY: The Institute for Socioeconomic Studies.

Lawrence, William J., and Stephen Leeds. 1980. *An Inventory of State and Local Income Transfer Programs*. White Plains, NY: The Institute for Socioeconomic Studies.

Lerman, Robert I. 1973. "The Family, Poverty, and Welfare Programs: An Introductory Essay on Problems of Analysis and Policy." In U.S. Congress, Joint Economic Committee, Subcommittee on Fiscal Policy, *Studies in Public Welfare*, Paper no. 12, Part 1. Washington, DC: U.S. Government Printing Office.

Lewis, Gordon H. 1983. "The Day Care Tangle: Unexpected Outcomes When Programs Interact." *Journal of Policy Analysis and Management*, 2(4):531-547.

Lewis, Gordon H. and Richard J. Morrison. 1983. "Coordinating Income Transfer Programs." *Journal of Policy and Information*, 7(1):93-124.

Lurie, Irene (Ed.) 1975. *Integrating Income Maintenance Programs*. New York: Academic Press.

Lynn, Laurence E., Jr. 1977. "A Decade of Policy Developments in the Income Maintenance System." In Robert H. Haveman (Ed.), *A Decade of Federal Antipoverty Programs*, New York: Academic Press.

MacDonald, Maurice. 1977. *Food, Stamps, and Income Maintenance*. New York: Academic Press.

MacDonald, Maurice and Isabel Sawhill. 1978. "Welfare Policy and the Family." *Public Policy*, 26:89-119.

Marmor, Theodore. 1971. "On Comparing Income Maintenance Alternatives." *The American Political Science Review*, 65:83-96.

McClung, Nelson. 1970. "Estimates of Income Transfer Program Direct Effects." In *The President's Commission on Income Maintenance Programs, Technical Studies.* Washington, DC: U.S. Government Printing Office.

McLanahan, Sara. 1985. "Charles Murray and the Family." Pp. 1-8 in Sara McLanahan, Glen Cain, Michael Olneck, Irving Piliavin, Sheldon Danziger, and Peter Gottschalk, *Losing Ground: A Critique.* Special Report Series, SR #38. Madison, WI: Institute for Research on Poverty.

Mills, Gregory B. and John Logan Palmer. 1983. *The Deficit Dilemma: Budget Policy in the Reagan Era.* Washington, DC: Urban Institute.

Mirengoff, W. 1978. "CETA After 4 Years: Achievement and Controversy: Record Reviewed." *Labor Law Journal*, 29(8):518-521.

Mirer, T. 1975. "Alternative Approaches to Integrating Income Transfer Programs." In I. Lurie (Ed.), *Integrating Income Maintenance Programs*, New York: Academic Press.

Moles, Oliver C. 1979. "Public Welfare Payments and Marital Dissolution." Pp. 167-180 in G. Levinger and O. C. Moles (Eds.). *Divorce and Separation.* New York: Basic Books.

Morrison, Richard J. 1984. *Microsimulation Analysis as an Input to Policy Development.* Ottawa, Canada: Department of National Health and Welfare. Processed.

Morrison, Richard, William Bradley, et al. 1978. *MAPSIT: Modular Analysis Package for Systems of Income Transfer*, Version 4. Ottawa, Canada: Department of National Health and Welfare, Technical Report, Policy, Planning, and Information Branch.

Morrison, Richard, William Bradley, Robert Ellis, et al. 1985. *MAPSIT: Modular Analysis Package for Systems of Income Transfer*, Version 5. Ottawa, Canada: Department of National Health and Welfare, Technical Report, Policy, Planning, and Information Branch.

Moynihan, Daniel P. 1973. *The Politics of a Guaranteed Income.* New York: Random House.

Murray, Charles. 1984. *Losing Ground: American Social Policy 1950-1980.* New York: Basic Books.

National Advisory Council on Economic Opportunity. 1980. "Critical Choices for the Eighties." *Clearinghouse Review*, I:703-720.

National Health and Welfare Canada. 1985. *Child and Elderly Benefits: Consultation Paper.* Ottawa, Canada: Department of National Health and Welfare Canada. January.

Office of Family Assistance. 1985. *Characteristics of State Plans for Aid to Families with Dependent Children under the Social Security Act, Title IV-A: Administration, Eligibility, Assistance Payments.* Washington, DC: U.S. Department of Health and Human Services, Social Security Administration. SSA Pub. No. 80-21235.

Office of Management and Budget. 1986. *Budget of the United States Government, 1987.* Washington, DC: U.S. Government Printing Office.

Office of Management and Budget. 1985. *Special Analyses: Budget of the United States Government, 1986.* Washington, DC: U.S. Government Printing Office.

Orcutt, Guy, Steven Caldwell, and Richard Wertheimer, II. 1976. *Policy Exploration Through Microanalytic Simulation.* Washington, DC: Urban Institute.

Organization for Economic Co-operation and Development. 1978. *The Tax/Benefit Position of Selected Income Groups in OECD Member Countries.* Paris: Organization for Economic Co-operation and Development.

Palmer, John Logan and Isabel Sawhill (Eds.). 1982. *The Reagan Experiment.* Washington, DC: Urban Institute.

Palmer, John Logan and Isabel Sawhill (Eds.). 1984. *The Reagan Record: An Assesment of America's Changing Priorities.* Cambridge, MA: Ballinger.

Plotnick, Robert D. 1977. *The Real Cost and Net Redistributive Impact of Cash Transfers.* Discussion Paper #398-77. Madison, WI: Institute for Research on Poverty.

Ross, Heather L. and Isabel V. Sawhill. 1975. *Times of*

Transition: The Growth of Families Headed by Women. Washington, DC: Urban Institute.

Sadowsky, George. 1977. *MASH: A Computer System for Microanalytic Simulation for Policy Exploration.* Washington, DC: Urban Institute.

Sanger, Mary Bryna. 1982. "Generating Employment for AFDC Mothers in New York State." New York: New School for Social Research. Paper presented at the Association for Public Policy Analysis and Management, Minneapolis, Minnesota, October 28-30.

Schmundt, Maria, Eugene Smolensky, and Leanna Stiefel. 1975. "When Do Recipients Value Transfers at Their Costs to Taxpayers?." In Irene Lurie (Ed.), *Integrating Income Maintenance Programs*, New York: Academic Press.

Sen, Amartya K. 1970. *Collective Choice and Social Welfare.* San Francisco: Holden-Day.

Smith, Vernon. 1974. *Welfare Work Incentives: The Earnings Exemption and Its Impact upon AFDC Employment, Earnings, and Program Cost.* Lansing, MI: Michigan Department of Social Services.

Stein, Bruno. 1971. *On Relief: The Economics of Poverty and Public Welfare.* New York: Basic Books.

Storey, James. 1972. "Public Income Transfer Programs: The Incidence of Multiple Benefits and the Issues Raised by Their Receipt." In Subcommittee on Fiscal Policy, Joint Economic Committee, U.S. Congress, *Studies in Public Welfare*, Washington, DC: U.S. Government Printing Office.

Storey, James. 1982. "Income Security." In J. Palmer and I. Sawhill, *The Reagan Experiment.* Washington, DC: Urban Institute.

Sulvetta, Margaret. 1976. *An Analyst's Guide to TRIM: The Transfer Income Model.* Washington, DC: Urban Institute.

Usher, C. and J. Griffith. 1983. *The 1981 AFDC Amendments and Caseload Dynamics.* Durham, NC: Research Triangle Institute.

van Praag, Bernard M. S. 1983. "Some General Structural Problems in Social Security." Pp. 38-64 in Uwe Reinhardt, Bernard M. S. van Praag, and Gail Wilensky, *Aging, Health Care, and*

Social Security: Three Essays. Laxenburg, Austria: International Institute for Applied Systems Analysis.

Viscusi, W. Kip and Richard J. Zeckhauser. 1977. "The Role of Social Security in Income Maintenance." Pp. 41-64 in Michael J. Boskin (Ed.), *The Crisis in Social Security: Problems and Prospects.* San Francisco: Institute for Contemporary Studies.

Watson, J. W. Henry, Marc Hollander, Michael Dost, and Mark Forman. 1981. "Tax Rates and Poverty Traps in the U. S. Welfare System: Before and After the 1981 Changes in the Law." Paper presented at the annual meeting of the Association for Public Policy Analysis and Management, Philadelphia, Pennsylvania. Chicago: University of Chicago, Committee on Public Policy Studies.

Weicher, John (Ed.). 1984. *Maintaining the Safety Net: Income Redistribution Programs in the Reagan Administration.* Washington, DC: American Enterprise Institute.

Wilensky, Gail. 1970. "An Income Transfer Computational Model." In *The President's Commission on Income Maintenance Programs, Technical Studies.* Washington, DC: U.S. Government Printing Office.

INDEX